American Standards

Studies in the
Postmodern Theory of Education

Joe L. Kincheloe and Shirley R. Steinberg
General Editors

Vol. 192

PETER LANG
New York • Washington, D.C./Baltimore • Bern
Frankfurt am Main • Berlin • Brussels • Vienna • Oxford

American Standards

Quality Education
in a Complex World

The Texas Case

E D I T E D   B Y

Raymond A. Horn, Jr.
& Joe L. Kincheloe

PETER LANG
New York • Washington, D.C./Baltimore • Bern
Frankfurt am Main • Berlin • Brussels • Vienna • Oxford

Library of Congress Cataloging-in-Publication Data

American standards: quality education in a complex world,
the Texas case / edited by Raymond A. Horn, Jr. and Joe L. Kincheloe.
p. cm. — (Counterpoints; vol. 192)
Includes bibliographical references and index.
1. Education—Standards—United States—Case studies. 2. Education—
Standards—Texas. 3. Education—Texas—Evaluation. I. Horn, Raymond A.
II. Counterpoints (New York, N.Y.); vol. 192.
LB3060.83.A44   379.1'58'0973—dc21   00-052040
ISBN 0-8204-5505-9
ISSN 1058-1634

Die Deutsche Bibliothek-CIP-Einheitsaufnahme

American standards: quality education in a complex world -
the Texas case / ed. by: Raymond A. Horn, Jr. and Joe L. Kincheloe.
–New York; Washington, D.C./Baltimore; Boston; Bern;
Frankfurt am Main; Berlin; Brussels; Vienna; Oxford: Lang.
(Counterpoints; Vol. 192)
ISBN 0-8204-5505-9

Cover design by Roymieco Carter

The paper in this book meets the guidelines for permanence and durability
of the Committee on Production Guidelines for Book Longevity
of the Council of Library Resources.

Printed in the United States of America

American Standards is dedicated to the tens of thousands of children who have been left behind in Texas.

Table of Contents

PART ONE

STANDARDS IN AMERICA

Chapter 1

"Goin' Home to the Armadillo": Making Sense of Texas Educational Standards

Joe L. Kincheloe

Recently, I was sitting in a meeting about educational standards in New York City listening to the usual litany of concerns about the subject. Almost asleep in my familiarity with the standards and standard clichés, I was startled awake by a reference to Texas. As a southerner who is sensitive to educational reference to the motherland, I carefully listened as a school leader spoke with great reverence about the "Texas model." Not accustomed to hearing "Yankees" speak so positively about anything remotely connected with Southern education, I marveled as the spokesperson waxed eloquent about the brilliant success Texas had achieved via the state's standards reform. He wanted New York—yes, New York—to emulate the Texas model and share in the educational glory of the innovative Texans.

It was at that point that I knew I would have to be involved in a book on the Texas standards reform. When my friend, Ray Horn, called to tell me about what was happening in Lone Star pedagogy, I suggested we collaborate on a project. Ray put together the entire project in no time. The subject of the Texas reforms is timely, he understood, and demanded immediate attention. As Donnya Stephens, Sharon Spall, and Sandra McCune describe in chapter 14, the nation is carefully watching the Texas reforms. Speaking on the standards movement in various locales in the nation over the last year or so, I have been amazed by the numerous references my audiences make to the Texas case and the almost universally positive view they hold of it. I thought I was going to have to run from one audience member in the Midwest when I questioned the validity of some of the claims made for Texas student academic improvement. Convinced of the unqualified success of the reforms, he refused to entertain my skepticism about the meaning of the increases in performance.

Thus, while "the eyes of Texas are upon you," the nation's eyes are on Texas education at the beginning of the twenty-first century. What has particularly caught the national attention is the "objective" proof of educational improvement—higher achievement test scores, specifically, higher scores on Texas's student assessment instruments. Americans, Texans in particular, have always been impressed by quantitative data. They like to achieve higher numbers than their competitors—Texas 38, Oklahoma 34 is a good example. In the year 2000, Texans have been quick to point out that Texas school students both White and non-White, have outscored similar students in comparable states. The set of actions that has contributed to this reality is the subject of *American Standards: Quality Education in a Complex World—The Texas Case*. Ray Horn, the contributors, and I lay out a description of these actions, asking a variety of questions about them, their effects, the interpretations of their meanings, and their relevance for Texas and the rest of the country in the continuing efforts to improve education in the U.S.

Old Wine, New Bottles, and Other Clichés: The Same Old Song

What struck me as I studied the Texas case was the amazing similarity between the contemporary conversation in Texas and the history of educational discourse in the U.S. since the late nineteenth century. As Danny Weil delineates in chapter 2, the history of American education has been marked by a never-ending debate about educational purpose, proper pedagogical methods, and reliable modes of assessment of educational progress. What is the purpose of American education? To adjust a group of obedient citizens to the needs of business? To create a cadre of critical democratic citizens with the ability to ensure the good health of American democracy, protect justice for all, and understand the insidious ways dominant power operates to undermine these possibilities? What are proper pedagogical methods? Are they teacher-centered and grounded on the successful delineation of an unchanging body of monocultural truth? Are they student-centered, contextually informed, flexible, and designed to engage students in the critical analysis of bodies of knowledge as well as building students' ability to conduct research and produce their own knowledge about the world? What is a reliable mode of assessing educational progress? Does it involve a measurement of how many facts students are able to remember and provide when requested? Does it involve the ability to engage in meaning-making activities that illustrate a wide body of knowledge, analytical and logical skills, a desire to learn more, and the ability to teach oneself?

I must admit my allegiances. Like John Dewey, Maria Montessori, Boye Bode, W. E. B. DuBois, George Counts, Myles Horton, Paulo Freire, Maxine Greene, and many others whose work precedes mine, I tend to answer the preceding questions with the second choices provided. You need to know up front that I am very concerned with producing critical, analytical, socially committed, imaginative, democratically minded, higher-order thinking researcher-scholars who can rethink and improve any aspect of the world with which they are involved. It is through these lenses that I observe the Texas case and the issue of educational standards in general. With these commitments in mind I will try to convince you of the legitimacy of my perspective in my two chapters in this book. In chapters 1 and 21, I promote what I refer to as "standards of complexity." Whether we like it or not, the debate over the contemporary Texas reforms is a continuation of an old conversation.

For example, Horace Mann and many of his business supporters in the first system of public schools in Massachusetts in the 1840s established an educational experience designed to produce a skilled and "safe" labor pool for an industrializing nation. While Mann sincerely spoke of a need of an educated citizenry for a democratic society, the schools he designed overtly operated to rid new immigrants of radical notions about egalitarianism and the rights of labor. Any effort to understand the origins of state-supported public education in the U.S. must take into account the influence of industrial leaders and their concerns with the control of their low-wage workers. Emerging in this common school crusade in the mid-nineteenth century was a conflict about the purposes of education in the U.S. that can be traced throughout the remainder of the nineteenth century and through the twentieth century, to the first years of the twenty-first century and the Texas standards reforms—the debate concerning education for social control and regulation versus education for democratic participation. Early in the twentieth century, teacher advocate Margaret Haley recognized this dynamic:

> Two ideals are struggling for supremacy in American life today: one the industrial ideal, dominating through the supremacy of commercialism, which subordinates the worker to the product, and the machine; the other, the ideal of democracy, the ideal of educators, which places humanity above all machines, and demands that all activity shall be the expression of life. (quoted in Tyack, 1974, p. 257)

In contrast to the advocates of social regulation for industrial needs; democratic reformers in the late nineteenth and early twentieth centuries argued that schools could be used to promote human freedom and to strengthen democracy. Perceiving the power of emerging corporations as a threat to the traditional American political values of liberty, justice, and the pursuit of happiness, these educational reformers maintained that a citizenry well educated in democratic principles could protect the spirit and future of American freedom. Schools, they argued, should serve as the cornerstone of both local communities and the larger democratic society. The most well-known and articulate spokesperson for this "progressive" perspective was philosopher John Dewey. Dewey viewed education as an academically rigorous, child-centered, democratically conscious endeavor. Each child, he thought, had to see the connections between the information presented and questions posed at school, and the larger society beyond. As educational historian Henry Perkinson (1991) maintained, "For Dewey . . . the school was to be the model for the larger society precisely because democracy, participant democracy, is nothing more than people engaging in joint activity to solve their common or shared problems" (p. 186).

Dewey's educational vision ran into problems with many Americans. First, it was openly critical of the strongest powerbrokers in the nation, the corporate leaders. They could exert tremendous pressure to undermine Dewey's efforts. Second, unlike corporate-supported schools for social regulation that were cheap and efficient to run, Dewey's schools were labor intensive and expensive. Third, evaluations of success were easy for "factory model" schools for social control; students either knew prescribed fragments of data or they didn't. Dewey's assessment model was much more complicated as students were asked to perform higher orders of cognitive abilities and to apply their learning to real-life situations. Again, such evaluations were labor intensive, required much higher levels of educator expertise, and were costly. And fourth, Dewey's proposals for educational excellence were complex and were often misunderstood by the American public. Many Americans viewed education as little more than as the process of accumulating a body of unexamined, unproblematic "facts." Dewey's discussions of the development of a curriculum that was related to student experience so as to engage the pupil's interest, curiosity, and commitment seemed an incomprehensible waste of time and money in the eyes of many. Others viewed such ideas as an abrogation of the need to learn "basic knowledge" about the world. Needless to say, with exceptions here and there, the advocates of schooling for social regulation for business needs generally won the struggle for the educational hearts and minds of Americans (Allison, 1995; Kincheloe, Steinberg, & Slattery, 2000; Brosio, 1994).

The Texas standards reform is important, therefore, not only for its relevance to the Texas community and its students and teachers, but for its connection to the larger history of education in the U.S. and its influence on the future of schooling around the country. The way we make sense of the reforms, the way we interpret their meaning, will inform policy leaders and educational policy makers for years to come. Will Texas be seen to represent some final victory for a back-to-basics form of teacher-centered, test-driven education or will it represent the failure of such a rationalized, decontextualized, and culturally insensitive mode of pedagogy? The jury, of course, is still out. One hopes that, *American Standards: Quality Education in a Complex World—The Texas Case* will make a positive contribution to this interpretive process. In the following sections of this chapter I explore eight educational issues raised by the Texas case.

The Larger Educational Issues Raised by the Texas Case

1. *The Acceptance of Technical Rationality.*
As Danny Weil details in chapter 2, Texas standards reforms have followed the lead of business efficiency models that came to prominence in the early part of the twentieth century. With the Reagan reforms of the 1980s, such educational models asserted themselves across the country, making test scores the most important product of teaching. As Weil puts it:

> Transformed into classroom managers overseeing student-workers, teachers become further disengaged from the nature of teaching, as they were galvanized to follow prescribed "teaching recipes" in the form of pre-formulated lesson plans. With the rise of prepackaged instructional materials, intellectual engagement with the curriculum had now become, for many teachers, a luxury, as they were transformed into mere managers of learning.

Technical rationality is a form of exaggerated reason that involves an obsession with means in preference to ends. Such a technicalization process is more interested in method and efficiency than in any larger sense of purpose. In Texas, political and educational leaders fall into the trap of technical rationality when they come to value high test scores more than the development of rigorous academic abilities and valuable understandings of the world and students' relationship to it. Instead of asking questions of educational purpose in a democratic society, Texas leaders of the standards reforms have often focused on *how to* raise test scores. Raising test scores may have little to do—there may in some cases be a negative influence—with the attempt to produce an academically rigorous education for students from all racial, ethnic, and class backgrounds.

When such a technical rationality shapes an educational system, questions of why we might choose to be educated or what are the characteristics of an educated person are dismissed. In such a rationalized context, learning is broken into little pieces of data to be memorized for the test. Such "factoids" are considered in conceptual isolation, and teaching for understanding is sacrificed. The only value of the data learned is its use to answer test questions. After the test is taken, such decontextualized information is soon forgotten. In the technical rationality of teaching to expert-produced content standards, Texas educational leaders have assumed in their test-driven mind-set that teaching and learning are never more than the sum of their parts. Houses from these perspectives are no more than the nails and lumber that go into them, and education is no more than the average number of objectives mastered. Many educators have referred to this fragmentation process as "bitting." It is not hard to imagine a Texas classroom caught in the bitting process. Students copy information from chalkboards and overhead projectors and skim textbooks to find information fragments that will answer both the questions in the study guides and the practice tests. Children listen (when they're not talking); they respond when called upon; they read fragments of the textbook; they write short responses to questions provided on worksheets.

They rarely plan or initiate anything of length or conceptualize their own projects. They rarely even write essays that aren't strictly pre-designated. They are learning to be deskilled, to be passive, to be citizens who are governed, not citizens who govern. They are being taught not to seek deep structures that move events, but to examine only the surface level of appearance. They will not understand the concept of how their consciousnesses have been shaped or how the world actually operates. They will perceive little reason to become scholars or to question the fragmented "truths" with which they are provided. Their unquestioning acceptance of this data is all important. Students or teachers who raise scholarly questions about the genesis of the official data throw a monkey wrench into the technically rational process and, for the good of the bureaucratic system, cannot be tolerated. Thus, the very nature of scholarly skepticism and inquisitiveness is undermined. Those students and teachers who exhibit the qualities essential to democratic citizenship tend to be punished.

All phases of such an educational process depend on the technically rational concern with measurable results of particular teaching strategies. Does the strategy serve to raise scores? No questions are asked of issues such as the following: the worth of raising the scores, the meaning of improved scores, the tacit view of politics embedded in them, the educational and social side effects of viewing their improvement as the primary goal of teaching. Such questions seem *verboten* in the Texas system. Value dimensions, political and ideological dimensions of educational practice are eclipsed by the power of technical rationality. No room exists for spontaneous innovation, expanding on student interests, or connecting teaching and learning to local issues and community problems. Fidelity to the data included on the test is supreme, and nothing must divert our single-minded objective.

> Social studies teacher Mr. Wilson: Turn in your study guides to pages 23–25. I want you to answer the questions on the Era of Good Feelings taken from chapter 6 of your textbook.
> Student Charles: But, Mr. Wilson, war has broken out in the Middle East. What do you think caused the invasion of Syria?
> Mr. Wilson: Charles, that has nothing to do with our lesson. Let's get to work on the assignment.
> Charles: I thought this was social studies. I don't see why we can't study the war.
> Mr. Wilson: I'm not going to tell you to get to work again, Charles.

Such scenes are not unusual in the test-driven, technically rational classroom. In such cases students learn important lessons about the irrelevance of school to the world.

In technically rational forms of knowledge production, research begins only with the delineation of a well-formed problem. In the contemporary Texas school, the improvement of test scores constitutes the well-formed problem. The complexity of the teaching and learning process with its differing social and cultural contexts, students with unique problems and abilities, the complications of motivation, the emotional and affective dimensions of teaching and learning, the multidimensional nature of scholarship and higher-order thinking, and many other dynamics are dismissed in the narrow rationality of the effort to improve test scores. In this context the system tends to focus on what may be the least important but the most easily (and cheaply) measurable aspects of the educational process.

A medical analogy might be in order. In the technically rational world of contemporary medicine, doctors are subjected to some of the same forces as teachers. Technological innovation in medicine has produced machines that inexorably fix the attention of both doctor and patient on those aspects of an illness that are measurable. The human dimensions of the illness that are at least of equal importance are neglected. Doctors must rebel if they are to serve their patients effectively; they must not allow a science of measurability to dictate what techniques they use, no matter how effective a technique might be in addressing the particular variable measured by the high-tech equipment purchased at great cost by the hospital administrators. The doctor must never lose sight of the patient as a human being with unmeasurable but yet important feelings, insights, pains, and anxieties (Wiggins, 1989). In education, the technology of the standardized tests often moves us to forget that students are human beings with unmeasurable yet important characteristics. Such a test-driven mentality hides the understanding that the most important aspects of the educational process—the ability to analyze, interpret, see dimensions of a situation that others have not seen, discern the existence of problems where others saw equilibrium, transfer understandings derived from our setting to a completely different locale, apply knowledge and skills gained to the salvation of human problems—do not lend themselves to easy measurement.

2. *Reductionism, Fragmentation, and Abstract Individualism.*

Teaching and learning are inherently complex entities. A form of destructive reductionism has dominated the Texas conversation about standards and has distorted both the education system and, importantly, the public view of how education operates. Entering a classroom one discovers that a wide variety of students with different backgrounds, special needs, different home experiences, diverse strengths and weaknesses, and changing moods and dispositions occupy those bizarre school desks. Teachers operating with a recognition of complexity appreciate the complicated task of understanding these diverse students and teaching to their individual needs and concerns. Such teachers learn to deal with the unanticipated complications of the everyday classroom, in the process appreciating that no generic form of teaching applies to all students in all contexts. No matter how straightforward the legislated content goals that may be articulated, these complexity-sensitive teachers know that no top-down technical fix will solve the everyday pedagogical dilemmas they confront.

In addition to the daunting perplexity of the teaching act, educators sensitive to complexity understand that curriculum development and knowledge production are also thorny tasks. Because of such realities I use the phrase *standards of complexity* to describe the types of educational improvements that are needed in the effort to avoid technical rationality and reductionism and to produce a truly rigorous system of teacher education and successful and inclusive elementary and secondary schools. Standards of complexity understand that even as information is being gathered/constructed by researchers, it is being analyzed and interpreted. A reductionist view of knowledge like the one used in the Texas standards reforms assumes that only after one knows "the facts" is one ready to analyze.

Such a view misses the important point that what we designate as the facts is an act of interpretation—in the case of positivistic research it is an unconscious act of interpretation. Reductionistic knowledge producers often assume that knowledge is a static or inert entity—writers of elementary and high school content standards often take this viewpoint. Knowledge production operating with an understanding of complexity proceeds tentatively, ever mindful of ambiguity and uncertainty. When we know for certain, little need exists for us to pursue alternative ways of knowing, to become rigorous scholars. "Deviant ways of seeing" are dismissed as irrelevant—they are not viewed as an important source of new insight and educational innovation (Romanish, 1987; Schon, 1987). Scholarship begins at the point where these understandings of the complexity of knowledge work emerge. Such insights guide the goals of standards of complexity.

One of the major problems of the Texas standards movement and U.S. schooling in general involves the inability to understand this notion of complexity, the inability to deal with ambiguity, to perceive ambiguity as a valuable characteristic. Without such an understanding educational leaders have continually sought naive and simplistic answers to the complex social and cognitive questions that confront education—reflecting the reductionistic predisposition to seek certainty in its inquiries about human and educational affairs. Standards of complexity attempt to overcome our socially engrained discomfort with the enigmatic, our desire for something we can all subscribe to together, our need for a shared certainty.

In chapter 3 Ray Horn describes this reductionism as a bounded approach. As employed in Texas standards, this bounded approach demands that a problem such as student achievement is viewed only within the boundary of the existing system—for example, the educational system. Such a reductionistic perspective fragments our view of the educational cosmos as it erases the impact of other systems on the way students perform. Horn's point is essential in understanding the reductionism of Texas standards: educational reform that is always economically, politically, and culturally driven is removed from its economic, political, and cultural context. Thus, the forces that shape student achievement are simply not understood by policy makers.

If the educational system itself operates and sets standards in a reductionistic cosmos, it becomes more and more difficult for teachers to escape the cognitive and pedagogical fallout of such a process. Thus, teachers are acculturated and rewarded for rote-based memory work, the teaching of unrelated fragments of data, and standardized lessons for cookie cutter students. As Glenda Moss reports in chapter 12, Texas standards have done little to expand student thinking ability. When teachers have transcended such cognitive reductionism and developed cognitive abilities that appreciate multiple-systems complexity, they are much better suited to encourage higher-order thinking on the part of their students. Such a high-complexity teacher tends to challenge student thinking, as he or she expects more factual and conceptual support for student argumentation, greater analytical divergence, and more self-analysis in light of the concepts under study. The high-complexity teacher is better able to establish more pervasive and authentic interactions between students and students, and students and teachers. Such interaction heightens self-awareness, as students (and teachers) are attuned to the power of their own words and those of others, and the nature of the contexts and codes and the ways they construct the meaning of information.

These higher-complexity teachers tend to operate on a sophisticated level, as they encourage the active interpretation and negotiation necessary to the process of teaching, learning, and expanding the cognitive abilities of students. As they gain the power to reconstruct their own ways of thinking, they are better able to help their students reinterpret their traditions and reinvent their futures together in solidarity with other self-directed human agents. Teachers who are comfortable with ambiguity and prefer complexity operate at an ideological level that seems to be more tolerant, flexible, and adaptive and employ a wider repertoire of teaching models. They are better equipped to enter a twenty-first-century world where certainty and memorization are sacrificed in order to overcome bureaucratic definitions of the deskilled role teachers often play in standards-driven schools. This complex view of teacher consciousness helps us move beyond the negative consequences of the quest for certain learning, as teacher educators and teachers themselves begin to imagine more rigorous educational futures. If the act of teaching followed the reductionistic pattern and was constant and predictable, teachers could act on empirical generalizations, and teacher educators would know exactly what teachers needed to know to perform successfully. But teaching is not constant and predictable—it always takes place in the microcosm of uncertainty (Schon, 1987).

This notion of standards of complexity may strike those who have operated only in a reductionistic school system as strange and unsettling. "Just give the students the content standards and then test them to see if they 'mastered' them," they might tell us. "What's so damned complex about that?" In such a mind-set, complexity is irrelevant because we all know that the purpose of science is to produce universal laws/truths and the purpose of education is to pass those truths along to students. What's the problem here? This is the way it has always been or seems to have been. Reductionistic educators have harbored grand ambitions: to provide, for example, the *truth* about the nature of entities such as intelligence or culture. Psychologist Donald Fiske, arguing the Cartesian position, contends that psychologists and social scientists must ignore all of this concern with complexity and focus on the discovery of the regularities in the behavior of social objects. Strongly disagreeing with our notion of complexity, Fiske argues that social laws exist and can be discovered. The regularities to which he refers are the building blocks of social laws. In other words, Fiske contends that our search for the laws of society and the universal practices of education must start small with microscopic methods of investigation. The objects of inquiry, he says, must be small objects and short temporal periods. Fiske is confident that years and years of such microscopic research will eventuate in an accurate portrayal of social and educational reality (cited in Frankel, 1986).

Fiske rejects our complex conception of disorder. It is this reductionistic discomfort with uncertainty that motivates the construction of logocentric designs: build more jails and get the deviants into them; reestablish old-fashioned discipline and solve school management problems; allow administrators to determine what textbooks teachers should use and adopt them; inquire into what strategies improve test scores, then require teachers to use them; give principals and deans more responsibility to fire people; pass a law or a constitutional amendment that requires citizens to respect the flag; do research that is simple, orderly, and elegant and produces verifiable data; devise questionnaires that soothe our quest for certainty by subtly requiring respondents to answer questions in ways that prove that the world is stable and predictable; as a research analyst, assume that the word and the deed are consistent.

All of these designs are based on the assumption of common frames of reference. They are all based on the reductionistic notion of the simplicity of the lived world. The fact that they are arrived at in a way that reflects the tacit dominant ideology of a time and place is not considered in the quest for certain knowledge of the world of education. Thus, in its assurance, its refusal to examine the assumptions that guide it, the reductionistic quest for certainty often obscures more than it uncovers (Gordon, Miller & Rollock, 1990). It provides teachers and students with a collection of fragmented, unconnected, often inaccurate data to be memorized and regurgitated on a standards test. Even when students do well on such an exam, little education may have taken place. Rote memorization after all is the lowest level of human cognition.

In the context of this educational reductionism, complex understandings of the forces that shape student relationship to the institution of schooling are also dismissed. The social, cultural, and economic dynamics that construct the educational consciousness of students are ignored in a manner that results in a punitive and blame-the-victim mentality. Horn is again informative, as in chapter 8 he writes of the way responsibility for student failure in the Texas system is placed squarely on the shoulders of individual students. There is no racism or class bias in the standards-driven Texas system; the bounded reductionism that abstracts (removes) individual students from the social and cultural context that shapes them and the dominant culture that constantly interacts with them shields the system from responsibility for the "losers" in the standards game. In this world of abstract individualism everyone starts at the same gate, equal opportunity prevails. Of course, equal opportunity is of minimal benefit in a system stacked against African Americans and Mexican Americans.

The socially decontextualized view of the individual and the complex process of identity formation held by the proponents of content standards in Texas are disconcerting. Our identity and our consciousness are formed by the cultural forces of race, class, gender, and place; the influence of such factors is profound as they construct boundaries, limitations, and possibilities in our various relations. They help shape the kind of friends we have, the work we do, the mates we choose, and the goals we pursue. Our interactions with our families, churches, peer groups, workplaces, and, of course, schools help shape our identities. As if these forces were not enough, our consciousness is constructed by our involvement with changing technologies, the mass media, and the popular culture they help produce—a popular culture designed to directly address our cultural positions and to reinforce and subtly change/exploit our world views.

If we do not appreciate these dynamics, we are lost in our efforts to understand the relationships of students—especially minority students and those from economically marginalized homes—to school in particular and education in general. Simply put, young people's views of themselves as students are socially constructed in particular ways. The discussion and analysis of such central features are not contemplated by the Texas educational leaders.

Embedded within the naive notion of abstract individualism is a historical amnesia. In the public conversation about Texas standards, minority students who score low on the tests, for example, have no connections with the past; they live in a freeze frame of the present. The school and its students in this conception are jerked out of history. What exists has always been, as school cannot be seen as an evolving institution that grows and falters through the years, as one aspect of several social, cultural, and pedagogical systems converging. In this decontextualized domain we have no way of understanding the motivations of individuals or the purposes of school. We are incapable of self-analysis, for we have no grounding that empowers us to see where we or those around us originated. In the same way we are incapable of critical analysis of school purpose, for we have no idea why schools do the things that they do. These are the conditions under which the Texas standards have been developed and debated.

In this context, Texas educational and political leaders would be well advised to study the sociological notion of totality. Totality is a concept that views social analysis as always taking into account both the particularity of individual experience and the generalization of socioeconomic and cultural patterns. Human beings are entwined in countless ways in this totality which in the micro-domain involves place and individual consciousness, and in the macro-realm includes psychological, social, political, and economic patterns: for example, in psychology, patterns of learning styles; in socioeconomics, patterns of school performance along the lines of class, race, and gender. Educators interested in questions of justice and democracy must attend to both the particularistic and the general, and especially the various levels of interaction between them—this is the totality, this is how we get to the lived world of students.

The totality implies a radical reconceptualization of both the socio-educational research act and teaching itself. It not only directs our attention to the ways that socioeconomic and ideological forces construct consciousness but also to how individual children, real-life boys and girls, respond to such construction in their home life, peer groups, and school. If Texas's educational leaders are sincerely interested in improving the quality of education for economically marginalized and African American and Mexican American students, they will study concepts such as sociological totality and apply them to the effort to make sense of the complex social dynamics that confront education in the state.

3. *Dumbing Everyone Down via Standards.*

One of the most unfortunate features of the Texas standards is that their operationalization tends to stupidify rather than enlighten. Rationalized, fragmented, and decontextualized data inserted into young minds do not scholars make. Indeed, the very meaning, purpose, and inspiration of learning are undermined in the process. Unfortunately, the process of digesting the curriculum so it can be taught for tests is a manifestation of a dumbed-down pedagogy that often graduates academically naive and misled students. In twenty-first-century Texas, the Texas Assessment of Academic Skills (TAAS) test drives all instruction, all school activities. Lisa Bertrand in chapter 5 and other authors in this collection question just what has been learned when a student passes the TAAS. Other authors point to a narrowed curriculum—especially in predominantly minority schools—and teacher views of test-driven standards pedagogy as encumbrances to good teaching.

Thinking, teaching, and learning from the perspective of advocates of reductionistic standards are improved by following specific procedures and seeking easy-to-measure psychometrically influenced goals. These procedures operationally define quality learning—arbitrarily define it, I might add—and break it into discrete pieces; we first learn, for example, the symbols of chemistry, the place of the elements on the periodic chart, the process of balancing chemical equations, and the procedure for conducting a chemical experiment. Students march through these procedures memorizing the necessary data and pre-delineated processes without any consideration of why they are engaged in the activities, not to mention the role of chemistry in the world. As Glenda Moss writes in chapter 12, subjects are reduced to their relationship to the tests—not their importance in the world. Standards reductionists use basal texts and worksheets. They know it is far easier and less rigorous to write a chemistry worksheet based on the fragmented knowledge of the discipline with a list here and isolated facts there than to encourage sophisticated, applicable, and challenging chemistry experiences.

It is much more important to engage chemistry students in an understanding of what real-life chemists do, how knowledge is produced in the discipline, the historical development of the subject, the important debates within the field, and how chemistry has or has not contributed to making the world a better place. Chemists do not sit around memorizing fragmented data for a multiple-choice test. Indeed, it is far easier for a reductionistic chemistry program to train teachers and students to follow specific, predefined, never-changing steps of prearranged "experiments" and rote memorization of factoids than to encourage a reflective stance toward student experiences, the role of chemistry in the world, the relations between chemistry and other academic subjects, and the discourse of chemistry as a discipline. There is no reason why such rigorous and sophisticated abilities cannot be taught.

Albert Einstein was literally horrified by such reductionistic methods of teaching science (Kincheloe, Steinberg, & Tippins, 1999). He would be doubly horrified by science teaching in standards-obsessed Texas. Again in chapter 12, Glenda Moss reports one Texas teacher's description of a senior kinesiology seminar designed to encourage higher-order engagement with the discipline digresses under the pressure of test-driven standards to a rote-based preparation for the fragmented questions of the ExCET test (the Examination for the Certification of Educators in Texas). The standards of complexity advocated here are grounded on the assertion that the *whole* of learning is greater than its fragmented individual parts. Indeed, it is only when the relationship between these parts is studied and understood by everyone involved in the teaching, learning, and evaluation process that complex, rigorous education can take place.

Standards of complexity reject reductionistic task analysis procedures for teachers derived from scope and sequence charts. They reject definitions of intelligence grounded upon a quantitative measurement of how many facts and associations a student has accumulated. Standards of complexity understand the contextual specificity and idiosyncrasy of learning, noting that there are many paths to quality teaching and learning. One of the best ways, for example, to teach students higher orders of cognition involves a detailed knowledge of the contexts from which such students emerge and the particular ways in which they engage in the search for meaning. What is important in a student's life? How might these concerns connect with the curriculum? These are examples of questions on which a rigorous and engaging pedagogy is constructed.

Such a pedagogical orientation involves educating teachers as scholars and researchers who are empowered to make decisions about their own professional practice. Armed with such scholarly abilities, teachers become professionals in the same sense as doctors and lawyers. In this context, students benefit dramatically as they gain the opportunity to model self-directed scholarly behavior. The complex curriculum is removed from the dumbed-down prison of fragmented content testing, and the possibility of student reflection about the intersection of the social and physical worlds with their lives is encouraged. In such a new situation, standards of complexity enable schools to produce better citizens, better workers, better family members, and better agents of social justice.

Texas standards make several mistakes, but possibly their most fatal flaw may involve the attempt to improve education without improving *scholarship*. After all the technically rational studies are collated, all the standardized tests are taken, and all the school rankings have been ordered, teaching and learning will be primarily scholarly activities. This means that teachers must be able to create an environment where scholarship can thrive and analytical thinking can develop. Teacher education institutions—not only schools of education but schools of liberal arts and sciences as well—must make sure teachers graduate from bachelor's, master's, and doctoral degrees as scholars capable of analysis, synthesis, research, and other forms of academic work.

Educational leaders must make sure that teachers possess these abilities and are given classroom opportunities to teach them. In this context educational leaders must understand—much better than they seem to in Texas—the numerous ways that school structure, reform proposals, and the standards themselves subvert both the acquisition of the abilities and the opportunity to use them and teach them in the classroom. Leaders must protect teachers, especially the best and the brightest, from the assault on their psyches and professional dignity that they will face in schools that are governed by top-down content standards, reductionistic goals, and high-stakes test scores.

Analytical, synthetic, interpretive, and research abilities, understanding the context in which education takes place, the ways students learn, the larger social and cultural role of education, and the historic purposes of education are basic teaching skills in the twenty-first century. Standards of complexity demand that teachers possess such abilities and be able to use them in classrooms so they can be passed along to students. Teachers so equipped will be able to take data, larger concepts, methods of knowledge production, and social and educational theoretical insights and adjust them to the demands of diverse learners and learning situations. Such rigorous teachers must by necessity be committed to independent critical thinking rather than to an unanalyzed allegiance to prespecified, fragmented data.

Such teachers in their pre- and inservice professional education engage in contextual studies including macro-social analyses, research into youth culture, explorations of the relationship between politics and education, and inquiry into economic needs as articulated by a variety of individuals from diverse social and ideological locales. Such contextual studies enable them to formulate and discuss questions of educational purpose. When scholarly teachers are able to formulate and contemplate such questions and to discern their relationships to classroom practices, they are ready to assume a larger role in redefining the nature and spirit of what an educator's role does. Such intellectually capable, self-directed, empowered teachers will create a workplace in which scholarly work is nurtured and teacher's input into the conceptualization of their own teaching is jealously guarded. Incompetent and authoritarian administrators and dumbed-down standards will not survive very long in such a rigorous and democratic setting.

Teachers who recognize the complexity of the educational task and possess these scholarly skills will ask compelling questions of schooling. They will be seekers of patterns, revealers of hidden agendas and ideologies, and agents of educational progress. Only teachers who possess those abilities and are allowed to use them will be able to teach them to students. An aviation teacher who cannot herself fly an airplane is not my choice of a flight instructor. Rigorous teachers will demand modes of student and teacher evaluation that go beyond the supervisory assessment of classroom cleanliness and order and fidelity to the test-driven, fragmented curriculum.

First, the new complex form of evaluation will demand evaluators who themselves possess the aforementioned scholarly skills; second, it will respect the creative abilities of good teachers to develop practices that help students learn such abilities and the knowledge that accompanies them; third, it will respect the diversity of individual teacher goals given the different social and cultural locales and the different needs and abilities their unique students bring to their classrooms; fourth, such evaluation and the process it initiates facilitate the efforts of teachers to work out the relationship between curricular conception and execution; and fifth, it observes and aids teachers in their never-ending attempt to make sense of the plethora of diverse elements that continually shape and reshape a learning environment.

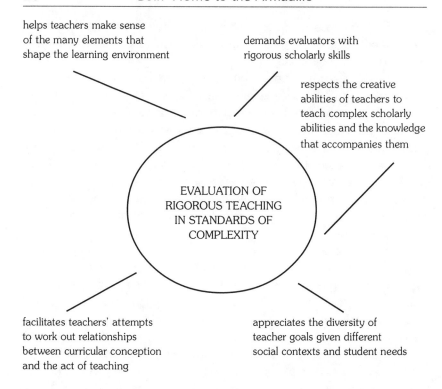

helps teachers make sense
of the many elements that
shape the learning environment

demands evaluators with
rigorous scholarly skills

respects the creative
abilities of teachers to
teach complex scholarly
abilities and the knowledge
that accompanies them

EVALUATION OF
RIGOROUS TEACHING
IN STANDARDS OF
COMPLEXITY

facilitates teachers' attempts
to work out relationships
between curricular conception
and the act of teaching

appreciates the diversity of
teacher goals given different
social contexts and student needs

Rigorous teachers who refuse to allow themselves or their students to be dumbed down will hold subject matter up to critical inquiry. Contrary to the right-wing proponents of top-down, reductionistic standards, education based on these complex principles does not refuse to teach subject matter: standards of complexity refuse to teach subject matter poorly. Teachers in higher education, for example, while often possessing a command of a body of disciplinary information, sometimes do their students a disservice by failing to question the significance of such data in the overall education of the individual. The educational studies promoted by standards of complexity are profoundly concerned with questions about the meaning of the knowledge of a discipline; where it came from and who produced it, its connection to the lived world, its role in education, its place in a particular individual's course of study, and other knowledges about the same subjects and why they have not been taught.

When educational and political leaders, concerned citizens and parents, teacher educators, and teachers and students themselves begin to view teaching and learning as complex scholarly activities, they automatically begin to think of such questions. As members of a scholarly profession, educators examine great teachers and reform movements from the past, and they study the interrelationship connecting political climate, educational purpose, and the teaching process. As educators note the diversity of purposes and processes utilized by successful educators in different historical periods and cultures, they begin to recognize the repressive attempt to foist rationalized, fragmented data, and test-driven teaching methods on teachers.

They recognize the pathology of educational bureaucracies, as these bureaucracies attempt to standardize the educational process and render its work quantitatively measurable. High educational standards do not necessitate standardization; indeed, in a process as complex and idiosyncratic as education, standardization demands an irrational dismissal of the all-important relationship between context and purpose. Where we are teaching and the needs of those we are teaching should always be important factors in shaping what we are trying to accomplish and how we go about it. Texas standards reformers have not learned this essential lesson, as their standardized requirements are removed from the contexts that give them meaning. As the pep rallies commence, the dumbing down continues.

4. *Standards as Part of Right-Wing Reeducation Project.*
In chapter 3 Ray Horn writes about the "essential values and agendas of those in control" of Texas standards. He is referring to the fact that nothing about the standards reforms in Texas (or anywhere else) is politically or ideologically neutral. Americans have not yet realized that any attempt to reform education, to develop standards, or even to teach a class is grounded on a set of political and ideological assumptions. Certainly the positions put forth in *American Standards: Quality Education in a Complex World—The Texas Case* are politically and ideologically inscribed. We are quick to admit our assumptions.

We believe in the following: equal educational opportunity, the centrality of education that promotes democratic values and civic participation, the confrontation of the racism, sexism, and class bias that distort student performance, the ill-advisability of standardized education, the importance of examining how knowledge is produced and certified for curricular inclusion, the limitations of monocultural perspectives on the world, and higher-order thinking as a cognitive *process* of interpreting and analyzing rather than the commitment of a large body of facts and formulae to memory.

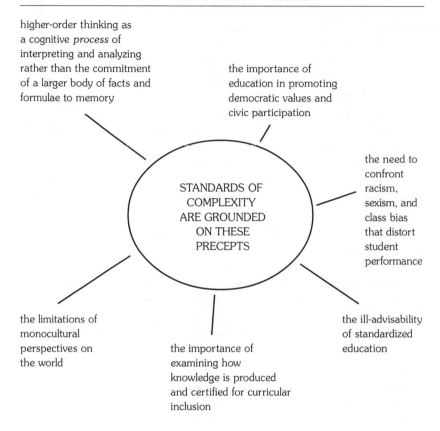

higher-order thinking as a cognitive *process* of interpreting and analyzing rather than the commitment of a larger body of facts and formulae to memory

the importance of education in promoting democratic values and civic participation

STANDARDS OF COMPLEXITY ARE GROUNDED ON THESE PRECEPTS

the need to confront racism, sexism, and class bias that distort student performance

the limitations of monocultural perspectives on the world

the importance of examining how knowledge is produced and certified for curricular inclusion

the ill-advisability of standardized education

The point that needs to be made here involves the preferability of exposing the values and assumptions upon which educational systems are built rather than claiming the protection of neutrality and objectivity. And the latter claim is exactly the one that leaders of the Texas standards movement have made. My objective here is to expose the larger political movement out of which the standards reforms emerge and to offer some alternative political possibilities for standards based on scholarly complexity and concerns with social justice.

The Texas standards movement is part of a larger right-wing reeducation movement of the past twenty-five years. Sensing that the Civil Rights, women's, gay, and anti-Vietnam War movements of the 1960s and 1970s had weakened traditional forms of power in American society, right-wing political, social, religious, and educational leaders worked hard to "take back" or "recover" traditional power relations in U.S. society. In education progressive efforts to racially integrate and address the needs of African

American, Latino, Native American, and economically poor students of all ethnicities and backgrounds were framed as efforts to destroy standards in American schools. Rhetorical analysis of the speeches of many political and educational leaders from the mid-1970s onward reveals patterns of calls for a return to the "quality education" of "the past"—the past used to signify a time before all of these egalitarian movements damaged our standards.

The reeducation movement (Apple, 1996; Gresson, 1995) referenced here does not merely refer to formal education and schooling but to the ideological common sense of the American people. The success it has achieved has revolved around its ability to depict American institutions and the American (that is, patriarchal European White) culture under threat. In an adept manner, right-wing advocates have been able to connect these concerns to the visceral, affective, everyday concerns of many Americans. In many educational research projects in which I have been engaged over the past two decades, I've heard numerous White parents of public school students rail about "all the effort the teachers are giving to help the Black students. They take all the school's time and money."

Upon examination of the schools referred to by these parents, I found time and again that the overwhelming mass of time and resources was relegated to the most economically privileged White students. Such parents had internalized the right-wing reeducation program's concern with the threats to Whiteness—signified as "us." What such individuals perceived had little relation to the lived world. Indeed, from the early 1980s to the beginning of the twenty-first century, the gap between White and non-White wealth widened, and opportunities for non-White professional mobility declined. The picture painted by the right-wing reeducators provided a very different understanding of the world (Kincheloe, 1999).

In the new political universe, great anger was directed at the "liberals" in the educational establishment who were wasting time and money trying to teach those groups that many reeducators designated as unteachable (Herrnstein & Murray, 1994; Kincheloe, Steinberg, & Gresson, 1996). If African Americans, Latinos, and the poor simply cannot learn, rightwing leaders argued, then there is no reason to study issues such as social context, youth culture, and multiculturalism. In the eyes of the reeducators these analyses waste time and effort. In classic reductionistic logic, simply teach the great facts of Western culture, emphasize the achievements of the scientific method, and devise multiple-choice tests to *confirm* the "superiority" of the culturally and economically privileged. Decontextualized school standards that are easy to statistically manipulate for good public relations fit the needs of the reeducators perfectly.

The reeducation has successfully rewritten history and re-created public memory in a manner that justifies educational, social, and political policies that perpetuate the growing inequality of Western societies. As Danny Weil explains in chapter 2, such policies are grounded on an effort to protect an uninhibited free market economics that is designed to raise the salaries of corporate leaders while harming the non-White and poor in the name of economic efficiency. Many Americans have accepted the reeducators' contention that any form of government aid to the poor is harmful to the social and economic health of the larger society. Reeducation has involved acceptance of the superiority of the privatized market economy, the absurdity of egalitarian programs, and the un-Americanness of multiculturally sensitive school curricula.

In this reductionistic, decontextualized manner the right-wing reeducators renewed efforts to adjust the poor and non-White to an unjust society. Education in this conservative conception has little to do with civic responsibility and social justice, as those who challenge unequal opportunity are labeled unpatriotic whiners and complainers. As a group that often speaks of its fear that pluralism and a diversity of curricular perspectives are divisive, are tearing apart the American social fabric, it is ironic that the reeducators employ the binary "we" and "they" so often. "We," they argue, are the true Americans who want standards in our schools; "they" are the multiculturalists who want to teach anti-American material and perpetuate an "anything goes" curriculum. "They" want to pamper the shiftless and lazy members of society who once may have been victims of discrimination but now want something for nothing (Kincheloe & Steinberg, 1997; Allison, 1995; McLaren, 1994, 2000).

The role of the teacher as scholar, researcher, and educational expert promoted by standards of complexity does not fit well in the plans of the right-wing reeducators. Many of the Texas standards reform leaders are not comfortable with teachers with too much academic freedom—the reform leaders want to control the politics and ideology of what is taught. Such leaders join in the reeducation project, as they promote a view of the teacher as technician who passes along information and belief structures provided by standards formulators and test makers. Under the banner of teaching as the "transmission of the best of our cultural heritage," excluding, as dangerous, social, cultural, political, economic, and religious understandings from other cultures, right-wing reeducators deskill and deprofessionalize teachers. It is hard for me to imagine the fact—although I do acknowledge its existence—that in the twenty-first century right-wing reeducators are afraid to allow diverse cultural perspectives into American classrooms. What an interesting commentary on the state of the American psyche.

In the ideological context constructed by the right-wing articulation of standards reform, well-regulated teachers do not need to help students interpret, question, relate, or apply the information transmitted to them. What need is there for scholars in the teaching profession? Indeed, in contemporary Texas education, scholars get in the way, impeding the orderly transmission of the "facts." The politically inscribed story of Western superiority can be transmitted and then scientifically assessed to make sure that teachers are performing their jobs properly. The ideological dimension of the standards reform is illustrated by the philosophical/political disjunction between the PD ExCET (the Texas teacher test on one's knowledge of professional education) and the teaching strategies promoted by the test-driven curriculum. The teacher knowledge test is grounded on a learner-centered perspective that takes the context of learner and learning into account.

Thus, such a pedagogy tacitly rejects the right-wing notion of an abstract individual totally in charge of his or her learning circumstance. Assumed within the PD ExCET is a belief that teachers must understand the individual learner and his or her context in order to devise an effective educational strategy. Right-wing standards advocates reject this concern with the importance of different social and cultural contexts and individual differences, opting for a test-driven pedagogy that is taught in the same way to everyone. Of course, as most Texas teachers understand, if the economically disadvantaged students in Oakcliff in Dallas are simply taught without reference to socioeconomic context in the same way students from across town in affluent Highland Park are taught, the outcome can be easily predicted. The privileged are further privileged, and the disadvantaged are removed from the school and, most importantly, the testing pool. Voila! Texas test scores are improved and right-wing political goals are furthered. Indeed, with "proof" of improved education, the right-wing, decontextualized, test-driven educational reforms are viewed as "what works" in raising school performance.

When right-wing, decontextualized, test-driven, one-size-fits-all modes of education drive school practice, a bizarre process is unleashed that devours many disadvantaged students. As poor and racially marginalized students carry their cultural baggage into the upwardly mobile middle class culture of right-wing schools, their poverty is viewed as a badge of failure. One poor African-American child learned this lesson in her first experiences in school, as evidenced by her response to the question, "what is poverty?" "Poverty," she said reflecting the values she had absorbed at school, "is when you aren't living right." The blame for poverty in the context of a right-wing abstract individualism rests on the shoulders of the poor—a key lesson in the reeducation curriculum. Such a lesson takes its psychic toll on economically poor students, moving them all too often to reject the academic world and the culture that surrounds it, as a means of self-protection.

Many school leaders still have trouble understanding that the poor are not stupid. Often, students from working-class and lower-socioeconomic class homes do not ascribe importance to academic work in the same way as middle- and upper-middle-class students do. Working-class and poor students often see academic work as unreal, as a series of short-term tasks rather than as something that has long-term importance for their lives. Real work, they believe, is something you get paid for after its completion. Without such compensation or long-term justification, these students often display little interest in school. This lack of motivation is often interpreted, of course, as inability or lack of intelligence. Poor performance on the TAAS in Texas or other standardized tests around the country is viewed as scientific conformation of the inferiority of such students.

It happens every day in Texas and around the country. Educators—with the aid of right-wing psychologists such as Richard Herrnstein and Charles Murray and their White-supremacist-funded eugenics research in *The Bell Curve* (1994)—mistake lower-socioeconomic-class manners, attitudes, and speech for a lack of academic ability. Research reports that many teachers place some students in low-ability groups or recommend their placement in vocational or special education because of their *class* background. Their rationale involves the poor students' social discomfort around students from a higher class background; lower-socioeconomic-class students, right-wing scholars imply, should be with their own kind. The standard practices of American schooling are too often based on a constricted view of the human capacity for development and an exclusive, reductionist understanding of human diversity. Intelligence in this view is defined operationally as one's performance on an IQ test, not as the unique and creative accomplishments one is capable of in a variety of venues and contexts. The social context and power relations of the culture at large and the school culture in particular are central in the attempt to understand these dynamics of student performance (Oakes, 1988; Nightingale, 1993; DeYoung, 1989; Woods, 1983; Kincheloe, Steinberg, & Hinchey, 1999; Kincheloe, Steinberg, & Villaverde, 1999).

Research on the education of low-status groups in other countries provides some important insight into the performance of marginalized students in American schools. In Sweden, Finnish people are viewed as inferior—and the failure rate for Finnish children in Swedish schools is very high. When Finnish children immigrate to Australia, however, they do well—as well as Swedish immigrants. Koreans do poorly in Japanese schools, where they are viewed as culturally inferior; however, in American schools, Korean immigrants are very successful (Zweigenhaft & Domhoff, 1991). The examples are numerous, but the results generally follow the same pattern: Racial, ethnic, and class groups that are viewed negatively or as inferiors in a nation's dominant culture tend to perform poorly in that nation's schools.

Democratic educators attend to the lessons of these findings in their attempt to undermine the class bias that consumes their students. Such research helps dispose of the arguments that school failure results from the cultural inferiority of the poor or the marginalized. It teaches us that power relations among groups (class, race, ethnic, gender, and so forth) must be considered when the performance of various students is studied. Without the benefits derived from such understandings, brilliant and creative young people from marginalized backgrounds will continue to be relegated to the vast army of the inferior and untalented. This is the very type of contextual information that right-wing reeducation has tried—quite successfully—to repress. Numerous right-wing attempts to shut down schools of education have been motivated in part by the teaching of these types of studies. Teachers who understand these and thousands of other contextual insights cannot approach their professional tasks in the same way. Moreover, they cannot view in a positive light the top-down, technically rational, decontextualized standards reforms that ignore such insights.

5. *Standards as Part of Recovery of White Supremacy.*
No matter how much Texas standards advocates may want to deny it, the chronicle of standards in the state is a racial story. As Ray Horn discusses in chapter 8, African Americans and Hispanics/Latinos have suffered high dropout rates and high TAAS failure rates. The most important aspect of this story involves the lack of interest educational and political leaders have shown in these dynamics and their general disregard for these demographic groups. Inseparable from the right-wing reeducation effort is a sociopolitical dynamic that Aaron Gresson (1995) has labeled "the recovery of White supremacy." The attitudes and policies of the

Texas standards reformers can be even better understood when viewed within this disturbing framework.

A key aspect of what Gresson refers to as the rhetoric of White recovery of the perceived losses of the Civil Rights movement involves the portrayal of White victimization and the blaming of non-Whites for social and educational problems. Spokespeople for the White recovery speak often about their victimization by affirmative action, immigration policies, and the newfound power of a *dominant* non-White minority. Ronald Reagan, George Bush, Bob Dole, Pat Buchanan, John Silber, and other spokespeople have gained political clout by invoking the rhetoric of recovery. That such a position could gain such widespread acceptance and support seems incredulous in light of the overwhelming (and continually growing) power of White people—White males in particular.

In the effort to historicize White victimization, Whites seeking recovery have referenced their immigrant grandparents' stories of struggle, assumed the status of European ethnic minorities, and revived ethnic practices long abandoned by second-generation descendants of immigrants. Using these signifiers of historical struggle, such Whites can deny attributions of White privilege and White political and economic dominance. In this context, Whiteness is constructed as a signifier of material deprivation and a litany of present-day grievances. Everyone but White males get advantages, the argument goes, as non-Whites undermine White progress by exploiting White guilt about a long-dead White racism.

Such a rhetorical construction, Gresson contends, is a form of vampirism, as Whites positioning themselves as victims suck the blood of moral indignation from Blacks, Latinos, and Native Americans and use it to reposition themselves in a new racial order. "They" won't even let us have our own clubs and White organizations, White students protest, with the blood of moral indignation dripping from their mouths. Democratic educators ask why many White students have such difficulty recognizing the long-term White domination of most existing school organizations. Why do they consistently miss this power dynamic? They have been reeducated to recover their White supremacy, to reclaim their White privilege.

While the Civil Rights movement failed on a variety of levels, it did produce a public facade of civility on matters of race and a genuine effort on the part of many Whites to rethink their racial consciousness. The architects of the recovery of White supremacy had to reshape the cultural representation of blackness in a way that would elicit White fear while not exposing the architects themselves as racists. With these guiding concerns, right-wingers rhetorically positioned Blackness as the opposite of family values, morality, nostalgia, authority, safeness, and prosperity. Facilitating their efforts to avoid the racist label, the politicos embraced upper-middle and upper-class Blacks with "cultivated tastes," "class," and "pedigree."

The Republican Party's enthusiastic celebration of Colin Powell and George Bush's embrace of Clarence Thomas are excellent examples of this aspect of recovery politics. Since racism no longer played a role on the contemporary political landscape, as recovery proponents including Dinesh D'Souza maintained, no reason existed for structural adjustments to take care of the disadvantages of racism and social inequality. In this racial context there is no need to address the failure and dropout rates of African Americans and Latinos in Texas schools—they have no one to blame but themselves since racism is a pathology of a distant past.

The White recovery project in the 1990s was championed by a new breed of talk radio hosts—Rush Limbaugh, G. Gordon Liddy, Oliver North, and many others—who successfully worked to make racism respectable. As they played to their audience's racial fears, they fanned fires of White supremacy to the degree that many of the political policies they advocated subverted the fundamental assumptions of democracy and egalitarianism (Giroux & Searls, 1996). The recovery rhetoric struck a resonant chord with White audiences, as the narrative was deftly articulated by individuals who appeared neither confrontational nor bitter. How could jovial, self-effacing Ronald Reagan be peddling a politics of hate, Whites wondered, when he's such a wonderful man. Like Reagan, they too could express their racial anger and antagonism without thinking of themselves as intolerant bigots. In this context the medium of television, with its magical ability to represent and disseminate morally repugnant messages without appearing to be mean-spirited or intolerant, worked in tandem with the recovery project. As reporters presented the words and messages of racial hate, they conveyed them with such low affect and media congeniality that the sting of their hurtfulness was airbrushed away.

These issues constitute the basis of the right-wing reeducation and the concomitant recovery of White supremacy. The Texas standards reforms with their crass insensitivity to racial minorities could only thrive in this climate. Right-wing politics in the twenty-first century, Joyce King (1996) contends, depends on a folklore (ideology) of White supremacy that moves White people to accept the degradation of the poor non-White as a natural process. Indeed, the rhetorical abilities of neo-racists rose to the challenge of the recovery project, employing phrases such as "new species" to describe poor, ghetto-raised Blacks.

Racial scapegoating was raised to a new aesthetic form, as right-wing commentators on TV claimed that racial integration's infusion of non-White students and the multiculturalist programs devised to accommodate them have destroyed "our" schools. Using declining SAT (Scholastic Aptitude Test) scores as their empirical proof, analysts painted a picture of schooling run amok, with unqualified teachers teaching silly multiculturalist curricula. Employing a pretzel logic, Herrnstein and Murray did their part for the recovery, maintaining the party line about non-Whites' role in undermining quality education and causing SAT scores to fall. Interestingly, such an argument contradicted their previous assertion that cognitive ability is innate and cannot be raised by educational intervention. Apparently, Black and Latino students possess the uncanny ability to make everyone dumber by their mere presence.

In this context we can gain a better sense of why, as Dina Townsend reports in chapter 7, 54 percent of Texas students are non-White, yet only 24 percent of teachers are members of minority groups. We can better understand why the numbers of Hispanic students with limited English proficiency have dramatically increased in the 1980s and 1990s while at the same time no money has been allocated to hire more educational personnel to help them. Of course, this is an important factor in the high Hispanic failure rate on the TAAS and high dropout percentage. Since many Hispanic students are not allowed to take the test, the failure rate for the group could be much higher.

The sobering differences between White and non-White TAAS passing rates would not exist in a racially just society. Either non-White students would receive learning assistance and help with test-taking skills, or new pedagogies and progressive forms of assessment would be developed that did not discriminate against African American and Latino students. The amazing aspect of this racial dynamic is that such pedagogies and assessments could be developed that would be simultaneously *more rigorous* and *more fair*. In the political climate of White recovery, however, we can hardly discuss these possibilities without right-wing charges of "playing the race card," "coddling the slackers," "not teaching content," "punishing hard-working White students," "tearing down American institutions," "not teaching the basics," and other signifiers of the educational expression of the White recovery.

6. *The Philosophical Confusion of the Standards Movement—The Need for a Compelling Social Vision.*
Outside of the effort to improve test scores, it is rare in the Texas standards movement to overhear a discussion of educational purpose. Reduc-

tionistic forms of curriculum development, it is safe to argue, have rarely involved the formulation of pedagogies consistent with social values and democratic precepts. Indeed, in Texas such forms of analysis are repressed; philosophical discussions of purpose and educational strategies consistent with larger purposes are ridiculed as impractical and irrelevant. Such anti-intellectualism often undermines good teachers' work in a variety of ways. Ray Horn's insight into these matters is helpful, as he writes in chapter 3 about the need to develop educational standards that are consistent with diverse and democratic communities. How, he asks, can we create schools and communities that further the goals of equality and meet the needs of a multicultural society. Standards of complexity take these essential features of education into account, exposing in the process the multidimensionality of the pedagogical process.

Standards of complexity take the task of educational leadership and curriculum development very seriously. Such reconceptualized standards see the development of a democratic social and educational vision as one of their primary tasks. The reason such a task is so important involves the fragility of contemporary democracy and its vulnerability to the abuses of power and oppression. Without a democratic vision with an egalitarian set of commitments, students must constantly resist reductionistic schooling's effort to adapt them to the brutality of the neo-social Darwinist landscape. While in no way rejecting the need for students and other citizens to understand the nature of the existing world so that they can negotiate its dangers, advocates of standards of complexity maintain the importance of exposing individuals to alternatives, to visions of what can be.

Without such visions we are doomed to the perpetuation of the structural inequalities and the political passivity of the status quo. This is why advocates of context-savvy complex standards seek to connect their democratic vision to rigorous scholarly work. In such a pedagogical effort, teachers, writers, theologians, and other cultural workers create a new history, as they work to revitalize a democracy dissipated first by industrialization and then by the new world produced by the communications revolution of the last half of the twentieth century. Analyzing democratic issues historically, philosophically, and pedagogically, in relation to this new information world and as a benchmark for educational purpose, constructs a vision of education for democracy and civic courage.

Such a curriculum is grounded on the assumption that self-directed education undertaken by self-organized community groups is the most powerful form of pedagogical reform. Standards of complexity in this context seek to build a coherent social and economic vision that addresses

the philosophical confusion of the Texas standards. Such complex democratic standards understand that an educational system philosophically
divided against itself with a unitary, one-dimensional form of high-stakes
assessment cannot long stand. When teacher testing is based on a child-
centered educational psychology, a constructivist form of knowledge that
recognizes the importance of an individual's social location in shaping his
or her perspective on the world, and the importance of a pedagogical
model of democratic cooperative learning, but student, school, and school
district success is based on a teacher-centered, rote-memorization-based
psychology, a positivistic form of knowledge that deems an individual's
social location irrelevant in learning essential final truths about the world,
and a social Darwinist, abstract, individualistic, competitive pedagogy,
then a variety of disjunctions emerge.

"What are we trying to accomplish?" confused teachers ask. "Why do
many of our teachers seem to resist our efforts to improve test scores?"
confused administrators ask. And, unfortunately, little conversation takes
place because in neither group have individuals been provided the philosophical background to delve into the disjunctions. Few know what is
going on in this land of confusion. Standards of complexity attempt to
bring these larger issues out of the shadows into the sunlight of public
conversation. How does that affect educational purpose? educational
quality? Educational success? The performance of middle- and upper-
middle-class White students? The performance of African American and
Latino students? Such questions should be asked and debated publicly,
among political leaders, among educators, among the citizens of Texas
and the U.S. at large. Such questions constitute the life blood of a functioning democracy and a democratic system of education.

Standards of complexity in this context become a "pro-democracy"
movement that attempt to promote forms of conversation, thinking, and
action that retrieve the impetus for educational change from business and
industrial elites. Grounded on a conception of solidarity with the oppressed
and the excluded, this curriculum seeks to connect with democratic organizations dedicated to a politics of social justice. Here students can become part of social movements where they can employ their rigorous
scholarship, their research and pedagogical skills to build new forms of
democratic consciousness and social action. Advocates of democratic standards of complexity understand that only an education that is intrinsically
motivating by its connection to the lived world will produce rigorous scholars and much-needed lifelong learners. Cheerleader-led pep rallies will
not be needed to provide motivation for students who see their efforts

making a difference in the world, making Texas and the U.S. a better place in which to live.

Such a lived-world-grounded, research-based, content-applying education can revolutionize current Texas students' view of school knowledge as data produced by disembodied experts in remote locales. The knowledge produced in complex standards is an outcome of democratic cooperation, a manifestation of what happens when world/community events are questioned in light of a historical consciousness intersecting with personal experience. In an academically rigorous pro-democracy movement, school teachers address forms of subordination that create inequities among racial, class, and gendered groups. Such practitioners align their teaching and learning in relation to forms of civic courage and link their pedagogies to confronting the forces that undermine Texan and American democracy and to addressing the needs of those excluded from the benefits of equal citizenship.

In the context of this vision of reform, advocates of standards of complexity understand the threat to public education and democracy itself posed by reductionism, technical rationality, the reeducation project, the recovery of White supremacy, and philosophical confusion. These problematic dynamics themselves are a manifestation of the destruction of the rigorous thinking that standards of complexity seek to promote. In many ways the crisis of reductionistic, technical standards can be viewed as a crisis of thinking, of cognition—an inability to conceptualize democratically, to imagine what democracy might imply in building social and educational institutions and in the activities of everyday life. Marked by a dominant power-saturated mode of thinking that is concerned with the standardization of things human and the rational management of everyday affairs, reductionistic, technical, standards-driven education has found itself trapped within a prison of nihilism (let's learn fragmented data so we can do well on the TAAS test and beat Kilgore High School) and a culture of manipulation.

Education in Texas and around the U.S. in the early twenty-first century has become a pawn of powerful interests who attempt to use it to further their own self-centered political and economic interests. Pushed and pulled by such powerful corporate interests, schools are not moved by educational and political visions that value the cultivation of the human spirit but by self-serving and unarticulated impulses that seek to control that spirit in the name of excellence and quality. Thus, schools, as most teachers will testify, are immersed in a *crisis of motivation*. In my interviews even with successful high school students their overt devaluation of the intrinsic merit of what they have learned, or more traditionally, the good students' inability to articulate a value for reductionistic learning outside of its "preparation for college," illustrates the reasons for the motivational crisis. "Quick, bring in the cheerleaders and the pep rallies." No cheer can pull students out of the maze of fragmented information.

After all the monetary incentives, trophies for winning scores, and certificates of recognition for individual test success are presented, classrooms in test-driven Texas schools will remain spiritless places—venues where intimidated, rule-following teachers face groups of students who have rarely been exposed to articulations of the intrinsic value of rigorous learning or the relation of education to the responsibilities of democratic citizenship. Such an educational nihilism can be addressed by educators, political leaders, parents, and concerned citizens who are able to articulate a democratic vision of individual development and social improvement (no matter where one comes from). When schools fail to meet the particulars of the vision, they must be held accountable. One standard within the standards of complexity, for example, asks the question of equity: are students from all social and economic sectors benefiting from the educational reforms implemented? If the answer is no, then schools cannot be deemed to be achieving high standards. High standards—or in Texas, high test scores—for the privileged few are not good enough. Authentically excellent education demands a *much higher* standard.

7. *Loss of Local Control of Education—The Dismissal of the Insights of Those Closest to the Teaching and Learning Process.*
In chapter 16, Sandra Lowery and Janiece Buck unambiguously document the recent decline of local control in Texas school districts and individual schools. The irony, the authors point out, of such a centralizing power play is that it has taken place—as most contemporary power plays do—in the name of democratic values. Decentralized and democratic concepts such as "site-based management" and "local decision making" have been used as smokescreens for top-down, antidemocratic, imposed content standards and teacher/school accountability measures. It is important to note, contrary to the protestations of Texas standards advocates, that rigorous educational standards can be developed that do not *standardize* school practice, in the process taking away local decision making about ways of dealing with local contingencies. Standards of complexity in their concern with diverse contexts zealously defend the sanctity of local educational decision making.

Such centralization and its accompanying attempts at control of teachers and students are as old as American public education itself. Referring to our previous discussion of Horace Mann's crusade for public education in Massachusetts in the 1840s and the educational movements of the early twentieth century devoted to schooling for the human capital needs of business, social regulation and control have always been central features of American education. The most important and effective manifestation of schooling for social control has involved the use of scientific management techniques based on forms of technical rationality discussed earlier. The forms of regulation used in the Texas standards reforms fit into this category.

In the first decades of the twentieth century, scientific management influenced schooling to such an extent that power relations among administrators, teachers, and students were profoundly affected. When behavioral psychology was added to the pedagogical recipe, teachers began to be seen more and more as entities to be controlled and manipulated. In the spirit of the times, psychologist Edward Thorndike announced that the human mind is an exacting instrument given to precise measurement. Teachers, he concluded, are not capable of such measurement, and therefore the formulation of instructional strategies and curriculum development should be left to experienced psychologists. It is no surprise that such reductionists soon won the battle for the soul of the school, shaping its ambiance with their control of instructional design (Popkewitz, 1987).

Though subsequent decades have witnessed an evolving sophistication of their strategies, the forces of efficiency, productivity, and scientific management unleashed by Frederick W. Taylor and Thorndike have helped shape the history of twentieth- and early twenty-first-century American schooling. In many schools and in varying degrees, efficiency, rationalization, productivity, and technology have achieved an almost divine status. In the situations most affected by these dynamics, teachers have taught subject matter that had been broken into an ordered sequence of separate tasks and "factoids." Trained to follow a pretest, drill work, posttest instructional model, teachers have efficiently followed a rationalized pedagogy that has insidiously embedded itself as part of their "cultural logic"— a logic that serves to tame their pedagogical imagination. No thought is necessary, it's just common sense to assume that if you want to teach somebody something, you simply break the information into separate pieces, go over the pieces until the learner has mastered them, then test him or her to make sure the pieces have been "learned" (Goodman, 1986). Sound familiar?

In the more centralized and rationalized schools of the twentieth century, many teachers were induced to internalize as common sense a pedagogical approach that broke the complex task of teaching into a series of simple steps that even unskilled laborers can perform. In this way, teachers were *deskilled*. As Taylor put it to one of his workers: "[You're] not supposed to think; there are other people paid for thinking around here" (Wirth, 1983, p. 12). The need for the judgment of the worker/teacher would be eliminated in Taylor's system. The deskilling of teaching was thus rationalized; the *conception* of the pedagogical act was separated from its *execution*. Teachers did not need to learn the intricacies of subject matter, nor did they need to understand the sociohistorical context in which the knowledge to be taught was produced.

All such teachers needed to do was to identify the subject matter to be transferred to the learner, break it into components, present it to the student, and test him or her on it. It was a strategy as right as rain, so commonsensical it defied the need for justification. What need was there for local control of schooling when teachers were implementing the dictates of experts? What was important here was that the very politicized subject of local control did not even need to be broached—the centralization of power had already taken place without public knowledge. This from the power wielder's perspective was the beauty of technicalized, rationalized forms of control: The changes did not have to be negotiated in the messy and unpredictable public forum of democracy. What an insidious way of undermining American democracy and democratic public education.

A brief examination of the teacher manuals that accompanied reading textbooks illustrates the deskilling of many teachers and the insidious loss of local control of education. In the 1920s, small manuals contained brief professional educational discussions and bibliographies for students. The pamphlets emphasized the teaching of reading. Fifty years later the manuals had added scores of pages that included complete scripts (about four pages per day) specifying exactly what teachers were to say, where to stand as they said it, and how to test and evaluate their students. The manuals of the 1970s were not as concerned with the teaching of reading as they were with the teaching of specific skills needed on standardized tests (Popkewitz, 1987).

It seems obvious what happened here. The technical management of teaching with its accompanying deskilling initiated a vicious circle of harm to the profession and to the democratic control of education. As teachers were deskilled, they lost more and more autonomy. As many of them became accustomed to the loss of autonomy, it was argued that they were incapable of self-direction. While in no way should we romanticize work conditions for nineteenth- and early twentieth-century teachers, teachers later in the century were subjected to forms of control unimagined by previous teachers. Technically rational teacher education often serves to enculturate teachers into this deskilled, politically passive role. Prospective teachers learn to be supervised in courses that teach them to meticulously write behavioral objectives and lesson plans in the "correct" format.

Enculturated into an academic culture of passivity, many teachers found themselves in workplaces that imposed both teaching objectives and test-ing and evaluation procedures. As a result, such teachers had little input into what to teach, how to teach it, or how to judge the outcome. Such a system was an insult to teacher dignity and democratic education, as it assumed that teachers and the public they served were too ignorant to be permitted to decide such matters. Such teachers became the pawns in a cult of expertise—just as Thorndike envisioned it—taking orders from ex-perts conversant with the language of efficiency and scientific manage-ment. In such systems some teachers did grow lazy and apathetic. But are we surprised, when they suckled at the breast of passivity and grew up professionally in a bureaucratic system that discouraged initiative? Rigor-ous and responsible teachers found themselves too often branded as pa-riahs, outsiders who were banished because of their "bad attitudes" and their reluctance to become "team players" (Kamii, 1981).

Thus, the Texas standards movement has precedents that go back decades. "Standards" is just another word for curriculum guides and state mandates. This has all been tried before—and it failed miserably. The Texas standards movement is simply the newest effort to centralize the control of schools, using charges of teacher incompetence and claims of excellence to justify technical, rationalistic, and easily measured and ma-nipulated outcomes. In the centralized and technically rationalized pro-cess, input into teaching and learning is covertly taken away from those closest to and with the most intimate knowledge of the students in the classroom and their specific locations in the web of reality. When this takes place, not only has a central tenet of democracy been subverted but also a central principle of a good pedagogy: instruction should always be designed around the needs of learners.

Despite the increasing forms of technical control found in the last third of the twentieth century, numerous teachers still had the power to escape rationalized (and irrational) forms of control. In many places, especially in Texas, teachers could close their classroom doors and remain fairly undis-turbed. Texas standards reforms and those who imitate them are shutting down this escape valve. Teachers, students, and local communities seeking to have input into their local schools are finding the task more and more difficult. The opposite of highly centralized, rationalized, and standardized education is not some haphazard, unprepared, inferior form of teaching.

The form of pedagogy we propose in standards of complexity is flexible but rigorous, locally controlled but in touch with the knowledge production of various academic disciplines, concerned with content acquisition but also attentive to the multiple knowledge forms produced by individuals from diverse cultures, political/ideological perspectives, and paradigms. Such concerns allow the promotion of a democratic rigor—a high-quality education that seeks not to restrict, regulate, and contain students and teachers but to engage them in understanding new levels of thinking of better ways of being human. I personally find this possibility extremely exciting and highly motivating to the students I have taught in elementary, secondary, and undergraduate classrooms and all the way to graduate school.

8. *The Quest for Good Public Relations and Image Construction Takes Precedence over the Production of a Genuinely Rigorous Education.* By the very nature of the standardized evaluation procedures used in Texas and in the U.S. in general, the public gets a distorted picture of what is happening in the Texas standards movement. Here I will briefly discuss the general distortions of standardized testing as well as comment on the intentional manipulations of Texas evaluation procedures. The Texas assessments are much more interested in controlling the public's opinion of the success of the reforms than honestly assessing what is happening in Texas education as a result of the reforms.

Standardized tests of fragmented content knowledge measure the most menial modes of human cognition. They reveal very little about whether or not students can or do engage in serious scholarship, whether they have an understanding of the complexity of an issue. Unable to measure higher-order thinking, standardized tests typically miss the cognitive abilities that great thinkers, innovative analysts, and individuals who make great breakthroughs in theoretical and/or practical domains possess: the abilities to see the world from a new vantage point, to ask previously unasked questions, to reveal hidden erroneous assumptions, to discern unnoticed relationships between/among various entities, to perceive flaws in the structure of disciplines of knowledge, and so on. Standardized tests deemphasize such difficult-to-measure but important abilities, while easy-to-measure but trivial abilities gain center stage. Education that is driven by such tests is undermined, reduced to low-level functions, computation, and busywork with little connection to the passions and complexities of human beings.

Reductionists attempt to refute such ideas by arguing that basic knowledge must be learned first and then built upon in a step-by-rigid-step process. Such reductionism falls into a fallacy of linearity that assumes that human beings learn in rationalistic manner. Socio-cognitive research (Kincheloe, Steinberg, & Villaverde, 1999; Henriques et al., 1984; Wertsch, 1991; Wertsch & Tulviste, 1992; Cannella, 1997; Shotter, 1993) reports that humans operating in everyday, out-of-school learning situations rarely learn in this step-by-step manner. Thus, the attempt to force students into the rationalistic mode actually undermines learning. Such rationalistic methods operate especially to destroy the meaning and purpose of learning. As researchers Linda McNeil and Angela Valenzuela (1998) insightfully point out, the TAAS test goes against most research findings on student learning. As they maintain, student "learning is not linear, it builds on what children already know and understand . . . must engage children's active thinking, and . . . must engage many senses" (p. 9).

The TAAS does none of these things. It reinforces one reductionistic mode of learning involving the mastery of arbitrarily chosen fragments of data. When the TAAS drives the curriculum, students are discouraged from building a comprehensive content grounding in a subject area, their understanding of a subject is not germane to teaching, their previous knowledge about an area is irrelevant, and they don't get to engage in the high-level task of producing their own knowledge. Where TAAS-preparation has displaced a more contextualized, student-centered, higher-order skill-based curriculum, the quality and rigor of learning decreases. When school leaders claim that an improvement in standardized test scores is an accurate sign of educational progress, they focus their attention on numbers. If the scores are allowed to stand as irrefutable proof of learning success, we dismiss the reality of cognitive reductionism, the lack of well-being of students, and their inability to find meaning and significance in classroom activities. When we find that the TAAS has destroyed the fragile learning environment of a school, such a change can hardly be described as progress.

These are the very issues that are excluded from the public conversation about Texas standards. If schools are to ever improve, these are the issues we must confront. As long as these dynamics are unchallenged, the Texas public and unfortunately the American public gain a perverted picture of what is happening in the state's educational reform. The wrong lessons will be learned, and other state and national reforms will be based on a pedagogical charade. As PR concerns overwhelm the hard work and conceptual insight needed to produce an equitable *and* rigorous education, a tendency for shady manipulation of statistics about Texas educational improvement has emerged. The following four distortions raise numerous questions about the integrity of the state's accountability process. Texas standards reforms give the impression of school improvement because of

a. Test score increases based on a better method of identifying who does poorly on tests. In this context, note that special education students in Texas are exempted from the test. We can raise any state's test scores by identifying the worst test takers and then exempting them from the process.
b. Test score increases due to focusing attention and resources on the group most likely to pass the test—the so-called bubble children. Such actions do raise test scores and TAAS passage rates but do little to improve the system or assist those in most need.
c. Test score increases involving cheating and unethical practices. There are numerous reports of teachers providing correct answers, administrative personnel changing incorrect answers, and school principals removing weak students from classes on testing days.
d. Underreporting of dropout rates—twice the number of Texas students drop out of school as the number reported by the state. The rate is particularly high among African American and Hispanic students. In addition to a bad reporting system in school districts, the state uses statistical manipulations to reduce the dropout rate reported to the public. Students who drop out of school, for example, because they did not pass the TAAS test are not reported as dropouts.

Conclusion: Standards of Complexity

The following chapters will provide more detail and conceptual expansion of these and other concepts concerning the Texas standards reforms. It is our contention that the standards conversation in Texas and across the U.S. has been disappointing in its relation to the effort to produce an equitable, just, rigorous, and life-enhancing system of education for the twenty-first century. In chapter 21 I will return to these issues, offering a foundation for the types of rigorous educational standards I have referred to in this introductory chapter—standards of complexity. In addition to recognizing the intrinsic complications of the teaching act itself, standards of complexity reject the standardization impulse of instrumental rationality, embracing instead a rigorous form of contextualized, purpose-driven scholarly practice.

Such a pedagogy is aware of the relationship between the new social conditions of the early twenty-first century and the goals of schooling. It is particularly interested in the emerging new information environment and its need for more sophisticated, ethical, and visionary knowledge workers, regardless of the vocational path they have chosen. Well-educated individuals of the future must understand these dynamics and, thus, must have access to an educational system that avoids the pitfalls of reductionism. Standards of complexity learn from the mistakes of the Texas reforms. Here rests the purpose of *American Standards: Quality Education in a Complex World—The Texas Case*.

References

Allison, C. (1995). *Present and past: Essays for teachers in the history of education.* New York: Peter Lang.

Apple, M. (1996). Dominance and dependency: Situating *The Bell Curve* within the conservative restoration. In J. Kincheloe, S. Steinberg, & A. Gresson (Eds.), *Measured lies: The bell curve examined.* New York: St. Martin's Press.

Brosio, R. (1994). *The radical democratic critique of capitalist education.* New York: Peter Lang.

Cannella, G. S. (1997). *Deconstructing early childhood education: Social justice and revolution.* New York: Peter Lang Publishing.

DeYoung, A. (1989). *Economics and American education.* New York: Longman.

Frankel, B. (1986). Two extremes on the commitment continuum. In D. Fiske & R. Schweder (Eds.), *Metatheory in social science: Pluralisms and subjectivities.* Chicago: University of Chicago Press.

Giroux, H., & Searls, S. (1996). The bell curve debate and the crisis of public intellectuals. In J. Kincheloe, S. Steinberg, & A. Gresson (Eds.), *Measured lies: The bell curve examined.* New York: St. Martin's Press.

Goodman, J. (1986). *Constructing a practical philosophy of teaching: A study of preservice teachers' professional perspectives.* Paper presented to the American Educational Research Association, San Francisco.

Gordon, E., Miller, F., & Rollock, D. (1990). Coping with communicentric bias in knowledge production in the social sciences. *Educational Researcher, 19* (3), 14–19.

Gresson, A. (1995). *The recovery of race in America.* Minneapolis, MN: University of Minnesota Press.

Henriques, J., et al. (1984). *Changing the subject.* New York: Methuen.

Herrnstein, R., & Murray, C. (1994). *The bell curve: Intelligence and class structure in American life.* New York: The Free Press.

Kamii, C. (1981). Teachers' autonomy and scientific training. *Young Children, 31*, 5–14.

Kincheloe, J. (1999). *How do we tell the workers? The socio-economic foundations of work and vocational education.* Boulder, CO: Westview.

Kincheloe, J., & Steinberg, S. (1997). *Changing multiculturalism: New times, new curriculum.* London: Open University Press.

Kincheloe, J., Steinberg, S., & Gresson, A. (Eds.). (1996). *Measured lies: The bell curve examined.* New York: St. Martin's Press.

Kincheloe, J., Steinberg, S., & Hinchey, P. (1999). *The post-formal reader: Cognition and education.* New York: Garland Publishing.

Kincheloe, J., Steinberg, S., & Slattery, P. (2000). *Contextualizing teaching.* New York: Longman.

Kincheloe, J., Steinberg, S., & Tippins, D. (1999). *The stigma of genius: Einstein, consciousness, and education.* New York: Peter Lang.

Kincheloe, J., Steinberg, S., & Villaverde, L. (Eds.). (1999). *Rethinking intelligence: Confronting psychological assumptions about teaching and learning.* New York: Routledge.

King, J. (1996). Bad luck, bad blood, bad faith: Ideological hegemony and the oppressive language of hoodoo social science. In J. Kincheloe, S. Steinberg and A. Gresson (Eds.), *Measured lies: The bell curve examined.* New York: St. Martin's Press.

McLaren, P. (1994). *Life in schools: An introduction to critical pedagogy in the foundations of education.* White Plains, NY: Longman.

McLaren, P. (2000). *Che Guevara, Paulo Freire, and the pedagogy of revolution.* Boulder, CO: Rowman & Littlefield Publishers.

McNeil, L., & Valenzuela, A. (1998). *The harmful impact of the TAAS system of testing in Texas: Beneath the accountability rhetoric,* [On-line]. Available: <http://www.law.harvard.edu/civilrights/conferences/testing98/drafts/mcneil_valenzuela.html>.

Nightingale, C. (1993). *On the edge: A history of poor black children and their American dreams.* New York: Basic Books.

Oakes, J. (1988). Tracking in mathematics and science education: A structural contribution to unequal schooling. In L. Weis (Ed.), *Class, race, and gender in American education.* Albany, NY: SUNY Press.

Perkinson, H. (1991). *The imperfect panacea: American faith in education, 1865–1900* (3rd ed.). New York: McGraw-Hill.

Popkewitz, T. (1987). Organization and power: Teacher education reforms. *Social Education, 39,* 496–500.

Romanish, B. (1987). A skeptical view of educational reform. *Journal of Teacher Education, 38* (3), 9–12.

Schon, D. (1987). *Educating the reflective practitioner.* San Francisco, CA: Jossey-Bass.

Shotter, J. (1993). *Cultural politics of everyday life.* Toronto, Canada: University of Toronto Press.

Tyack, D. (1974). *The one best system: A history of American urban education.* Cambridge, MA: Harvard University Press.

Wertsch, J. (1991). *Voices of the mind: A sociocultural approach to mediated action.* Cambridge, MA: Harvard University Press.

Wertsch, J., & Tulviste, P. (1992). L. S. Vygotsky and contemporary developmental psychology. *Developmental Psychology, 28* (4), 548–57.

Wiggins, G. (1989). A true test: Toward a more authentic and equitable assessment. *Phi Delta Kappan, 70* (9), 703–713.

Wirth, A. (1983). *Productive work—in industry and schools: Becoming persons again.* Lanham, Maryland: University Press of America.

Woods, P. (1983). *Sociology and the school: An interactionist viewpoint.* London: Routledge and Kegan Paul.

Zweigenhaft, R., & Domhoff, G. (1991). *Blacks in the white establishment.* New Haven: Yale University Press.

Chapter 2

Couching the Standards Debate in Historical Terms: Developing a Dialectical Understanding of the Standards Debate Through Historical Awareness

Danny Weil

Introduction

Any understanding of the politics of the current standards debate, its recent emergence, challenges, and promises must be understood within the socio-historical context that spawned it. Historically, we can find a critical rethinking and reexamination of intelligence and educational standards in a multitude of educational and psychological theoretical pursuits throughout the twentieth century. These include the social functionalism of the factory school, Dewey progressivism of the early 1900s, critical pedagogy, notably in the persona of Paulo Freire, neo-functionalism, critical thinking insights, post-structural psychoanalysis, and Vygotskian understandings of cognition and theories.

Yet unfortunately, as educational author and reformer Herbert Kliebard has lamented, school change movements generally fail to understand the history of educational reform in the United States. According to Kliebard,

> New breakthroughs are solemnly proclaimed when in fact they represent minor modifications of early proposals, and, conversely, anachronistic dogmas and doctrines maintain a currency and uncritical acceptance far beyond their present merit. (Kliebard, 1970, p. 259.)

Kliebard calls upon educators to examine new and popular school reform proposals from a historical perspective. For our purposes, this examination will specifically focus on the historical development of education as these developments affect the debate regarding educational standards.

Educational Purpose: *Why Do We Teach?*

There are many points of view regarding the role or purpose of schools in society, what they should teach, and how the teaching and learning should be assessed. The aim of this chapter is not to give a prolonged or detailed characterization of the myriad frames of reference on the subject. However, characterizing at least some of these points of view in terms of how the debate is currently viewed is essential to engage in a truly meaningful dialogue about assessment and standards. Currently, popular political debates regarding literacy, standards, and assessment continue to concentrate on anecdotal evidence and attention-seeking headlines that really do little or nothing to help teachers, their students, or their students' parents move toward a genuine curriculum of thinking and learning. Furthermore, many parents and community members continue to labor under old paradigms of what it means to be literate, intelligent, and assessed. These paradigms are fueled and nurtured by an ignorant and demagogic media that continues to separate assessment from learning while seeking to frame the complex issue of education in terms of either back-to-basics or outcome-based education (whether in public schools or private schools.

American Industrialism and the Twentieth-Century Development of the Factory School

The end of the Civil War and the years that immediately followed brought unbridled economic growth and development to post-Civil War America. New scientific and technological developments fueled the expansion of markets and configured a deeply changing America. More and more Americans began to move to large urban centers, leading to the increased development and expansion of cities. Coupled with immigration, the increased urbanization and industrialization of the late nineteenth century and early twentieth century brought rapid growth to American industry and a new concentration of economic power in the hands of industrialists and corporations.

With immigration changing the political and cultural landscape of America in the late 1800s, larger urban centers were not only growing, but for the first time they were growing with people other than White Anglos (Kincheloe, 2000, p. 151). Along with this rapid growth came the need to assimilate these newly arriving immigrants into the melting pot of "mainstream" American life. An obvious and logical forum for this was the public school. Work in urban centers during this time in history was largely relegated to factory work, so the emerging of the American public school began to resemble the factory as well. There were bells to sound the beginning of classes, desks bolted to the floor in regimented rows, strict discipline, and a rigidly imposed social order (Kincheloe, 2000, p. 151).

The costs of building these new factory type schools were justified in the minds of the public by appeals to the "national interest." The argument was simple. Immigrant children were in the United States because the United States needed the labor of their parents to become rich and prosperous. The market rationale at the time also argued that educating these "immigrant children" would bring a positive return on the investment, that is a more productive work force and a more competitive America. One leading educational functionalist at the time, Ellwood Cubberley (1916), wrote:

> Our schools are, in a sense, factories in which the raw products (children) [his parentheses] are to be shaped and fashioned into products to meet the demands of life. The specifications for manufacturing come from the demands of twentieth century civilization, and it is the business of the school to build its pupils according to the specifications laid down. (p. 338)

If the public school represented the factory, the students themselves were little more than the raw material or objects of production; they were seen as the products to be fashioned by the public school system. In the emerging modern public schools of America, children, especially immigrant children, were to be trained to follow directions and routines, learn proper English, and develop rudimentary "basic skills," such as reading, mathematical, and writing skills. Schooling, in a sense, developed as a center for socialization and indoctrination as America entered the industrial age.

Post-Civil War America also saw market interests and business concerns rapidly permeate public schools. Not only was the curriculum of public schools immersed in the growth, regulation, and maintenance of urbanization and the rise of industrialization and factory existence, but the schools were also implicated in the development of a modernist conception of knowledge and intelligence.

Between 1880 and 1920, as the factory-style public school system emerged, so too did the philosophy specifying that the reality and life of both students and teachers needed to be scientifically oriented and regulated

(Kincheloe, 2000, p.153). Standardized tests were developed during this period and emphasized sorting and categorizing mechanisms that would place students on specific curricular tracks. Modern rationalism and specific, delineated ways of knowing emerged, as the measurement of intelligence and the new standardized tests, such as the Stanford-Binet test, were designed to calibrate and classify students according to emerging modernist notions of intellectual behavior. These instruments of assessment also gave specific direction to teachers as to what they should be doing in their classrooms.

The IQ test had its origins in France where Alfred Binet attempted to study and recommend procedures for educating mentally retarded children (Binet & Simon, 1905). The test itself was forged in the fires of the actual material conditions of early twentieth-century capitalist France and reflected the values, interests, needs, and focuses of not only Binet himself but the cultural and socioeconomic milieu within which he found himself.

Binet proposed, in 1905, a 30-item scale of intelligence, a set of norms, so to speak, to measure what contributes to classroom achievement. After Binet's death in 1911, the Stanford-Binet IQ test revised Binet's earlier normative scale. The test has been revised many times since its inception and is still generally considered the measure of intelligence in Western societies.

Formalist reason, Cartesian-Newtonian science, and the techno-rationalist necessities of the emerging industrial revolution, coupled with the need to develop a psychology or managerial science of the mind, all influenced and the theoretical development and practical implementation of the normative scales used in the IQ test. Considerations of historical reality are necessary to understand any assessment, not simply the IQ test; the development, use, and analysis of assessments is always historically situated and must be understood against the specific socioeconomic conditions from which the assessments arose. This allows us to see why and how intelligence has been defined and how this definition has implications for the ways we organize educational occasions for students and productive opportunities for teachers. It also affords us an insight into the role of standards and assessment.

The Development of Functionalist Theory

The burgeoning industrial capitalism of the late 1800s and early 1900s needed schooling to preserve, extend, and legitimize the economic relations of production and the new forms of unprecedented consumption. Consequently, during this period we see the rise and development of an educational philosophy called social functionalism; education organized, implemented, and controlled to meet the functional needs of society's business and economic interests. These needs could be identified with what was necessary in the workplace and then taught and assessed. The assessment would be metaphorically similar to assuring quality control, much like quality control assurance of products.

Directly associated with the social functionalism of schools was an excessive preoccupation with the values of productivity, efficiency, and thrift (Goodman, 1995, p. 6). With the development of the assembly line, and specifically the contributions of Frederick Taylor to the new science of business management that was being realized on assembly lines, efficiency, productivity, and speed began to capture the imagination of the American public. Factory work relied on workers who could follow instructions, take simple directions, and work swiftly to increase production with maximum efficiency.

Industrial production proceeded at levels previously unheard of, and the power and ideology of industrialized production became the infatuation and ideology of America during this period. It is hard not to see the parallel between this historical time period and today. Although contemporary production has shifted to technological and service work as America enters into the "third wave," or post-industrialism, infatuation with technological, cybernetic tycoons and the ideology of efficiency and "lean production" now dominates American culture. School-to-work programs are important offerings of many public schools and have arisen partly in response to the demands of the new social functionalism designed to prepare students for the changing needs of production in the twenty-first century.

The social functionalism prevalent in the philosophy of early twentieth-century educational discourse, along with a preoccupation with speed and efficiency, was described by leading reformer Franklin Bobbitt, one of the key social functionalists in the industrial-age school restructuring movement. Bobbitt claimed as early as 1912:

> It is helpful to begin with the simple assumption to be accepted literally, that education is to prepare men and women for the activities of adult life; and that nothing should be included which does not serve this purpose. . . . The first task is to discover the activities which ought to make up the lives of men and women; and along with these, the abilities and personal qualities necessary for proper performance. These are educational objectives. When we know what men and

women ought to do then we shall have before us the things for which they should
be trained. (p. 259)

The activities to which Bobbitt (1912) refers were tied to necessities due
to changes in the relations of production and consumption that were
exploding at the time.

And not only did the industrial age have an impact on the purposes
and goals of education, but the social functionalism of the time also affected staffing patterns, curricular construction, and instructional design
(Goodman, 1995). What Callahan (1962) referred to as the "cult" of efficiency and productivity had an effect on every aspect of schooling.
Taylorism (a term taken from Frederick Taylor, the father of the assembly
line), as the modern science of business management, was rapidly being
implemented in school production as well. With educational goals restructured and defined as increasing productivity in schools, in essence,
increasing, the quantity of what students learn, the factory school began
to predetermine outcomes and then plan backwards to restructure education so that these outcomes could be reached. Bobbitt declared as early
as 1913:

> The third grade teacher should bring her pupils up to an average of 26 correct
> [addition] combinations per minute. The fourth grade teacher has the task, during
> the year that the same pupils are under her care, of increasing their addition
> speed from an average of 26 combinations per minute to an average of 34 com-
> binations per minute. If she does not bring them up to the standard 34, she has
> failed to perform her duty in proportion to the deficit; and there is no responsibil-
> ity beyond the standard. (pp. 21–22)

Specifically stated learning objectives that could be measured, controlled, and regulated became the language of educational discourse. These
objectives were tied to what was needed or what was functional within
the emerging industrial society. With an "objectives first" approach to
education and schooling, curriculum underwent unique changes. Educators at the time were not only concerned with efficiency and production,
but they also believed strongly in the practice of differentiated staffing
(Goodman, 1995). Knowledge acquisition was fragmented into disciplines
and subjects, much like the work on assembly lines in industrial factories.
The important goal for the social functionalists and efficiency educators
of their day was to reduce the number of educational workers by maximiz-
ing their instructional efficiency. Thus, just as Taylor advocated in the
factory, no one person was ever to be responsible for too many tasks.
Scientism and the instrumentalist approaches of functionalist educators

divided teaching into distinct and differentiated tasks performed by distinctive individuals.

The reconfiguration of the school day and the redesign of curriculum during the industrial revolution in the early part of the twentieth century helped shape what we know now as the large, urban public school and the accompanying public school curriculum. As we shall see, Bobbitt's appeal to link school to work was not much different from the positions taken by certain educational policy makers and business leaders today. And just as Taylorism and the new science of business administration influenced the conception and organization of schooling during the early twentieth century, contemporary changes in production, consumption, and business management theory exert a tremendous influence on the standards debate today.

Progressive Educational Responses
to the Factory School

Although the factory style of education of the latter part of the nineteenth century and early part of the twentieth imposed a functionalistic, industrial education on all American citizens (African Americans, Native Americans, newly arriving immigrants, and Anglos) it was not without its critics.

Even though the prevailing wisdom of the time argued for impersonal factory schools grounded on modernist approaches to curriculum and teaching, many educators protested. They not only saw the factory school as an impersonal social arrangement, they saw industrial society and the factory itself as an impediment to human development. Margaret Haley, union organizer and teacher-activist at the time, made the following observation:

> Two ideals are struggling for supremacy in American life today; one the industrial ideal, dominating through the supremacy of commercialism, which subordinates the worker to the product, and the machine; the other [the] ideal of democracy, the ideal of educators, which places humanity above all machines, and demands that all activity shall be the expression of life. (quoted in Tyack, 1974, p. 257)

Educators like Haley opposed what they viewed as the rigid and impersonal social order imposed by factory life. Haley, like many of her contemporaries, felt that the rise of corporations and corporate power were far more menacing to American life than the role of government (Kincheloe, 2000, p. 159). These educational progressives wanted schooling to create educational experiences for children that expanded their involvement in citizenship activities and civic responsibility; and to this end, they argued, public education must construct its mission and purpose.

Besides Haley, one of the most prominent progressive educators and philosophers during the early part of the twentieth century was John Dewey. Like Haley, Dewey (1938/1976) argued against reducing schooling to mere functionalism (boring and repetitive tasks designed to prepare students for future work). Dewey's argument against social functionalism maintained that the role and purpose of education should be to prepare students to live fully in the present, not simply to prepare for the future. Like Boyd Bode, another progressive educator of the time, Dewey argued that for schooling to become merely a preparatory institution for future market needs was dehumanizing and denied children the opportunity to find relevancy and meaning in their lives. Dewey (1938/1976) commented:

> The ideal of using the present simply to get ready for the future contradicts itself. It omits, and even shuts out, the very conditions by which a person can be prepared for his future. We always live at the time we live and not at some other time, and only by extracting at each present time the full meaning of each present experience are we prepared for doing the same thing in the future. This is the only preparation, which in the long run amounts to anything. (p. 49)

Dewey (1940) himself was very clear regarding what he and other progressives conceived of as the purpose and objective of education:

> The problem of education in its relation to the direction of social change is all one with the problem of finding out what democracy means in total range of concrete applications; domestic, international, religious, cultural, economic, *and* political . . . The trouble. . . is that we have taken democracy for granted; we have thought and acted as if our forefathers had founded it once and for all. We have forgotten that it has to be enacted anew with *every* generation, in *every* year, in *every* day, in the living relations of person to person, in all social forms and institutions. Forgetting this . . . we have been negligent in creating a school that should be the constant nurse of democracy. (pp. 357–358)

Dewey was convinced that democracy was not a "thing" that is found, but an idea that is perpetually created. His notion of education rested upon a citizenry concerned with developing the ability to visualize the type of society its members wished to live in. Dewey and his progressive contemporaries continued to argue against social functionalism and for a different conception of schooling and educational purpose. They looked to assessment to measure how students think, not what they think.

Although the debates between progressive educators like Dewey, Bode, and Haley, on the one hand, and Bobbitt and Cubberley, on the other, were intense and controversial, in the end it was functionalism that triumphed over progressivism.

There are many reasons for the triumph of social functionalism in the educational debates of early twentieth-century America, not the least being the cost of subsidizing and operating public education as an enterprise. Progressive educational ideas would have required new structural configurations of school, an emphasis on quality education as opposed to the education of quantities of students, new assessments, and more creative and innovative curricula. Social functionalist approaches to education, on the other hand, were less expensive precisely because, within the factory style school, students could be "produced" on an educational assembly line in much larger numbers than by the craftsmanship required by progressive education (Wirt & Kirst, 1992). Similarly, with standardized tests, quality control could be rigidly fixed without variation.

Perhaps even more importantly, the progressive agenda for education was highly controversial and threatened the elite agenda of control and power that was taking shape in industrialized, modernist America. With the emergence of union activism, socialist movements, the creation of the Soviet Union in 1917, and the so-called Red scare and the Sacco and Vanzetti trial of the 1920s, the last thing that policy makers in either education, business, or politics wanted was an education for social liberation and individual realization. Business interests, policy makers, and politicians were worried that opening up education to such things as personal awareness, democracy, social exploration, and critical analysis might compel the public to examine the social, cultural, and economic relations that governed their lives. This could pose a considerable threat to power, authority, and control and was of little value to the captains of a market society undergoing a huge economic expansion, technological revolution, and industrialization. The notion of education for social function and control was far more pragmatic in an emerging industrial world where commercialism relied on disciplined workers and responsible consumers. Socialization and indoctrination were to be the norm for schooling, and tests and measurement instruments were developed to assist in assuring that this indoctrination and socialization became the objects of education.

As a result, Dewey's progressive ideas gained little support from administrators and other educational policy makers. And so, although the debates between progressives and social functionalists reigned as educational discourse during the early part of the twentieth century, schools were to be increasingly organized on factory models and their curricula wedded to organizational and intellectual endeavors that promoted education as preparation for work.

The argument between the educational functionalists and educational progressives is as heated today as it was in the beginning of the twentieth century; perhaps even more so. The issues that confronted educators in the early twentieth century (curriculum construction, access to quality education, the education of minority children and newly arriving immigrants, race, gender equity, social class, market capitalism, technological innovation, work, efficiency, and production, and the purpose and goals of education) represent similar but different challenges, much as they did close to one hundred years ago.

The Post-World War II Period and the Politics of Public Education

Public education in post-World War II America would experience some of its most dramatic challenges and changes. In the context of the Cold War, McCarthyism, economic prosperity, suburban development, technological innovations in consumer goods, the advent of television and television advertising, the growth of the Civil Rights movement, and the rapid development of scientific innovation and discovery, controversial and rancorous debates arose over the role of education and universal access to school facilities.

Perhaps the most important event that marked post-World War II social, racial, and educational politics was the 1954 Supreme Court decision, *Brown v. Board of Education*. Until this time, what was referred to as the separate-but-equal doctrine, set forth as law in the famous *Plessy v. Ferguson* case, governed relations between Blacks and Whites. The *Brown* decision swept *Plessy* away forever, declaring the separate-but-equal doctrine "inherently unequal" (*Brown v. Board of Education*, 1954). Further clarifying its position on the matter, the Court intervened in a follow-up decision by stating that public school systems that had been segregated until that time now had to become desegregated (*Brown v. Board II*, 1955).

The court decision also brought up the issue of "states' rights" versus federal control—an issue as old as the Civil War itself. Many conservative southerners felt that decisions regarding local issues should be left to the states and local government bodies, and not mandated by the federal government. The Supreme Court decision in *Brown* was seen at the time by many conservatives as a federal invasion of states' rights.

Another important post-World War II event that was to have a massive impact on the nation's school systems and continued public debate over education was the advance of the Soviet Union into space, with the 1957 launching of the sputnik. Following the Soviet success, American leaders reacted with shock and disbelief, arguing that the Soviet Union now had a military advantage over the United States. Business leaders, military leaders, and educational policy makers scrambled to assign the blame to American public schools. With the permissiveness of the 1960s in everything from rock and roll music to new ideas regarding sexuality and conformity, blaming public education for not preparing the United States for global and economic competitiveness was convenient, and attacks on public education intensified (Kincheloe, 2000, p. 164).

With the launching of Sputnik and the perception of Soviet superiority in matters of technology and military development, the federal government began to become more involved in the legal and economic realities of public education. The National Defense and Education Act was passed, and educational emphasis was now focused primarily on science, mathematics, foreign languages, guidance, career counseling, and vocational endeavors. The federal government also appropriated and spent massive sums for the construction of schools.

Worried that the Soviet Union was achieving technological and military dominance over the United States, educational policy makers saw their role as that of the custodians of the public educational system. Education was now to be perceived as a vehicle for gaining necessary skills for the promotion of the "national interest" and was directly linked to defeating Communism at any cost. For the first time in its history, the United States government declared education a national preoccupation and a national interest. The public schools were still organized as large factories, but they were factories that were now more preoccupied with the regulation of the curriculum. In this atmosphere of political fear and educational purpose tied to military and technological preparedness, the former voices of progressive education were muted and silenced.

The efforts to promote an educational marketplace through privatized school choice can be traced directly to the work of conservative economist Milton Friedman in the 1950s. Unlike proponents of public education who sought restructuring and reform of factory-style public schools, Friedman, in 1955, proposed that every family be given a federal "voucher" of equal worth, to be used for each child attending any school. Under the proposed plan, the voucher would offer public funds that would allow families to choose any school that met minimal governmental standards. Parents could also add their own resources to the value of the voucher, and schools would operate like businesses, setting their own tuition and admission requirements (Friedman, 1955).

Not only did Friedman's proposal fail to attract public interest at the time, but the prevailing ideology argued that a simple re-tooling of the curriculum and the addition of advanced placement classes would remedy whatever problems were associated with public education. Further, with the *Brown* decision, any primacy of states' rights over federal law in the form of state-imposed segregation was now illegal. Although Friedman voiced his support for integration at the time, by asserting the primacy of freedom over equality, Friedman's proposal would directly or indirectly further segregation ("Rethinking Schools," 1996). Even though it was rejected by the public at the time, the Friedman proposal would return with a vengeance in the late 1980s and early 1990s.

The post-World War II era in education is significant to any understanding of the current debates regarding public schools and specifically charter schools. Issues regarding states' rights, race, market initiatives, and "failing American schools," so predominant in the educational discourse of the 1950s, are among the topics that the educational community faces today. They are apparent in the debate over standards in contemporary Texas.

The Decade of the 1960s and the Politics of Standards

If post-World War II America experienced conformity in the 1950s, the 1960s were anything but conformist. The changes in educational policy during the 1960s and the issues discussed in the debate over educational purpose and access must be situated and understood within the context of the political activism and resistance of the decade. Antiwar demonstrations, the Civil Rights movement, boycotts, the emergence of the gay liberation movement in 1969, multiculturalism, feminism, assassinations of political leaders, and the multiple marches on Washington all worked directly to change the conception of America and American consciousness. And the decade of the 1960s was to have a dramatic and far-reaching impact on educational issues and schooling as well.

One of the most important political events of the 1960s was the passage of the Civil Rights Act of 1964. Not only did the passage of the act guarantee African Americans access to all public facilities, but it empowered the United States government to assure compliance with the act by bringing discrimination suits against any institution or local governmental body found to discriminate. According to estimates, almost 99 percent of Black students in the eleven southern states still attended segregated schools (Orfield, 1969, p. 45). Such schools were now to be stripped of any federal aid.

Another consequential legislative enactment in the 1960s was the passage of the Elementary and Secondary Act of 1965. Signed into law by President Johnson as part of the War on Poverty, the act would provide another nail in the coffin for segregated schools by bringing even more African Americans into the mainstream of public schooling.

With the fight over desegregation often becoming violent, the Supreme Court once again was forced to act with its 1968 decision in *Green v. City School Board*. The issue involved the so-called "freedom of choice" plans that had been adopted by some southerners as a way of avoiding desegregation. The *Green* decision outlawed these schemes as barriers to desegregation, further assuring that schools would be desegregated in accordance with the *Brown* decision.

The late 1950s and the decade of the 1960s saw an increasingly desegregated school system in America, and immense changes in public education occurred during this time in the South. For the first time, African Americans were allowed to attend public schools with Whites, albeit at times under the protection of the National Guard. Universal access to education sprang from the struggle for equality and justice on behalf of African Americans, workers, students, feminists, and other groups.

The 1960s also witnessed the beginning of intense debates over the school curriculum. The roots of what is currently termed the "multicultural" movement in education are in the radical challenges put forth by progressive educational forces in the 1960s and early 1970s. The movement toward a multicultural curriculum originated largely from America's culturally subjugated and marginalized groups, such as African Americans, Mexican Americans, Native Americans, and women. Proponents of multiculturalism criticized schools for their practices with regard to admission of people of color; they condemned the academic establishment for its subservience to business interests; they reprimanded schools for their racist, sexist, and culturally biased curriculum; they criticized hiring practices for women and minorities; they exposed the pernicious practice of tracking; they lambasted the curriculum for its claim of neutrality; and they labored assiduously to assure beneficial entitlement programs such as bilingual education and Title VII mandated educational programs.

Proponents of multiculturalism argued that a lack of understanding and acceptance of racial differences was a recognized problem both for teachers and students alike (Stent, Hazard, & Rivlin, 1973, p. 73). From within the multicultural educational community there were calls to directly address issues of prejudice and discrimination within the curriculum. Multicultural theorists argued that schools should not seek to dissolve the cultural differences within our pluralistic society but instead should celebrate these differences in an atmosphere of educational inquiry. Therefore, they pointed out, schools should be oriented toward the cultural enrichment of all students through programs aimed at the preservation and extension of cultural pluralism. They put forward the idea that cultural diversity was a valuable resource that should be recognized, preserved, and extended, and they argued that only by directly confronting racism and prejudice could society assure an understanding and appreciation of human dignity (Weil, 1998).

The movements and educational struggles that took place during the 1960s and early 1970s produced a new language of educational critique. Coupled with the critiques of schooling was a call for the abolition of inequality in school financing and for a commitment to federal funding for educational programs. The struggle for universal access, changes in the curriculum, and the passage of social legislation profoundly changed American public education. These movements lent new currency to the progressive calls for a democratic educational purpose that had started with Dewey. Old progressive arguments and positions regarding the role and purposes of education that had been silenced by the Cold War of the 1950s began to reemerge in the national debate. American identity itself was under reconsideration as diversity and an understanding of difference became intense objects of controversy and debate. This was to be especially true in universities that at the time were agitated sites of militancy and resistance.

Conservatism, the 1980s, and the Politics of Standards

The 1970s marked the first time that the National Education Association (NEA), the nation's largest teachers' union, endorsed a candidate for the presidency of the United States. President Jimmy Carter received the endorsement of the largest teachers' union in his bid for the presidency in 1976. Carter owed this backing to his intent to establish a cabinet-level department of education. The NEA had lobbied for such a national cabinet-level department since World War I. Now, finally, with the union's endorsement, Carter raised education to the cabinet level in 1980.

While Jimmy Carter proved to be more conservative than many observers had expected from an "education president," there is little doubt that Ronald Reagan, Carter's successor, left a lasting conservative ideological stamp on American public education.

Considering the Department of Education an unnecessary expense and perceiving it as an infringement of states' rights, Reagan sought to abolish the department directly after his 1980 election. Invoking free market enterprise and the logic of market forces as the panacea for American social and economic troubles, Reagan and his administration embarked on restructuring social policy, including education, to reflect the primacy of market solutions (Lugg, 1996).

Calls for the abolition of the Department of Education met with severe resistance. This made it impossible for conservatives to abolish the department. As a result, the Reagan administration sought to reconstitute the Department of Education, transforming it into a source of support for controversial policies like organized prayer, public and private school choice, and school vouchers. As a result, blistering attacks were leveled against public education, teachers' unions, and the curriculum.

It was in 1983 that the best-publicized educational achievement of the Reagan administration was presented in the form of a book-length report, *A Nation at Risk*. Issued by the National Commission on Excellence in Education (NCEE), the report provided a scathing critique of the public education system, arguing that American education had become a bastion of mediocrity. The report concluded that the state of American education was actually threatening the nation's future economic growth. With its dire predictions and warnings, *A Nation at Risk* once again focused public attention on the issue of education as an economic issue. As educational urgency took on market features, progressive educational concerns were not considered a priority (National Commission on Excellence in Education, 1983).

After the *A Nation at Risk* study was released, scores of magazines and newspapers lamented the supposed "failure of public education." That year, *Newsweek* rushed a scathing story to press asking if the schools could be saved. The sum of the report was that progress from generation to generation was being "shattered" by the mediocre condition of American schools ("Saving Our Schools," 1983, pp. 50–58).

Responsibility for the recessionary economic crisis that plagued America during the early 1980s was placed squarely on the public educational system. Public education was now looked at as an inhibitor of economic growth (Shor, 1986, p. 108). Like the Sputnik scare decades prior, *A Nation at Risk* was used to sound a wake-up call to educators and policy makers. This time, instead of Soviet superiority in outer space, it was the influx of quality goods from Japan that was considered the threat to national security. America's ability to compete globally, it was argued, was jeopardized by a public educational system that simply did not work.

To prove the mediocrity of the school system, the NCEE turned to an analysis of the Scholastic Aptitude Test (SAT) scores to make its point. The NCEE pointed to the long SAT score decline from 1963 to 1980. They also began to publicly compare U.S. education to other Western school systems. Exploiting political patriotism and economic nationalism, the *Nation at Risk* report pointed out that America would continue to be the preeminent country only so long as material benefits and great ideas were available. The report argued that the nation's national security was in jeopardy as long as public schools jeopardized this (National Commission on Excellence in Education, 1983).

In June 1983, another report, entitled *Action for Excellence: A Comprehensive Plan to Improve Our Nation's Schools*, was published by the state governors' group, the Education Commission of the States (ECS). Often referred to as the "Hunt Report" after Governor James B. Hunt of North Carolina, the report continued to echo the notion that American schools were failing (Action for Excellence, pp. V, 3).

The alarms did not stop with the Hunt Report. The next major statement regarding the state of public education was issued in September 1983 with the National Science Board (NSB) report. In its dramatic study, *Educating Americans for the 21st Century,* the NSB documents warned that:

> The nation that dramatically and boldly led the world into the age of technology is failing to provide its own children with the intellectual tools needed for the 21st century. . . . Already the quality of our manufactured products, the viability of our trade, our leadership in research and development, our standard of living, are strongly challenged. Our children could be stragglers in a world of technology. We must not let this happen; American must not become an industrial dinosaur. We must not provide our children a 1960's education for the 21st century world (National Science Board, 1983).

The exigencies of education were once again being linked to the nation's economic readiness, or lack of it. The 1980s built the case for a super functionalism. Instead of the rudimentary skills required by the social functionalism of industrialization, the new information and technological revolution in American society needed a different type of worker with different kinds of skills. Preparing students for the twenty-first-century technological and cybernetic revolution, or the "third wave," became the mantra of reports like *A Nation at Risk*. Calls for a "back-to-basics" focus were similar to the "objectives first" clamor in the early 1900s. The National Science Board defined the new cognitive-economic relationship between school and work in the following way:

> Alarming numbers of young Americans are ill-equipped to work in, to contribute to, profit from and enjoy our increasingly technological society. Far too many emerge from the nation's elementary and secondary schools with an inadequate grounding in mathematics, science, and technology. This situation must not continue. . . . We must return to the basics, but the "basics" of the 21st century are not only reading, writing, and arithmetic. They include communication, and higher problem-solving skills, and scientific and technological literacy (National Science Board, 1983, introduction).

The new basics, now called "ultra basics," included science, computer studies, higher-order reasoning, social studies, foreign languages, and academic English. Schools were now to place these basics at the core of their curriculum. While the "second wave" of educational restructuring was established for the industrial age of the 1900s, the "third wave" restructuring movement of the 1980s would focus on preparing students for the information/technology age.

Educator Larry Hutchins (1990) expressed the new "third wave" functionalist restructuring argument as follows:

> The old design worked relatively well for the society it served; it brought schooling to millions of immigrants [who]. . . were needed to stoke the engines of the industrial society. Today's society no longer requires such a work force. We need people who can think and solve problems using information and technology (p. 29).

Maintaining the American empire, creating better goods and services, dominating world markets, and creating the new workforce of the future were all interwoven into the calls for a new and radical restructuring of schools. Any discussion as to what type of society Americans wished to create, or the relationship between school, democracy, culture, and the emerging cybernetic society, was conspicuously absent from the concerns of third wave restructionists. Furthermore, as in the efficiency production arguments of the industrial age, teachers were encouraged to develop curricular goals based on step-by-step procedures and time schedules (Goodman, 1995).

During the 1980s, the educational reform movement increasingly found expression in a language of business efficiency and productivity, and in the application of management theories to educational enterprise. More than at any other time, test scores became the main products of schools. Students became the workers who created these products using instructional programs given to them by the "educational organization." Teachers were transformed into shop managers who presided over students' production; school principals became the plant managers who managed the school personnel; and specialists, such as social workers or school counselors, were employed to handle students' emotional needs (Goodman, 1995, p. 11). Transformed into classroom managers overseeing student-workers, teachers became further disengaged from the nature of teaching, as they were galvanized to follow prescribed "teaching recipes" in the form of pre-formulated lesson plans. With the rise of pre-packaged instructional materials, intellectual engagement with the curriculum had now become, for many teachers, a luxury, as they were transformed into mere managers of learning.

Third Wave Restructuring at the End of the Millennium: School Choice and the Politics of the Charter Movement

The development of the new educational discourse of business productivity and efficiency in the 1980s set the stage for our current educational controversies at the beginning of the new millennium. As America exited the 1980s, unregulated capitalist markets monopolized mainstream thinking. Sure that market solutions were the remedies for all of society's ills, economists and other pundits advised America to concentrate on market solutions to social problems in order to compete vigorously in the global arena. Unregulated markets and privatization were seen as essential for all those interested in American progress.

With the fall of the Soviet Union in 1991, this vision of America, one of unregulated markets and capitalist hegemony, became the primary vision for education as well. Public schools were not only continually perceived as failing or mediocre, but the argument now began to suggest that public schools would better serve American citizens if they were forced to compete with schools that were privatized. As the argument went, schools need to develop students in the way that corporations develop products. School-choice proponents now claimed that the government should provide vouchers to pay for the schooling that students or their parents wished to choose. The idea, claimed voucher adherents, was that private and public schools could then compete for the most academically able students. The schools that prepared students for the emerging information/technology-driven market in the most efficient manner would benefit from "natural selection" (Kincheloe, 2000, p. 171). Friedman's proposal for privatized education was now accepted.

Economic Conservatives and the
Neo-Functionalist Argument

The educational foundations of our society are presently being eroded by a rising tide of mediocrity that threatens our very future as a nation and a people. . . . We have, in effect, been committing an act of unthinking, unilateral educational disarmament.

—A Nation at Risk

The prevailing point of view at this time, one that embraces both economic and neo-functionalist assertions and that resonates throughout the media, seems to be that school is merely a training ground for the requirements of market civilization (that is, preparation in school is preparation for work). Now, with dramatic changes in the nature and relations of the forces of postmodern capitalist production, contemporary neo-functionalists have refashioned and rely on notions of intelligence that, though formal in nature, seek to expand the parameters of formal psychological theories to include such things as critical thinking skills, problem solving, and decision-making capabilities.

Part of the problem, according to the neo-functionalists, is what they refer to as failing *government schools*. They go on to argue that the cybernetic economy of information and knowledge will necessitate the cultivation and harvesting of the best decision-making and problem-solving capacities among capitalist workers and managers. They describe managers and workers as knowledge workers who are able to use new technology, and they advocate that students be educated to fashion large amounts of information and data into patterns from which they might make plausible inferences about business issues. They see problem-solving and decision-making skills, within the context of postmodern capitalist society (and its political, social, and economic arrangements) as the new sphere of intelligence. Adaptation to change, lifelong learning, thinking outside of the box, flexibility, proactive thinking, open-minded thinking, intuitive thinking and a host of other business and managerial psychobabble expressions are marshaled to point to the "new intelligence" needs of the postmodern capitalist global order (American Management Association, 2000).

Fundamentally, this means that students go to school for the purpose of learning how to compete in a capitalist global society, and they are taught job skills they are told are essential for getting ahead. The National Skills Standards Board (1996), containing members appointed by President Bill Clinton, adopts this position in its discussion of standards:

The National Skills Standards Board is building a voluntary national system of skill standards, assessment, and certification that will enhance the ability of the United States to compete effectively in the global economy.

From this point of view, education, beginning in primary school, should be designed to create producers and consumers who accept and adapt to the business models inherent in capitalist society as well as the power relations that govern them. The new political discourse of conservative neo-functionalism discusses education only as it relates to markets, national identity, global competition, increased productivity, and unbridled consumption. Nothing is said about helping students relate to the world in critical ways. For economic conservatives, schools serve national and market forces (not people).

Even for those CEOs and neo-functionalists who bemoan the current state of education as an antiquated testimony to the past and talk about the need for critical thinking, their goal is also clearly tied to the bandwagon of individual economic necessity. Former CEO of Apple Corporation, John Sculley, at Bill Clinton's 1992 Economic Conference stated this quite succinctly:

We are still trapped in a K-12 public education system which is preparing our youth for jobs that no longer exist. A highly skilled work force must begin with a world class public education system which will turn out a world class product. . . . It is an issue about an educational system aligned with the new economy and a broad educational opportunity for everyone. Our public education system has not successfully made the shift from teaching the memorization of facts to achieving learning of critical thinking skills. . . . It's America's choice: High skills or low wages.

According to the new gospel of neo-functionalism, there is a need not only for a different kind of production under Post-Fordism but for a different kind of worker (the knowledge worker). This is the worker who is adaptable and amenable to multi-task work environments and who has a theoretical understanding of systems and how they function, who can work in teams, who can accept new managerial authority. This is the worker who can form data into patterns and then interpret them so as to increase company profits, who can operate within wider frames of reference, who seeks out new information from multiple sources, and who can solve business problems and make business decisions. For neo-functionalists and their economic conservative counterparts, the new millennium is foisting upon us new market-driven cognitive demands and different productive relations, and schools must be ready to accept and meet the challenge if people want to get ahead and if America truly wants to be able to compete.

Former Labor Secretary Robert Reich (1992) makes similar arguments in his book *The Work of Nations:*

> We are living through a transformation that will rearrange the politics and economics of the coming century. There will no longer be national economies at least as we have come to understand the concept. All that will remain rooted within national borders are the people who comprise the nation. Each nation's primary asset will be its citizens' skills and insights. (p. 3)

For neo-functionalists like Reich and Sculley, the rhetoric is clear: less desirable jobs will not exist in the U.S. but will be shipped overseas to third world countries—the new assembly line of global capitalism. More complex, intellectually challenging work, they argue, will become the norm in the United States. Of course, there will be winners and losers. However, this time the winners and losers will not only be within nations, but will actually be nations themselves. The message the neo-functionalist, neo-liberal agenda promotes is very clear: global economic necessities demand an educational system tied to the skills and training necessary to compete in the new millennium of a cybernetic global capitalism. Critical thinking is important only as it relates to creating critical capitalist mass—designing better products, boosting productivity, fashioning better customer service, creating stronger national identity, and creating a new class of disciplined consumers. Preparing citizen-consumers for this "new world order" becomes the *raison d'être* of education and educational sites.

From both the economic conservative and the neo-liberal perspective, educational assessment and "world class standards" in education must be linked to what it means to be successful in the new global economy. Through their efforts, economic conservatives and neo-liberals have created standard and assessment think-tanks, such as Achieve Incorporated, a nonprofit organization, created by a group of CEOs and the National Governors Association, that is currently co-chaired by IBM's Chief Executive

Officer, Louis Gerstner, Jr., and Governor Tommy Thompson of Wisconsin, as well as the *National Education Goals Report* launched in 1989 as a result of the controversy over the 1983 report, *A Nation at Risk*. The *Goals Report* (National Education Goals Panel, 1991) announces its mission as follows:

> By the year 2000, American students will leave grades 4, 8, and 12 having demonstrated competency in challenging subject matter including English, mathematics, science, history, and geography; and every school in America will ensure that all students learn to use their minds well, so they may be prepared for responsible citizenship, further learning, and productive employment in our modern society (p. 2).

By adopting what they like to call "world class standards," corporate and business leaders are working to identify what Post-Fordist, neo-functionalist skills will be necessary for the workplace of the future (Mid-Continent Regional Educational Laboratory, 1997). The clamor to define world class standards and skills has been linked to America's desired continued dominance in the world economy, and both economic conservatives and neo-liberal policy makers have tied the development of these standards to American market competitiveness.

Diane Ravitch (1996), recognized as one of the chief architects of the modern standards movement, has stated the economic conservative and neo-liberal rationale for standards:

> Americans expect strict standards to govern the construction of buildings, bridges, highways, and tunnels; shoddy work would put lives at risk. They expect stringent standards to protect their drinking water, the food they eat, and the air they breathe. Standards are created because they improve the activity of life. (pp. 8–9)

What is ironic is how this neo-instrumentalism and neo-functionalism has been redefined and refashioned to convey the appearance of progressive dialogue; as a call to arms for change from the so-called new school reformers—the new corporate business and managerial elites. Although the functionalist rationale has changed to that of neo-functionalism, what really has changed are the historical necessities of capitalism, not thinking regarding the role of schools. The contemporary reformers, the neo-functionalists, still cling to an educational theory and practice allied with the needs of commercial interests and organized according to business organizational theories and practices. The difference at this historical juncture is simply how they define the new functionalism and instrumentalism in face of postmodern capitalist changes in the relations and forces of production.

The Purpose of Education Is to Inculcate Basic Skills

Another argument that we hear today among conservative educational reformers is the argument that schools must stick to the business of educating children in basic skills. This is nothing new. What is new, however, is how these basic skills are being redefined in face of the changes in the relations and forces of production in postmodern capitalist society. What was basic in Bobbitt's time is not so basic today according to neo-functionalists. Where basic skills were once tied to an industrial society, they are now being recast in terms of the cybernetic-information society; the society we find ourselves in at the beginning of the twenty-first century.

And not only have basic skills been redefined and updated to meet the exigencies of postmodern capitalist development, we now find that critical thinking and Socratic questioning have been hijacked from progressive educational theory and practice and are now being taught as the type of intelligences businesses believe worker-managers will need in the twenty-first century (Spitzer, 1999).

Indeed, the whole notion of examining and reexamining cognition has now become a major preoccupation of managerial programs, business educational theories, and teacher education training classes. Michael Molenda captures this well when he states:

> Learning achievement is the crucial product of the educational system. Schools obviously attempt to perform many functions in American society, including socialization of youth into the community. However, the primary and unique requirement expected of schools is the attainment of the knowledge, skills, and attitudes specified by state and local boards of education. . . . It is what Reich (1991) and others insist is the vital element for economic survival. (quoted in Goodman, 1995, p. 10).

Of course, what the neo-functionalists don't tell us is that the development of systematic, collaborative, evaluative, and abstract thinking through schools modeled after effective and efficient business organizations (Reich, 1992, p. 3) is really designed to develop a cognitive elite—a post-modern managerial class. From their point of view, the successful acquisition of capital and the smooth operation of technological control, authority, and maintenance should be the object of education (thus their neo-functionalism). The rhetoric they choose to embrace is one of citizen inclusivity and an end to the so-called *digital divide* (a Jeffersonian, democratic education for all). Yet as we can see by examining any number of their programs, their inclusivity is much like that of a private country club which admits its members in accordance with rigid, privileged, class, gender, and race-based criteria. It is affirmative action for the affirmed.

For the first time, in a real way, the notion of public education itself is being questioned by a new generation of social functionalists. And while the educational discussions and debates in the past focused on how to bring America's public school system up to speed, the new functionalist arguments actually question the very efficacy, existence, and necessity of public schools. Education is now being conceived of as a "marketplace" and a new language of "choice" begins to emerge to define the terms of the debate. Progressive educational concerns regarding the role of democracy, equity, and social justice have been marginalized and even purged from educational discourse in favor, once more, of competitiveness, efficiency, and productivity needs. The new rhetoric of privatized schooling and "choice" defines the terms of the debate, and Americans are now embroiled in a controversy over the continued existence of public education itself.

Summary

Understanding the historical nature of American schooling and the controversies that have surrounded and continue to encompass educational purpose is crucial to understanding the current standards debate. Through meticulous dialogue and an exchange of diverse points of view in an atmosphere of civility and inquiry, the standards debate in this country will be enriched, and we as American citizens can begin to design a curriculum and educational standards that meet the needs of our citizens in their quest for happy and productive lives. Without historical understanding and a critical and rigorous dialogue about educational purpose, the standards debate in this country promises to hold our nation's children hostage to a neo-functionalism that prepares students only for the necessities of postmodern capitalist life. We need to ask ourselves as a nation: Is this what we really want?

References

The American Management Association (2000). *Catalogue of classes.* New York, NY.

Binet, A., & Simon, T. (1905). Methodes nouvelles pour le diagnostique de niveau intellectuel des anormaux. *L'annee psychologique.*

Bobbitt, F. (1912). The elimination of waste in education. *Elementary School Teacher, 12,* 259–271.

Bobbitt, F. (1913). Some general principles of management applied to the problems of city school systems. In S. C. Parker (Ed.), *Twelfth Yearbook of the National Society for the Study of Education.* Chicago: University of Chicago Press.

Brown v. Board of Education. 347 U.S. 483, 74 S. Ct. 686 (1954).

Brown vs. Board II. 349, U. S. 294, 75, S. Ct. 753 (1955).

Callahan, R. E. (1962). *Education and the cult of efficiency.* Chicago: University of Chicago Press.

Cubberley, E. (1916). *Public school administration: A statement of the fundamental principle underlying the organization and administration of public education.* Boston: Houghton Mifflin.

Dewey, J. (1940). *Education today.* New York: Greenwood Press.

Dewey, J. (1976). *Experience and education.* New York: Collier Books (Original work published1938).

Friedman, M. (1955) The role of government in education. In Robert A. Solow (Ed.), *Economics and the Public Interest.* New Brunswick, NJ: Rutgers University Press.

Goodman, J. (1995). Change without difference. *Harvard Educational Review 65* (1), 1–29.

Green v. City School Board. 391 U.S. 430 (1968).

Hutchins, L. (1990). *Achieving excellence.* Aurora, CO: Mid-Continent Regional Laboratory. (ERIC Document Reproduction Service No. ED 370 157)

Kincheloe, J. (2000). *Contextualizing teaching.* New York: Longman.

Kliebard, H. (1970). The Tyler rationale. *School Review 78* (2), 259–72.

Lugg, C. A. (1996). *For God and country: Conservatism and American school policy.* New York: Peter Lang.

Mid-Continent Regional Educational Laboratory. (1997). Aurora, CO.

National Commission on Excellence (1983). *A nation at risk.* Washington, DC: USA Research.

National Education Goals Panel. (1991). *The National Education Goals Report.* Washington, DC. (ERIC Document Reproduction Service No. ED 334 281)

National Science Board Commission on Precollege Education in Mathematics, Science, and Technology. (1983). *Educating Americans for the 21st century.* Washington, DC.

National Skills Standards Board (1996). *Discussion of standards.* 1441 L. Street NW, Suite 9000, Washington, DC. 20005.

Orfield, G. (1969). *The reconstruction of southern education: The schools and the 1964 Civil Rights Act.* New York: Wiley Interscience.

Ravitch, D. (1996). *National standards in American education.* Washington, DC: The Brookings Institute.

Reich, R. (1992). *The work of nations.* New York: Vintage Press.

Rethinking Schools. (1996). *Selling out our schools: Vouchers, markets, and the future of public education.* Milwaukee, WI. (ERIC Document Reproduction Service No. ED 398 343)

Saving our schools. (1983), May 9). *Newsweek,* 50–58.

Sculley, J. (1992). *Critical thinking: Why it matters so much.* Speech given in Arkansas.

Shor, I. (1986). *Culture wars: School and society in the conservative restoration.* Chicago: The University of Chicago Press.

Spitzer, Q. (1999). *Heads you win: How the best companies think.* New York: McGraw-Hill.

Stent, M., Hazard, W., & Rivlin, H. (Eds.). (1973). *Cultural Pluralism in Eduation: A Mandate for Change.* New York: Appleton-Century Crofts.

Task Force on Education for Economic Growth, The Education Commission of the States. (1983). *Action for excellence: A comprehensive plan to improve our nation's schools.* Washington, DC. (ERIC Document Reproduction Service No. ED 235 588)

Tyack, D. (1974). *The one best system: A history of American urban education.* Cambridge, MA: Harvard University Press.

Weil, D. (1998). *Towards a critical multicultural literacy: Education for liberation.* New York: Peter Lang.

Wirt, F. M. & Kirst, M. W. (1992). *Schools in conflict: The politics of education* (3rd ed.). Berkeley, CA: McCutchan.

Chapter 3

The Question of Complexity: Understanding the Standards Movement in Texas

Raymond A. Horn, Jr.

Complexity problematizes America's search for quality education. The problems arise when the inherently complex nature of educating children intersects with the agendas of economic, political, ideological, and modernistically oriented interest groups. One outcome of this intersection is the urban myth that quality education can systemically exist in American society.

Besides the impossible task of defining quality education, any subsequent large-scale implementation would also be impossible. Impossibility is a strong term but appropriate when speaking idealistically about quality education for all. The ideal educational system would guarantee the development of *every* child into a fully literate, fully functioning, and critical adult. Unfortunately, all segments of our society, at one time or another, would disagree with one or more of these characteristics of a quality education. Certain economic, political, and ideological interest groups would undoubtedly disagree with the need for advanced literacy (currently defined as a college education) for *all* children. The current economic and class structures would certainly be at risk if *all* individuals because of their level of literacy had the same expectations for a good life. Certain economic, political, and ideological interest groups would undoubtedly disagree with the need for all children to become fully functioning adults—fully functioning in that their level of understanding and skill would give them the power to act to realize their expectations for a good life. Certain economic, political, ideological, and religious interest groups would undoubtedly disagree with the need to develop critically thinking adults who would consider the implications of their own and others' exercise of power on race, gender, age, and social class. Finally, there are those who would agree with the need for educating children to become fully literate, fully functioning, and critical adults. However, these people cannot achieve this kind of quality education because the reductionist and systematic techniques that they employ actually work against the creation of quality education.

This dismal but realistic portrayal of the barriers to attaining the previously defined quality of education is assuredly a portrayal of the complex world in which we live. To understand the standards movement in America and its potential for success requires an examination of the standards movement in the context of complexity.

The Texas case study that follows is ironic in the postmodern sense in that many people truly aspire to create a condition of quality education for all children, but the methods that they employ to create this condition and their attempt to accommodate the diverse interest groups are the reasons for their failure to attain quality education for all children. The more regulation there is, the more accountability structures there are, the higher the standards are raised, the more the supporters of quality education move further from their goal. This ironic situation is an outcome of the failure to view educational reform as a systemically complex process.

As you will discover, the Texas standards initiative is a highly organized and rigorously pursued initiative that has been going on for a long time. This is not a piecemeal, one-shot-and-done, fly-by-night initiative. You will also discover that even though it is a highly organized and systematic initiative, it is not systemically complex.

Complexity

Complexity is not the same as a high degree of systematic organization. Any systematic initiative that is pursued with rigor will attain highly complicated functioning and structure. The Texas movement is characterized by a complicated bureaucracy of governmental agencies, standards, accountability tests, and accountability procedures for public schools and state universities, as well as for all stakeholders in the educational system, including students, teachers, administrators, school board members, and university personnel. In a traditional sense, this is a complex system; however, a more technical definition of the word "complex" proves the Texas system systematically complicated, not systemically complex.

The argument will be advanced that dealing with change in a complex human system, such as the education system, involves a level of complex understanding that includes considerations of systems design, critical multiculturalism, community, and the form of conversation that is relevant to the kind of organizational community that is the desired outcome of the change effort. Other concepts could be added to this list of considerations; however, these are the basic structures of the landscape of educational change.

In another sense, if one were to tell the story of an educational change, these considerations would surface in questions like: Who designed the change? To what extent was the change designed? Whose voice was excluded from the design process? What will be the effects of the change on all the different groups of stakeholders in the system? Does the change foster inequity? What type of community is promoted by the change? What type of conversation characterizes the system? Does this conversation promote a critique of the change that enhances equity? These are just some of the questions whose answers are essential in the facilitation of large-scale change in a multicultural social system. Inherent in these questions is the moral and ethical consideration of the effects of the change.

These questions represent a very short list of essential questions that need to be asked about any change initiative at any point in its development or implementation. These few broad questions illustrate the high degree of complexity inherent in any change initiative. To address this complexity requires a concomitant high degree of contextualization, which can best be attained through post-formal thinking.

As you examine the case of the standards initiative in Texas, utilize the model of complexity as a series of lenses that will generate additional questions, not only about the Texas situation, but also about your own interest in standards. To facilitate your questioning process, specifically relating to the American standards movement, short synopses will be presented about systems design, critical multiculturalism, community, and conversational form. An overview of post-formal thinking will provide an additional method that can lead to an understanding of the complex nature of the standards movement in America.

Systems Design

When people think about American standards, it is usually in relation to the curriculum and instruction in their local school district that is designed to increase student achievement on a standardized state-mandated test.

The systems view recognizes the local school district as a subsystem embedded within a series of larger subsystems that comprise their systemic environment (Banathy, 1992, p. 40). To broaden the narrow view requires people to understand that the standards and their effects are not related just to their local school district but to other systems within their systemic environment. In addition, any changes in these other systems will interact with those produced by the standards initiative within the local school district. The changes emanating from other subsystems can intensify or diminish the effects of the standards.

Some other educational subsystems included in the systemic environment are other school districts, regional service centers to the school districts, institutions of higher education, and the state agency governing education. In addition, the systemic environment includes the community system, within which the educational systems are embedded. Subsystems within the community can be centered on elements of the community such as industry, business, groups of retired people, law enforcement organizations, ethnic and racial groups, social agencies, and local governments. All of these community systems interact with the educational system to some degree.

For instance, in Texas, local school districts are intensely focused on meeting the student achievement, attendance, and dropout goals of the standards movement as established by the educational governing body in the state of Texas, the Texas Education Agency (TEA). If these goals are not met, as determined by the TEA school rating system, severe consequences can ensue for the school district, administrators, and teachers. Therefore, there is an inordinate amount of pressure on all stakeholders to succeed. As you will see in the case study that follows, minority categories, as established by the TEA, represent the greatest challenges in meeting these goals.

Concerning the interaction between subsystems within the systemic environment, if a local industry expands its production facility and relocates 200 families into a community, all systems within the community will be affected. In the case of one Texas community, all of the new families were Mexicans who spoke limited if any English. Besides the effects on other community systems, the effect on the local school district was extensive in that it involved expansion of the facility, of bilingual support, and of faculty positions. The short-term and long-term ability of the school to meet the standards requirements was weakened. Also, negative feelings toward the Mexican minority in the community were intensified as more resources had to be reallocated to accommodate this growing segment of the population, already seen as problematic in relation to the attainment of the district's standards goals.

Another example of systemic interaction concerns juvenile delinquency, youth gangs, and dropout rates. As you will see in later chapters, student attrition, or the student dropout rate, is significantly related to standardized testing in Texas. As testing becomes more rigorous, dropout rates soar. Students who are no longer part of the school system are more susceptible to juvenile delinquency, youth gang activity, and youth violence. From a systemic perspective, this impacts the legal, law enforcement, and social systems in a community as well as all of the stakeholders who must pay the various costs of social deviance. On a deeper level, dropping out exacerbates the isolation of the individual student, or in the case of Texas, where the dropout rates are highest for African Americans and Hispanics, the isolation of a category of people from mainstream culture.

Related to student attrition in public schools is another type of attrition that occurs at the university level. In Texas, to become a teacher requires the passing of a certification examination, which is a standardized test administered by the state. If a person fulfills all of the teacher education requirements and graduates from the university, that person can still not teach until the certification exam is passed. If the exam has high failure rates for African Americans and Hispanics, the effect is that these groups of people will be underrepresented in the teaching profession and also in educational administration and higher education. In this case student attrition doesn't mean abandoning a course, it means having one's progress toward a professional goal terminated, even though a degree at an accredited institution has been attained. Once again, we can see the systemic effect of one aspect, in this case the nature of a standardized test, of a system, not only on that particular system, but also on other systems in the same systemic environment.

Besides the interactions of community and school systems within the systemic environment, the systemic environment is embedded within the larger geopolitical environment. Decisions by governmental and business policy makers who exist outside of the systemic environment directly affect the systems within the systemic environment. In our previous example, the decision to create standards was not a local decision but one mandated by the state government and developed by the TEA, an agency outside of the local systemic environment. The decision to relocate certain people was a decision generated by a corporate process including decision makers in other parts of the country or world. The Mexicans, who are utilized because they are cheap labor, are cheap labor because of international and national financial and economic policies. Both educational and economic policies are influenced by geopolitical events such as presidential politics and the culture wars between the Right and the Left.

Whether a school in Texas is labeled "exemplary" or "low-performing" is dependent more upon the interactions of all of the systems in the societal system than the scores of perhaps 25 children out of 150 children in one racial category. To understand the significance of a change like the standards movement in America requires the broader systemic view. Systems thinking refers to the narrow view as a bounded approach (Banathy, 1996). A bounded approach occurs when, to understand a problem, such as student achievement, the identification of the problem and the plan for change are contained within the boundary of the existing system, such as the school district. This narrow view dismisses all of the significant effects of the other systems on the achievement of students. A simplistic and narrowly contextualized scenario is created, and an equally simplistic and narrow solution is developed. Much of the conversation about standards in America is intensely politically and economically driven, yet at the same time denies the political and economic influences on student achievement.

Another benefit of utilizing systems design thinking to understand American standards is in the continuity of understanding that occurs. For instance, once awareness is reached about the interrelationship between all societal systems, then the means by which control of this interrelationship is manifested can be understood. Systems theorists (Ackoff, 1981; Banathy, 1996) have identified four ways that people work with change. The Texas standards movement is an example of the reactive orientation, or "back to the future." According to Bela Banathy the general attitude of reactivists is one of dissatisfaction with the present, a longing for the past, and a desire to return to what was (1996, p. 38). The organizational mode and culture is one of "past experience-focused orientation" in which "we have a tendency to rely on old, well-proven, and familiar organizational forms" (Banathy, 1996, p. 39). Culturally, "the vision of the organization is defined at the top," and "there is an official culture—the culture of management—and an employee culture, which is often very different from the official culture" (Banathy, 1996, p. 39). Russell L. Ackoff (1981) identifies the attraction of this orientation in that it "maintains continuity and seeks to avoid change; and it preserves tradition, protects familiar grounds, and maintains a feeling of stability and security" (Banathy, 1996, p. 39). As you read the Texas case study, utilize this reactive orientation lens to discern which aspects of Texas education have changed and which have not. Utilize this, along with the other multiple lenses that are offered, to broaden your critique to include societal attitudes and agendas as well as educational technology and procedures.

In the context of systemic change, the standards movement in Texas is not a design change but a restructuring movement. Restructuring "means taking a structure of a system and reorganizing it by rearranging its parts in a different configuration" (Banathy, 1996, p. 21). Wrongs are corrected "by changing relations among the parts, by redefining the role played by people in the system, or redefining the role of the components of the system" (Banathy, 1996, p. 21). Change can occur, but a new system is not created.

The difference between restructuring and designing a new system is evident in the Texas model. Banathy identifies this distinction as the difference between the "old story" and the "new story" (Banathy, 1996, p. 45). In the old story there remains a fixed, bureaucratic structure that is status-laden and rigid, where power resides at the top. People are motivated and manipulated, and their compliance is valued. The change initiative is focused on problems, and people are blamed for failure. Past hierarchies and regimens are reinforced; people work within constraints imposed by those in charge, and progress is measured incrementally. The change is technology and capital based and is linear, logical, and reductionist. There is an emphasis on high volume and "doing it the right way" as determined by those in charge. Those in the change initiative are driven by survival needs and motivated by production. Success is determined by external acknowledgment; related environments are adversarial and competitive, and the goals are to succeed and to go ahead (Banathy, 1996, p. 45).

The new story that evolves out of the design model, and is characteristic of design, differs from the old story in this way. Structures in the new story are flexible, dynamic, functional, and evolutionary. Power is shared by empowerment, which causes inspiration and caring for others. Creative contribution is valued, with a focus on creating opportunities that support learning from failure. The long-term perspective is taken, and innovation and novelty are nurtured. The ideal is sought and, consequently, progress occurs by leaps. The change is people- and knowledge-based, and is further characterized as dynamic, intuitive, and expanding. There is an emphasis on high value, which comes from encouraging learning and exploring. There is a desire to develop, to fulfill the self, and the motivation to change comes from personal and collective satisfaction. Success is determined by the individual; related environments are cooperative and supportive, and the goals are aimed at creating integrity, and individual and collective identity (Banathy, 1996, p. 45).

As you can see there are sharp distinctions between a design culture and a traditional modernistic culture. There are pockets of design culture within the educational system of Texas; however, the argument will be made that the standards movement in Texas is essentially one embedded in a reactive orientation and simply represents the old story. As some read the following case, they will agree that indeed this is the situation. However, they will ask what is wrong with this old reactive story. To answer their question, we must continue to broaden the complexity of our critique. It is not enough to understand the mechanism of change, or once again our understanding will be held ransom to the reductionist view. The mechanics and structure of change are but two elements in the understanding of change. In relation to the standards movement in Texas, we must also include the effects of the change on society. The intent is not to condemn a standards movement but to promote standards of a reasonable complexity that work to create an egalitarian society.

Critical Multiculturalism

Like many other states, Texas is a multicultural society. With its proximity to Mexico and its antebellum history, the population of Texas is quite diverse, especially in relation to Hispanics and African Americans. As in many other states, African Americans and Hispanics represent not only the largest minority groups, but also the most socioeconomically impoverished. This social and economic poverty is poignantly represented in the academic achievement, school attendance, and student attrition rates in Texas education. Because of this, along with the poor Anglo-Americans, these minority groups are most visible in the problem detection process of the standards movement.

The term multiculturalism elicits many definitions and opinions; however, for our purpose the important considerations are that multiculturalism is the reality in American society and more important than defining or debating the existence of multiculturalism is deciding how we respond to it (Kincheloe & Steinberg, 1997, p. 2). In relation to the standards movement, the nature of the response to the multicultural nature of our society is the critical lens that adds complexity to our understanding of the standards movement. This lens is considered critical because the act of responding is an act of power.

Multiculturalism doesn't only refer to African Americans; it reflects the cultural and economic diversity of America. Also included are Hispanic American, Native American, Asian American, and economically disadvantaged Anglo American cultures. Often overlooked is the middle and upper Anglo American culture. This group is often not included in the multicultural rainbow because, since its members represent the dominant culture, they are considered the norm to which all others are compared. Many other cultures exist in America, however, those typically recognized in a discussion of standards, as in Texas, include African American, Hispanic, White, Native American, Asian/Pacific Islander, Male, Female, and Economically Disadvantaged. The aim of Texas's disaggregation of student achievement scores, school attendance, and student attrition rates into these racial and socioeconomic groups is undoubtedly not to discriminate against certain groups but to better assess and support the academic development of all children. However, as in all things, the outcome, not the intent, is what is important.

How change is managed often subverts the intent of the change. Whether the goal is to develop critical thinking skills in all students, or to increase the academic achievement of disenfranchised groups, the potential success of the change in accomplishing the goal depends upon the interpretation and implementation of the goal by the stakeholders in the system. In a hierarchical system, in which those at the top have rigid control, require success, deny stakeholder participation in the design of the system and in policy decision making, a mechanical and reductionist (focusing on parts instead of the whole) process is created that actually works against the intended outcomes. In the Texas case study, you will discover how, out of the necessity to survive the pressure of the test, the standards are implemented in such a way that goal attainment, involving such goals as critical thinking and academic achievement, is actually decreased in some situations. This denigration of the goals of a standards movement is especially critical to those minority cultures that need these goals the most.

One outcome of technical standards movements that focus simply on performance on a standardized test is what Paulo Freire called "banking education." Freire explains that "education thus becomes an act of depositing, in which the students are the depositories and the teacher the depositor [who] makes deposits which students patiently receive, memorize, and repeat" (1996, p. 53). It is once again ironic that in a time when there is a shortage of high-tech workers who need to be able to work creatively and autonomously, education reverts to the factory model of education, in which students mechanically memorize and recite decontextualized knowledge, and obediently rely on the teacher who is the center of instruction.

One final concept that is central to all discussions of critical multiculturalism is that of oppression of minority cultures by the cultural majority. Oppression is also a central issue in any discussion of standards. Standards in various forms may imply a compulsion for sameness or a tolerance and celebration of difference. The thin red line that the proponents of standards walk deals with the determination and promotion of oppressive or non-oppressive knowledge, values, and identities. If knowledge, values, and identities are viewed as curriculum, the same line exists for instructional practice and assessment. The development and application of curriculum, instruction, and assessment can be overtly or inadvertently oppressive. Those who determine and implement the standards are exercising power through the knowledge, values, and identities inherent in their standards. The outcome of this exercise of power can be to oppress difference or to allow difference to democratically participate in the construction of knowledge, values, and identity.

In this case, identity refers to the construction of a person's self. What messages are sent to children through the knowledge that they receive, through their effectiveness in receiving the knowledge, and through the contradiction of their indigenous knowledge by the "official" knowledge provided by the "authority"? Similarly, what messages are sent by the values embedded in the knowledge and embedded in the value messages sent in relation to the child's success in mastering the knowledge? Language is central to the construction of identity. What messages are sent about the cultural identity of children when their native language or culturally appropriate pattern of speech is disregarded or deemed problematic by those in charge? Those in charge of creating and implementing standards have great power over the construction of a child's identity, which in turn means that they have great control over the child and the culture from which the child comes. If the knowledge and values of the child's cultural tradition are absent from the standardized curriculum, or rendered invisible by those in charge, what effect will this have on the child? If these messages denigrate the child's culture, then the critical question is merely whether this oppression is intentional.

As systems design provides one lens to broaden our view of American standards, critical multiculturalism provides another. Critical multiculturalism creates additional complexity by adding power to the mix; power in relation to human culture. Systems design raises questions about structure and organization in relation to change. Critical multiculturalism raises questions about equity in relation to race, gender, and socioeconomic status. Both add to our growing understanding of the standards movement.

Community

Prevalent in recent educational research is the idea that successful schools are communities of learners. In essence, this is a response to the factory model of education that became predominant at the beginning of the twentieth century. Prior to the intrusion of the factory model, the values of the school and community were equivalent, in that the school was seen as an extension of the community (Cremin, 1988; Kliebard, 1995; Tyack & Hansot, 1982). As scientific management models were promoted and the "cult of efficiency" dominated the organization and structure of schools, not only did the relational connection of school and community change, but the idea of schools *as* communities also changed (Callahan, 1962; Cuban, 1984; Kliebard, 1995). John Dewey's (1916) idea of schools as communities has not only been revived but also extended with many variations (Alexander, 1999; Palmer, 1993). A leading promoter of this trend is Thomas Sergiovanni (1994), who sees schools as communities that are "not based on contracts or commitments" but on shared values and relationships (p. 4). Sergiovanni' s (1994) emphasis on shared values is related to the Gemeinschaft community theorized by the German sociologist Ferdinand Tönnies (1887/1957), who distinguished between Gemeinschaft, a more sacred community, and Gesellschaft, a more secular society. The shared values and commitments that bind each type of community are as different as the values and commitments of a community as a neighborhood and a community as a factory.

This discussion of community is important for our purpose in that the differing ideas of community can be used as lenses to broaden the complexity of our understanding of standards. Different types of standards will affect school communities in different ways. Technical standards and standards of complexity will have uniquely different effects on all types of school community. In her analysis of the root metaphors of educational community, Lynn G. Beck (1999) presents a great variety of concepts behind school community that lead to the many different ways that people strive to organize themselves. Each type of standard will either negatively or positively reinforce each of these concepts, which are used by people to better understand and promote their concept of community. In other words, the operational ideal would be to foster compatibility between the type of standards and the type of community that a society wants to create.

For instance, we previously discussed the multicultural aspect of our society, as recognized by the State of Texas through its student achievement categories. With the addition of the community lens, questions can now be raised, such as, What kind of school community do we want to develop that can appropriately respond to the needs of a multicultural society? What impact will certain kinds of standards have on this kind of school community? The interrelationship of standards, community, and multiculturalism is critical due to the impact that all three have on the construction of knowledge, values, and identity in children. For example, to return to the situation of the relocation of Mexican workers in Texas, where do these people fit in that school's definition of community? Does that Texas school seek to accept them by including their culture in their Anglo-dominated community, or is the only place for Mexicans in that community a place for those who emulate Anglo values and attitudes? Add to these questions the effects of the organizational structure and the hidden knowledge and values inherent in any type of standards, and we have a very complex situation with significant implications for everybody in that school system.

The implications of the relationship between multiculturalism and the type of standards to be employed are especially significant for schools that want to develop egalitarian communities. Joel Westheimer (1999) identifies five common features of community identified by contemporary theorists, which can be seen to be seminal to egalitarian community: shared beliefs, interaction and participation, interdependence, concern for individual and minority views, and meaningful relationships. Egalitarian school communities are first affected by the organizational structure of the standards. A rigid and controlling standards structure, rather than a flexible and empowering one, is a contradiction to the essential structure of an egalitarian community. The school community that strives to be egalitarian can resolve this contradiction by developing a strong collective mission centered on meeting the requirements of the technical standards. Unfortunately, this mission will be defensive and survival oriented in nature due to the overriding need to avoid the negative consequences that arise from poor student achievement on a technical standardized test. On the other hand, flexible and empowering standards of complexity will promote a generative mission enhanced by its inherent compatibility with critically oriented complex standards.

A recent research study concerning eight predominantly Hispanic schools along the Mexican/American border between Brownsville, Texas, and Laredo, Texas, confirmed the potential effectiveness of learning communities in dealing with the complex mix of minorities and technical standards (Reyes, Scribner, & Scribner, 1999). The study centered on high performing Hispanic schools that also included all of the problems of poverty, unemployment (exceeding 10 percent), underemployment, and the disruption of education due to the transience of migrant/seasonal farm workers. Reyes, Scribner, and Scribner (1999) found that in the context of Texas standards these schools were high-performing due to practices that they described as characteristics of a learning community. They found that the success was based on these practices: collaborative governance and leadership, community and family involvement, culturally responsive pedagogy, and advocacy-oriented assessment and quality control. These dimensions suggest an obviously egalitarian orientation driven by the multicultural aspect of these school communities.

In reviewing this research, it becomes evident that the Texas Assessment of Academic Skills (TAAS) plays a central factor in the development of this strong collective mission. In an analysis of the mathematics instruction, Reyes and Barbara Pazey (1999) describe in detail all of the traditional and innovative pedagogical practices of these schools. What is interesting is how TAAS dominates the curriculum, instruction, and assessment of these schools. How these school communities have organized themselves to meet the requirements of the TAAS is instructive; however, for our critical purposes it is the domination of TAAS that is significant in our understanding of the implications for the meanings that children construct, and for the effect that the state has on the organizational structure and institutional focus of a school. The work of Reyes and Pazey (1999) is especially poignant in showcasing how the knowledge, values, and identities inherent in the TAAS have total access to the school and all of the people connected with the school. Undoubtedly, this would be the case with any type of standards. The salient question is have the stakeholders in our school systems (parents, teachers, administrators, school board members, students, and non-parent adults) carefully and critically deconstructed and evaluated the knowledge, values, and identities that have unrestricted access to our children and through them to ourselves? Is this what we want in our schools?

An additional point that increases the complexity of our understanding of standards is that the actual Texas standards are called the Texas Essential Knowledge and Skills (TEKS). The irony is that the TAAS (the test) is

not yet aligned with the TEKS. Therefore, the *test* itself is directly affecting every aspect of these school systems. It is not enough to look at just
the standards and anticipate their effect on the knowledge, values, and
identities of our children. We must also be concerned about the knowledge, values, and identities that are promoted by the testing instrument,
which may be different from the standards.

Up to this point, two types of standards have been simplistically identified—technical standards and standards of complexity. However, to further complicate the issue, a distinction must be made between the actual
standards and the tools used to measure these standards. An analysis
of the two types of standards might show a degree of conceptual similarity; however, how the actual standards are translated into the testing
instrument is significant in understanding the complex issue of American
standards.

Conversation

To add to our understanding of the complexity of American standards,
we need to appropriate a basic human activity as an additional lens. Conversation is a ubiquitous activity in all societal systems. In other words,
conversation occurs within all levels of a school system and permeates all
boundaries between those levels. In addition, there are types of conversation that can be used as indicators of the type of community that characterizes a school system.

Patrick M. Jenlink and Alison Carr (1996) identify four types of conversation: discussion, dialectical, dialogue, and design. Discussion and
dialectical conversation are similar and the most frequently occurring types.
They are characterized by disciplined, logical, and emotional argument
used to promote ideologies and beliefs. Unfortunately, this type of conversation invariably results in the polarization or alienation of some people.
People who engage in dialectical conversation "are threatened by anyone
who thinks differently from them, and so regard it as their responsibility
to convert others to their view" (Avers, Broadbent, Ferguson, Gabriele,
Lawson, McCormick, & Wotruba, 1996, p. 32).

On the other hand, dialogue and design facilitate the development of a
"oneness"—a shared culture sustained by morally committed people. In
dialogue, people examine their personal assumptions and then suspend
them; thus opening new spaces where new meanings can be constructed
(Bohm, 1992; Horn & Carr-Chellman, 2000; Jenlink & Carr, 1996).
Dialogue requires a respect for other views and recognition that the
intended outcome is the development of community. The distinction

between dialogue and design is that when engaged in design conversation, people focus on creating something new. When engaged in creating change through design conversation, the participants are committed "to change of the system rather than change within the system" (Jenlink & Carr, 1996, p. 35). In the context of current restructuring efforts, design conversation would lead to something new: not just a reshuffling of a school schedule and minor conceptual changes in curriculum and instruction, but a new concept of curriculum, instruction, and school administration.

Dialogue and design are generative in that, through critique, newness and difference are welcomed. Discussion and dialectical conversation purposefully promote one position in opposition to other positions. Like dialogue and design, another type of conversation, post-formal conversation, facilitates the discovery of newness and difference. Post-formal conversation (Horn, 1999a) can be a dialogic and design type of conversation, but its distinction is that the conversation is guided by post-formal thinking, which will shortly be explained in detail. The distinctive element that characterizes this type of conversation is the inclusion of power. As conversation occurs, considerations of power are always in the forefront. A post-formal conversation about American standards would include a continuous assessment of how the standards will affect the power relationships among all of the stakeholders in the social system. Power, like conversation, is ubiquitous—it is everywhere in human activity.

All of these conversational types are evident in any system; however, the absence of some or the predominance of others is a strong indicator of a corresponding type of community. For instance, an analysis of a community that strives to be egalitarian would reveal spaces for dialogic, design, and post-formal conversation. A commitment to egalitarianism requires an ongoing critical probing of the community's origins and processes, as well as a need to understand the obvious and hidden patterns and contexts of the community's activity. A community that recognizes and includes the diversity of its' multicultural nature welcomes all stakeholders to participate in this post-formal conversation.

Banathy's "old story" metaphor for restructuring is indicative of the type of system in which discussion and dialectical conversation would predominate. A system like this would only welcome multicultural diversity into its conversation if the diversity was in a form that was compatible with the mandates of those in control. Any incompatible difference that emerged would be dealt with in a dialectical manner.

The argument has been made concerning the link between community, multiculturalism, and conversation; but what about standards? Is there a link between the type of standards and the type of conversation that is generated in the school community? Does the type of test used to measure student achievement of the standards generate or facilitate a particular type of conversation? If a type of conversation represents a type of mindset, what mindsets do the different types of standards promote? The answers to these questions will be as complex as our understanding of American standards. As we saw in the research concerning high-performing Hispanic schools where it is possible to develop a learning community in response to rigid technical standards, so it is possible to utilize dialogue, design, and post-formal conversation to respond to the dialectical conversation of a technical standards movement. Obviously, if the essence of standards of complexity is to think critically and to include difference, then there is a natural compatibility with dialogue, design, and post-formal conversation.

As you read about Texas standards, employ the lens of conversational analysis as another tool to move to a complex understanding of the effects of standards on school communities. This lens also has the potential to clearly reveal the relationship between the schools and the governing body that implements and regulates the standards. The conversational relationship between the governing body (such as the nation, state, or school board) and the schools is an indicator of the values and attitudes of those in control. A rigidly mandated standards initiative that allows no room for negotiation not only indicates the kind of society valued by those in control but also contradicts the essence of any critical thinking or egalitarian values included in the standards. Common sense requires an essential pattern of continuity between what is said and what is done, and when there is a contradiction between the "talk" and the "walk," the essential values and agendas of those in control become evident.

Post-Formal Thinking

So far, four lenses have been provided to increase the level of complexity in understanding American standards. However, to continue the metaphor, these lenses will take us only so far. How we think about what we see is also critical in broadening our understanding. The lenses add complexity, but how do we process this complexity?

Formal thinking of the modern age relied upon analysis and synthesis, isolating variables, controlling the factors that disrupted and complicated the process of understanding. The modernist tradition separated reality into dualistic opposites, such as emotion and reason, or the knower and the known. Our postmodern society requires a more complex process that more closely approximates the complexity of reality. We know that factors/variables can't be separated or controlled without losing the context that gives them meaning. We know that dualisms like emotion and reason can't be separated; that reality can't be compartmentalized. If we have learned anything from our study of ecology, quantum mechanics, and chaos theory, it is that life is interrelated, holistic, and wholly unpredictable. American standards are also like this. What then is a post-formal process that allows us greater insight into complex situations?

The aim of post-formal thinking (Horn, 1999b; Kincheloe & Steinberg, 1999) is to broaden our understanding of complex situations by broadening our inquiry into the complex reality of that which we seek to understand. Unlike the myth of formal modernistic thinking, which claimed absolute truth can be discerned, post-formal thinking understands that, due to the dynamic, ever-changing condition of reality, understanding is also an ongoing process.

The four explanational categories of post-formal thinking must be understood as interactive, integrated, and ongoing. Post-formal thinking is a continuing process, not a mechanism to reach an end-state. In relation to our study of American standards, our post-formal thinking about standards is viewed as co-evolutionary with the standards movement. In Texas, the standards movement has evolved from its inception in the 1980s to the present, and this evolution will continue as the state of Texas strives to create quality education. Our thinking must evolve along with the changes in Texas standards, or our understanding will stagnate and become irrelevant. The four categories that characterize post-formal thinking are intended as *moving* guideposts that require continuous reflection.

Etymology
Etymology is the study of origins, and understanding any standards movement requires a critical study of how the standards came about. What are their antecedents? Who originated the idea/process? What was the agenda of these people? How has knowledge about standards been produced? How have social forces shaped our understanding of standards? What were the original problems that created the apparent need for standards? How have those problems changed over time? All of these questions deal with the origins of knowledge, values, ideology, and hidden agendas.

They are some of the etymological questions that a post-formal thinker would ask about standards.

Patterns
Patterns imply continuity, regularity, and once again, agendas. What are the surface patterns of a standards movement in relation to its organization, structure, and implementation? What are the hidden patterns, the deep structures, and the tacit forces that need to be made visible? How can we penetrate the "curtain of ostensible normality" (Kincheloe, Steinberg, & Hinchey, 1999, p. 68) that cloaks deep and hidden realities? What metaphors are used to promote standards and what metaphors can be used to more critically understand the patterns created by a standards movement, and the patterns that superficially represent the movement? Discovering and critiquing these patterns leads to a more complex understanding of American standards.

Process
Process indicates new ways of reading the world. Transcending the simplistic notions of cause and effect (Kincheloe, Steinberg, & Hinchey, 1999, p. 76) requires the use of a toolbox of methodological diversity. Seeking the truth in a postmodern world requires the use of all kinds of quantitative and qualitative methods. Statistical analysis and postmodern deconstruction both have a situational applicability. The eclectic array of methods used by the critical post-formal researcher may include ethnography, textual analysis, semiotics, psychoanalysis, content analysis, poststructural feminist perspectives, contextual analysis, critical hermeneutics, interviews, survey analysis, and phenomenology (Kincheloe, 1998, pp. 1198–1199).

True post-formal thinkers never met a method that they didn't like or couldn't use for some purpose. The inherent complexity of American standards requires an equally complex process of reading the world.

Contextualization
Contextualization is what makes a story, in book or movie form, a good story. What are the circumstances? How does one particular setting or place create a different understanding of a similar phenomenon that occurs elsewhere? Would a standards model in one place be appropriate for another place? What are the broader temporal, spatial, or ideological aspects? How is indigenous knowledge utilized and valued? Who are the "players" in the story? What is their interest, and how do they achieve

that interest? How have the standards affected all of the people in the system? What are the benefits and the costs? Who pays the costs and reaps the benefits? Are the standards relevant to our current and future needs? How can they be changed to accommodate our needs? What are the moral and ethical implications of the standards? These questions represent an exceedingly short list of contextual questions. A post-formal thinker generates contextual questions that provide a wealth of information. A post-formal thinker searches for and values details.

A Post-Formal Analysis of Texas Standards

Why should we post-formally analyze Texas standards? The answer lies in the critical center of post-formalism. Unlike the enervating relativism of postmodernism, post-formalism is critically centered on paradigms of social justice and caring. As we utilize diverse processes to discern the deeper implicate (complex and hidden) levels of understanding, we do so through a critical lens that is centered on the promotion of social justice and caring for others. Of course, a postmodern inquiry would contest the possibility of this center and contest even more the ability to achieve a just and caring state. However, within this postmodern context, adherents of post-formalism strive to uncover the contradictions within our own beliefs and actions and those of our society that promote injustice and a lack of caring. An egalitarian-centered post-formalism recognizes the dynamic, ever-changing nature of reality, also expressed by the idea that there are no real answers, just probabilities of degrees of understanding or highly contextualized approximations of reality.

How do we do post-formal analysis? By employing the previously identified diverse processes in a critical analysis of the context and etymology of standards in Texas, we can discern patterns on two levels. The first level of pattern recognition quickly yields simplistic answers that are the product of formal reductionist analysis. This is the explicate order that David Bohm (Bohm & Edwards, 1991; Bohm & Peat, 1987) identified: an order or layer of patterns that are explainable through the formalistic reductionism of modernism. In other words, these are the simple answers that become apparent when a complex holistic phenomenon is reduced to its parts (decontextualized or separated from all else that contributes to its meaning/identity), and formal analytical processes (scientific method) are used to discover "answers." Unfortunately, this is where many stop.

On the other hand, post-formal analysis continues, examining the context and etymology of the phenomenon, pushing into the second level of patterns. Here the patterns become more complex and holistic, characterized by descriptors such as interrelated, nested, embedded, and interactive. This level of hidden patterns is Bohm's implicate order: a dynamic and inherently more abstract level than the formal abstraction of the explicate. On this level, no concrete answers or truths are found; instead, complex understanding mirrors the complexity of the organization and structure of the patterns. What also extends this level's abstractness from the formal to the post-formal is our concern for social justice and caring. As our egalitarian center mediates our understanding of the phenomenon, our examination of the phenomenon is extended from a limiting formal analysis of its context and etymology of the phenomenon to a broader critical analysis.

What then is a post-formal analysis? It is the use of a diversity of processes to analyze the context and etymology of a phenomenon in order to discern the explicate (shallow and easily visible) and implicate (deep and hidden) patterns inherent in the phenomenon. This is what we will do with the standards initiative in Texas. Many processes will be employed to expand our understanding of the context (circumstances and setting) and the etymology (origins) of the Texas standards movement. From this process, patterns of behavior and thought will emerge; some will be simple and shallow and others will be complex and deep. But, through all of this analysis our purpose will be to make clear the implications of this initiative in relation to justice and caring for all of the people affected. These diverse processes used to examine the degree of equity and caring that characterizes the relationships of those affected by the Texas standards make up post-formal analysis.

American Standards and the Case of Quality Education in Texas

A Historical Context

Contemporary educational reform efforts are often seen as the results of events that occurred in the early 1980s. The publication of *A Nation at Risk* in 1983 (National Commission on Excellence in Education) and the Carnegie Report in 1986 (the Carnegie Task Force on Teaching as a Profession), prompted a public debate that rapidly became ideologically polarized and continues today. However, long before these events during the Reagan presidency, the State of Texas had not only conducted its own educational research but also initiated a standardized testing sequence that has resulted in the current batch of standardized tests: the Texas Assessment of Academic Skills (TAAS), the Texas Academic Skills Program (TASP), the Texas Oral Proficiency Test (TOPT), and the Examination for the Certification of Educators in Texas (ExCET).

In 1968, during the term of Governor John Connally, the Governor's Committee on Public School Education commissioned the Subcommittee on Goals to research and recommend goals for public education in Texas. Through funding provided by an ESEA Title III grant, this committee published its findings in December 1968 (Operation PEP, 1968). To complete its task the committee relied on three sources of information: a study of the educational goals of Maryland, Pennsylvania, Massachusetts, and Oregon; a review of educational goals in Texas from 1876 to 1963; and an analysis of "historical landmarks" in public education in the United States from 1635 to 1966.

Additionally, to discern the future needs of society, two conferences held in 1966, designed to forecast the future, were reviewed. One conference, sponsored by the American Management Association, met in New York to consider the theme, "Educational Realities." Another conference, held in Denver, Colorado, was a joint research project of eight western states and had the theme of "Prospective Changes in Society by 1980." The areas related to education reported by this conference were a need for greater technical competence in the working force due to growing automation; an increasing urbanization with accompanying problems of waste disposal, transportation, housing, and racial unrest; and increasing psychological tensions and political irresponsibility.

The subcommittee concluded that in 1966 Texas represented a blend of the past and the future in public education. "Because of the wide degree of local autonomy and the variance in local resources among school districts in Texas, some schools are not far removed in concept and practice from those of decades past. Others are already launched into space-age programs utilizing an impressive array of new techniques and technological tools" (Operation PEP, 1968, p. 16).

After reviewing innovations current at that time, the subcommittee further concluded that "clearly, these innovations in subject matter, technology and technique are altering some of the traditional concepts of education, challenging what has been called the 2 x 4 x 6 limitations: two covers of a book, four walls of a classroom, and six periods of a school day. But there is as yet no evidence that these innovations alter the basic goals of public education" (1968, p. 16).

These two quotations contextualize the subcommittee's and subsequently the State of Texas' decision to move toward a standardized, high-stakes testing situation. The wide diversity in the quality, practice, and focus of education across the State of Texas obviously suggested a need for some sort of standard that would provide educational continuity. In the second quotation, the subcommittee's review of educational innovation current at that time suggests an understanding that the traditional concepts of education are fair game in a change initiative. However, it is especially interesting to note the subcommittee's adherence to what it explicates as the "basic goals of public education." In other words, the change that occurs must be designed to promote these "basic goals."

The subcommittee identifies these goals as those proposed by John W. Gardner, Secretary of the Department of Health, Education, and Welfare, at the New York conference. Gardner listed these basic goals as teaching a young person "to exercise his critical capacities, his capacity for reasoning, his curiosity"; developing citizenship knowledge and skills so individuals know how to function in society; enabling young people to earn their living, to be competent; and giving children an understanding of the shared values that hold society together (Gardner, 1966).

This emphasis on critical thinking, citizenship, and shared values is evident, not only in the goals determined by this subcommittee but also in the current Texas standards initiative. Future versions of the standardized tests are targeted to be more focused on assessing critical thinking skills such as problem solving, and more aligned with the critical thinking standards in the Texas Essential Knowledge and Skills (TEKS), which are the actual standards for public school students. The other two emphases, citizenship and shared values, very much still reflect the traditional (nonpluralistic) European/White contextualized knowledge base and attitudes. And the assessment instruments and procedures also reflect this traditional bias. A case can be made that to promote the traditional definitions of citizenship and shared values, the state-mandated standards, assessments, and accountability structures are primarily designed to assimilate minority views into the culture represented by the majority, rather than to build an egalitarian, pluralistic society.

This is evident in an examination of the six specific, detailed goals recommended by the subcommittee, which deal with intellectual discipline, economic and vocational competence, citizenship and civic responsibility, competence in human and social relations, moral and ethical values, and self-realization, and mental and physical health. These goals are the antecedents of the current standards initiative in Texas. From intellectual discipline comes the imperative to "provide all children with knowledge of the traditionally accepted fundamentals, such as reading, writing and arithmetic" (Operation PEP, 1968, p. 18). Also, this goal proposes that each child should develop "the power to think constructively, to solve problems, to reason independently, and to accept responsibility for self-evaluation and continuing self-instruction," and that educators should "help each child gain access to the accumulated culture and knowledge of man" (p. 18). Concepts like "accumulated culture" and "knowledge of man" are vague, innocuous terms with which most people can agree. Culture and knowledge are, however, significant battle zones in the "culture wars." A reading of the historical context of this time period in Texas supports a traditional interpretation of these terms.

From the economic and vocational competence goal comes the necessity to

- help all students understand how to function effectively in the American economic system,
- provide every student with usable vocational skills which will equip him to find employment in the event he finds it impracticable to continue his education; and
- offer guidance and counseling to help every student decide what he should do upon completion of high school.

From citizenship and civic responsibility comes the need for schools to "emphasize the American heritage and the responsibilities and privileges of citizenship," and "help equip each child for intelligent participation in the democratic processes through which this country is governed" (p. 19).

These goals represent the foundation for the knowledge base of the Texas standards and the conceptual attitude of the policy makers of the Texas standards initiative. These goals, in conjunction with a report by the Educational Testing Service (1965), provided the key foci for the subsequent Texas standards initiative that would begin with the Texas Assessment of Basic Skills (TABS).

In 1975, essential objectives (standards) for mathematics and reading were developed "as the result of a series of public hearings held in each of the 20 education service centers. The writing objectives were developed during the summer and early fall of 1979 by a special committee of Texas Education Agency and school district specialists from across the state. The Educational Testing Service of Princeton, New Jersey, collaborated with the committee in the development of objective specifications for measurement purposes" (Texas Education Agency, 1980, p. 28). In 1979, a contract was negotiated with the Educational Testing Service for the development of further tests.

In 1979, the 66th Texas Legislature mandated that with the 1979–80 school year, the Central Education Agency (now the Texas Education Agency) would adopt and administer an appropriate criterion-referenced assessment instrument designed to assess minimum basic skills and competencies in reading, writing, and mathematics for all pupils at the fifth-grade level. By February and March 1980, 433, 520 students in grades 5 and 9 had been tested (TEA, 1980).

A final historical note, to further contextualize our understanding of the development of Texas standards, is that in 1978 a report was issued by the National Education Association (NEA), warning about the implications of standardized testing for minority students. The NEA reported the extent of standardized testing in the United States (that in 1975 at least 200 million achievement test forms were used and that this represented only 65 percent of all educational and psychological tests administered), and the effects on African Americans and Hispanics. The NEA reported a number of cases in which minorities were significantly affected by a standardized test. In one case, 50 percent to 300 percent more Blacks and Mexican Americans were identified as mentally retarded than could reasonably be expected from their proportion of the population (Griffin, 1978, p. 5). In another, NEA cited the reduction of Black teachers in South Carolina from 43 percent to 29 percent in 1975 due to the use of the National Teacher Examination to assess teacher performance.

The NEA joined a number of other prominent national organizations in calling for a moratorium on the use of standardized tests. They expressed their doubt that this would happen since, at that time, educational testing was a $300-million a-year industry. They completed their report by listing the results of standardized educational tests:

A. The majority of the students are grouped by ability.
B. Low achievers are grouped together and deprived of the stimulation of high-achieving children.
C. Principals and school superintendents are regularly judged by and rewarded for their pupils' performance.
D. Students are admitted to or rejected by a course, college, or professional school on the basis of test results.
E. Test results determine curriculum and instruction.
F. Scores are permanently attached to student records.

G. The results maintain the differential status of population subgroups.
H. Test results legitimize the dominance of the Anglo cultural tradition.
I. Tests tend to calm parents who are seeking to change educational programs.
J. Cities, school districts, and schools are compared and allocated resources on the basis of test results (Griffin, 1978, pp. 9–10).

In concluding, the NEA recommended alternatives ranging from multiple measures of validity to the inclusion of multicultural perspectives and the utilization of multiple assessment alternatives. Without question, this report, and others like it, were essentially disregarded by the TEA, as evidenced by the same issues resurfacing in the court case that will be examined in a later chapter.

The Current Context

As the new millennium begins and Texas standards continue to evolve, this evolution will be shaped by the continued concern about the effects of standards on minorities, the continuing student attrition problem, the significant teacher shortage looming on the immediate horizon, and the equitable reallocation of resources for public schools. The chapters in part 3 will further explicate the concerns about minorities and student attrition.

The teacher shortage will have an immediate impact on the Texas standards initiative. At this time, there are predictions of a 40,000-teacher shortage within the next two years. This number may be conservative, due to the retirement of the baby boomer generation and due to the rising standards in teacher certification programs, which will be the focus of a chapter in part 2. Rising admission standards for teacher preparation programs, as a response to the state's stringent certification requirements and the consequences of low scores on the standardized test, will also make it more difficult for minorities to become teachers. In addition, the current level of Texas teacher salaries will further exacerbate the shortage as prospective teachers continue to be enticed by superior reimbursement into the non-education sector. Teacher retention will continue to be a problem, as Texas already has great difficulty in keeping beginning teachers from moving to the private sector.

Concerning the equitable allocation of resources, the State of Texas provides additional funding through grant programs to compensate for the economic inequity between school districts. However, no decision has been made to guarantee statewide economic parity through fundamental changes in the state funding structures. Maintaining current funding structures guarantees a continuation of the primary focus of educational change as being on the student.

José A. Cardenás, the director of the Intercultural Development Research Association (1998), characterizes the focus of educational change, in relation to raising student achievement, as either directed at input (the resources provided), process (the use of the resources), or output (the results of the process). A focus on input would require an equitable redistribution of resources. The importance of an input focus on raising student achievement is evident in Cardenás' comment that "it is embarrassing to hold school systems responsible for realistic inputs when the state system of school finance makes no pretense of providing equitable or equal resources for acquiring these inputs" (1998, p. 2). Process evaluations require a focus on the teaching-learning and teacher-pupil interaction process.

To a degree, both of these influences on student achievement are only a small part of the Texas standards initiative; however, the overwhelming emphasis for change is on the student. Cardenás contests this emphasis. "What is important is the amount that the student learns. This is grossly unfair to the student. The student may have some impact on what is learned, but the student has no impact on input (the adequacy of resources) nor on process (the quality of instruction)" (1998, p. 17). Cardenás further maintains that "school systems and professional organizations have developed a line of defense that assumes that resources are adequate, everything done by the school is proper, and if a student fails to learn, the student and only the student must be held accountable" (1998, p. 17). Cardenás is of the opinion that the State of Texas has defaulted on its professional responsibility and allowed "the standardized test to make critical educational decisions instead of using extensive information on what is best for the individual student. The state did the same thing in requiring successful performance on the TAAS as a condition for graduation. Accountability is based solely on one output measure, student performance, without consideration of input and process" (1998, p. 18).

The professional development and teacher evaluation structure, the Professional Development and Appraisal System (PDAS), supports Cardenás' proposition. Developed in 1995, the PDAS links teacher evaluation to student performance. "We believe the system has the potential to positively impact student achievement. The performance link focuses on TAAS-related objectives, attendance, and students in at risk situations, allowing the system to appraise all teachers on their contributions to the overall improvement of the school" (TEA, 2000). Of the eight domains against which the teacher is evaluated, four directly refer to student progress: active, successful student participation in the learning process; learner-centered instruction; evaluation and feedback on student progress; and management of student discipline, instructional strategies, time, and materials—in relation to the students under the teacher's immediate instruction. An additional domain links teacher evaluation to "improvement of academic performance of all students on the campus (based on indicators included in the Academic Excellence Indicator System [AEIS])" (TEA, 2000). In other words, if students, under the immediate supervision of a teacher, or the whole school or campus, do poorly, as indicated by the AEIS/TAAS, the teacher will receive a poor evaluation. However, the primary focus and direct pressure to achieve still fall upon the student. Another implication of this relationship between the teacher and student achievement is the limitation placed on the teacher as an autonomous professional. Without the state mandating a specific pedagogical method, it is indirectly controlling the teacher's pedagogy. If the child doesn't succeed, your job is in jeopardy. Therefore, you must teach to the test, and the most efficient way is through techniques that accommodate mass repetition and memorization. This factory system pedagogy sacrifices the teacher's ability and desire to individualize instruction to accommodate unique individual academic needs. In addition, there is less space for other types of instruction, even if they are superior methods in improving the quality of student learning.

Critics like Cardenás raise questions about issues that will affect the development of the standards movement in Texas. A systemic and post-formal analysis of these issues will be essential in their resolution. To begin this analysis, *American Standards* offers a different perspective on the pursuit of quality education by the State of Texas.

American Standards

American Standards will examine the Texas standards initiative by providing a variety of perspectives on this unique phenomenon. *American Standards* is a collage of broad, sweeping strokes and intense personal experiences. The purpose of the collage is to avoid an exclusively structural analysis of Texas standards. The addition of individual stories and interpretations provides a unique perspective.

The focus of part 2, "Standards and the Texas Public Schools, " deals with the structure of the standards and the effects of the standards on the

Texas public schools. An overview will be provided of the structure and systemic nature of standards as they apply to Texas. The techniques employed by educators to meet the standards tested by the TAAS will be reviewed, along with the effect of the TAAS on minority populations. This will be followed by a discussion of the relationship between the TAAS and student attrition in Texas schools.

Part 3 focuses on standards and the Texas universities. Once again, the section will start with an overview of the structure and systemic nature of standards in relation to higher education. An analysis of the standardized test given to perspective teachers and an analysis of the accountability system used to rate Texas universities will be provided. Other topics include the impact of standardized testing on academic departments in a Texas university, the effects of the decision to increase the accountability level of the standardized test, and the impact of the test on minority students in higher education.

Part 4 moves from public education and higher education to other voices and concerns about standardized testing in Texas. A detailed overview of the standards and the accountability structures will provide a comprehensive overview of the systemic complexity of the Texas system. A discussion of the issue of the systemic alignment of curriculum, instruction, and assessment will follow. A different view will be presented as to the effect of the public school standards movement on private education in Texas. A detailed analysis of a legal challenge to the TAAS test will be followed by a closer look at TAAS gains.

The complexity of the Texas standards initiative does not allow a definitive presentation of all aspects or all views on the Texas model. Instead, this book hopes to create critical conversation about the model, and problematize the reader's understanding of standards in Texas and in America in general. To achieve this purpose, the reader is initially provided with commentary about standards in general, and given critical lenses that can be used to gain a deeper understanding of this phenomenon. The rest of the book will focus on the standards situation in Texas. The section on higher education will focus more specifically on one state university in Texas and its struggle to meet the standards.

References

Ackoff, R. L. (1981). *Creating the corporate future.* New York: John Wiley & Sons.

Alexander, G. C. (1999). Schools as communities: Purveyors of democratic values and the cornerstones of a public philosophy. *Systemic Practice and Action Research, 12* (2), 183–193.

Avers, D., Broadbent, M., Ferguson, T., Gabriele, S., Lawson, T., McCormick, S., & Wotruba, D. (1996). Design conversation and systems design: Group report. *Proceedings of the Eighth International Conversation on Comprehensive Design of Social Systems, Pacific Grove, California,* 1–42.

Banathy, B. H. (1992). *A systems view of education: Concepts and principles for effective practice.* Englewood Cliffs, NJ: Educational Technology Publications.

Banathy, B. H. (1996). *Designing social systems in a changing world: A journey toward a creating society.* New York: Plenum Press.

Beck, L. G. (1999). Metaphors of educational community: An analysis of the images that reflect and influence scholarship and practice. *Educational Administration Quarterly, 35* (1), 13–45.

Bohm, D. (1992). *Thought as a system.* New York: Routledge.

Bohm, D., & Edwards, M. (1991). *Changing consciousness.* San Francisco: Harper.

Bohm, D., & Peat, F. (1987). *Science, order, and creativity.* New York: Bantam Books.

Bowles, S., & Gintis, H. (1976). *Schooling in capitalist America: Educational reform and the contradictions of economic life.* New York: Basic Books.

Callahan, R. E. (1962). *Education and the cult of efficiency: A study of the social forces that have shaped administration of the public schools.* Chicago: The University of Chicago Press.

Cardenás, J. A. (1998, October). School-student performance and accountability. *Intercultural Development Research Association, 25,* (9), 1–2, 17–19.

Carnegie Task Force on Teaching as a Profession. (1986). *A nation prepared: Teachers for the 21st century.* Washington, DC: Carnegie Forum on Education and the Economy.

Cremin, L. A. (1988). *American education: The metropolitan experience.* New York: Harper & Row.

Cuban, L. (1984). *How teachers taught: Constancy and change in American classrooms, 1890–1980 (2nd ed.).* New York: Longman.

Dewey, J. (1916). *Democracy and education.* New York: The Free Press.

Educational Testing Service. (1965). *A plan for evaluating the quality of educational programs in Pennsylvania.* Princeton, NJ: Educational Testing Service.

Freire, P. (1996). *Pedagogy of the oppressed.* New York: Continuum.

Gardner, J. (1966). *Education for what?* [Filmed interview]. American Management Association Conference on "Educational Realities," New York.

Griffin, A. H. (1978). *Standardized testing: Implications for minority students.* Washington, D.C: National Education Association.

Horn, R. A. (1999a). The dissociative nature of educational change. In J. L. Kincheloe, S. R. Steinberg, & P. Hinchey (Eds.), *The post-formal reader: Cognition and education* (pp. 349–377). New York: Garland.

Horn, R. A. (1999b). Joe L. Kincheloe: Teacher-as-researcher. *Educational Researcher, 28* (4), 27–31.

Horn, R. A., & Carr-Chellman, A. A. (2000). Providing systemic change for schools: Towards professional development through moral conversation. *Systems Research and Behavioral Science, 45* (3), 255–272.

Jenlink, P., & Carr, A. A. (1996). Conversation as a medium for change in education. *Educational Technology, 36* (1), 31–38.

Kincheloe, J. L. (1998). Critical research in science education. In B. Fraser & K. Tobin (Eds.), *International handbook of science education* (pp. 1191–1205). Boston: Kluwer Academic Publishers.

Kincheloe, J. L., & Steinberg, S. R. (1997). *Changing multiculturalism: New times, new curriculum*. London: Open University Press.

Kincheloe, J. L., & Steinberg, S. R. (1999). A tentative description of post-formal thinking: The critical confrontation with cognitive theory. In J. L. Kincheloe, S. R. Steinberg, & P. Hinchey (Eds.), *The post-formal reader: Cognition and education* (pp. 55–90). New York: Garland.

Kincheloe, J. L., Steinberg, S. R., & Hinchey, P. (Eds.). (1999). *The Post-formal reader: Cognition and education*. New York: Garland.

Kliebard, H. M. (1995). *The struggle for the American curriculum: 1893–1958* (2nd ed.). New York: Routledge.

National Commission on Excellence in Education. (1983). *A nation at risk*. Washington, DC: U.S. Government Printing Office.

Operation PEP: A State-Wide Project to Prepare Educational Planners for California. (1968, December). *Goals for public education in Texas: A report by the subcommittee on goals to the Governor's committee on public school education*. Redwood City, CA: County Office of Education.

Palmer, P. J. (1993). *To know as we are known: Education as a spiritual journey*. San Francisco: HarperSanFrancisco.

Reyes, P., & Pazey, B. (1999). Creating student-centered classroom environments: The case of mathematics. In P. Reyes, J. D. Scribner, & A. P. Scribner, (Eds.). *Lessons from high-performing Hispanic schools: Creating learning communities*. (pp. 94–130). New York: Teachers College Press.

Reyes, P., Scribner, J. D., & Scribner, A. P. (1999). *Lessons from high-performing Hispanic schools: Creating learning communities*. New York: Teachers College Press.

Sergiovanni, T. J. (1994). *Building community in schools*. San Francisco: Jossey-Bass.

Texas Education Agency. (1980, November). *Texas assessment of basic skills: Statewide and regional results as reported by the commissioner of education.* Austin, TX: Texas Education Agency.

Texas Education Agency. (2000). Professional development and appraisal system. *Texas Education Agency* [On-line]. Available: http://www.tea.state.tx.us/PDAS/

Tönnies, F. (1957). (C. P. Loomis, ed. and trans.). *Gemeinschaft und gesellschaft [Community and society]* New York: HarperCollins. (Original book published in 1887)

Tyack, D., & Hansot, E. (1982). *Managers of virtue: Public school leadership in America, 1820–1980.* New York: Basic Books.

Westheimer, J. (1999). Communities and consequences: An inquiry into ideology and practice in teachers' professional work. *Educational Administration Quarterly, 35* (1), 71–105.

PART TWO

STANDARDS AND THE TEXAS PUBLIC SCHOOLS

Chapter 4

The Texas Accountability System Past, Present, and Future Through One Educator's Lens: A Continuing Journey Toward System Improvement

Betty J. Alford

As I was driving in the rain on a cold day with my car heater not working, I couldn't wait to arrive at my destination. Looking out the window at a lonely field, I thought, "It's a miserable day outside." Later that same day, after a wonderful meal and warm conversation at my parents' home, I walked outside onto the back porch and again gazed out across an empty field. If anything, the rain was heavier, and the day was drearier. However, from the warmth of our home, the view seemed lovely. I couldn't help but think, "What a difference perspective makes."

The Texas State Accountability System is like the above anecdote. Where an individual is sitting, as he or she views the accountability system, shapes his or her perspective. For example, in schools that have mastered the Texas Assessment of Academic Skills (TAAS), the state's high-stakes testing instrument, educators talk about the schools' educational program not being "driven by the TAAS." These schools may be focusing on the advanced placement program as a driving force of secondary school reform, or on another advanced academic measure. One educator summarized this perspective by saying that some schools are moving "beyond the tide of the TAAS." Other educators in schools that are on the Low-Performing list generally view the accountability system as the primary focus for the school. In these schools, professional development is directed at the improvement of TAAS scores, and curriculum discussions center on the TAAS. In the words of one educator, "Everything else is on hold until after TAAS testing." Another educator from a Low-Performing school commented, regarding campuses that received high ratings primarily through exempting large numbers of special education students, "It's a good game if you know how to play it." How an educator views the accountability system is mainly a matter of perspective, and this is influenced by the local context.

Like many goals in education, the state's accountability system remains a moving target. As a total quality management consultant once commented, "What we consider quality keeps changing." In like manner, what we perceive as acceptable in the state's accountability system keeps changing, as well it should. Our society is not static. The needs of the twenty-first century keep emerging. Our knowledge, as educators, of what students should know and be able to do in today's global society keeps growing. States across the nation have implemented standards-based reform (Wilson & Rossman, 1993). Texas is no different. In this state, educators continually wrestle with the question, "What do students need to know and to be able to do?" as a pivotal focus, and "How can we use the accountability system as a lever for achieving this focus?" What has emerged in Texas is not a perfect accountability system but a system in the process "of becoming." This system has, however, helped to bring about improvement in student achievement by serving as a catalyst for increased student learning (Grissmer & Flanagan, 1998). As Grissmer and Flanagan (1998) emphasized, "If we average the gains across all grades and subjects [for the National Assessment of Educational Progress (NAEP) Reading and Mathematics tests], North Carolina and Texas show the highest average gains among all states" (p. 6). The report further asserts, "The assessment results in Texas when averaged across grades show larger gains for Hispanic and black students than for non-Hispanic white students—although white students are also making significant gains" (p. 8). This report further notes, "From 1990 to 1996, large gains were also made by students on the state assessment test [TAAS]" (p. 9). The accountability system was influential in the achievement of these results by Texas public school students (Grissmer & Flanagan, 1998).

One principal of a Low-Performing school described the accountability rating as published in the local paper as "magic dust." Upon receiving the Low-Performing rating, educators who had been content for years to maintain the status quo suddenly recognized that change was needed. Teachers who had been working hard and were eager to regain a reputation of excellence attacked the problem with vengeance. Standardized test results, which had previously been relegated to boxes in the hall, became a matter of public concern. Suddenly, educators were studying closely the disaggregation of the data and looking closely at the results of each student subgroup to determine areas of strength and weakness. Action plans were formulated, and support systems were established, such as after-school tutorials and in-school tutoring. The test results and the test processes were closely scrutinized. Educators were looking for answers to questions such as, "Who was declared exempt? How did the English as a Second Language students fare? How did the gifted and talented students do?" and "What makes a difference in raising scores?" The search had begun.

Early results revealed some common patterns. A greater percentage of small schools versus large schools were declared exemplary. Schools with a high percentage of high socioeconomic level students largely received higher ratings on the system. Attention then began to turn to "What makes some schools of predominately low socioeconomic level students perform well?" Increasingly, attention turned to schools that were achieving increased student learning for all subgroups, Hispanics, African Americans, Whites, and Economically Disadvantaged, as models for other schools. The results of the Texas Accountability System began to win acclaim, as did those of the North Carolina system. The characteristics of the Texas and North Carolina systems were identified as follows:

- establishing clear teaching objectives by grade through statewide learning standards;
- implementing new, statewide assessment closely linked to the clear learning standards;
- establishing a system of accountability with both sanctions and rewards linked to the assessment results;
- establishing a comparative system of feedback on test score performance at the state; classroom, school, and district level that can be used for diagnostic purposes
- emphasizing strongly that students are expected to meet the standards;
- deregulating the teaching and school environment and giving teachers and administrators more local control and increased flexibility in determining how to meet the standards;
- sustaining the system of assessment and accountability without significant changes over several years;
- explicitly shifting resources to schools with more disadvantaged students.

(Grissmer & Flanagan, 1998, pp. 19–20)

These characteristics were cited as influential in increasing student learning in schools.

As I reflect upon the Texas Accountability System, I am reminded of my own experiences with the state's accountability system in considering ways in which key factors of the system have evolved, the merits and challenges of the system, and possible future directions. In this report, I will share these reflections as a way of providing an overview of the Texas Accountability System—past, present, and future—in hopes that my reflections will prompt others' to ask "How do we improve learning for students? What does continuous improvement really mean?" and "How can we uniquely contribute to increased student achievement?" These reflections are not shared as a final treatise on the Texas Accountability System but rather as a reflective beginning toward greater understanding of the evolution of this system with its accompanying merits and challenges. I hope that my reflections will spark further dialogue and meditation on ways to improve student learning by others who also are intensely interested in helping more students gain an equitable opportunity to learn and to achieve outstanding results.

Overview of the Texas Accountability System

The Legislative Role in the Texas Accountability System

In providing a retrospective overview of the Texas Accountability System, a chronology of key dates is useful (see Table 1). Abelmann and Elmore (1999) suggest that the purpose of an assessment and accountability system is to improve the learning of all students. In Texas, by statute the accountability system was designed to improve student performance (Texas Education Code (TEC): 35.063 accreditation standards; and TEC: 35.041 academic excellence indicators). The first statewide testing program for Texas was adopted in 1979–80 and implemented in 1980–81 with the Texas Assessment of Basic Skills (TABS) Test. The test was essentially designed to be used for diagnostic purposes to enable educators to better meet students' needs. In the early 1980s, an influential committee chaired by H. Ross Perot, a business executive, was formed to examine education. The committee's recommendations were included in House Bill 72, passed by the legislature in 1984, which resulted in increased graduation requirements, a no-pass, no-play measure for student athletes, the requirement for each student to pass an exit-level competency test in order to receive a school diploma, and a maximum five-day absence rule per semester. Additionally in 1984, House Bill 246 resulted in the

Table 1 Timeline of Changes in the Texas Accountability System

1980–84	The Texas Assessment of Basic Skills (TABS) was implemented for grades 3, 5, 7, and 9 for reading, math, and writing, and for grade 1 for math and language arts.
January 1984	A statewide curriculum framework, the Essential Elements, was established.
1984–89	The Texas Educational Assessment of Minimum Skills (TEAMS) test was administered, replacing TABS.
1984	House Bill 72 created the regulation that students must pass a state exit test as well as passing their courses to get a high school diploma.
1984–85	Districts were first required to make a performance report available to the public.
1987	The first class graduated under the requirement of passing the exit-level Texas Educational Assessment of Minimum Skills (TEAMS) exam.
1989	The State Board of Education (SBOE) rules allowed exemptions for Limited English Proficient (LEP) students.
1989	The Academic Excellence Indicator System (AEIS) was established by the Texas Legislature, which also directed the SBOE to adopt and report a set of campus- and district-level indicators of student performance
1989–90	Through 1994–95 and 1997 through the present: Monetary awards for students academic performance were provided to schools by state appropriation.
1990	The monetary awards for increased student performance were administered by the Governor's Educational Excellence Awards Committee.
1990–91 to the Present	The Texas Assessment of Academic Skills (TAAS) was administered to students replacing the TEAMS test. Before 1992–93 the grades tested were 3, 5, 7, 9, & 11. Since 1993–94, grades 3–8 and 10 are given reading and mathematics tests only while grades 4, 8, and 10 are also given writing tests.
1991–1992	The first TEA desk audit of schools on the accountability system was held.
1992–93	The testing date was changed so that tests would be administered to students in the spring (April) not in fall (October) each year.

Table 1   (Continued)

1991	The monetary awards began to be administered by the Texas Education Agency (TEA) as part of the Texas Successful School Award System.
1992	AEIS reports were grouped into base categories, additional categories, and report-only indicators.
1993–94	The Texas Learning Index was added to the testing reports to provide a comparison of the performance of each individual student from year to year.
1993	The accountability system was first used to determine district accreditation.
1994	A Spanish version of the TAAS was adopted by the SBOE (Over 90% of LEP students in Texas speak Spanish).
1995	The State began releasing the TAAS annually for students, educators, parents, and others.
1995	Accountability status was based on AEIS reports.
A.	End-of-course exams in science and social studies were phased in, with Algebra I, Biology, I, English I, and U.S. History being phased in.
A.	The Principal's Initiative of $5,000 for campus improved scores was to begin but was rescinded before any awards were made.
A.	The Texas Education Agency began annually releasing TAAS tests except for field-tested items.
1996	Beginning in 1996, special education students who are exempted from TAAS must be given an alternative assessment.
1996	The Texas Essential Knowledge and Skills (TEKS) were adopted by the State Board of Education as the new curriculum framework for Texas.
1999	Special education and Spanish TAAS takers were included in the campus and district score ratings.
1999	Students can access spring 1999 grades 3–8 released TAAS tests and answers on the web. The exit-level released TAAS can be taken on-line for practice and scored.
1999–2000	A one-time postponement of end-of-course tests can be provided for Limited English Proficient (LEP) students who have been in the U.S. three years or less, and the three-year exemption rule for LEP students

Table 1   (Continued)

	will apply only to immigrant LEP students who have been in the U.S. three years or less.
2000	Beginning in spring 2000, reading proficiency tests in English (RPTE) will be administered to Limited English Proficient (LEP) students.
2000	Senate Bill 103 of the legislature mandated development of a new exit-level 11th-grade test to cover English-language arts, writing, math, science, and social studies. Senate Bill 103 also required new 9th- and 10th-grade tests. The new test will be administered in 2003.

establishment of a statewide curriculum framework of Essential Elements (EE's) of instruction established for each grade level and subject area. The legislative push for accountability had truly begun. *A Nation at Risk*, published in 1983, had created alarm nationally that the United States was not preparing students for the global society, and Texas was not exempt from the rising concern that schools must strengthen academic programs and graduation requirements in order to remain competitive in a world market (Wilson & Rossman, 1993).

Again, the legislature played a key role in the state's accountability system with the passage of Senate Bill 1, which incorporated many ideas from a strategic plan developed largely by businessmen. Senate Bill 1 in 1990 provided further support and clarification of the state's accountability system (Grissmer & Flanagan, 1998) in requiring both campus and district ratings. The school's academic performance data is compiled for an overall rating and ratings for African American, Hispanic, White, and the Economically Disadvantaged subgroups. Rewards and sanctions are provided based upon overall scores and upon the student subgroup scores on the Texas Assessment of Academic Skills (TAAS) test results, dropout data, and attendance reports. The emphasis of Senate Bill 1 was on achieving the end results of increased student learning for each subgroup as well as for all students. Recommendations for how districts and campuses should reach the goal of increased student learning was not specified.

Philosophical Basis of the Accountability System

Philosophically, the Texas Accountability System is grounded in the belief that all students can learn. This tenet of the effective schools movement is reflected in both the design of the accountability system and the rewards and sanctions which are imposed. Yet, as Asa Hilliard (1999) suggests, even more important than the philosophy that all students can learn is the belief that "Every teacher can make every child succeed, and all teachers can learn" (p. 79). The state's accountability system is also based on the idea of efficacy and supports the belief that educators have the power to impact learning by all students. The guiding principles of the accountability system are listed as follows:

- Student Performance: The system is first and foremost designed to improve student performance.
- Recognition of Diversity: The system is fair and recognizes diversity among schools and students.
- System Stability: The system is stable and provides a realistic, practical timeline for measurement, data collection, planning, staff development, and reporting.
- Statutory Compliance: The system is designed to comply with statutory requirements.
- Appropriate Consequences: The system sets reasonable standards for adequacy, identifies and publicly recognizes high levels of performance and performance improvement, and identifies schools with inadequate performance and provides assistance.
- Local Program Flexibility: The system allows for flexibility in the design of programs to meet the individual needs of students.
- Local Responsibility: The system relies on local school districts to develop and implement local accountability systems that complement the state system.
- Public's Right to Know: The system supports the public's right to know levels of student performance in each school district and on each campus.

(Texas Education Agency, 2000a, pp. 1–2)

These principles are reflected in the components of the accountability system as well as in a communication by the commissioner of education. As Texas was being honored as one of twelve states recognized for educational progress by the National Education Goals Panel, Commissioner Nelson stated,

> Texas has been able to improve academic performance because the citizens in this state made up their minds that all students can learn, then they supplied the funding, the classroom resources and the will power to make that statement a

reality. We are determined to leave no student behind as we approach this new century. (Texas Education Agency, 1999c, p. 1)

The emphasis of the accountability system on increasing all students' performance is further illustrated by Commissioner Nelson's comments following U.S. District Judge Edward Prado's court ruling supporting the state's exit-level testing requirement in order for students to receive a high school diploma:

> Our testing program, coupled with our nationally recognized school accountability system, is clearly causing schools to focus on academic achievement and pushing performance up. We still have an achievement gap between our minority and white students but thankfully, it is shrinking. We will continue to work to eliminate that gap. (Texas Education Agency, 2000b, p. 1)

Two former commissioners, Skip Meno and Mike Moses, also reiterated the philosophical belief that all students can learn. The constant theme expressed by Commissioner Meno and listed as the slogan for the Texas Education Agency was "Equity and Excellence for all Students." Commissioner Moses continued this emphasis on promoting the attainment of high educational learning goals for all students. When a record number of Texas school districts and campuses earned the ratings of Exemplary and Recognized in the Texas accountability rating system, Commissioner Moses stated, "I am very proud of Texas educators and parents. They are clearly embracing our goal that all children can learn. No group of students will be left behind. A school will be held accountable for all students-its highest achievers and its special needs students" (Texas Education Agency, 1999b, p. 6). The philosophy, expressed in the *Accountability Manual for Texas* and reinforced by present and former commissioners of education, emphasizing increased student performance is also reflected in the evolution of the statewide testing system to a test reflecting higher-order thinking skills from a test whose purpose was to measure minimum skills.

Evolution of the Statewide Testing System

The testing instrument used to determine whether students have learned the essential elements designed for Texas schools has evolved since statewide standardized criterion-referenced testing was begun in Texas with the Texas Assessment of Basic Skills (TABS) test in 1980, a test which continued to be administered through the school year of 1983–84. The new test, implemented in 1984–85 and administered through the 1988–

89 school year, was entitled the Texas Educational Assessment of Minimum Skills (TEAMS) test. Although TEAMS was more difficult than TABS, both tests were designed to address student acquisition of minimum skills. Beginning in 1984, grades 1, 3, 5, 7, and 9 were tested. I can recall as a parent of a first grade child in 1985 comforting my teary-eyed son who was quietly crying the night before the TEAMS test. When I asked him what was wrong, he replied, "If I fail the test tomorrow, I'll fail first grade." I vividly remember hugging him and assuring him that he would not fail first grade, that he was already reading well, and that he would do fine on the test. Unfortunately, this scenario may have been repeated in more than one household. After 1988–89, however, first-grade students were no longer tested in the statewide assessment system. In 1991, Senate Bill 7 further strengthened the accountability reporting method to include publication of the results of every school, not just of school districts, and to require statewide testing of students in grades 3–8 and at the exit level (10–12). Reading and mathematics are tested in each of these grades with writing also assessed at grades 4 and 8 and the exit level. In addition, end-of-course examinations were established.

With the advent of the Texas Assessment of Academic Skills (TAAS) test, administered in the school year 1990–1991 until the present, the emphasis in the testing system changed. The emphasis was no longer on the assessment of minimum skills. Instead, the test was designed in such a way that critical thinking and higher-order reasoning skills were required for test mastery. Differences between the TAAS and the TEAMS test were readily apparent in the longer reading passages that replaced the short answer responses of the TEAMS test. In math, a greater emphasis was placed on word problems with extraneous information included, with a decreased emphasis on rote computation. Thinking back on my experiences as a new middle school principal at the time of the TEAMS test, I remember that it was relatively easy for our campus to raise TEAMS scores through focused efforts on this task. Teachers attended multiple writing workshops and learned holistic scoring and ways to teach writing prompts. For example, after one year of concerted effort, our scores rose in fifth grade from 46 percent to 83 percent passing writing and in seventh grade from 86 percent to 90 percent passing writing. We were a small school, and I hired an excellent math teacher who taught all seventh-grade math classes. She concentrated on improving TEAMS math scores, and our scores rose in one year from 78 percent to 97 percent passing.

As the TAAS test became part of the statewide testing system in 1990–91, however, schools had to learn new ways to prepare students for these more difficult tests. Although many consultants and others began to market TAAS preparation materials, clarity in ways to better prepare students for the TAAS test was not fully attained until 1995 when Texas was required by the Texas Legislature to release the previously scored TAAS tests for teacher and parent perusal. However, even as educators gained increased understanding of the statewide standardized test, overall results from schools with a high percentage of high socioeconomic level and low minority student populations were higher than schools with low socioeconomic level and primarily minority student populations. Growing interest emerged in studying schools that had been designated as Low-Performing but that had improved to become Recognized or Exemplary. These studies did not find magic tricks or packaged programs of teaching as causes for success. Instead, factors such as a focus on academic achievement, acceptance of no excuses, experimentation, inclusivity, a sense of family, collaboration and trust, and a passion for learning and growing emerged as reasons for success (Lein, L., Johnson, J.F., & Ragland, M., 1996). In an additional study, factors of urgency, responsibility, and efficacy emerged as common themes from analysis of data. In this study of high-performing districts that primarily included students of low socioeconomic backgrounds, the following factors emerged:

- First, district leaders created in their community a sense of urgency for the improvement of academic achievement.
- Secondly, district leaders created an environment in which improving academic instruction became a responsibility shared by everyone at every school.
- Finally, district leaders recognized that high expectations need to be accompanied by high-quality support. (Ragland, Asera, & Johnson, 1999, p. 21)

These findings were consistent with Newmann's and Wehlage's (1995) study of schools nation-wide that were particularly effective in improving the performance level of students. They found that these schools had administrators who established a professional learning community, focused on student work (through assessment), and modified their instructional practices to get better results. The Texas School Improvement Initiative training suggests that student success on the TAAS in schools with a high percentage of low socio-economic students includes a campus-wide commitment to the task, analysis of the student data, and formation of campus improvement plans focusing on building capacity to meet areas of need. These recommendations are in keeping with King and Mathers (1997) contention that

> An accountability system that does not stress meaningful professional development will not have teachers' and parents' support. Similarly, reform agendas will not advance without school level leadership. Finally, issues of equity and excellence must be addressed. (p. 175)

The Texas standardized testing program is continuing to evolve with TAAS II scheduled for implementation in 2003. As in the past whenever the statewide criterion-referenced test has undergone major revision, a new name has been proposed (Texas Education Agency, 2000c). Changes in the TAAS test are in progress. In 1997, the State Board of Education in Texas approved the Texas Essential Knowledge and Skills (TEKS) for the State of Texas as the new curriculum framework for schools. The TEKS replaced the former Essential Elements as the statewide curriculum. The TEKS were developed by educators and underwent extensive review and refinement. They reflect both a greater emphasis on critical analysis and higher-order thinking skills and an emphasis on increasing student learning. While the Essential Elements focused on what the teacher would teach, the TEKS focus on what the students will learn. The emphasis on student learning is evident in the wording of the TEKS, which are divided into student knowledge and skill statements and student expectations. The TEKS are being phased into the TAAS test; the TAAS test in 1999 was based only on the TEKS elements that were also the EEs, and full implementation of the test based on the TEKS is planned for 2001. For math, more multiple-step questions will be included on the 2000–2002 tests. In 1999, the legislature mandated the development of a new exit-level 11th-grade test, to include English, language arts, writing, math, science, and social studies, in the test required for a high school diploma. The English language arts part of the new 11th grade exit test will include concepts from English III and writing. The mathematics section will include algebra I and geometry. The social studies test will include U.S. history, including early American history, and the science test will include biology and integrated chemistry and physics. Senate Bill 103 also required the creation of new 9th-and 10th-grade tests. In 2003, the TAAS II tests will be administered.

The Evolution of the Statewide Accountability Rating System

Just as the state standardized testing program has evolved, the state's accountability rating system has changed over time. In 1989, the Academic Excellence Indicator System (AEIS) was established by the Texas Legislature. The legislature directed the State Board of Education (SBOE) to adopt and report student performance for campus and district levels based on indicators of student information, staff information, district information, and program information. This indicator system has been used to rate districts and campuses, and these ratings are the basis for rewards, sanctions, and public information. Districts are rated as Exemplary, Recognized, Acceptable, or Low-Performing on student performance by all subgroups: Hispanics, Whites, African Americans, and Economically Disadvantaged.

Rewards for System Improvement

Rewards are provided for annual improvement in performance of all students and improvements made by each of the four subgroups in performance if schools are in the Acceptable category. Outstanding performance awards are given for Exemplary and Recognized schools. The first awards, provided in 1992–93, ranged from $25,000 to $175,000. The first reward system for campuses and districts rated as high-performing was administered by the Governor's Educational Excellence Awards Committee in 1990. Beginning in 1992, however, the Texas Education Agency (TEA) became the agency to administer the rewards that were a part of the Texas Successful Schools Award System. The monetary reward system has used state appropriations from 1989–90 through 1994–95 and from 1997–98 to the present to disburse funds to schools in recognition of high student performance. The monetary rewards are to be used for academic purposes and cannot be used for athletic purposes. From 1995 to 1997, although the AEIS was administered, no funds were appropriated, so monetary rewards were not provided to schools. Recognizing the vital role of leadership to school improvement in 1995, the legislature established that the principal of a school that was high-performing or that had improved markedly would receive $5,000. In a state in which site-based decision making had been mandated by the Texas Education Agency and a philosophy of team empowerment had been espoused in state leadership training sessions, rewarding only one person for a school's improvement was not a popular idea. The reward was rescinded before the award was provided.

The first year that the AEIS group performance indicators were divided into three—base indicators, additional categories, and report-only indicators—was 1992. The TAAS testing results, dropout rate, and attendance rate by subgroups are included in the base indicators on which monetary rewards are based and accountability ratings are made. Additional categories such as student performance on the SAT-I or ACT and the percentage of students taking the SAT-I or ACT are used to provide acknowledgment to a district but do not affect a school's accountability rating. Other additional indicators include the percentage of students taking end-of-course tests, students' completion of advanced courses, students' completion of the recommended high school program, the results of Advanced Placement (AP) and International Baccalaureate (IB) examinations, and equivalency between performance on the exit-level TAAS and the Texas Academic Skills Program (TASP) test. To receive acknowledgment on an additional indicator, a school and district must also be rated Acceptable or higher. The report-only indicators are not used for rating purposes but supply pertinent profile information on students, programs, staff, and finances, such as the percentage of students in special education or gifted and talented programs, other special programs, and staff demographics including years of experience, ethnicity, and sex. Just as there have been changes in the AEIS system indicators, the rating system has evolved. Beginning in 2000, 50 percent of the student population for each of the four subgroups must pass the TAAS in order for the campus to receive an Acceptable rating, up from 45 percent in 1999.

Sanctions of the Accountability System

In addition to rewards based on the state's AEIS system ratings, a campus or district can receive sanctions based on the ratings. Since 1984–1985, districts and campuses have been required to make a performance report available to the public. With the emergence of the AEIS system in 1990, districts and campuses have been provided a school report card that is to be mailed to all parents. In addition, all schools must hold a school board hearing to publicize the AEIS report each year. Schools that are designated as Low-Performing must also hold a public hearing at the school to explain to parents and other interested individuals both the school's rating and the campus plan to improve the scores. Beginning in 1991–92, the state also established a system whereby a division of TEA would perform a desk audit of Low-Performing schools to determine whether a campus visit was needed. The 73rd Legislature in May 1993 required the state to use the AEIS report to determine district accreditation, a practice that continues to the present. If a school is rated as Low-Performing according to the TAAS ratings, the dropout ratings, or the attendance ratings for any of the four subgroup populations, a monitoring team will visit the school to review the campus improvement plan and to provide recommendations. If a campus is Low-Performing for two years, a specific intervention team will again visit the school. A third-year Low-Performing rating may result in a monitor being assigned to the campus. A plan for closing or reconstituting a campus could result if the school were Low-Performing for a fourth year. Needless to say, the AEIS system of sanctions contributes to the high-stakes testing system. Principals, superintendents, and school boards recognize that they are accountable for student results. As students must pass the exit test in order to receive a diploma from school, they also recognize the relationship of their performance on TAAS to their future.

Concerns in Implementing an Equitable Accountability System

Provision for Students with Special Needs

With a high-stakes testing system, it is essential that students with special needs be accommodated to prevent unfairness. For this reason, the state allows safeguards both for students with special needs and for campuses with high student-mobility rates. If a student qualifies for special education, the Admission, Review, and Dismissal (ARD) Committee determines whether the student is exempt from the TAAS test. Prior to 1996, special education students were not required to take an alternative form of the test. However, beginning in 1996–97, special education students must be given an alternative assessment. In like manner, there have been changes in the reporting of data about special education students. Prior to 1999, special education students who took the TAAS were not included in determining the campus accountability rating, though they were included in the attendance and dropout ratings. In 1999, special education TAAS data were also included in determining the campus rating, a practice that continues to the present. In considering this change, concerns that exemptions for special education might increase were voiced. A Texas School Improvement Initiative (TSII), which trains public school, service center, and university educators to serve as members of the peer review team required for TEA monitoring visits to Low-Performing schools and for district effectiveness compliance visits, cautions educators to question the percentage of special education students above the state's percentage of special education students. In 1999, an increase in the number of special education students exempted under the system was reported. Former Commissioner of Education Mike Moses stated,

> I am disappointed that we saw the number of special education students who were exempted from taking the TAAS test increase to 144,473, up from 106,529 last year [1998]. I have been very vocal for years about the need to include as many students as possible in the accountability system. I know that in years past some special education students who were not working on grade level took the TAAS test purely for diagnostic purposes. Obviously last year, when the stakes became higher, the educators and parents who sit on each special education student's Admission, Review and Dismissal (ARD) committee and determine the individual education plan for that student took a harder look at whether it was appropriate to test the student. Some clearly decided that the TAAS was not appropriate for these students . . . . Despite the increase in the number of special education students who were exempted from the TAAS, I am very pleased that 84 percent of the students who took the TAAS test this year were included in the accountability system in contrast to 76 percent in 1998. That percentage increase is due to the inclusion of the special education and Spanish TAAS takers in the accountability system. (Texas Education Agency, 1999b, p. 6)

In addition to the encouragement by the Texas Education Agency to provide exemptions only for special education students for whom the TAAS test is inappropriate, the public media has also served as an impetus for district consideration of the number of special education students who are exempted from TAAS. Schools that have received Recognized or Exemplary status and that also exempt excessive numbers of students from the state testing have been criticized in the media. An Alternative Assessment for Special Education students was field-tested in 1999–2000. This assessment was provided to students in grades 3–8 who are "receiving instruction in the TEKS though not at grade level" (Texas Education Agency, 2000c, p. 7).

Limited English Proficient (LEP) students also require the accommodation of special needs, and again safeguards are established in the accountability system to attempt to avoid abuse of the modification. Ninety percent of the Texas Limited English Proficient students are native language speakers of Spanish. Since 1986, the SBOE rules have allowed for LEP students to be exempt from the TAAS test and take an alternative assessment. In 1994, a Spanish version of the TAAS was adopted by the State Board of Education. This test can be administered to students no more than three times in order to assess whether students are making satisfactory progress in acquiring minimum skills in Spanish even while they are learning English. However, the results are not included in determining the school's accountability rating. In the third-grade TAAS test, campuses are discouraged from exempting LEP students who entered a school in the first grade in the United States as these students have had two years to learn English. Particular difficulties are faced by Limited English Proficient students who enter the U.S. schools in high school as the exit test must be passed in English before a student is eligible for a high school diploma. But, exemptions from end-of-course examinations are allowed for one year. The Reading Proficiency Test in English (RPTE) was given in 2000 to LEP students in grades 3–12. LEP students must take the RPTE each year until they take the TAAS in English in order to assess progress in reading level in Spanish and knowledge of English.

King and Mathers (1997) state that "low-performing schools and student groups may be most affected by accountability systems" (p. 161). Often, these schools and student groups also reflect a high mobility rate. One administrator described the school's student turnover rate as "104% with children entering and leaving the school several times during the course of the year" (McCarthy & Still, 1993, p. 64). The Texas Accountability System addresses the fairness issue of holding schools accountable for student performance when the student may only have been enrolled in the school briefly, by using the performance data only of students who were enrolled in the school on the last Friday in October and who took the spring TAAS test. Campuses are responsible for determining the placement of a student who moves. If a student does not enroll in another school or a graduate equivalency degree program after transferring from the district, that student is counted as a school dropout and impacts the school's accountability rating. As a result, in some districts, more careful record-keeping of transfer students and dropout prevention and recovery programs have been implemented. Limited English Proficient students are included in the attendance rate and dropout rate base indicators for a campus.

Challenges and Merits of a Statewide Accountability System

Possible problems with a state testing program include the possibility that the curriculum may be narrowed; unethical or illegal practices may become more prevalent, and morale problems and division among persons on a campus may occur (King & Mathers, 1997, p. 162). Texas has not been immune to any of these problems. For example, unethical tampering with school assessment data influenced a change in the Texas Penal

Code which now makes it a "3 rd degree felony to tamper with a government record that is a published school record, report, or assessment required under Chapter 39 of the Texas Education Code. If the intent of the tampering is to defraud or harm another, then the offense is a felony of the second degree (Texas Education Agency, 2000a). However, the positive results achieved by the system of increasing student performance have contributed to its continuance. Furhman (1999) argues that new accountability systems are different from more traditional systems with regard to one or more of the following factors:

> District/school approval is being linked to student performance rather than compliance to regulations; accountability is focused more on schools as the unit of improvement, continuous improvement strategies involving school-level decisions around specific performance targets are being adopted, new approaches to classroom inspection are being developed; more categories or levels are being developed; school-level test scores are being publicly reported; and more consequences are being attached to performance levels. (p. 1)

In the Texas State Accountability System, each of these factors is present.

Has the state's accountability system made a difference in student performance? I would answer, "Yes, definitely." In 1999, Texas was one of twelve states honored for its progress toward the National Education Goals and received commendations for progress in meeting goal three, "established by the number of students scoring at the 'proficient' level on the National Assessment of Educational Progress (NAEP) in reading, math, science and writing and on performance on Advanced Placement exams" (Texas Education Agency, 1999c, p. 1). The *1999 Interim Report on Texas Public Schools* cites the following commendations:

- In looking at all students included in the accountability system from 1994 through 1999, students have made tremendous gains on the TAAS tests, especially in mathematics. Minority students and economically disadvantaged students have made especially impressive gains. For example, between 1994 and 1999, 8th grade African American students posted a passing rate that was 20.9 percentage points higher in reading, 40.5 percentage points higher in mathematics, 25.9 percentage points higher in writing, and 17.5 percentage points higher in all tests taken. At Grade 4, from 1994 to 1999, Hispanic students increased their passing rates in reading by 18.4 percentage points, mathematics by 35.8 percentage points, writing by 6.3 percentage points, and all tests taken by 30.1 percentage points. At Grade 10 between 1994 and 1999, students who were identified as economically disadvantaged improved their passing rates in reading by 19.2 percentage points, mathematics by 31.3 percentage points, writing by 14.6 percentage points, and all tests taken by 29.1 percentage points.

- The number of districts and campuses that received exemplary and recognized ratings from the state accountability system continued to increase over the previous years. The number of districts rated exemplary increased from 14 in 1995 to 122 in 1999, and the number of districts rated recognized increased from 137 in 1995 to 383 in 1999. The number of campuses rated exemplary increased from 255 in 1995 to 1,120 in 1999, and the number of campuses rated recognized increased from 1,004 in 1995 to 1,843 in 1999. These increases were in spite of the accountability standards being raised and more students being included over this time period.
- The average SAT I score for the Class of 1998 was 992, the same as for the Class of 1997. The average ACT composite score was 20.3 for the Class of 1998, up slightly from 20.1 for the Class of 1997. In 1998, the numbers of both SAT I and ACT-tested graduates were up from the previous year—up 6.8 percent for the SAT I and 9.7 percent for the ACT in Texas. These surpass the national increase of 4.1 and 3.7 percent, respectively.
- In comparing Texas to the nation, Texas showed higher increases in the number of students taking the Advanced Placement or International Baccalaureate (AP/IB) tests than was the case nationally. Across grade levels, there was a 16.5 percent increase from 1998 to 1999 in the number of Texas students meeting the criterion score, which was higher than the 12.5 percent seen at the national level.
- Texas 8th grade students participated in the 1998 National Assessment of Educational Progress (NAEP) writing test for 8th graders nationwide. Texas students registered a passing rate of 88 percent, compared to the national average of 83 percent. In a state-by-state comparison, 8th graders in Texas, Connecticut, Maine, and Massachusetts demonstrated the highest average writing performance among the 35 states participating in the NAEP writing assessment.
- From 1997–98 to 1998–99, the number of students taking the Algebra I end-of –course examination increased (from 17.4 percent to 18.0 percent) and the percentage of students passing increased from 35.9 percent to 43.4 percent. The majority of students taking the Biology, English II, and U.S. History examinations passed—

76.4 percent, 72.7 percent, and 69.8 percent, respectively. These figures are based on all students included in the AEIS State Performance Report.

(Texas Education Agency, 1999d, pp. vii–viii)

Both in criterion-referenced testing and nationally-normed testing, the influence of the Texas Accountability System is evident.

Is the Texas Accountability System a perfect system? No, it is a system that is evolving. The TAAS test, dropout rate, and attendance rates have been base indicators for the system, but they are insufficient alone. The number of students completing the Recommended or Distinguished Graduation Plans and the number of AP/IB tests taken by students are examples of other important additional indicators of success for secondary schools. As an educator commented to the deputy commissioner of education during a meeting at our university, "The accountability recognition ratings need to be strengthened for the secondary school levels." Under the accountability system for the 1998–99 school year, schools had to have a student passing rate of 90 percent on the TAAS, a dropout rate of 1 percent or less, and a 94 percent attendance rate for each subgroup and for all students in order to be named exemplary. In order to be recognized, schools had to have a 70 percent passing rate on the TAAS, a dropout rate of 3.5 percent or less, and a 94 percent attendance rate for each subgroup and for all students. In order to be acceptable, schools had to have at least 45 percent (increasing to 50 percent for 2000) passing the TAAS, a dropout rate of no more than 6 percent, and a 94 percent attendance rate for all subgroups and for all students (Texas Education Agency, 1999a). Where do we go from here? It is hard to predict, yet, it appears unlikely that the accountability system will go away. It seems more likely that the accountability system will be strengthened, particularly for secondary schools. The exit-level TAAS currently measures predominately only eighth-grade to early ninth-grade concepts and is not a sufficient measure of student performance in high school. The commissioner of education has appointed a commission for the purpose of studying ways to strengthen secondary school performance.

I end the chapter as I began with the premise that what one thinks of the Texas Accountability System is largely a matter of perspective. One of my former students who failed to graduate from high school was a diligent, polite, soft-spoken, Hispanic student who spoke perfect English but who refused to disobey her father's wishes and be tested for special education. She failed the exit math test each time, despite intensive tutoring by our best math teacher. This student would probably say that the exit-level testing system did not help her. For the Hispanic, African American, White, and low socioeconomic level students across the state who have influenced the increasing scores for these subgroups, I would have to answer, "Yes, unequivocably, the accountability system has been helpful. It has helped us to focus on the needs of all students rather than adopting a Lake Woebegone philosophy reflected by the statement, 'Overall, we're above average.'" The disaggregation of data to analyze the performance needs of subgroups and individual students together with the rewards and sanctions has contributed to improved learning for students.

I began this chapter with an analogy of a drive down the road. This, too, seems an appropriate way to end. Most of us have experienced a ride with children. "Are we there yet?" is the often-repeated inquiry. "No," a parent might reply, "but we are closer than we were." The same could be said for the Texas Accountability System. "Are we there yet?" "No, but we are now further down the road." Some might suggest that we abandon this path altogether, but most would probably say, "Let's continue the journey because we are going down the road for the good of children." The system was designed to promote student learning. Whether, in fact, this proves true will be influenced by our continued reflective analysis of the accountability system, its benefits and challenges, and our ongoing work toward continual improvement.

References

Abelmann, C. & Elmore, R. with Even, J., Kenyon, S., & Marshall, J. (1999). When accountability knocks, will anyone answer? *Consortium for Policy Research in Education Research Report Series RR-42*, University of Pennsylvania. Graduate School of Education.

Fuhrman, S.H. (1999). The new accountability. *Consortium for policy research in education: Policy briefs*. University of Pennsylvania: Graduate School of Education.

Grissmer, D. & Flanagan, A. (1998). *Exploring rapid achievement gains in North Carolina and Texas: Lessons from the States*. Commissioned by the National Education Goals Panel. V-36.

Hilliard, A., III. (1999). Keynote address by Dr. Asa Hilliard, III, October 19, 1998: Colloquium on student achievement in multicultural school districts. *Equity and Excellence in Education 32* (1) 79–86.

King, R.A. & Mathers, J.K. (1997). Improving schools through performance-based accountability and financial rewards. *Journal of Education Finance*, 23 (2), 147–176.

Lein, L., Johnson, J.F., & Ragland, M. (1996). *Successful Texas schoolwide programs: Research summary*. Available from the Charles A. Dana Center, University of Texas at Austin, 2901 North IH-35, suite 2.200, Austin, Texas 78722–2348.

McCarthy, J. & Still, S. (1993). Hollibrook accelerated elementary school in *Restructuring schooling: Learning from ongoing efforts in education,* ed. Joseph Murphy & Phillip Hallinger. Corwin Press, Inc. Newbury Park, California. 63–83.

Newmann, F. & Wehlage, G. (1995). Successful school restructuring. (Madison: Center on Organization and Restructuring of Schools, University of Wisconsin, 1995), and Karen Louis and Sharon Kruse, eds. *Professionalism and community*. Thousand Oaks, California. Corwin Press.

Ragland, J.A., Asera, R., & Johnson, J.F. (1999). *Urgency, responsibility, efficacy: Preliminary findings of a study of high-performing Texas school districts*. Available from the Charles A. Dana Center,

University of Texas at Austin, 2901 North IH-35, suite 2.200, Austin, Texas 78722–2348.

Texas Education Code. 35.041. academic excellence indicators. *Texas school law bulletin*. Austin, TX: West Publishing.

Texas Education Code. 35.063 accreditation standards. *Texas school law bulletin*. Austin, TX: West Publishing.

Texas Education Agency (1999a). *Accountability manual: The 1998–1999 accountability rating system for Texas public schools and school districts*. Austin, TX: Author.

Texas Education Agency (2000a). *Accountability manual: The 1999–2000 accountability rating system for Texas public schools and school districts*. Austin, TX: Author.

Texas Education Agency: Division of Communication. (1999b). Record number of schools earn state's highest rating: Accountability. *Texas education today*. XIII (1) 5–6. September-October. Texas. Author.

Texas Education Agency: Division of Communication. (1999c). Press release: Texas one of 12 states to be recognized for educational progress by the National Education Goals Panel. December 1.

Texas Education Agency. Office of Policy Planning and Research (1999d). *A report to the 76th Texas legislature: 1999 interim report on Texas public schools*. Publication number (GE00 600 01).

Texas Education Agency: Division of Communication. (2000b). Federal court upholds legality of TAAS graduation requirements. *Texas education today*. XIII (3). 1,4. January-February. Texas. Author.

Texas Education Agency: Division of Communication. (2000c). Changes in testing program to occur over the next four years. *Texas education today. XIII* (4) 1,7, & 8. March-April. Texas. Author.

Wilson, B.L. & Rossman, G.B. (1993). *Mandating academic excellence: High school responses to state curriculum reform*. Teachers College Press. New York, NY.

Other Sources for Background Information

Texas Education Agency: Research and Evaluation Division, Office of Policy Planning and Research. (1996a). *The development of accountability systems nationwide and in Texas: Statewide Texas educational progress: Study Report No. 1.* 1–47. (GE 6-601-07). Texas: Author.

Texas Education Agency: Office of Accountability and School Accreditation. (1996b). *Integrated district and campus planning and site-based decision making: A resource guide provided by the commissioner's statewide advisory committee on site-based decision-making and planning.* Texas. Author.

Texas Education Agency: Research and Evaluation Division, Office of Policy Planning and Research. (1997).*Expanding the scope of the Texas public school accountability system: Report Number 9,* June 1997. 1–13 (GE 7-601-7). Texas: Author.

Texas Education Agency: Research and Evaluation Division, Office of Policy Planning and Research. (1999). *Results of college admissions testing in Texas for 1997–1998 graduating seniors.* August 1999. 1–26. Texas: Author.

Chapter 5

Promoting Student Success Through the Mastery of the Texas Assessment of Academic Skills

Lisa A. Bertrand

In order to fulfill Texas legislative requirements, all teachers, building level administrators, and district superintendent evaluations now reflect student performance as measured on the state-mandated Texas Assessment of Academic Skills (TAAS) test. The TAAS test, a criterion-referenced assessment, is administered in grades 3–8 in addition to the exit-level test at the 10th-grade level. The TAAS test measures student mastery of academic skills in the areas of reading, writing, math, science, and social studies. All students in grades 3–8 and the 10th-grade are given the reading and math portions of the test. Writing is administered at the fourth-grade, eighth-grade, and exit levels and science and social studies tests are administered in the eighth grade. An individual mastery score of 70 percent or better is needed to pass the TAAS test, and district and campuses are assigned an accountability rating that reflects passage rates for all student populations on all portions of the tests administered. Campus ratings ranging from lowest to highest status are Academically Unacceptable/Low-Performing, Academically Acceptable/Acceptable, Recognized, and Exemplary. For the academic year of 1999–2000, at least 90 percent of all campus student populations had to master the TAAS to receive the Exemplary rating. In order to receive the Recognized rating, at least 80 percent of all student populations had to master the TAAS. At least 50 percent mastery was expected for all student populations in order to receive the Academically Acceptable/Acceptable rating, and if a campus's mastery level was below 50 percent, a rating of Academically Unacceptable/Low-Performing was assigned to that campus.

Recent legislation now connects student performance on the TAAS to professional performance evaluations. Yearly evaluations for all teachers and campus principals now reflect the accountability rating that is assigned to the school. For teachers, in Domain 8 of the Professional Development and Appraisal System (PDAS), points are added to the total domain score that reflects the accountability rating of the campus. As an example, if a school receives an accountability rating of Recognized, a teacher will receive an additional four points to add to her Domain 8 total. Therefore, this total score very much reflects student performance on the TAAS and becomes an important dimension of each teacher's evaluation.

For principals and superintendents, as a part of the administrators' comprehensive evaluation, a formula is utilized that reflects the TAAS mastery of all student populations. For principals, campus information is included in the evaluation; for superintendents, information regarding the performance of all schools in the district is included. Again, TAAS performance of students is an important dimension of administrators' evaluations.

With student performance connected to professional performance evaluations, school districts across the State of Texas have enhanced their efforts to improve the yearly student TAAS scores. District and campus efforts are not only focused on the achievement rating of Academically Acceptable, but efforts are now underway to reach the even higher accountability ratings of Recognized and Exemplary. Again, to be a Recognized-rated campus, 80 percent of all students must pass all portions of the TAAS test; to be rated Exemplary, 90 percent of all students must pass all portions of the test.

In order to achieve these higher levels of passage rates on the TAAS test, Texas schools have implemented various strategies and techniques to improve student performance. Curricular and instructional areas are addressed as well as staff development and student motivation. The purpose of this chapter will be to explore these various areas by highlighting the strategies and techniques that both elementary and secondary Texas schools utilize to improve student performance on the state-mandated TAAS test. Concluding thoughts will address a critical view of the benefits and possible pitfalls of the testing process.

Curriculum in the state of Texas is driven by the newly implemented Texas Essential Knowledge and Skills (TEKS), with instructional efforts reflecting strategies to master these skills. In order to assess mastery of this state curriculum, the TAAS test, which is now aligned with the TEKS, is administered. As a means to chart mastery and improvement, many schools utilize benchmark assessments administered throughout the year to prepare for the spring administration of the TAAS test. Previously administered copies of the state-released TAAS test are administered as practice tests in the fall, usually in September, and then again at the beginning of the second semester in January. Test results are then disaggregated by individual student to assess the target areas that need to be addressed before the final test is administered. From these test results, students are tagged for additional intensive instruction in small groups or on a one-to-one instructional basis.

Previous test results are also used to develop curricular and instructional strategies for improved student performance. Districts may order an individual item analysis of the previous year's test performance for each student. These individual reports can be reviewed by the receiving teacher as well as with each student. Goals can then be set for the students with the idea of improving performance on the subsequent grade level TAAS test.

Test-taking strategies are taught and practiced throughout the year. Students are taught to show all their work, especially when working math problems, and to break down lengthy reading passages into smaller portions. In the reading area, students are taught to number the paragraphs in each passage, underline key words, and support their answer choice by labeling answers in the margins of the passage. To help with organization in the writing area, students are taught to outline and format their ideas according to the mode of the presented prompt.

Strategies are also shared with parents. Many Texas schools, both elementary and secondary, host parent seminars that focus on test content as well as the strategies needed in order for students to master the TAAS objectives. By providing hot dog or spaghetti dinners for parents, along with babysitting services, faculty members entice parents to attend evening sessions. Most sessions last from one to two hours and are held throughout the school year.

Schools also communicate with parents through three weekly progress notes and school newsletters. Many administrators write monthly letters to parents with the intent not only to distribute school news but to also educate parents by suggesting strategies and techniques that can be used at home. With state mandates in place, teachers are required every three weeks to report to parents the progress of students who are failing or in danger of failing a subject; however, many schools choose to report progress for every student more frequently. This method of communication helps to keep parents constantly informed of progress, with a special emphasis placed on TAAS-related skills and objectives.

Strategies relating to time on task are important in the grades where the TAAS is administered. Intensive instruction throughout the day is delivered during regularly scheduled lessons. Teachers develop lessons from a variety of resources such as textbooks (which are aligned with the Texas curriculum), materials provided by state and regional agencies, materials purchased from private sources, and teacher-made materials. When visiting any classroom in the state of Texas, files upon files of materials can be found in the possession of the teacher. With accountability a large concern, teachers are continually on the lookout for new and improved materials that may provide just the edge needed for their students to master the TAAS objectives. Teachers are also very much aware of the fact that time on task does make a difference relative to student achievement.

With regard to time on task, altering the school schedule is another strategy that Texas educators utilize to enhance student performance. At the elementary and middle school levels, tutorials are held during regular class enrichment time. Students are pulled from classes for 30 minutes to an hour for intensive daily instruction on the TAAS objectives. To further address TAAS mastery, districts offer extended day and extended year opportunities for students needing additional academic assistance. Grant money is awarded by the Texas Education Agency to implement these additional programs. As an example, students may extend their regular school day by up to two hours to receive instructional support in the content areas tested by the TAAS test. Most often, these areas involve language arts and math. Students may also be assigned to extended year classes held during the summer to aid in skill retention. Grant money for these programs targets students in grades 1–8.

In preparation for the February administration of the TAAS fourth-grade writing test, one elementary school altered its schedule to initiate a Camp Write-a-Long. For eight instructional days, students in the fourth grade brought sleeping bags, tents, pillows, and camping supplies to school and set up camp in their classrooms. Following the activities of the day, under the direction of the fourth-grade teachers, students were asked to write about their experiences. The formats for the writing assignments were based on the compositional modes tested at the fourth-grade level. These same modes are again tested at the eighth-grade level; therefore, this type of activity is viewed as beneficial for students of all abilities.

At the secondary level, several East Texas high schools have initiated a yearlong testing preparation program that reflects an altered instructional schedule. Committees of parents, students, teachers, and administrators meet together as a task force to form a plan for improvement. Activities listed in the plans include scheduling provisions for evening and Saturday tutorials as well as peer-tutoring sessions sponsored by National Honor Society members.

In addition to this extra time allotted for instruction, all subject area teachers in these same East Texas high schools have been trained to provide daily instructional "sponge" activities during the first 15 minutes of each period. Teachers in grades 9 and 10 provide activities relative to mastery of the TAAS objectives, while junior and senior instructors focus on ACT/SAT preparation. The reasoning behind this comprehensive subject-area instructional approach stems from the fact that all teachers will be evaluated according to the campus accountability rating; therefore, all teachers are held accountable for the TAAS scores—from the vocational agriculture instructors to the athletic period instructors, all teachers prepare students for the TAAS test.

As a last effort to review TAAS objectives, both elementary and secondary schools may alter the master schedule immediately prior to the administration of the test. Full-day comprehensive instruction takes place as students are reviewed on all TAAS objectives. Most schools strive to make this an enjoyable time by providing snacks and treats in a somewhat unstructured environment. Students focus on last-minute improvements of their individual mastery levels. For secondary students, passage of the TAAS is required in order to receive a high school diploma.

In order to learn how to provide curricular and instructional strategies appropriate for the mastery of the TAAS objectives and to deliver specialized instruction during an altered schedule, teachers and administrators attend a variety of staff development sessions. Most yearly campus plans for improvement, which are required by the Texas Education Agency, indicate that a majority of the staff development sessions held on each campus are devoted to TAAS improvement. As mentioned above, teachers in several high schools that provide daily sponge activities attended training before the school year began. Many of these teachers had never administered the TAAS test and were unfamiliar with the format and content of the test. They were trained to address all TAAS objectives, assess for mastery of these objectives, and provide follow-up tutorials for students not achieving mastery.

On both the elementary and the secondary level, content-area teachers attend staff development sessions to hone their skills at providing instruction. Sessions are sponsored by the Texas Education Agency, the regional service centers, district-level content area coordinators, and private organizations. Math problem solving, composition writing techniques, and reading comprehension strategies are areas often addressed through staff development. As part of their goals for improving student achievement, many school districts develop a yearly calendar of staff development sessions based on prior TAAS test scores. As an example, if students are consistently scoring lower in the four areas that assess number operations on the math portion of the TAAS test, staff development sessions will then be planned for the teachers delivering instruction in this area.

The three areas of curriculum, instruction, and staff development all connect to help teachers and administrators implement strategies and techniques to improve student achievement, but what motivates the students to master the skills needed to pass the TAAS? In the State of Texas, motivational activities range from the distribution of small tokens, such as pencils, to holding a city-wide rally with a celebrity featured as a motivational speaker.

Motivating students to master the TAAS objectives leading to a passing score on the test is a major focus of Texas educators throughout the entire school year. With the intensive training provided during the school year in preparation for the test, incentive programs are very much part of the plans for improvement.

In many schools, staff members are assigned a student or small group of students to mentor throughout the year. Constant contact is made between student and teacher to support the learning process. Positive notes, praise, and encouragement from the teaching staff help to motivate the students to persevere in their efforts to improve upon their skills. One elementary principal schedules an individual conference with each student after the mid-year benchmark test is administered. The focus of this conference is to discuss how the student performed on the mid-year measure and to encourage and support the student in his efforts to improve before the actual TAAS test is administered.

The awarding of homework passes, which, in essence, satisfies the requirement for individual homework assignments, and the awarding of extra credit are also ways in which teachers help to motivate students to learn the TAAS objectives. One elementary school offers Friday treats to those students who do well on their weekly benchmark tests. Continual improvement is the focus of all teaching and learning efforts.

Motivation becomes even more important during the last few weeks before the TAAS test is administered. On the elementary level, many first- and second-grade classes, which are not involved in the testing process, adopt upper-grade classes to support them in their efforts. Posters relaying positive messages, special notes, and banners are made for the adopted classes. Walking through the hallways and upper-grade classrooms right before the TAAS test is administered, a visitor can observe these encouraging messages posted for all students to view.

Pep rallies and pre-TAAS events are also popular throughout the state. Students, teachers, and administrators plan very special performances to help motivate students. Cheers and songs are adapted to reflect the TAAS experience. These performances, which usually include costumed students, teachers, and administrators, are a big part of the pep rallies. Parodies and skits are additional examples of activities included in these motivational events.

Local businesses and parents also play a part in the motivation of students. In order to support and encourage student efforts, prizes are donated. These prizes may include small tokens, such as candy, snacks, and pencils, or larger prizes of movie passes, computers, and jam boxes. One East Texas high school, through donations by local businesses, ensures that every 10th-grade student is awarded some type of prize prior to the administration of the TAAS test.

In one East Texas area, TAAS improvement was not only the focus of the school district but also filtered into the community. A city-wide pep rally was held in the high school stadium to help motivate the students to perform well on the TAAS test. High school students served as masters of ceremony, with speeches given by former students on the struggles needed to pass the TAAS in order to graduate. Younger students were involved in skits and songs that were performed to increase the motivation of elementary students, while the high school cheerleaders yelled rousing cheers that led to the participation of all members in the audience. As a highlight of the evening, a former high school graduate of the local school district, who was then a member of the Dallas Cowboys football team, gave a motivational speech to encourage all students to do their best on the test.

These motivational activities, along with a focus on curriculum, instruction, and staff development, all enhance student performance throughout the school year. With so much emphasis on the TAAS test in Texas schools, one would wonder about the benefits and possible negative issues that arise relative to the administration of the test.

Most teachers and administrators alike state that even without a state-mandated measure of achievement, the same objectives would be taught in the classrooms. Reading objectives that relate to such skills as summarization, identifying the main idea and details of a passage, and determining if a passage is fact or fiction are relevant at any grade. Accountability is not always seen in a positive light, but educators state that it leads to interventions that might not otherwise take place. By benchmark testing throughout the year, student learning is monitored on a consistent basis in preparation for the final TAAS test. TAAS preparation is not only seen as a way to reach those students who are at risk of not passing the test, but the preparation is also viewed as a way for average and above average students to improve their skills year after year.

Another benefit of the TAAS test affects students that plan to enter higher educational settings. Those students who score in the higher range of mastery on the reading, math, and writing portions of the exit-level of the TAAS test are exempt from the Texas Academic Skills Program (TASP). The TASP is an entrance examination required of those students entering state-sponsored as well as most private Texas higher educational facilities.

Possible negative effects of the TAAS test are also mentioned by Texas educators. First, the third-grade level is the first time many students will take a standardized test. Teachers spend a great deal of time teaching the test format to students in addition to teaching them how to "bubble in" their answers in the test booklet. For students at the fourth-grade level, the test booklet is provided with a Scantron sheet on which to record answers. This is the first time that many students take a test where they have to address the question in the test booklet and then transfer their answers onto an answer form. Instruction in Scantron use is certainly time on task, but is it a worthwhile task for nine- and ten-year-old children? Most educators agree that academic instruction is lost due to the emphasis on training the students to record their answers in the correct manner.

Second, what happens when a student at any grade level passes the benchmark test at the beginning or the middle of the year? Is there a limit put on their learning, since these students will continue to receive TAAS preparation at their grade level throughout the year? Teachers are trained to differentiate instruction; however, with the emphasis on accountability and the drive to have more and more students pass the test in order to achieve higher ratings, many students will continue to sit through preparation lessons in the regular classroom. Instructional focus is centered on those students who have not mastered the objectives, with little emphasis placed on enhancing the learning for those students who already perform well on the benchmark measures.

Third, with a heavy emphasis on reading and math in the grade levels in which the TAAS is administered, one would wonder how much time is allotted to other subjects. In the levels below eighth grade, the science and social studies tests are not administered, so unless a teacher integrates these subjects into the reading and math areas, these disciplines usually take a back seat to the tested areas. In the schools that alter their schedules to include tutorials and intensive instruction on the TAAS objectives in addition to regular instruction, this extra time allotted to the TAAS objectives must certainly affect the learning time in other subject areas.

Fourth, the question can be asked, just because a student passes the TAAS test, does that ensure that he or she is fully prepared for instruction at the next grade level? If a student passes the exit level of the TAAS, does that imply that he or she is prepared for higher education or the work force? To answer these questions, during the 76th Texas legislative session in 1999, policymakers passed Senate Bill 103, which in essence, altered the current assessment system. By the 2002–2003 school year, the exit-level test will be moved from grade 10 to grade 11 and a more rigorous content-level test is expected. Senate Bill 103 also adds tests in reading and math at the ninth-grade level, science at the fifth-grade level, and writing at the seventh-grade level. The new writing test at the seventh grade replaces the eighth-grade test, and the eighth-grade science test is eliminated. Even with these changes in place, educators continue to ask if mastery of these standards is sufficient to prepare a student for the next grade level or life beyond the high school experience.

Finally, a policy that now affects students enrolled in kindergarten relates to the connection between promotion and the mastery of the TAAS objectives. When the 1999–2000 kindergarten students reach the third grade, a state mandate now in place states that these students must master the reading portion of the TAAS to be promoted to the fourth grade. The policy will then follow this group as they proceed from grade to grade. In other words, during the 2002–2003 school year, all third-grade students must pass the reading portion of the TAAS test to be promoted. Even though the State of Texas is providing great amounts of money for teacher training in the area of reading for kindergarten through second-grade teachers, educators continue to question what will happen when the policy is actually implemented during the 2002–2003 school year. A question that arises is whether large numbers of students will be retained in third grade in Texas schools due to their failure to meet mastery levels on the reading portion of the TAAS test.

In conclusion, it would seem that accountability is here to stay in the state of Texas. Now, because of the connection between student performance and professional evaluations, educators across the state are focused on improving student performance. Not only are they satisfied with achieving an Academically Acceptable rating, but schools in all areas are striving to meet the standards that will earn the elite status of Recognized or Exemplary. Curricular and instructional strategies, in addition to staff development and student motivation, all contribute to the understood goal of being the best. As evidenced by this monumental drive toward excellence, Texans really do strive to be "bigger and better" at what they do—even as it relates to the Texas Assessment of Academic Skills.

Chapter 6

The Administrator's Caper

Robert Low
Raymond A. Horn, Jr.

The Context

Imagine the pressure, the stress, and the consequences. At least your pay increase, and probably your job, is riding on the performance of the students in your school on the Texas Assessment of Academic Skills (TAAS). As an administrator, you diligently do all of the things mentioned in chapter 6; however, in your heart you know that all of that isn't enough.

Your problem may reflect the complexity of the educational situation in Texas. Perhaps your school or school district's profile is the ultimate nightmare of all student achievement—low funding, a high-poverty area (65% or more of your students are on the free and reduced lunch program), a traditional and culturally engrained lack of regard for academics, high percentages of African Americans and Hispanics (a problem because not only are they traditionally economically and socially oppressed groups in Texas, but they also score low on the TAAS due to test bias and language), an inexperienced faculty (due to Texas' inability to retain certified teachers in the profession, and the consequent need to hire people who are not trained teachers), and an aging, inadequate facility.

For whatever reason, you decide to take the low road to success. The following fictional scenario reflects a reality in Texas that is, of course, not prevalent but does occur. For instance, in 1999, the Texas Education Agency audited 17 school districts concerning their dropout data, and sanctioned four for reporting bad data. In September 1999, Texas Comptroller Carole Keeton Rylander created a task force to investigate TAAS cheating and erroneous dropout rates. The *Houston Chronicle* reported that the call for an investigation started with the cheating scandal that "erupted during the last school year when 11 districts statewide were asked to investigate schools that were suspected of tampering with answer documents to the TAAS. Houston, one of the 11, already had started its own investigation and eventually found evidence of wrongdoing at half a dozen schools in the district. Disciplinary action was taken against two principals, three teachers and a substitute. Fort Bend and North Forest also found some evidence of test tampering after the state-ordered investigations" (Markley, 1999, p. 18A). This led to the resignation of a veteran principal and teacher in the Fort Bend School District.

In April 1999, the Austin Independent School District was indicted by a Travis County grand jury on 16 counts of tampering with governmental and student records. The school district faces fines of up to $160,000, and the deputy superintendent could face up to a year in jail and a $4,000 fine or both ("Austin," 1999). The indictment involved the TAAS records of 16 students who were either Hispanic or Economically Disadvantaged. The allegation is that school officials changed the identification numbers of students who performed poorly on the test, knowing that their test results would be deleted by the TEA computer system ("Austin," 1999).

The purpose of this chapter is not to highlight these disingenuous, unethical, and illegal practices but to use them to highlight the significant effect that TAAS has on Texas education. All of the practices mentioned in the scenario have been tried. Some of them are now no longer feasible due to a change in who must take the TAAS.

As of spring 2000, school districts in Texas have been "required to test nearly every student including children who would have been exempt in the past for language deficiences" (Markley, 2000, p. 37A). Even though districts will be allowed to continue their exemption of severely handicapped students from taking the test, they will have to test all students with limited English skills, the exception being immigrants who have been in the country less than three years (Markley, 2000, p. 37A). However, in 2001 this rule will be tightened to exempt only immigrants who have arrived within the year. As Texas Education Commissioner Jim Nelson reported, scores on the TAAS will drop. The previously described changes will narrow the illegal and unethical options but will further heighten the pressure on school administrators.

Of course, we see reactions like this in the high-pressure world of business, where the intense pursuit of profit drives some people to unethical and illegal practices. As state governments and other interest groups push for technical standards and a return to the factory model of education, the ethical and moral focus of education will also more closely approximate the ethical and moral behavior and concerns of the world of business. An important question is, do we want our educators focused on the positive growth and development of the children or on artificial and culturally arbitrary technical standards?

The Scenario

Robbie Benet is a middle school principal and is considered to be bright, ambitious, and a real "go-getter." He has decided to improve his TAAS (Texas Assessment of Academic Skills) scores for his eighth grade this year in order to enhance his career. He has called another principal from a different school district, Hollis James of Collusion High School, who just happens to be at lunch discussing the TAAS with an assistant principal from Backwater High School, Randall Godfrey. Robbie is 28 years old and out to be the youngest superintendent in his district's history. Hollis is 50 years old and has been a successful administrator at Collusion for many years. Randall is in the early part of his administrative career, even at 36, because he pursued another career, in business, for several years.

Robbie: Hollis?

Hollis: Yes, who is this?

Robbie: Hey! This is Robbie, Robbie Benet. I was hoping to catch you with a few minutes on your hands. I have something I want to discuss where I need your attention and wisdom.

Hollis: Robbie, how's the whiz kid? What do you want to talk about?

Robbie: Hollis, I want to improve my TAAS scores this year, and I want your opinion on my ideas as to how I can "help" my students do better.

Hollis: I have just the man in my office to help us "plan" on how to help our kids. Do you know Randall Godfrey from Backwater?

Robbie: Sure! We were in the cohort together at UT [University of Texas].

Hollis: Well, he has several ideas about "cheating" on the TAAS, or shall I say "enhancing our chances"?

Robbie: Well, my idea is to add an extra digit to my students' social security numbers so the computer will throw them out or make them not gradable.

Hollis: That's already been done! That Lee Worth over in Salina got caught doing that very thing! Here let me put you on speakerphone so that Randall can tell you about it.

Randall: Hey Robbie, how has that pretty wife of yours put up with you for so long?

Robbie: Because I'm a genius! Ha! Say, bud, what's the story on the Salina principal? I thought adding digits to the social security numbers was a really good idea. How did he get caught?

Randall: He got greedy. He changed too many students' numbers and the grading committee got suspicious because there were so many "computer errors." He should have varied the number and the position. He was trying to cheat but didn't think it through.

Robbie: Well, what else can I do? What other "ideas" do you guys have?

Hollis: I have asked students in the past just not to show up on TAAS days. Most of them don't want to be bothered with the test anyway. I've even suspended students for discipline reasons, if I felt they wouldn't do well on the TAAS test. Last year, I asked a father to keep all 10 of his kids at home. There hasn't been one of them pass yet. I just flat out asked him to keep them from coming to school. No one even missed those discipline problems, so no one asked any questions. However, you have to be careful who and how many you ask not to show.

Randall: I can't believe you did that and got away with it! How many years have you been doing that?

Hollis: I'll never tell and you better not either!

Randall: I won't, because I'm going to use that this year. I need to keep many of my ESL [English as a Second Language] students from taking the test and bringing my scores down. I know I can get their parents to keep them home. I'll just threaten them with the INS [Immigration and Naturalization Service]!

Robbie: I love that idea! I don't have as many ESL problems as I do special education students who have somehow qualified to take the TAAS but will never pass it. They are going to kill my scores!

Hollis: Wait a minute! Labeling students as special education students before the 10th grade TAAS can be a tremendously successful way of getting them not to take the test. You have just got to get them re-tested and decide their "tests" make them too low to take the TAAS.

Robbie: I've tried that. But, I've got this young "bleeding-heart" who thinks all children are really trying and should not be judged too severely by their IQ scores. She is the only special diagnostician and her word is "law."

Randall: Not if she gets fired or "decides to leave" before the exemptions are decided upon!

Robbie: You guys are vicious!

Hollis: No, just trying to save our jobs in a state that has gone TAAS overboard!

Randall: No one in Austin cares whether our kids have a wonderful, nurturing experience in school anymore; they are only interested in whether all the socioeconomic groups are passing the TAAS.

Hollis: Robbie, you have got to get 20% more of those students labeled as exempt from the TAAS. That will raise your scores tremendously. If you have to, change the scores on the IQ tests.

Randall: Another way I have heard of is to retain the students in the eighth grade. As you know, there is a high correlation between eighth and tenth grade TAAS scores. Students will either be remediated in your TAAS remediation classes or they will eventually drop out of school and not be TAAS takers anyway. Either scenario will be a winner as far as you are concerned. Of course, this really works better at the high school test level.

Robbie: Yeah, that's good, but I need something either to stop the eighth graders from taking the test altogether or to enhance their scores after they have taken the test.

Hollis: Have you got any teachers who are "ambitious" enough to help you "cheat"?

Robbie: Yeah, I've got several that I know are really anxious about how low their particular subject has scored in last few years on the TAAS. Especially two math teachers and a social studies teacher who was so embarrassed last year when her students only scored a measly 45%.

Randall: There's another solution to your problem! Talk to these teachers; there are many ways for them to "enhance" the scores because they are right there in the room with the tests and the students. They have so much opportunity to "help" the students with their answers!

Robbie: Like what?

Hollis: One thing they can do is to change the answers on the answer sheet itself. I know of a teacher at my school who looked at an extra copy of the test and knew what the answers should be. As the students turned in their tests, she checked the answers and changed some of the lower students' answers. Since she was helping me out, I certainly didn't say anything.

Randall: That will work fine if you are careful not to change too many answers. The testing center in Austin gets suspicious if there are too many erasures.

Robbie: That's great! What about getting a teacher to bubble in the answers herself? Say, for instance, in the case of an absent student or a student who gets "sent to the office for something" after he has started the test? Will that work?

Hollis: Why not? Choose your teachers and students carefully and it should work.

Robbie: Thanks guys, y'all have been a big help!

Even though the names in the preceding conversation are fictitious, the ideas are not. The ideas to circumvent TAAS have been taken from the newspapers and various conversations and stories. One could shrug all this off with the idea that some people will do almost anything to keep their jobs. However, for most of us a deeper paradox exists. Is the TAAS process itself actually above reproach?

There exists in this state, indeed this country, a multitude of educational leaders who want to do the right thing for the educational benefit for all students. Should there be so much invested in a single measurement? Should there be an opportunity for multiple measurements of different types?

References

Austin ISD indicted in TAAS probe: Official, system accused of manipu-
    lating test data. (1999, April 7). *Houston Chronicle*, p. 17.

Markley, M. (1999, September). New state task force to probe TAAS
    cheating, dropout data. *Houston Chronicle,* p. 18A.

Markley, M. (2000, April). New rule likely to lower TAAS scores. *Hous-
    ton Chronicle,* p. 37A.

Chapter 7

An Unfair Graduation Requirement: Why Hispanics Are at a Disadvantage in Passing the TAAS Test

Dina Townsend

When all Hispanic students have access to the same education starting in preschool, then one test can be administered to determine whether or not a student should graduate from high school. The high-stakes TAAS test is not a fair graduation requirement because not all Hispanic students receive the same education as do other students in our Texas schools. Besides, the Limited English Proficient (LEP) students, who are not as well prepared as other students, are at a great disadvantage in passing the TAAS.

This chapter explores the following reasons why many Hispanic students are at a disadvantage in passing the TAAS. These reasons are teacher training, Hispanic culture, the lack of Hispanic educators, bilingual education, and poverty and parental participation.

Background Information

The rapidly changing demographics of Texas make the high failure rate of Hispanic students a problem in all Texas schools. During the 1996–97 school year, there were 3,828,975 students attending 6,875 public schools in Texas. In Texas schools, 46 percent of all students are Anglo; 37 percent are Hispanic; 14 percent African American, and 3 percent "Other" in terms of ethnic group (Texas Education Agency, 1997). In spite of the fact that 54 percent of all students in Texas are ethnic minorities, only 24 percent of all teachers are members of minority groups. Additionally, 11 percent of all students are in bilingual English as a Second

Language (ESL) education programs (Texas Education Agency, 1997). The first step of all ESL students is to learn the English language, followed by learning the subject matter. Since having to learn English is truly a disadvantage to the Hispanic student, it is not surprising that Hispanic students do not have high rates of success on the TAAS test.

Evidence from TAAS results indicates that students belonging to diverse groups do not pass the TAAS at the same rate as White students. The Mexican American Legal Defense and Education Fund (MALDEF) maintains that as many as 85 percent of students who have failed the TAAS have been Mexican Americans or African Americans, and they have failed the three-part test in reading, writing, and math at more than double the rate of White students. Therefore, TAAS test results reveal Hispanic students do worse than their White counterparts. In addition, schools focus on the "bubble" students (those on the edge of passing the TAAS) rather than on students who need much more help reaching the passing score of 70. The students who need more help but are often not bubble students include many Hispanics along with other Limited English Proficient students. These are the students who fall through the cracks.

The children of migrant and seasonal farm workers in Texas, whose parents make a living by following the harvest schedules of various agricultural crops throughout the country, have special needs that place them at a great disadvantage in terms of accessing regular school systems. The problems faced by these families and their children include severe poverty, lack of continuity in schooling, transportation problems, poor nutrition and health, language, and cultural barriers. It is important to note that about 80 percent of the migrant and seasonal farm worker population is Hispanic American. It's understandable then that migrant students lacking continuity in schooling do not have the skills required to pass the TAAS.

According to the U.S. Census Bureau, the nation's Hispanic population has grown almost five times faster than the non-Hispanic populations in the last ten years. This growth has particular consequences for the nation's public schools. In 1968, there were about 2 million Hispanic school-age children in this country; by 1986, that number had more than doubled to 4,064,000 (Orfield, 1988). In addition, the U.S. Hispanic population is highly concentrated in certain regions and major cities. For instance, in Texas, 25. 5 percent of Houston's population is Hispanic, 54.3 percent of San Antonio's, 77.4 percent of El Paso's, and 91.7 percent of McAllen-Edinburg-Mission.

In relation to the growing Hispanic population, there are very significant racial disparities in the passing rates of the TAAS. On the 1996 exit-level test, statewide only 60.7 percent passed all tests. However, for Hispanics the total was 45.1 percent. The number indicates that Texas Hispanic students are not prepared to pass the TAAS test when they are required to take it. In a lawsuit against the Texas Education Agency (TEA), Mexican American Legal and Educational Fund (MALDEF) maintained that biases against Hispanics and African Americans make them more likely than Anglos to fail the TAAS.

MALDEF further maintained that the TEA is implementing invalid, discriminatory, standardized tests as requirements for high school graduation. Because of the nature of the TAAS, the TEA denies diplomas to Mexican American and African American students at a rate significantly higher than it denies diplomas to Anglo students. This is done without sufficient proof that use of the tests will enhance the education or life opportunities of these students. The TAAS test results in a significant and irreparable reduction in the ranks of Mexican American and African American high school graduates.

Teacher Training

Fair and equitable education for Limited English Proficient (LEP) students in Texas schools involves being taught by individuals who are properly trained and certified to teach those students. The problem is that the number of certified bilingual education teachers is not adequate for the number of Limited English Proficient (LEP) students enrolled in Texas public schools. In 1997, of the 3.7 million students enrolled in Texas public schools, only 11 percent were enrolled in bilingual education or ESL programs (TEA, 1997), and in relation to the growing Hispanic population, many more should have been enrolled. Not only must teachers be trained to teach LEP students, but also Texas schools must employ the needed number of certified bilingual education teachers if LEP students are to be expected to pass the TAAS test.

In addition, Limited English Proficient (LEP) programs must be staffed with teachers who not only are appropriately trained in effective instructional practices to promote Hispanic student success but also possess caring attitudes. Teacher attitudes and expectations regarding the quality of instruction determine the success of all students.

Also, the quality of instruction for Hispanic students needs to be improved. Most teachers of LEP children do not use instructional materials specifically designed for LEP students (Planning and Evaluation Service, 1995). Instructional strategies employed by effective bilingual teachers include specific methods that target LEP students. Appropriate LEP instruction introduces content instruction in English using a sheltered approach to teach challenging academic content (that is, math, science, and social studies) in English. Instructional materials, teacher presentation, and classroom interaction are adapted so that learners can understand and participate (Short, 1991). The quality and effectiveness of a program depend on the ability of the teachers to provide instruction in English that is accessible to English learners, the academic content being simplified (Short, 1991). The program should be designed so that students always have additional opportunities to master critical skills. Teachers in effective classrooms follow a general process that addresses a variety of learning styles. Furthermore, teachers in successful LEP programs stress hands-on learning activities that are active, collaborative, and of high interest and relevance to all students. Technological aids should be made available in both Spanish and English.

Teachers of LEP students should know techniques that integrate students' culture and experiences in the curriculum and prevent or address issues of intolerance, prejudice, and bias. Hispanic students need instructors who can challenge them academically and set high expectations. Unfortunately, only 80 percent of LEP teachers are trained to do so (U.S. Department of Education, 1995).

When entering school, LEP students require time before they can "catch up" to native speakers. In the meantime, English speakers are moving ahead in their acquisition of vocabulary and other features of the language. Unless LEP students in Texas are offered additional, enriched, and accelerated curriculum, it will remain very difficult for these students to pass the TAAS test.

Hispanic Culture

Hispanic Americans are united through customs, religion, language, and values. Family commitment, which involves devotion, a powerful support system, and a duty to care for family members, is of foremost importance in a majority of Hispanic families. This strong sense of a caring commitment for other family members conflicts with the mainstream U.S. emphasis on individualism (Vasquez, 1990). In fact, Hispanic culture's emphasis on cooperation in acquisition of goals can result in Hispanic students' uneasiness with our country's traditional classroom competition. In other words, the Hispanic families' emphasis on cooperation, rather than on individualism, becomes a barrier to the Hispanic students' achievement.

Furthermore, I observed that children learn best when the classroom curriculum reflects the history and culture of the students. Knowledge of a student's background is important in assessing how students learn best. When teachers comprehend cultural differences, classroom environments become conducive to enhanced learning.

It is also important to understand how cultural background influences LEP students' approaches to test taking. Skilled and culturally knowledgeable teachers must create meaningful and successful lessons tailored to the backgrounds and experiences of their students. When teachers lack sensitivity to cultural and language diversity, a student may feel alienated from the school system. Consequently, logic dictates that more Hispanic staff members are needed to serve as models for Hispanic students.

Lack of Hispanic Educators

This does not imply that an educator must be Hispanic or Spanish-speaking to be a good and effective instructor of Hispanic students; however, there are too few Hispanic teachers, counselors, and administrators. Consequently, there are few school professionals who are linguistically, culturally, and socially sensitive to the needs of Hispanic students. This also leaves Hispanic youth without personnel to serve as role models. It should be obvious that positive educational outcomes are enhanced when schools are staffed with sufficient Hispanic personnel to serve as mentors as well as models for Hispanic students. Hispanic staff members will be sensitive to Hispanic students' needs and will encourage awareness of the importance of bilingual education in the school environment.

Bilingual Education

Bilingual education programs develop native-language proficiency in order to enable LEP students to make a transition to all-English instruction; this transition occurs while receiving academic subject instruction in their native language. In order to learn to speak, children must participate in a particular learning community; the grammar, social rules, and cognitive challenges of the children's linguistic community are interwoven to shape their language abilities (Rogoff & Wertsch, 1984). Unfortunately for many Hispanic students in Texas, neither bilingual instruction nor LEP programs are available in our schools. Consequently, Hispanic students clearly do not acquire the skills to pass the TAAS, which depends upon a correct understanding of language.

From 1984 to 1994, the number of LEP students increased by almost 70 percent, yet the numbers of qualified bilingual teachers did not increase. Failure to provide full bilingual instruction in academic subjects to LEP students is one of the disadvantages. Hispanic students. Lack of appropriate instruction contributes to the high TAAS failure rate for Hispanics. Clearly, LEP students do not have access to the same education as other students, making them vulnerable to failure in the TAAS.

The TAAS has a particularly negative effect on students of Limited English Proficiency. With 37 percent of all students identified as Hispanic, it is reasonable to assume that these students should be identified and given the opportunities to become successful in our schools. The Network of Regional Desegregation Assistance Centers, reports that the state agencies' bilingual education departments do not closely monitor school districts for compliance with the Title VI requirements. The TEA requires the public school system to provide bilingual education programs in the elementary grades when district enrollment exceeds 20 LEP students with limited English proficiency in any grade. ESL instruction must be provided to these students when bilingual education is not offered. Many Texas schools are not fully compliant with the intent of the Title VI requirements because they do not use the federal funds to employ staff who know the LEP strategies and who have the knowledge to address the cultural issues in the classroom. Because of this, Hispanic students remain limited in their English language ability, and therefore find it difficult to pass the TAAS. Even though some reports suggest that 70 percent of Hispanic students pass the reading test, in reality, many Hispanic students are exempted by school administrators from taking the TAAS. Indeed, if all Hispanic students took the TAAS at the 10th-grade level, the results would be significantly worse.

Poverty and Parental Participation

Other reasons for Hispanic students' TAAS problems are levels of parental education, parental poverty, and lower levels of parental involvement in schools. The voices of parents of Hispanic children are rarely heard at school. Among these parents, school experiences, linguistic difficulty, and different cultural practices have produced a body of knowledge about

Hispanic involvement in school settings that frequently goes unacknowledged (Finders & Lewis, 1994). Consequently, it is not that Hispanic parents do not care about the success of their children or value their education; many times it is other issues, like their own lack of education and their poverty, that get in the way of Hispanic parents participating in their children's educational future.

Many people attribute the low level of participation to a failure on the part of the parents to place an appropriate value on education. There does not appear to be any research to support this claim. De La Rosa and Maw emphasize that "Hispanics are extremely concerned about education issues; national polls and research reveal that the Hispanic community places a high value on education" (1990, p. 97). Despite the fact that Hispanic parents value education, however, the majority of parents fail to become actively involved in the educational process of their children.

The lack of participation by parents in the education of their children is a significant obstacle to Hispanic student success. According to Clark (1983), the parents of "low achievers" had lower expectations regarding the roles of both themselves and their children in the child's education, when compared to the parents of "high achievers." It means that parents of low achievers considered education to be the sphere of the teacher. This also means that parents feel it is inappropriate to become involved in school. One suggestion is that educators begin to deal with these issues in which minorities become trained to serve as advocates for their own children as they progress through the public school system.

The failure to involve parents is closely related to many other factors affecting Hispanic education and the low numbers of Hispanic students passing the TAAS test. Many Hispanic students not passing the TAAS test are affected by school professionals who are linguistically, culturally, and socially insensitive to their needs. These same school professionals fail to relate effectively to the parents of the Hispanic student population.

For many parents, their own personal school experiences create obstacles to involvement. Parents who have dropped out of school do not feel self-assured in the schools. This situation becomes even more complicated due to the language barrier and lack of literacy skills. Even parents who speak fluent English often feel inadequate in school contexts. Not all Hispanic parents feel comfortable in asking their own children to translate for them during a parent conference. In some instances, Hispanic males feel that this places the child in a position of equal status with the adult, which then creates a dysfunction in the family hierarchy.

Conclusion

Educators are forced to teach to the TAAS in order to meet state accountability standards in Texas school districts. School districts feel an urgent need to formulate strategies to increase the number of students passing the TAAS test. A tremendous amount of pressure to improve TAAS scores is seen at every level in Texas schools. Indeed, there is a focus on the TAAS at the elementary level, two years before the test is even given. In some middle schools, beginning in January, TAAS objectives become the curriculum. At the high school level, many schools require their teachers to teach little more than the TAAS objectives beginning in October.

Bubble students are then identified and TAAS tutoring begins. Claims that the TAAS test actually encourages Texas teachers to set higher academic standards for their students are unfounded. In reality, teachers regularly just drill their students to beat the TAAS. When education is reduced to test coaching, most real learning is eliminated.

More importantly, Hispanic and LEP students are generally not selected to receive intensified instruction, thereby creating an inequitable circumstance. Here then lies the worst of all evils. Hispanic and/or LEP students usually do not score high enough on a practice test to be identified as bubble students, and, therefore, will not receive intensified instruction in preparation for the TAAS test. In other words, in many schools a practice test is given to determine who should receive remedial TAAS instruction.

Finally, Texas educators must investigate factors involving the disadvantages created in each of our schools that impact our Hispanic youth. Many of the disadvantages that Texas Hispanic students face are the result of poor teacher training in relation to Hispanic students, a lack of teacher knowledge concerning Hispanic culture, the poverty in which many Hispanic children live, the lack of Hispanic parental participation in their children's schools, a lack of State commitment to bilingual education, and the lack of Hispanic educators. In order to close the achievement gap between White and Hispanic students, Texas educators must recognize these disadvantages.

References

Clark, R. M. (1983). *Family life and school achievement: Why poor black children succeed or fail.* Chicago: University of Chicago Press.

De La Rosa, D., & Maw, C. E. (1990). *Hispanic education: A statistical portrait 1990.* Washington, D.C: National Council of La Raza.

Orfield, G. (1988). The growth and concentration of Hispanic enrollment and the future of American education. Albuquerque, NM: National Council of La Raza.

Rogoff, B., & Wertsch, J. (Eds.). (1984). *Children's learning in the zone of proximal development.* San Francisco: Jossey-Bass.

Short, D. J. (1991). *How to integrate language and content instruction: A training manual.*Washington, DC: Center for Applied Linguistics.

Texas Education Agency. (1997). *Snapshot '97 School District Profiles.* Austin, TX: Texas Education Agency.

U.S. Department of Education. (1995). *Prospects: The congressionally mandated study of educational growth and opportunity: Language and minority and limited English proficient students* (Office of Educational Improvement Rep. No. 199). Washington, DC: Planning and Evaluation Service.

Vasquez, J. (1990). Teaching to the distinctive traits of minority students. *The Clearing House 63* (7), 299–304.

Chapter 8

Is Texas Failing to Equitably Educate Minorities?

Raymond A. Horn, Jr.

A Matter of Complexity

The question given above is reasonable and significant, especially in relation to the educational assertions of George W. Bush about the efficacy of standards and the court case brought by Hispanic and African American students against the state of Texas. It is also significant because of the relationship between the Texas Assessment of Academic Skills (TAAS) test and the student attrition situation in Texas. Also, as your understanding of the student attrition or dropout rate grows, always bear in mind the changing demographics of Texas, which reveal a significant rise in the Hispanic population across the entire state. Furthermore, there is great significance to the question given above because it invites simplistic answers that polarize opinions and mask the true complexity of any educational system and its effects on minority populations.

The gut response of the proponents of the Texas technical standards is to become defensive about the possibility of inequity and to further entrench themselves in vitriolic rhetoric against multiculturalism. Radical minority advocates can easily continue this polarization of the issue by attacking all aspects of the standards movement. Lost in this polemic conflict is a more realistic perspective that could generate higher-quality education that is indeed equitable. What is required to reach this realistic and equitable perspective is to embrace the complexity of the issue. To view the complexity, with the intent to arrive at an equitable perspective, requires a return to the critical lenses detailed in chapter 3. Utilizing these lenses is not merely an academic exercise but a way to avoid the narrow and simplistic reading that the issue of the TAAS and the student attrition rates commonly receive. If we are to avoid the polarizing political rhetoric and the narrow view offered by traditional research, we need to broaden our view of these issues by broadening *how* we look at them.

After becoming familiar with the ongoing problem of student attrition in Texas, we will post-formally analyze the implications of the relationship between the TAAS and the attrition rate for minority students in Texas and the critical implications of the dropout trend for all Texans.

Student Attrition Rates in Texas

First, there is not only a distinction between the terms "student attrition" and "dropout rates," but there is also a difference between the Texas Education Agency's (TEA's) numbers and those of the Intercultural Development Research Association (IDRA), a nonprofit organization whose purpose is to disseminate information concerning equality of educational opportunity in Texas and across the United States.

Essentially, an attrition rate includes all of the students lost over a period of time. A dropout rate can be crafted that excludes certain students for certain reasons from a tally of students lost from a system over the same time period. Taking the example of a ninth-grade class and following it to graduation, the strictest definition of attrition would include all of the students who did not graduate for whatever reason. Reasons could include transfers to other schools, early admission to college, admission to a health care facility, or death. Obviously, this definition is flawed in many ways as an informative statistic about student dropouts. On the other hand, student attrition statistics can be tightly defined and loosely monitored, thus once again creating problems in understanding the phenomenon of student dropouts. Also, dropout rates can be reported as longitudinal statistics covering a population group over a number of years or as a year-to-year indicator. The situation in Texas is one in which, due to the definitions used and inaccurate reporting, the dropout rates reported by the state have been proven to be inaccurate. John Suval (1999) reports that nobody knows for sure how many students drop out of Texas's public schools, and that one count places the state's dropout rate at less than 2 percent, another at more than 10 percent, and yet another at more than 40 percent. Suval attributes part of the problem to the difficulty in tracking down students who have withdrawn and the lack of agreement as to the definition of a dropout.

The IDRA reports that "according to TEA, the dropout rate has declined steadily for almost a decade. The reported annual dropout rate was

1.6 percent in 1996–97 and in 1997–98, down from 6.7 percent in 1987–88" (Johnson, 1999, pp. 8, 11). Unfortunately, the TEA's claim is invalidated by the inaccuracy of prior dropout data. The data are inaccurate because of the improper reporting of dropouts by school districts and a change in the coding of dropouts. Concerning the inaccurate reporting of data, a report prepared by the Texas state auditor "stated that underreporting of dropouts must be addressed by the TEA" (Johnson, 1999, p. 11). "As a result of inaccurate calculations and unverified counts, the state auditor estimated that the 1994 actual dropout rate was more than double the reported rate" (Johnson, 1999, p. 11).

In 1999, the TEA responded with its first dropout and school leaver report (TEA, 1999), which included unreported students for the 1996–97 school year and underreported students for the 1997–98 school year. "The school leaver report indicates that in many of the larger school districts, schools could not account for significant percentages of their pupils from one year to the next. Yet rather than counting these 'unreported students' as dropouts, the agency chose to disregard these numbers and continued to use official dropout numbers reflected in the data reported" (Johnson, 1999, p. 11). Roy Johnson reports that "the agency estimated that more than 55,000 students were underreported as dropouts or school leavers" (Johnson, 1999, p. 11).

In addition, in September of 1999, Texas Comptroller Carole Keeton Rylander created a task force to investigate TAAS cheating and erroneous dropout rates. This action was preceded by a TEA probe of dropout data in 16 school districts, including 6 in the Houston School District, which is the largest district in the state. Prior to this action the TEA gave two other school districts unacceptable ratings in 1999 because of their severe data-reporting problems (Markley, 1999, p. 18A).

Besides the improper reporting of dropout data, how dropouts are coded is critical in determining the validity of the statistics. The original mandate of the Texas Legislature in 1986 "requires that TEA collect and calculate longitudinal and annual dropout rates for students in grades seven through 12. The bill mandates that the state reduce the state-wide longitudinal dropout rate to not more than 5 percent of the total student population in grades seven through 12 by the year 2000" (Johnson, 1999, p. 8). Note that the 1.6 percent reported in the last two reporting years is significantly lower than the legislature's requirement. Also, note that the deadline of the year 2000 further directly contextualizes the TEA's compliance actions and indirectly those of the school districts pressured by the TEA to comply.

The state definition of a dropout is as follows: "A student is identified as a dropout if the individual is absent without an approved excuse or documented transfer and does not return to school by the fall of the following school year, or if he or she completes the school year but fails to re-enroll the following school year" (TEA, 1998). To accommodate this definition, the TEA established "leaver codes" in the three general categories of graduate, leaver, and dropout (Johnson, 1999). Prior to and including the 1996–97 school year, the state used 22 leaver codes; it increased that number to 37 for the 1997–98 school year. These codes are used to describe the circumstances of each student's departure from the school. One of the 37 codes was for graduation, 20 were codes that were not included in the dropout statistics, and the remaining 16 were reasons why a student dropped out. Some of the leaver codes that are not included in the dropout statistics included school transfers, leaving to go to college, admission to a health care facility, expulsion for criminal behavior, and removal by Child Protective Services. However, other codes that are not included in the dropout statistics are these: completed graduation requirements except for passing TAAS; withdrew but in alternative programs toward completion of GED/diploma; district has documented evidence of student completing GED; graduated previously, returned to school, left again; withdrawn by the independent school district; and GED previously, returned to school, left again.

A system of this complexity is fraught with peril in terms of validity. In its school leaver report, the TEA reported that in 1997–98 approximately 3.6 percent of the students who left the school system in Texas were underreported, compared to approximately 18.1 percent underreported in the previous years. TEA also reported that in some cases students were reported as leavers even though they were not enrolled in the system the previous year. TEA determined that a significant portion of this poor reporting was due to personal identification errors when the schools reported the data to the TEA. "In a statement, then State Education Commissioner Michael Moses acknowledged the problem with the large number of unreported student records and warned districts that next year's ratings might count these *desaparecidos* (lost students) as dropouts" (Johnson, 1999, p. 13).

Johnson (1999, p. 13) reports the following statistics that TEA failed to mention:

- Of the 1.7 million students in grades seven through 12 in 1996–97, an estimated 464,024 students were classified as "non-returning" students. The 27.2 percent non-returning rate translates into almost a half million students who did not return to the school of record.

- Of the 1.7 million students in grades seven through 12 in 1997–98, an estimated 434,042 students were classified as "non-returning" students. The 24.9 percent non-returning rate translates into almost a half million students who did not return to the school of record.
- The enrollment status of an estimated 245,933 students was not reported by school districts in 1996–97.
- An estimated 55,123 students were underreported as dropouts or school leavers in 1997–98.

Based upon their analysis of the inaccuracy of the TEA numbers, the IDRA determined that "in Texas over the last 13 years, the percent of students of all races and ethnicities lost from public school enrollment has worsened. It was 33 percent in 1986. Today, it is 42 percent" (Johnson, 1999, p. 1). In Texas between 1995–96 and 1998–99, 53 percent of Hispanic students and 48 percent of Black students were lost compared to 31 percent of White students (Johnson, 1999). "Two of every five students from the freshman class of 1995–96 left school prior to their 1998–99 graduation from Texas public schools. Though the attrition rate has remained relatively stable over the last few years, the rate is 27 percent higher than in 1985–86 when the attrition rate was 33 percent" (Johnson, 1999, p. 1). This is possible because "longitudinally, the attrition rate in Texas public schools has increased by nine percentage points from 1985–86 (33 percent) to 1997–98 (42 percent). Numerically, 151,779 students were lost from public high school enrollment during the period of 1995–96 to 1998–99 as compared to 86,276 during the period of 1982–83 to 1985–86" (Johnson, 1999, p. 1).

The IDRA has conducted comprehensive assessments of student attrition in Texas from the 1985–86 school year to the present. Their major findings from their 1998–99 report are as follows (Johnson, 1999, pp. 2, 8):

- From 1985–86 to 1998–99, more than 1.3 million students have been lost from Texas schools due to attrition.
- Black students and Hispanic students were more likely than White students to be lost. Hispanic students were 1.7 times and Black students were 1.5 times more likely than White students to leave school before graduation.

- From 1997–98 to 1998–99, Native American students, and Asian/ Pacific Islander students experienced a decline in attrition rates. The attrition rates of Blacks also declined from 49 percent to 48 percent while the attrition rates of White and Hispanic students remained constant at 31 percent and 53 percent.
- More males (45 percent) than females (38 percent) were lost between 1995–96 and 1998–99.
- Hispanic students (50.1 percent) made up the highest percentage of students lost from public schools in 1998–99. White students comprised 39.1 percent and Black students 16.8 percent.
- From 1995–96 to 1998–99, 25,526 Black students, 48,178 White students, and 76,096 Hispanic students were lost to attrition. These numbers do not include students who left to go to special schools such as military schools, state schools, and charter schools.
- Attrition rates for the following Texas counties in 1998–99 were as follows: Houston, 46 percent for Blacks, 26 percent for Whites, and 76 percent for Hispanics. Rates for Dallas were 51 percent for Blacks, 32 percent for Whites, and 64 percent for Hispanics. Bexar, the home of the University of Texas at San Antonio, had the following rates: Blacks—46 percent, Whites—28 percent, Hispanics—50 percent. Travis, the home of the University of Texas at Austin, had the following rates: Blacks—60 percent, Whites—34 percent, Hispanics—69 percent. Brazos, the home of Texas A&M, had the following rates: Blacks—53 percent, Whites—26 percent, Hispanics— 56 percent. Jasper had rates of 37 percent for Blacks, 28 percent for Whites, and 71 percent for Hispanics. Lubbock, the home of Texas Tech University, showed rates of 30 percent for Blacks, 18 percent for Whites, and 46 percent for Hispanics. Nacogdoches, the home of Stephen F. Austin State University, had a Black rate of 46 percent, a White rate of 24 percent and a Hispanic rate of 59 percent. El Paso had a Black rate of 41 percent, White of 26 percent, and Hispanic of 43 percent.

To once again clarify the context of these numbers, they represent the actual statewide *longitudinal* dropout rate; a rate that measures the loss of students over a period of time, such as that from 9th grade to 12th grade. Students are lost for a myriad of reasons, which are identified by the TEA as withdrew/left school due to the following: pursuing a job, joining the military, pregnancy, marriage, alcohol or other drug abuse problems, low or failing grades, poor attendance, language problems, age, homelessness, enrollment in alternative programs, entering college without evidence of pursuing degrees, expulsion for criminal behavior, not completing graduation requirements and not passing the TAAS, and reasons unknown.

As a comparison, the TEA reported dropout rates in 1996–97 of 29.4 percent for Whites, 17.6 percent for African Americans, and 51.5 percent for Hispanics. In 1997–98, the TEA reported rates of 28.1 percent for Whites, 18.7 percent for African Americans, and 51.3 percent for Hispanics. These numbers were distributed by the TEA's Public Education Information Management System (PEIMS), which can be accessed through the TEA's homepage at http://www.tea.state.tx.us/.

The Relationship Between TAAS and Student Attrition in Texas

This relationship can be viewed in at least two ways. First, does the TAAS contribute to student attrition? Secondly, are the TAAS and the student attrition rates actually manifestations of the same phenomenon? The first question implies that they are two separate entities with the TAAS having the capability of influencing the other. The second question implies that they are related in some way, perhaps, metaphorically, as cousins or siblings.

Concerning the first question, there is no doubt that the TAAS exacerbates the attrition problem; the real question is how significant is the effect? The State of Texas recognizes this effect by providing grant funds for programs aimed at retaining students in the 9th grade. State officials, public school administrators and teachers in conversation all assume a common sense posture in that students who do poorly on the 8th-grade and 10th-grade TAAS become at risk of dropping out before they graduate. Public school educators aggressively vie for the state 9th-grade retention money because they see the potential not only for decreasing their dropout rates but also for bettering their TAAS performance. The additional services made available by the additional funding work to achieve both goals—a lower dropout rate and higher TAAS scores. In relation to the recent court case involving the suit brought against the State of Texas by the Mexican American Legal Defense and Education Fund (MALDEF), testimony also indicated an assumption that there is a relationship between the TAAS and student attrition. Pertaining to the issue of significance, the paucity of empirical studies directly dealing with the extent of the effect of the TAAS on student attrition leaves room for ample research opportunity.

If the TAAS and the high student attrition rates (note that I am not calling them "minority" student attrition rates; this is because White rates in the 20 and 30 percent range are also unacceptable) are manifestations of the same phenomena, what are the patterns or paradigms of how we view this educational situation? Utilizing the multiple lenses detailed in chapter 3, we can enter the level of complexity necessary to answer this question. To do this we will attempt to discern deep patterns through an examination of context and etymology or the history and origins of the knowledge accepted and used by people in Texas concerning the implications of the TAAS and student attrition.

Patterns
An examination of the historical context of educational change in Texas uncovers a liberal intent, starting in the 1960s, to remedy educational ills through government intervention. In the case of Texas, the governor and legislature, undoubtedly influenced by the actions of the national government, took action by empowering regulatory agencies to assess needs and initiate change. However, due to the power of business and industry and to the Reagan Revolution, conservatives were able to quickly appropriate the government's intent to remedy educational ills as an opportunity to promote the conservative agenda. Therefore, in the culture wars of the 1980s, Texas education represented a conservative victory, and the power of the government was brought to bear on the educational system.

The pattern that emerged and has continued is the promotion of White Eurocentric culture and political control by the dominant White culture[1] through the control of the cultural capital[2] that can be used to gain political and economic status, and through the commodification[3] of the people involved in Texas education. Education represents the capital that people can gain to better themselves. The situation in Texas, as described in this book, clearly shows that certain segments of the population (African American, Hispanic, and poor White) are limited in their acquisition of cultural capital due to the high attrition rates, the TAAS as an exit-level test, and the technical standards tested by the TAAS.[4] The fact that for over a decade the high TAAS failure rates and dropout rates have gone unattended, and that the TEA has held its course indicates a disregard, whether unconscious or conscious, for these population groups.

How could human cost of this magnitude[5] become an acceptable part of a change initiative? Returning to the context of place, Texas history informs our understanding of this acceptance of human cost. An examination of the cultural, economic, and political history of slavery, segregation, integration, and resegregation[6] reveals the attitudes and world views that continue to contextualize the views that tolerate this human cost. My analysis by no means suggests that the understandings by which people lived up to the beginning of integration are the same as the understandings of people today. However, I am suggesting that past attitudes still affect the collective and unconscious understandings that justify current actions and beliefs. Specifically, the instrumental use of people was deeply engrained in the culture of Texas, as indicated by their Civil War decision and the consequent high level of later Klan activity. A detailed look at the historical clash of Mexicans and Texans would also greatly inform our understanding of the acceptance of Hispanic educational losses. This contextual analysis could continue with an examination of the history of and attitudes toward organized labor in Texas. But the end result is the recognition that there is an attitudinal pattern of acceptance of using/sacrificing people for a goal, which is manifested once again in the tolerance of such enormous human cost in the standards initiative. The belief that minorities will eventually benefit by the stringent and unrelenting enforcement of the technical standards system is a myth that will continue to add to the human cost.

But what about White dropout rates and White male TAAS scores? Is the Texas education situation simplistically a racial and ethnic situation? Statistics show that low socioeconomic-level White males have the same level of failure as the non-White racial groups. Poverty appears to be one of several significant variables. A further look at the historical context of Texas reveals a pattern of rugged individualism that was born in the exigencies of the frontier and achieved mythical levels in cultural stories. Individuals, through the strength of their personal character, prevailed over great odds, not only to survive but to build business empires. Survival of the fittest and natural selection characterized past generations of Texans. In light of this historical context, it is not surprising that one simple fact carried such enormous influence with the court in the MALDEF case—every student has eight chances to pass the test. Surely the responsibility must fall squarely on the shoulders of the individual students, especially if they don't have the will to prove themselves by mastering the standards and staying in school. In this scenario there is no racism, just the will of individuals to empower themselves through their own actions, and the complaints of those who can't accept at the socioeconomic level that they have earned.

Another pattern that emerges from our post-formal analysis is one dealing with input, process, and output as proposed by Cárdenas (1998), and previously explained in chapter 3. A conscious decision was made by the TEA and mandated by the legislature to target the students as the focus of the standards change initiative. The significance of this pattern is that the burden of the change is an affliction that weighs heavily on the students, not on those responsible for instruction, nor those responsible for providing enough funding to deal with the complexity of the situation.

As alluded to in chapter 3, a further pattern is that of how the State of Texas has responded to the multicultural nature of its society. Reflected in the racial and cultural disparity in the TAAS results and the dropout rates are the racial and cultural struggles in which members of the dominant culture are engaged. The brief historical context developed in this chapter provides only a glimpse of the contextual and etymological complexity of the ways this pattern is playing out. Through a critical multicultural lens, we see those of the dominant culture struggle to assimilate individuals who are different rather than to create an egalitarian, pluralistic society. We also see the power arrangements and the struggle of the dominant culture to maintain those arrangements. Unfortunately, the educational decisions that relate to these struggles significantly impact countless children.

Undoubtedly, others will contest the premise that these societal patterns relate to the TAAS and the dropout situation. However, the fundamental tenets of systems thinking support the premise. Society is comprised of subsystems and suprasystems that are systemically interrelated and embedded within the systemic environment—systems nested within systems. This dynamic concept of the structure of society further dictates that all systems are affected by every other system's actions. If a system is consciously designed by one group of stakeholders, and when implemented deleteriously affects certain other stakeholders in that system—in this case, the children—and action is not taken to remedy these deleterious effects, then the designers and implementers of the design are the culpable individuals. Their culpability lies in their awareness of these bad effects and their intent to take no direct and expeditious action to remedy the situation.

Through a post-formal analysis of conversation, a distinct conversational pattern emerges. The history of the standards initiative in Texas is characterized by only two conversational types—discussion and dialectical. In these types, emotion and reason are utilized by those in charge to promote their educational agenda and all the economic, political, social, and racial values and attitudes attached to the agenda. The rigid control exerted by the state through its regulatory agencies allows only a one-way flow of conversation about the standards and their effects. Since the state's way is the only way, all conversation is essentially either compliant in nature or adversarial. This assertion is supported by the necessity for the Hispanic community to seek relief through the court system. The conversational tone of the whole educational system is set by the state's conversational choice. Assuredly, there are schools in which educational leaders allow or promote dialogue, but even in these cases the potential of the dialogue is limited to the constraints set by the state's mandates. Assuredly, there are educational leaders who engage in design conversation, even focusing the design conversation to promote equity and caring; however, even in these cases, the potential of their idealized design is limited to the narrow confines of their own environment and further constrained by the state's mandates that intrude into that environment.

All of the previously identified patterns coalesce into a concern about the community patterns that are being established. The pattern that persists is the continuation and evolution of the factory system of education and the concomitant industrial sense of community. As discussed in chapters 2 and 3, this system of education has direct implications for the type of community in which we live. Do we want to live in a Gesellschaft kind of community in which people are separated and in which they instrumentally use each other? Do we want to design our own communities or let them be designed for us? Will our communities be inclusive of people who are different from members of the dominant, controlling culture, or will we promote a resegregation of people based on their difference? The answers to these questions directly relate to the answer to this chapter's title. As we continue to separate people through the TAAS and the dropout rate, we promote a notion of community that is inequitable, uncaring, and separatist.

Conclusion

There are undoubtedly other patterns, and even the ones that have been identified have not been explained in a depth that exposes the extent of their complexity. A more detailed and comprehensive post-formal analysis of explanations about minority achievement in school would have to include other factors, such as the following: poverty and related health care issues, academic coursework as in tracking, peer pressure, class size, the greater mobility or transience of the poor, teacher quality, administrator quality, parenting, preschool access, the threat of negative stereotyping about one's group, the summer effect or summer vacation, teacher expectations in relation to race and gender, the effects of excessive television viewing, and test bias (Viadero, 2000). A final issue is genetic inferiority. Periodically, this issue raises its ugly head, most recently precipitated by Murray and Herrnstein's *The Bell Curve* (19xx), and insidiously feeds the racist potential in many people. The specter of genetic inferiority silently provides private justification for continuing obviously discriminatory practices.

It is interesting to note that many of the explanations listed are being addressed through TEA programs. However, their positive effect is blunted by the TEA's inability to focus program design on a vision that is effectively and truly egalitarian and caring. There are many paradoxes in the Texas standards initiative. It seems that in many cases, one program negates the effectiveness of another. These paradoxes or contradictions occur because of the lack of a truly egalitarian and democratic vision and design. Also, the state fails to recognize these contradictions, and its puzzling behavior is explained by how we define the word "recognize." To not recognize a contradiction requires the state to either not be consciously aware of the contradiction or to be aware but to choose to be unresponsive.

The dropout rate and the TAAS results are related because they are both indicators of the cultural, political, social, and racial conditions and attitudes of Texas society. The dropout rate and the TAAS results are excellent assessors of the state's commitment to the various segments of its population, the distribution of power in the state, and the effectiveness of the educational system's ability to promote student achievement and retention. As you continue through this book, seek answers to the question: Is Texas failing to equitably educate minorities?

Notes

1   Dominant culture refers to the cultural group that is politically, socially, and economically in a position of power, and therefore has the ability to impose its beliefs, knowledge, traditions, and values on others in the society.

2   Cultural capital refers to Pierre Bourdieu's (Bourdieu & Passeron, 1977) idea that in a society there are cultural knowledge and patterns of behavior that if attained and followed increase the chance of success in that society. Just as the accumulation of capital (that is, money and other means of production) increases one's chance of financial success, the accumulation of appropriate language patterns, behavior habits, and attitudes increases one's chance of social, political, and economic success. What cultural traits are deemed appropriate and contribute to one's success are defined by the dominant culture.

3   Commodification refers to the notion that everybody is an object or commodity in the sense that everybody has a market value and becomes a tool of production and consumption. When people are seen as objects or means to a political or economic end, attrition rates in public schools and teacher certification programs are justified in a cost/benefit analysis. When people are treated as commodities or objects, they become depersonalized, which allows those in control to instrumentally use the people for the controllers' own interest just as they would use other objects. Human cost is relevant only as it applies to market value or instrumental value as defined by those in control.

4   Information that is uncritical in its intellectual requirements of students and requires only repetitive drill and memorization for mastery, does not lead to the knowledge base and skill level required for success in an information society. As explained in chapter 1, memorization is a necessary component of learning; however, when the entire educational experience of the student is heavily contextualized by this kind of learning, the child is not being prepared to attain success in the *upper* economic levels of the information society. The child is in fact being directed into lower socioeconomic levels.

5   To understand the magnitude of the human cost, consider the number of students who have not received a high school diploma since the inception of TAAS, the number of people who have dropped out of school, and the continuing deleterious effect on the lives of these people and their own children. The cost must include not only the number of people who have directly experienced failure, but also what they have been unable to attain in their lives because of this early failure. The TAAS as an exit-level test is truly a high-stakes test because of the continuing effect it can have on one's life. The TAAS and the dropout rate facilitate the systemic and transgenerational poverty that is prevalent in Texas.

6   Resegregation refers to the efforts of both the dominant culture and the minority cultures to separate themselves from each other. Resegregation occurs among

economic, religious, and political groups as well as between racial groups. The increase in home schooling, charter school enrollment, and private school enrollment is indicative of resegregation.

References

Bourdieu. P., & Passeron, J. (1977). *Reproduction: In education, society, and culture*. Beverly Hills, CA: Sage.

Cárdenas, J. A. (1998, October). School-student performance and accountability. *Intercultural Development Research Association Newsletter, 25 (9)*, 1–2, 17–19.

Herrnstein, R. J., & Murray, C. (1994). *The bell curve: Intelligence and class structure in American life.* New York: The Free Press.

Johnson, R. (1999, October). Attrition rates in Texas public high schools still high. *Intercultural Development Research Association Newsletter, 26 (9)*, 1–2, 8–15.

Markley, M. (1999, September). New state task force to probe TAAS cheating, dropout data. *Houston Chronicle, 98*, p. 18A.

Suval, J. (1999, April 12). Dropout rates hard to figure, officials note. *The Monitor.*

Texas Education Agency. (1998). *Texas dropout rates by ethnicity* [On-line]. Available: http//www.tea.state.tx.us/research/dropout/9798/appendb/state.html

Texas Education Agency. (1999, May 14). *1996–97 and 1997–98 returning and non-returning students in grades 7–12.* Austin, TX: Texas Education Agency.

Viadero, D. (2000, March). Lags in minority achievement defy traditional explanations. *Education Week* [On-line]. Available: http://www.edweek.org/ew/ewstory.cfm?slug=28causes.h19

PART THREE

STANDARDS AND THE TEXAS UNIVERSITIES

Chapter 9

Understanding Standards in the Republic of Texas: Through the Looking Glass of Complexity

Patrick M. Jenlink

"Dear, dear!" . . . [said Alice] . . . "I wonder if I've been changed during the night? Let me think: was I the same when I got up this morning? I almost think I can remember feeling a little different. But if I'm not the same, the next question is, who in the world am I? Ah, that's the great puzzle." (Carroll, 1871/1960, p. 37)

At the threshold of a new millennium, Texas is much like Alice's Wonderland, a place where people are caught in a flurry of political activity, while striving to understand the rapidly changing landscape amidst partisan politics and national agendas focused on challenging educational systems to better prepare more educators for public schools in the twenty-first century. Situated in the national discourses on quality education, with a history dating back some four decades, the educational systems of Texas are bound up in the chaotic forces of change brought on by accountability for educator preparation and student performance (ExCET and TAAS, respectively), and the increasing demands that standards impose on the public school and university. Relatedly, these same chaotic forces bring cause to question "What has changed?" " What will change?" "What can change?" In the now classic stories of *Alice in Wonderland* and *Through the Looking Glass,* written over a century ago by Lewis Carroll (1871/ 1960), I am drawn to the character of Alice as the world of education in Texas becomes "curiouser and curiouser" (p. 35) in the growing complexity and problematization brought on by standards and accountability.

While there are few incontrovertible facts in life, not unlike the situation in Alice's Wonderland, one thing seems fairly certain: accountability has captured the attention of the American public, and it is currently the primary subject of educational policy at the national, state, and local levels. As Olson (1999) notes, accountability is "a very American set of ideas" (p. 8). Relatedly, standards have become the topic of public discourse across America, and nowhere has this discourse had more impact than in the colleges of education in Texas. Texas is a state that is being surveyed by other states because of its accomplishments in accountability, as well as because it is the first state to implement an Accountability System for Educator Preparation (ASEP) (State Board for Educator Certification, 1999), but there is much about standards in Texas that is not as it appears, and more that warrants understanding.

This chapter will provide an overview of the structure and systemic nature of standards as they apply to the Texas universities in general and to Stephen F. Austin State University (SFA) in particular. SFA has one of the largest teacher and administrator preparation programs in Texas. Currently, SFA has completed its second year of "Accredited-Under Review" status assigned by the State Board for Educator Certification (SBEC) because of its percentage of low African American scores on the Examination for the Certification of Educators in Texas (ExCET). As I write text for this chapter, an unofficial notification has arrived from State Board of Educator Certification (SBEC) that SFA has raised scores to a satisfactory level and will likely be removed from "Accredited-Under Review" status, a status that has in many ways exacerbated the impact of the ExCET standards authorized by the Texas Accountability System for Educator Preparation (ASEP). The significance of being under review and the implications for the university's curriculum, instruction, and assessment will be explored. The exploration will be guided by the use of the metaphorical and critical lens of the "looking glass of complexity."

The *Looking Glass of Complexity*

"So she sat on, with closed eyes, and half believed herself in Wonderland, though she knew she had but to open them again, and all would change to dull reality. . . ." (Carroll, 1871/1960, p. 163)

The metaphorical use of the "looking glass" by Lewis Carroll gave the author a means by which to characterize the irrational and often problematic nature of life that Alice experienced in the fantasy world of Wonderland. While the stories by Carroll were originally penned for young children, they capture the fascination of all ages and provide a medium by which to critically examine the rational versus irrational worlds, bringing into question what is real, and what is constructed through actions and interactions in the world. From the different perspectives of a child's fantasy world, Lewis Carroll used the "looking glass" to reflect life inside a world turned upside down and constantly changing. The experiences of Alice as she tumbles down a rabbit hole into the chaotic world of the White Rabbit and the Mad Hatter characterize what might be interpreted as a space between order and chaos, a space that shifts and fluctuates between chaos and complexity. In our world of educator preparation and ExCET standards for assessing competency and proficiency, this space exists at the edge of our world where complexification of life is brought on by the smallest as well as the largest of changes. My adoption of the metaphorical lens *looking glass of complexity* provides a means and medium through which to illuminate and construct understanding of how standards in the "Republic of Texas" have turned the world of SFA upside down. I have chosen the "Republic of Texas" as a referent due in large part to the rich history of rugged individualism and heroic figures that have captured the attention of people in Texas and across the nation, giving way to a characterization of Texas as a world apart from others. A world that provides both conservative and counterpoint perspectives within the larger context of the standards discourse.

Complexity is an inherently subjective concept; what's complex depends upon the perspective from which you look. When we speak of something being complex, what we're doing is making use of everyday language to express a feeling or impression that we dignify with the label *complex*. But the meaning of something depends not only on the language in which it is expressed (the code or symbol system), the medium of transmission, and the message, but also on the context, origins of knowledge, patterns of cognition and culture, and processes that comprise the text—whether the text be the physical reality of the world, the practical setting of schools, or the world of educator preparation (Kincheloe & Steinberg, 1999). In short, meaning is bound up with the whole process of cognition, communication, and interaction with the text and doesn't reside in just one or another aspect of it. Understanding complexity and working in complexity are both difficult undertakings. In large part, this is due to the uncertainty that multiple contexts and cultural patterns often provide in contrast to rational logic and technical standards. Importantly, both understanding and working in complexity reside largely in the processes used to interact with the multiple systems that comprise the world around us. Systems are complex patterns of processes, patterns in which people interact with other people in human activity connected through social and cultural structures. I have often reflected on the work of Alfred

North Whitehead (1978), who provides a powerful explanation for understanding the interdependent nature of people and systems in his explication of the principle of process, "That *how* an actual entity *becomes* constitutes *what* that actual entity is; so that the two descriptions of an actual entity are not independent. Its 'being' is constituted by its 'becoming" (p. 23). It is by understanding the principle of process that we are able to begin to understand complexity.

As a result of understanding process, we know that the complexity of changing an educational system such as an academic department at SFA or a public school cannot be regarded as simply a property of that system and the change process. The system under consideration for change cannot be understood apart from its interaction with other systems or from the larger context that provides identity and meaning for all systems and processes involved. Rather, the complexity must be regarded as a dynamic new level of sophistication as each of these elements interfaces. As Waldrop (1992) notes, "you should look at systems in terms of how they behave instead of how they're made. . . ." (p. 293). What this view of complexity helps us to understand is that imposing standards like those characterized by the ExCET standards for educator preparation in Texas and at SFA means that levels of complexification are added that cannot be understood without examining the behavior of the systems involved within the systemic context of the state educational systems that are impacted by the implementation of these standards. In the section that follows, I will step through the *looking glass of complexity* to examine the changes and implications of standards in the world of educator preparation at SFA, a world bound up in the irrational and complex reality of implementing ExCET standards for educator preparation.

ExCET and the Wonderland of Educator Preparation at SFA
"Cheshire Puss," [Alice] began. . . ." Would you tell me, please, which way I ought to go from here?"
"That depends a good deal on where you want to get to," said the Cat. (Carroll, 1871/1960, p. 88)

Stephen F. Austin State University (SFA) is a regional institution in Deep East Texas with a population of approximately 11,400 students. Recently, SFA has experienced the impact of standards for educator preparation from the problematized position of being "Accredited-Under Review" for the past two years. "What does this mean, Accredited-Under Review?" one might ask. This status of accreditation reflects an accountability assessment of an institution of higher education in Texas (such as

SFA), whose pass rate, either of its first-year test takers and/or its cumulative (two-year) pass rate has fallen below an acceptable level (70 percent). The impact of an "Accredited-Under Review" status, while felt university-wide, was/is quite often viewed as the responsibility of the College of Education (COE). At SFA, the COE serves as the primary repository for educator preparation, with six academic departments hosting the majority of students in either initial and/or professional level certification programs at SFA. While other academic departments at the university are responsible for the content areas in each teaching field, the COE most often was/is viewed as the nexus of ExCET activity.

In reflection, this view of the College of Education as the responsible party was/is perhaps symptomatic of the underlying complexity and endemic nature of patterns of thought in the wake of standards. All too often in the critique of programs, individuals were/are willing to disavow their responsibility, displacing this responsibility so as to discharge the negative valance it might have on individual academic programs or particular courses and the faculty teaching these courses.

SFA, like most institutions in Texas that prepare educators for public schools, has certification programs for teachers, administrators, and other practitioners that fall under the ASEP guidelines. These guidelines include accountability standards for accreditation that govern and otherwise direct academic programs for certification. Data are collected at each point during the ExCET cycle (ExCET administration is typically conducted in five test periods in a cycle or academic year) to form a cumulative database that reflects the levels of success for first-time and repeat test takers. Data are disaggregated by ethnicity or minority representation, with each sub-population being a critical factor in the overall ExCET rating of the university.

The two-year period of "Accredited-Under Review" status for SFA began in the 1997–98 academic year. At that time, SFA was placed in "Accredited-Under Review" status based on the scores of the African American population of students who had taken the ExCET. While African Americans are only a very small percentage of the entire student population at SFA, the effect of the ExCET on African American students at SFA characterizes the often complex and problematic nature of standards. A closer analysis of the African American population results in a clearer understanding of how a small number within a sub-population (fewer than 15 students) falling below the acceptable pass rate (70 percent), can effect system-wide problems and ultimately compromise the accreditation status of the university. SFA stepped through the looking glass during these two years, finding life on the other side of the "Accredited-Under Review" status complex, paradoxical, and at times bordering on the absurd. While SFA has recently been given unofficial notice (August 21, 2000) that the "Accredited-Under Review" status has been lifted, life through the looking glass is not over, nor will it be over for some time. What is important to understand in the context of the two-year "Accredited-Under Review" period is the depth of complexity that was revealed, with the African American population viewed by some people early on as a default reason why SFA was placed under review.

At first glance, the problem seems rather simple and insignificant. After all, the African American students who take the ExCET (for all certification programs) are a relatively small percentage of the total population involved in the ExCET problem. Relatedly, the percentage of African American students who scored less than 70 percent on the ExCET was small in comparison to the total number of African American students, and yet this small number of students created a major ripple in the whole system. This ripple became very instructive in the larger flow of activity to solve the "Accredited-Under Review" problem. On one level, the African American students, as well as the larger African American community outside the university, were made sensitive to the negative nature of standards by the public focus and attention drawn to the issues. On a different but related level, as resources were diverted to address the ExCET concerns, there was a specific targeting of African American students as first-time and/or repeat test takers. Faculty time for mentoring and review sessions as well as fiscal resources were redirected to the ExCET problem, and often African American students were targeted for additional assistance. As I reflect on the issues of complexity that impacted the day-to-day functions of SFA and redirected our attention to developing and implementing strategies to address the perceived problems, I am aware that often African American students were pressed into a socially and politically untenable position by their access to resources provided, notwithstanding other actions taken. Relatedly, as SFA moved from its first to its second year of "Accredited-Under Review" status, there was a growing awareness that the standards had significantly influenced and redirected the lives and activities of faculty in departments, none more obvious than in the COE. As the structures of standards interacted with the patterns and contexts of the COE and SFA, African American students were placed in a high-profile position, a position that challenged issues of social justice and equity.

What is most instructive from an analysis of the African American experience is that technical standards and the respective languages of these standards tend to privilege one group of participants (White) at the expense of minorities. Standards like the Texas ExCET and other professional standards sponsored by external agencies at the state and national levels are not designed to be sensitive to issues of diversity, nor are these standards sensitive to addressing cultural biases such as language. In the latter part of the second year of "Accredited-Under Review" status, and as we move into our next academic year (2000–2001) (with the unofficial notice taking us off the list), we are confronted with yet another result of the ExCET crisis, that of a sorting and selecting factor that standards have created in the process of implementing strategies to solve a standards-induced problem. In the large-scale interplay between our faculty and the ExCET problem, minority populations were sorted and selected into special needs categories related to perceived success on the ExCET.

Retrospectively, my view of SFA's two years under review is not unlike my view of Alice's problems in Wonderland. SFA found that in attempting to change one element (such as policies for ExCET or admission requirements for entry to teacher preparation), its action most often resulted in a change that turned old patterns and processes upside down (classroom instruction, curriculum alignment, and assessment practices are three critical examples) and challenged the technical-rational nature of standards. Each action taken to offset the "under review" status served to illuminate and make problematic the underlying complexity of standards. Knowing which way to go, for SFA, much like Alice, depended upon where we wanted to get to in terms of our accreditation status. Ostensibly, our goal was to be removed from the "Accredited-Under Review" list but what we didn't understand was the complexity involved, overshadowed by the political pressures brought on by the "Accredited-Under Review" status. As we sought to move in one direction and then another, the complexity of the standards problems became more and more apparent.

But why should I continue to focus on the two years under review? I ask myself why the other side of the looking glass is still important. I query, as I reflect on the success of moving to 93 percent plus cumulative pass rate and pass rates of above 80 percent in sub-populations, a success that will result in our being removed from the political and academic encumbrance of the "Accredited-Under Review" status. It is perhaps the fact that the complex and problematic nature of standards and accountability does not allow us the luxury of stepping back through the looking glass to a sheltered view of the world, a view of the world that is simple and rational. Quite the contrary, applying technical-rational standards for certification to a world more characteristic of the irrational, topsy-turvy world of Alice's Wonderland only adds to the complexity of the real world of educator preparation, or a world that is as real as the moment. Technical standards decontextualize the preparation process for preservice and inservice teachers and often politically and academically result in the ideological values and beliefs of the standards being pressed on teacher educators and students alike. In the section that follows I will step back through the *looking glass of complexity* to look at the world of standards in educator preparation from the inside out, and I hope to provide some understanding of the structures and systemic nature of the ExCET standards.

Complexity of Standards—Standards of Complexity
"You will observe the Rules of Battle, of course?" the White Knight remarked, putting on his helmet too.
"I always do," said the Red Knight.
"I wonder, now, what the Rules of Battle are," [Alice] said to herself, as she watched the fight, timidly peeping out from her hiding place. (Carroll, 1871/1960, pp. 294–295)

Viewing standards, like those embodied in the Texas ExCET, from the technical-rational perspective in which they are grounded limits a participant's understanding of reality and certainly overshadows the complex and problematic nature of these standards. As faculty worked toward the implementation and articulation of standards into the day-to-day life of a department, its academic programs, and its practice, the irrational nature of applying technical standards became increasingly apparent. Stepping through the *looking glass of complexity,* I have found that the rules we learn on one side of the glass very seldom if ever apply on the other. Attempting to apply old rules as guides for making decisions concerning change often results in creating new problems and/or intensifying existing problems. To paraphrase Albert Einstein, we can no longer afford to apply to existing problems the same level of thinking with which the problems were created. If technical-rational thinking guided us into the ExCET crisis, then we need to change our thinking. As Alice found in Wonderland, we can not afford to assume that the patterns and processes that have guided our activities in the world outside will help us in a world guided by "Rules of Battle" that are irrational.

The complex nature of education and educator preparation must be examined from a view other than that of a world based on technical knowledge that sees educators as technicians. More importantly, we must not assume that a technical knowledge base of how to teach will sufficiently prepare teachers for the classroom. Relatedly, we cannot assume that standards for educator preparation, like ExCET, can or should provide the technical foundation from which to rethink teacher education programs in colleges of education. The complexity of standards is, perhaps more accurately, a reflection of the standards of complexity, applied as Kincheloe (this volume) has appropriately applied them to education.

The "Rules of Battle," as Alice noted, must be discerned from the actual experience of practice. For SFA, the ExCET policies became the "Rules of Battle" and were both formal and informal. On reflection, technical rules offer little application in complex systems like schools, and conversely, trying to teach "rules of teaching", as if there are explicit standards by which the world is governed, devalues and disadvantages the human condition of teaching. The ExCET policies that flooded SFA for the past two years, and which still pervade our world, became decision rules interpreted in the flux of activities among faculty, students, and administration responding to a rapidly changing world within SFA.

Kincheloe (this volume) examines the meaning of complexity from a post-formal perspective, suggesting that standards reflective of the Texas ExCET rarely take into account such issues as value differences, diversity of perspectives, and contextualization of teaching. Nor do these standards consider the importance of context in learning to teach, diversity of cognitive as well as cultural patterns, subjectivity and creativity, irrationality of life in schools, and language. The structures and systemic nature of standards call into question patterns and processes as well as the origins and types of knowledge and relatedly the contexts of educator preparation and practice.

Reflecting on the past two years of SFA's efforts to move off the "Accredited-Under Review" list suggests to me that Kincheloe's standards of complexity play an important, even critical, role in understanding standards like the ExCET, including their deep structures. Ideology, language, policy, curriculum, instruction, assessment, standards, students, and faculty each play an equal role in the complexification of human activity in educator preparation. Compounding this complexification are issues of social justice, equity, diversity, and caring, as these issues are all moved to the background at the expense of the political agendas of the agencies sponsoring standards. Concomitantly, the complexity of ExCET standards is directly related to the multiple contexts that faculty, preservice and inservice students (undergraduate and graduate alike), department chairs, and others are situated in as they work through the problematic nature of being placed in an "Accredited-Under Review" status, as well as the retrospective view of having this status lifted but knowing that the potential always remains for replacement back in the "Accredited-Under Review" category. This is particularly problematic as the State Board for Educator Certification (SBEC) and ASEP guidelines are in the process of raising the standard from 70 percent to 75 percent for number of students passing, narrowing the margin of success for SFA in the course of a single academic year.

The political as well as academic implication of a shifting accountability measure is that it holds the university, departments, faculty, and students hostage to standards that are ideologically grounded and politically motivated. Systematically, accountability measures and technical standards depersonalize teacher educators and teachers alike, diminishing the representation of their particular practice in the reporting of aggregate pass rates for their programs. Pass rates and mentoring ratios dominate the discourse of accountability as faculty engage in efforts to align standards of proficiency with instruction and curriculum, leaving a narrow margin of difference between accountability and pedagogy by subverting the focus of college courses to preparation for the ExCET at the expense of a more important responsibility, that of teaching how to be a caring educator.

Returning to Alice and her experiences through the looking glass, I have reflected on the timidity that she often portrays as she encounters figures like the Red and White Knights, the Queen, the March Hare, and the Mad Hatter. This same timidity is often experienced as faculty and students alike come face-to-face with those in positions of power and control, often not knowing whether, if at all, they should challenge the ideological foundations or the political implications of the standards; thus the timidity gives way to incremental normalization of the system, perpetuates inequalities, promotes acquiescence to questionable political decisions, and impedes action to change academic programs on a fundamental and systemic level.

Again, I am caught up in the reflections created by the *looking glass of complexity* and the ways my department and SFA have been drawn into a world made complex and problematic by the ExCET standards for educator preparation, standards focused on assessing proficiencies decontextualized from the practical world of classrooms and public schools. I am struck by the rules that have come into play as we have faced the ExCET crisis of being Accredited-Under Review, and the tension of knowing we could return to this status in the near future. This tension is a residue of our working through the complexity of issues that pervaded our world. I am equally struck by the resource intensity of the ExCET crisis that SFA has experienced and the way this crisis has displaced discourses of pedagogy and scholarship for teachers.

I'm unsure as to which is the more problematic, the ideological reconciliation (Burbules & Densmore, 1991) that some people have embraced as demands have exhausted faculty and students alike and otherwise made them victims of the ExCET or the false consciousness (Leistyna, Woodrum, Sherblom, 1999) which allows members to buy into the subversion of their practice by standards and the subordination of faculty to "become uncritical tools" (p. 19) of a standardized system. What is clear is that if standards draw members into either of these paths, then the humanistic side of educator preparation is at risk. Certainly, as we have struggled with the political impact and the threat of losing our accreditation, as well as the realization that this threat has influenced the public's perceptions of our credibility, the naive realism that we may have felt has been challenged and the conscious awareness of what standards can do has been significantly heightened.

During the past two years, the structures of standards, those related to policy as well as curriculum, instruction, and assessment, have received great attention, but I have to ask at what cost to teaching and learning and, perhaps more importantly, ask to what degree do we really understand how standardization of learning to teach (or be a principal or superintendent) reduces a preservice practitioner's access to quality education. Equally important is the pressing critical question concerning how standardization privileges certain groups of students while disadvantaging minorities. The complexity of standards—standards of complexity examination brings to the foreground a concern for the technicizing of education and the dedemocratizing of education. Measures of accountability that sort populations and marginalize sub-populations while simultaneously creating "a resource dependency and a hierarchical power structure which maintains that dependency" (McNeil, 1999, p. 10), place our educational systems and educator preparation programs at risk. The risk created by the "high-stakes" nature of ExCET has created an awareness that there are other structures to consider in the context of the standards problem.

Critically important in the discourse and practice of educator preparation are structures that are intrasubjective and intersubjective in nature. These structures are the relational foundation that profoundly impacts the lives of students and faculty, and from which we can take our bearings as we critically examine the complexity of standards. The intrasubjective structures refer to the internal meaning system that individuals bring to their work in the preparation of educators, and relatedly to the work of changing the educational system to create quality programs. Intrasubjective structures are "culturally derived meaning systems . . . often unexamined and unarticulated" (Eaker & Prillaman, 1994, p. 195). Intrasubjective structures are important to ensuring a caring and critically democratic community. These structures are often marginalized by the implementation of technical standards, as a focus on technical knowledge privileges codified knowledge and disadvantages creativity and diversity.

Intersubjective structures reflect the internal negotiation of ethical identity, the learned caring of socially responsible and responsive educators, and the continual negotiation that must go on between faculty members and faculty and student. These negotiations are "complex, multidimensional, and happen over time" (Eaker & Prillaman, 1994, p. 196). Intersubjective structures open up the opportunity for creating consciously constructed organizational cultures that support the identity and ethic of care within departments and across programs. The ideological grounding of standards often works against these structures, seeking to create a false consciousness that subordinates members into routines of normalization and a deficit of criticality in practice.

Both intrasubjective and intersubjective structures are woven together in the organizational text of a department as well as inscripted into the program culture and curriculum for educator preparation. When standards like the ExCET problematize the teaching and learning processes, these patterns are often revealed, and the consequences "of these standards become apparent and understandable" (Eaker & Prillaman, 1994, p. 197).

Reflecting on the SFA experience, and more specifically on the work within my department to address the "Accredited-Under Review" status, it is apparent that the ExCET crisis and the implications of teacher education standards have promoted an increased, measurable accountability, which essentially excludes or disregards the underlying organizational structures that are formed from the negotiated relations between the intrasubjective and intersubjective dimensions. Again, I am sensitive to the importance of Kincheloe's (this volume) standards of complexity: how these figure importantly into the texts of educator preparation, and how some structures related to standards are advantaged in the political and ideological negotiations while other structures related to issues of justice, equity, and caring are disadvantaged.

Uncertainty in the Looking Glass

"Who are *you*?" said the Caterpillar . . . . Alice replied, rather slyly, "I—I hardly know, sir, just at present—at least I know who I was when I got up this morning, but I think I must have been changed several times since then."

"What do you mean by that?" said the Caterpillar sternly. "Explain yourself!"

"I can't explain *myself*, I'm afraid, sir," said Alice, "because I'm not myself, you see."

"I don't see," said the Caterpillar. (Carroll, 1871/1960, p. 71)

Like Alice, I have given much thought to the question of who we are, and the simple answer is that I hardly know, but I think we have been changed several times by our experiences in the Wonderland of the ExCET. When we stand on either side of the *looking glass of complexity*, looking from outside in or inside out, we find that we seldom really know who we are, and that more often than not, who we think we are is confused by the complexity of standards brought to bear on our lives, our work, and our relationships with those around us. I think we have become more sensitive to the fact that in the past we believed we were less confused, and we were quite likely less informed. The impact of the ExCET standards has made us more informed and at the same time more confused at a higher level, in part due to our awareness of the deeply complex and problematic nature of the ExCET in the larger context of standards in Texas. It is perhaps those whose ideologies and political agendas shape and guide the ExCET who have served to keep us somewhat confused, as well as the state entities and systems like the State Board for Educator Certification, the Texas Educational Agency, and the Accountability System for Educator Preparation.

When I turn to ask someone in the department who we are in relationship to ExCET, much like Alice and the Caterpillar, there seems to be confusion at times as we attempt to respond, one to another. The changing policies and shifting contexts have given way to demands for new processes in the midst of political and intellectual challenges to existing views of knowledge, learning, and practice. The level of uncertainty that we have experienced is characteristic of a system that exists between the worlds of complexity and chaos, rationality and irrationality. We have stepped through the looking glass at SFA and found that the structures of standards are complex and problematic. We have also found, as Kincheloe stresses, that standards of complexity must be part of the text in which we work with preservice and inservice educators. Standards in America and Texas will most likely continue to dominate the public and political discourses for some time, reminding us that the looking glass of complexity offers a different view of the world.

References

Burbules, N. C., & Densmore, K. (1991). The limits of making teaching a profession. *Education Policy, 5* (1), 44–63.

Carroll, L. (1960). *The annotated Alice: Alice's adventures in wonderland & through the looking-glass.* New York: Clarkson N. Potter. (Original work published in 1871)

Eaker, D. J., & Prillaman, A. R. (1994). The tapestry completed (but not finished). In A. R. Prillaman, D. J. Eaker, & D. J. Kendrick (Eds.), *The tapestry of caring: Education as nurturance* (pp. 191–205). Norwood, NJ: Ablex Publishing Corporation.

Gallagher, C. (2000). A seat at the table: Teachers reclaiming assessment through rethinking accountability. *Phi Delta Kappan, 81* (7), 502–507.

Kincheloe, J. L. See your standards and raise your standards of complexity and the new rigor in education. In this volume.

Kincheloe, J. L., & Steinberg, S. R. (1999). A tentative description of post-formal thinking: The critical confrontation with cognitive theory. In J. L. Kincheloe, S. R. Steinberg, & P. H. Hinchey (Eds.), *The post-formal reader: Cognition and education* (pp. 55–90). New York: Garland.

Leistyna, P., Woodrum, A., & Sherblom, S. A. (Eds.). (1999). *Breaking free: The transformative power of critical power.* Cambridge, MA: Harvard Educational Review.

McNeil, L. M. (1999). *Contradictions of school reform: Educational costs of standardized testing.* New York: Routledge.

Olson, L. (1999). Shining a spotlight on results. *Education Week, 17* (17), 8–10.

State Board for Educator Certification. (1999). *1999 accountability system for educator preparation* [On-line]. Available. HTTP://WWW.SBEC. STATE.TX.US/GENINFO/RULES/CH229.PDF

Waldrop, M. N. (1992). *Complexity: The emerging science at the edge of order and chaos.* New York: Simon & Schuster.

Whitehead, A. N. (1978). *Process and reality* (Corrected ed.). (Edited by David Ray Griffin and Donald W. Sherburne). New York: The Free Press.

Chapter 10

Anatomy of an ExCET

Carolyn Davidson Abel
Charles F. Abel
Vi Cain Alexander
Sandra Luna McCune
Patricia Gathman Nason

Introduction

To be certified to teach in Texas, prospective teachers must pass one of
the two state-mandated professional development (PD) ExCET tests, the
Elementary PD ExCET or the Secondary PD ExCET, and at least one
content area ExCET test. Although the two PD ExCET tests are different
tests, they do not differ significantly from each other in the knowledge
base tested. The major difference between the two tests is in the grade
level of classroom situations presented in the test items. Of course, for
items dealing with developmentally appropriate practices, this difference
becomes a discriminating factor. Nonetheless, the State Board for Educator Certification (SBEC) offers one preparation manual for those seeking
elementary, secondary, or all-level certification. Therefore, for purposes
of discussion it is sufficient to discuss *the* PD ExCET and make no distinction regarding which level: elementary or secondary.

The Domains and Competencies
Purportedly, the PD ExCET is designed to measure proficiency in three
broad domains of content (SBEC, 1998):

- Understanding Learners (about 33 percent of the test)
- Enhancing Student Achievement (about 40 percent of the test)

- Understanding the Teaching Environment (about 27 percent of the test) (p. 5)

Within the framework of these 3 domains, 15 competencies further clarify the professional knowledge and skills that an "entry-level teacher" (SBEC, 1996, p. 235) should be expected to possess. Following is a listing of the domains, their respective competencies, and the state-produced explanatory paragraph on each.

Domain I: Understanding Learners
Competency 001: The teacher uses an understanding of human developmental processes to nurture student growth through developmentally appropriate instruction.

The teacher recognizes that students' developmental characteristics affect what and how they learn and that effective decision making about instructional content and methods takes into account individual students' level of development in the various domains (e.g., cognitive, social, emotional, aesthetic). The teacher is aware of expected developmental progressions and ranges of individual variation in each domain, knows how to foster growth in each domain, and understands how development in any one domain may affect performance in other domains. The teacher applies knowledge of human development to design instruction that helps students at various developmental levels make connections between their current skills and understandings and those that are new to them.

Competency 002: The teacher considers environmental factors that may affect learning in designing a supportive and responsive classroom community that promotes all students' learning and self-esteem.

The teacher understands how various external factors (e.g., conflict within students' families, peer relationships, gang- or drug-related community problems, malnutrition) may affect students' lives and their performance in school and knows how to create a learning environment that takes advantage of positive factors and minimizes the effects of negative factors. The teacher recognizes signs of stress in students (e.g., a sudden drop in grades, an increase in aggressiveness) and knows how to respond appropriately to help students deal with stress. The teacher understands factors inside and outside the classroom that influence students' perceptions of their own worth and potential (e.g., grouping practices, parent and teacher expectations, prior experiences in school), recognizes the effects of these perceptions on learning, and knows how to plan instruction to enhance all students' self-esteem and to create an environment in which all students feel safe, accepted, competent, and productive.

Competency 003: The teacher appreciates human diversity, recognizing how diversity in the classroom and the community may affect learning and creating a classroom environment in which both the diversity of groups and the uniqueness of individuals are recognized and celebrated.

The teacher is aware that each student brings to the classroom a constellation of personal and social characteristics related to a variety of factors such as ethnicity, gender, language background, exceptionality, etc. The teacher recognizes the instructional implications of student diversity and knows how to turn the diversity within and beyond the classroom to advantage by creating an environment that nurtures a sense of community, respects differences, fosters learning, and enhances students' understanding of the society in which they live.

Competency 004: The teacher understands how learning occurs and can apply this understanding to design and implement effective instruction.

The teacher understands how students develop knowledge and skills and recognizes instructional strategies that promote student learning (e.g., linking new information to old, fostering a view of learning as a purposeful pursuit, promoting a sense of responsibility for one's own learning). The teacher is aware of factors that affect learning (e.g., individual talents, learning styles, teaching styles, prior learning experiences) and can design instruction to facilitate learning in different situations and to help students learn how to learn and to monitor their own performance.

Competency 005: The teacher understands how motivation affects group and individual behavior and learning and can apply this understanding to promote student learning.

The teacher understands the importance of motivation to learning, knows how to help students become self-motivated, and is able to recognize factors and situations that are likely to promote or diminish motivation. The teacher is aware of the characteristics and effects of intrinsic and extrinsic motivation and knows how to use a variety of techniques (e.g., relating lessons to students' personal interests, allowing students to have choices in their learning, giving students control over their learning experiences, leading individuals or groups of students to ask questions and pursue problems that are meaningful to them) to engage students in learning activities and to help them develop the motivation to achieve.

Domain II: Enhancing Student Achievement
Competency 006: The teacher uses planning processes to design outcome-oriented learning experiences that foster understanding and encourage self-directed thinking and learning in both individual and collaborative settings.

The teacher understands the relationship between careful planning and student success in the classroom. In designing instruction the teacher takes account of factors relevant to instructional planning (e.g., learners' backgrounds, desired learner outcomes, content of instruction, integrated curriculum, input from students, available materials and resources, time and space constraints). The teacher chooses lessons and activities that reflect the principles of effective instruction and that help students achieve an in-depth understanding and acquire the will to set and accomplish their own long-term and short-term goals. The teacher makes use of collaborative processes (e.g., working with other teachers) in planning instruction and in designing individual and group activities.

Competency 007: The teacher uses effective verbal, nonverbal, and media communication techniques to shape the classroom into a community of learners engaged in active inquiry, collaborative exploration, and supportive interactions.

The teacher understands that communication takes place verbally, nonverbally, and through the use of media. Using a variety of modes and tools of communication, the teacher imparts expectations and ideas to create a climate of trust, respect, support, and inquiry. The teacher models effective communication strategies (e.g., monitoring the effects of messages, being a reflective listener, simplifying and restating, being sensitive to nonverbal cues given and received) and encourages students to communicate effectively in a variety of contexts. The teacher is a thoughtful questioner who asks questions that elicit different levels of thinking and recognizes that different ways of questioning achieve different purposes (e.g., promoting risk taking and problem solving, facilitating factual recall, encouraging divergent thinking, stimulating curiosity). The teacher appreciates the cultural dimensions of communication and knows how to foster effective, constructive, and purposeful communication by and among all students in the class.

Competency 008: The teacher uses a variety of instructional strategies and roles to facilitate learning and to help students become independent thinkers and problem solvers who use higher-order thinking in the classroom and the real world.

The teacher uses an array of instructional strategies to actively engage students in learning and constantly monitors and adjusts strategies in response to learner feedback. The teacher understands principles, procedures, advantages, and limitations associated with various instructional strategies (e.g., interdisciplinary instruction, cooperative learning, discovery learning) and appropriately chooses among alternative strategies to achieve different purposes and meet different needs. The teacher can vary his or her role in the instructional process (e.g., instructor, facilitator, coach, audience) in relation to the content and purposes of instruction and the levels of need and independence of the students. The teacher knows how to make instruction relevant to students' own needs and purposes and helps students acquire strategies and skills (including higher-order thinking skills, such as comparison, analysis, evaluation) that will be useful to them in the real world.

Competency 009: The teacher uses a variety of instructional materials and resources (including human and technological resources) to support individual and group learning.

The teacher knows how to enhance learning for all students through the appropriate use of instructional materials and resources (e.g., computers, CD-ROMs, videodiscs, primary documents and artifacts, AV equipment, manipulatives, local experts) and helps students understand the role of technology as a learning tool. The teacher evaluates the effectiveness of specific materials and resources for particular situations and purposes; selects appropriate materials and resources to address individual students' strengths and needs, learning styles, preferred modalities, and interests; understands the value of using multiple resources in instruction; and can manage the logistics of individual and collaborative use of limited materials and resources.

Competency 010: The teacher uses processes of informal and formal assessment to understand individual learners, monitor instructional effectiveness, and shape instruction.

The teacher understands the importance of ongoing assessment as an instructional tool and employs a variety of formal and informal assessment techniques (e.g., observation, portfolio, teacher-made classroom test, student self-assessment, peer assessment, standardized test) to enhance his or her knowledge of learners, monitor students' progress in achieving outcomes, and modify instructional delivery. The teacher is aware of the characteristics, uses, advantages, and limitations of different types of assessments; understands assessment-related issues such as those related to bias, reliability, validity, and grading; and knows how to select or construct and use assessment instruments for various purposes.

Competency 011: The teacher structures and manages the learning environment to maintain a classroom climate that promotes the lifelong pursuit of learning and encourages cooperation, leadership, and mutual respect.

The teacher knows how to promote student ownership of and membership in a smoothly functioning learning community whose members are responsible, cooperative, purposeful, and mutually supportive. The teacher facilitates a positive social and emotional atmosphere in the classroom, establishes and maintains standards of behavior, manages routines and transitions, maximizes the amount of class time spent in learning, and creates a physical setting that is conducive to the achievement of various goals.

Domain III: Understanding the Teaching Environment
Competency 012: The teacher is a reflective practitioner who knows how to promote his or her own professional growth and can work cooperatively with other professionals in the system to create a school culture that enhances learning and encourages positive change.

The teacher understands the importance of reflection and self-evaluation and recognizes personal factors (e.g., self-concept, attitudes toward authority, biases, sense of mission) that affect one's role as a teacher and the nature of one's interpersonal relationships with students. The teacher recognizes that he or she is a member of a learning community and knows how to work effectively with all members of that community (e.g., planning a new curriculum, working across disciplines, assessing school effectiveness, implementing site-based management plans). The teacher actively seeks out opportunities to grow professionally; knows how to use different sources of support, information, and guidance (e.g., mentor, principal, professional journals and organizations, inservice training programs) to enhance his or her own professional skills and knowledge; and is aware of the value of technology in promoting efficient time use and professional growth.

Competency 013: The teacher knows how to foster strong school-home relationships that support student achievement of desired learning outcomes.

The teacher is able to establish a relationship of trust with parents or guardians from diverse backgrounds and to develop effective parent-teacher partnerships that foster all students' learning and well-being. The teacher recognizes the importance of maintaining ongoing parent-teacher communication, is aware of factors that may facilitate or impede communication with students' families, and understands basic principles of conducting parent-teacher conferences (e.g., beginning and ending on a positive note, avoiding technical jargon) and knows how to work cooperatively with parents to devise strategies for use at home and in the classroom.

Competency 014: The teacher understands how the school relates to the larger community and knows strategies for making interactions between school and community mutually supportive and beneficial.

The teacher is aware of the significance of the school-community relationship and understands the value of working with local citizens to establish strong and positive ties between the school and the community. The teacher knows how to take advantage of community strengths and resources to foster student growth. In addition, the teacher is aware of problems facing the community (e.g., drugs, gangs, racism, crime, unemployment, poverty), understands how these problems may affect students' lives and learning, and is aware of resources and strategies that can help students cope with community problems.

Competency 015: The teacher understands requirements, expectations, and constraints associated with teaching in Texas, and can apply this understanding in a variety of contexts.

The teacher is familiar with the various expectations (e.g., those of school boards, principals, colleagues, parents, students) and constraints (e.g., legal requirements, ethical responsibilities) placed on members of the teaching profession and is aware of the multiplicity of roles that teachers may be called upon to assume (e.g., instructor, resource person, problem solver, curriculum developer, school spokesperson). The teacher understands the laws and guidelines relevant to education (e.g., those related to civil rights, special needs, confidentiality, child abuse) and ensures that his or her decisions and actions are in compliance with legal and ethical requirements and the legitimate interests of others. The teacher understands the structure of the Texas education system, recognizes types of authority and decision-making structures within the system (e.g., centralized systems, site-based management), and knows how to work within the system to address issues and make decisions appropriately. (SBEC, 1998, pp. 5–10)

Analysis of the Competencies and Implications

As one reads through the competencies and examines sample items for the PD ExCET, it becomes apparent that the test is based on a cognitive theory of learning that supports learner/child-centered instruction to ensure conceptual understanding. Furthermore, learning opportunities are offered in a utopian world of unlimited materials and resources. The results is "ExCET Land"—the perfect world for the education of Texas' school children. In ExCET Land, ideal teachers base instruction on their students' prior knowledge and facilitate learning through exploration and interaction with the environment; knowledge is constructed socially in a classroom that is reflective of a cooperative, democratic society. Technology is readily available and is integrated into the curriculum. Teachers foster a positive classroom climate that provides equal access for all learners, and they take into account the varied needs and characteristics of students. Instead of producing "cookie-cutter," look-alike students, they encourage individuality through the use of a variety of instructional strategies and classroom activities that address learning styles and cultural preferences. Teachers build on the learners' knowledge by including the students' experiences and language and by incorporating relevant, real-world contexts. Learners develop conceptual understanding as they explore, investigate, and discuss concepts. Furthermore, in ExCET Land, teachers do *not* teach to the TAAS test, the public school exam that their students will be taking, because their students do well without a TAAS-driven approach, and because they believe learning should go beyond the facts-based drill and practice methods commonly adopted by those whose focus is on improving TAAS scores. How does all of this play out? Examinees attending universities whose teacher preparation programs are based on the cognitive learning philosophy and the ExCET competencies should be better equipped to respond correctly on the test.

Another aspect of readiness for the test, however, deals with the fact that Texas teacher preparation programs are funded and encouraged by the SBEC and the Texas Education Agency (TEA) to provide a variety of internship experiences in public schools throughout the teacher preparation process. This often places examinees in classrooms where mentor teachers practice behavioral approaches to learning that are teacher-directed with fact-based curriculum, instruction, and assessment. This factory model of education with cookie-cutter results quickly becomes more "acceptable" to the examinee because of the modeling done by experienced teachers, their real experience in the classroom, and the lack of theory and practice coming together. Teaching for understanding quickly becomes an unattainable aspiration (it can happen only in ExCET Land); thus, for many, the competencies must simply be memorized in order to pass the test.

All the same, the set of 15 competencies, along with their underlying cognitive framework, drives the current PD ExCET, to the extent that language from the competencies can be found embedded in answer choices on the tests. Consequently, those offering ExCET workshops and producing remedial materials are forced to focus on this emphasis. Admittedly, developing a strong understanding of the competencies, including the language and vocabulary expressed in them, can play a role in successful performance on the current test and inform teaching under ideal conditions. Nevertheless, just as in geometry there is "no royal road," the same can be said for teaching in the classroom. Effective teachers must be able to adjust the context in which they find themselves; these contexts are not often similar to the scenarios presented on the ExCET.

The competencies outline the knowledge and skills the state feels beginning teachers in Texas should have acquired through their preparation programs. Thus, when examinees take the ExCET, they are expected to have a knowledge base of broad understandings, steeped in a student-centered cognitive theory of learning philosophy, that extend from knowing the cognitive, social, physical, and emotional developmental characteristics of students in various age groups (Competency 001) to a complete and thorough grasp of the ethical and legal requirements for Texas teachers (Competency 015).

Format of the Test and Sample Questions

The PD ExCET usually consists of 90 multiple-choice test items. Each test item requires the examinee to choose between four answer choices labeled A, B, C, and D. The examinee must mark his or her answer choices on a separate answer sheet. The 90 test items are grouped into Teacher Decision Sets of related items. Each Decision Set begins with an initial "stimulus," a short descriptive paragraph about a classroom situation, followed by two or more test items. Then more information is presented in the form of another stimulus which leads to additional test items, and so on. Typically, a Decision Set will have two or more stimuli for 6 to 15 questions. The classroom situations described in the Decision Sets may indicate a particular content area (for example, physical education); however, knowledge of that content area is not necessary in order to answer the item correctly. The entire test consists of the 90 four-option test items divided into 6 to 8 Teacher Decision Sets (McCune, Stephens, & Lowe, 1999).

According to the SBEC (1996), the Teacher Decision Sets are designed to "place candidates into meaningful, connected educational situations and challenge them with significant information to analyze, problems to solve, and decisions to make" (p. 238). For instance, a sample Teacher Decision Set from the state-produced *ExCET Examination for the Certification in Texas Preparation Manual: Professional Development* (SBEC, 1998) begins with the following stimulus.

> Julie Robinson is a new middle school physical education teacher. She is planning for her coed seventh-grade classes, each of which is expected to include about 40 students. (p. 12)

This sets the stage for the 14 questions that comprise this particular Decision Set. The reader now knows the setting is a seventh-grade physical education class. Next come four questions related specifically to that stimulus. Then a second stimulus is introduced, followed by five questions. Finally, the Decision Set ends with a third stimulus and five related questions.

The items on the test are formatted into two types: single-response items and multiple-response items. Single-response items require a single response which the examinee selects from the answer choices, A, B, C, or D, listed below the item. Following is an example from the Ms. Robinson sample Decision Set:

To promote an equitable environment in coed classes such as hers, it is most important for Ms. Robinson to:

    A. specify distinct expectations for male and female students that clearly reflect her sensitivity to gender-related differences.

    B. select a variety of activities that together address the interests and strengths of both males and females.

    C. develop separate criteria for evaluating the performance of male and female students for each activity.

D. avoid selecting any activities that are likely to appeal more to stu-
    dents of one gender than the other. (SBEC, 1998, p. 14)

A typical strategy for answering this type of question is to try to eliminate
the two least likely answer choices. In many cases on the official test,
there will be at least one answer choice that is glaringly incorrect. In the
above example, choices A and C stand out as unacceptable because they
promote discrimination based on gender—not a learner-centered notion
and, certainly, unsupported in today's "politically correct" society. Furthermore, they express the same approach: that the teacher should have
requirements for girls that are different than those for boys. Since these
two answer choices, in essence, duplicate each other, both of them should
be eliminated—there can be only one correct answer.

Now, the examinee must select between the two remaining answer
choices. One difference to note between choices B and D is that choice B
involves a teacher taking action—selecting appropriate activities, while
choice D is about teacher inaction—avoiding certain activities. A mindful
rereading of the question often can help the examinee make a final decision about which is the better answer choice. The question is asking what
is "most important" for "promoting an equitable environment." Which
answer choice best reflects how a teacher who embraces a cognitive theory
of learning would do this? For such teachers, a learner-centered approach
is proactive—teachers take action to create situations in which all learners
are given opportunities to be successful. Choice B is most consistent with
this idea.

In a multiple-response item, the item stem is followed by a set of
statements numbered with Roman numerals. The examinees are given
answer choices A, B, C, and D that offer various combinations of the
Roman numeral statements. Though any or all of the Roman numeral
statements may be correct, only one response option (A, B, C, or D) is
correct. Ostensibly, the purpose of this format is to present the common,
real-world situation of being faced with a problem and having a number
of plausible options, of which one, several, or all might be good solutions.
The following question in the Ms. Robinson sample teacher Decision Set
is an example of a multiple-response item:

In planning instructional activities for the coming year, Ms. Robinson should take
into consideration which of the following factors?
   I.   students' daily academic schedules
   II. state curriculum guidelines

III. learners' needs and interests
IV. available equipment and space
   A. I and IV only
   B. I, II, and III only
   C. II only
   D. II, III, and IV only. (SBEC, 1998, p. 13)

Using a systematic process works well when answering multiple-response questions. One such approach is as follows. First, examinees try to identify Roman numeral responses that are clearly incorrect or implausible and cross them out. If none stand out, then the examinee should consider that the correct answer choice may contain all four Roman numeral responses. Obviously, for the sample question under consideration here, this is not an option, since none of the answer choices contains all four Roman numerals. Therefore, the examinee should be able to eliminate at least one of the listed Roman numerals. For instance, students' daily academic schedules have little, if anything, to do with a teacher's instructional activities so Roman numeral I should be crossed out. When answer choices containing that Roman numeral are eliminated, we are left with choices C and D. These answer choices are examined to see which Roman numerals must now be considered. Since Roman numeral II is in both C and D, then only Roman numerals III and IV need be considered. If either one of these is acceptable, then choice C cannot be the correct response. Before making a final decision, it is a good idea to reread the question. The question wants to know what "factors" should be taken into consideration when "planning instructional activities." What about "learners' needs and interests" (III) and "available equipment and space" (IV). Should these be considered when planning instructional activities? From a child-centered point of view, "learners' needs and interests" rank high in importance when planning instructional activities. This leads to choice D as the correct answer choice. Most educators would agree that both "learners' needs and interests" and "available equipment and space" are important, even though the examinee need only identify one of these to answer correctly.

To further confound the examinee, the test offers priority-setting items in which the item stem requires the examinee to select from among the responses the choice that

- is *most* appropriate, is *most* important, etc.
- is *most* likely, is *most* probable, etc.

- *best* illustrates, *best* describes, etc.
- should be done *first*, is the *first* step, etc.

In this type of question, the examinee is faced with the possibility of more than one credible answer choice. The dilemma comes in deciding which is best. The following question in the Ms. Robinson teacher Decision Set about a special education student, Janine, who has a severe physical impairment, is an example of a priority-setting item:

With regard to Janine, it is most important for Ms. Robinson to ensure that planned activities:

A. focus on those areas in which her developmental problems are most significant.
B. permit her to participate with minimal teacher supervision.
C. are in compliance with her individualized education plan (IEP).
D. permit her to perform at a level similar to that of other students in the class. (SBEC, 1998, p. 24)

This question deals with legal requirements for Texas teachers, which preempt a philosophical framework—teachers in Texas, as elsewhere, must obey federal and state laws. Although answer choices A, B, and D are plausible actions a teacher might take, it is *most* important—because it is required by law—that the teacher comply with the student's IEP, choice C.

The above examples underscore the fact that reading comprehension and logical reasoning are important skills that examinees need for successful performance on the PD ExCET. This type of thinking is usually time-consuming and mentally exhausting. In recognition of this circumstance, teacher-preparation institutions are reluctant to allow their students to take more than one test per test-administration date, and many have implemented policies that prohibit students from doing so.

The PD ExCET is scored electronically. Ten of the test items do not count, because they are being tested for use on future tests—but the examinee does not know which 10. Usually only 80 questions are used to determine the score on the test. The State Board of Education has set 70 as the minimum passing standard. Currently (in 2000), to reach the passing standard, an examinee must correctly answer a minimum of 70 percent of the test items that count within the five-hour time frame allowed for the test. The score is based on the number of test items answered correctly, with no penalty for incorrect answers.

Future of the Test

It is important to mention that the SBEC is beginning the process of revising the professional development ExCET test (SBEC, 2000). Whether the strong cognitive theory of learning framework will prove dominant when the new test is developed is difficult to determine at this time. Proposed draft certification standards for professional development on which the new test will be based are currently available at www.sbec.state.tx.us/certstand/standards.htm (SBEC, 2000). The four proposed standards (for which competencies will be written as the process continues) are as follows:

Standard I. The teacher designs instruction appropriate for all students that reflects an understanding of relevant content and is based on continuous and appropriate assessment.

Standard II. The teacher creates a classroom environment of respect and rapport that fosters a positive climate for learning, equity, and excellence.

Standard III. The teacher promotes student learning by providing responsive instruction that makes use of effective communication techniques, instructional strategies that actively engage students in the learning process, and timely, high-quality feedback.

Standard IV. The teacher fulfills professional roles and responsibilities and adheres to legal and ethical requirements of the profession. (SBEC, 2000)

References

McCune, S. L., Stephens, D. E., & Lowe, M. E. (1999). *How to prepare for the ExCET: Professional development tests.* Hauppauge, NY: Barron's.

State Board for Educator Certification (1996). *A resource for understanding the ExCET tests: Development and implementation.* Austin, TX: Author.

State Board for Educator Certification (1998). *ExCET examination for the certification of educators in Texas preparation manual: Professional development.* Austin, TX: State Board for Educator Certification.

State Board for Educator Certification (2000). *Draft certification standards for professional development* [On-line]. Obtained February 28, 2000. Available: www.sbec.state.tx.us/certstand/standards.htm

Chapter 11

Accountability System for Educator Preparation: Standards and Data Analysis

Trinidad San Miguel

Introduction

Texas, the Lone Star State, is the first state in the nation to implement an accountability system for entities that prepare educators. This accountability system is called the Accountability System for Educator Preparation (ASEP), and it became effective September 1, 1998. When added to the already existing public school accountability system, this implementation in effect also gave Texas the only pre-kindergarten-grade 16 accountability system in the country (San Miguel, Garza, & Gibbs, 2000). The public school accountability system is administered by the Texas Education Agency, and ASEP is administered by the State Board for Educator Certification (SBEC).

Accountability in public education has been the focus of an enormous amount of current research (Bryk & Hermanson, 1993; Cohen, 1988; Darling-Hammond, 1991; Glickman, 1990; Harrington-Lueker, 1990; Hill & Bonan, 1991; San Miguel, 1996). In the educational setting, accountability means holding an educational entity responsible for student performance. Educational indicators and school delivery systems are two main accountability mechanisms advocated by leading educators and researchers (Smith, 1988; Brown, 1991; Burstein, Oakes, & Guiton, 1992; Bryk & Hermanson, 1993; Caldwell & Spinks, 1992; Kaagen & Conley, 1989; Odden, 1990; Richards, 1988; Wise, 1979; Darling-Hammond, 1991; Harrington-Leuker, 1990; Porter, 1993; Odden 1992). The report in 1983 entitled *A Nation at Risk: The Imperative for Educational Reform* by the National Commission on Excellence in Education triggered broad public concern about education, and it initiated a strong push for closer monitoring of the system, its schools, and its personnel.

Accountability Mechanisms

Bryk and Hermanson (1993) note that educational indicators are promoted as efficacious instruments with which to monitor educational systems, evaluate their programs, diagnose their troubles, guide policy formulation, and hold school personnel accountable for the results. Indicator data are seen as the newest tool for legislators and administrators to construct rational policies and better manage the numerous sub-units under their control. As Foster (1991) suggests, policy makers are reluctant to entrust the future of school to teachers and administrators without some clear method of assessing the effectiveness of their work.

The history of school delivery standards, though brief, resulted in 1991 from three task forces supported by the National Council on Education Standards and Testing (Lewis, 1992). Members of the task forces argued for a level playing field for students in any system of national standards and tests. They said, "It is only fair for students to have equal opportunities to learn if standards and assessments are to have high stakes attached" (100). Lewis comments that talk of a level playing field would inevitably lead to a debate over equalizing resources: equity. In essence, school delivery standards would include these premises: (1) the school has formally adopted a curriculum that is in line with national standards; (2) the curriculum is being taught in classrooms; (3) teachers understand the curriculum and are able to teach it; (4) teachers have access to curricular materials necessary to master the standards; (5) the school has instructional methods and policies in place to promote mastery by all students (including no tracking); (6) administrators are well prepared; and (7) the school has the libraries and laboratories necessary for learning.

In the Texas case, accountability has been extended to include educator preparation programs located in institutions of higher education (IHE) and alternative certification programs (ACPs) including regional education service centers, school districts and those run by IHE. Educator preparation programs and their host entities are now held accountable for the performance of their perspective educators (teachers and administrators) on the state examinations called the Examination for the Certification of Educators in Texas (ExCET), Texas Oral Proficiency Test (TOPT), Texas Assessment of Sign Communication (TASC), and TASC-American Sign Language (ASL). These state examinations and other functions are the responsibility of the SBEC.

The Texas State Board for Educator Certification

The SBEC was created in 1995 by the 74th Legislature to govern the standards of the education profession, and its mission is to "ensure the highest level of educator preparation and practice to achieve student excellence." The 15-member appointed board oversees all aspects of public school educator certification, continuing education, and standards of conduct. The certification board is guided by the philosophy that educators will create higher standards for preparation, practice, and conduct than others outside the profession would, and that educators will rigorously uphold these standards (SBEC, 1997).

The certification board is organized into five broad areas: educator preparation, assessment, accountability, certification, and professional discipline.

Educator Preparation

In the area of educator preparation, the certification board works primarily with entities preparing educators for certification in Texas. The work includes guidance in program development, approval, and implementation. The board currently serves 70 institutions of higher education with approved educator preparation programs, 28 alternative teacher certification programs, and 6 alternative administrator certification programs. The board also advises entities interested in initiating educator preparation programs. The certification board is involved in reviewing program approval procedures to streamline the process while maintaining the integrity of program review.

Assessment

State law requires that individuals pass examinations in the areas in which they seek certification. The certification board manages the development and administration of the ExCET, TOPT, TASC, and TASC-ASL testing programs. Individuals typically take the ExCET Professional Development test and additional tests in the academic disciplines in which they seek certification after completing a program of preparation for the specific certificate(s). These tests assess the prospective educator's knowledge of academic content and teaching, including understanding of learners.

Test development and review of current tests is ongoing. Passing standards are reviewed periodically by test development and review committees and their recommendations from these reviews are presented to the board. The board sets the minimum score required to pass each certification test. Assessment professionals work with school district and educator preparation program staff to identify committee members for test development and review activities.

Accountability

The certification board monitors the quality of educator preparation at university and alternative certification programs through the ASEP. The certification board uses assessment data (ExCET, TOPT, TASC, and TASC-ASL) and, in the future, will use the performance of beginning teachers to determine program quality and issue annual accreditation reports according to minimum acceptable performance levels established by the board.

Certification

The certification board is responsible for ensuring that educators are qualified to serve in the Texas public school system through the following: issuing educator credentials to applicants who have completed the appropriate degree and have a standard credential from another state; issuing educator credentials to applicants who have completed the requirements for certification at a Texas educator preparation program; certifying applicants adding further areas of certification based on completion of the appropriate examination(s); issuing paraprofessional certificates to educational aides and secretaries; assisting education service center personnel in authorizing emergency and nonrenewable permits for school districts and reviewing and approving hardship permits; analyzing and disseminating data on certificate and permit activity; coordinating criminal investigations of applicants; advising school district staff on assignment criteria for hiring appropriately certified individuals.

Professional Discipline

The certification board enforces standards of conduct for educators in the state. It reviews all complaints of misconduct. If a formal complaint is filed against an educator, the educator will be given an opportunity to be heard. Formal hearings involving educator misconduct are open to the public and a copy of the final decision on such cases can be obtained (SBEC, 2000).

Accountability System for Educator Preparation

Recently, the quality of academic preparation has been criticized nationally by the media. Many in higher education agree, and they believe that a connection between institutions of higher education and public schools needs to be addressed. According to Jennings (1989) much of the criticism hails from groups affiliated with institutions of higher education. Furthermore, John Goodlad in *Teachers for Our Nation's Schools* (1990) has led the call for "simultaneous renewal" in K-12 education and in universities and colleges, particularly in those purporting to prepare educators.

Authorized in 1995 with the passage of Senate Bill 1, the intent of the Accountability System for Educator Preparation (ASEP) "is to assure that educator preparation programs are held accountable for the readiness for certification of educators completing the programs. An educator preparation program is defined as an entity approved by the SBEC to recommend candidates for certification in one or more certification fields." Details of the ASEP are located at http://www.sbec.state.tx.us/geninfo/rules/ch229.pdf (SBEC, 1999b).

Entities meeting the above definition include universities, colleges, and public school districts and regional education service centers offering alternative certification programs. All entities are responsible for meeting accountability standards. When the educator preparation accountability system was implemented in September 1998, entities received one of three ratings: "Accredited," "Accredited-Under Review," or "Not Accredited." Entities initiating educator preparation programs are rated "Accredited-Preliminary Status," a rating which may be maintained for three years, after which time the entity is to be held accountable to ASEP standards. While the entity is rated "Accredited-Preliminary Status", it may recommend candidates for certification (San Miguel, Garza, & Gibbs, 2000).

The ASEP requires performance levels to be met for seven demographic groups (All Students, African American, Hispanic, White, Other, Male and Female). For educator preparation entities, the stakes are high. For example, an entity failing to meet performance standards for three consecutive years will be rated "Not Accredited." Texas Administrative Code Chapter 229 allows the SBEC executive director to appoint an oversight team to make recommendations and provide assistance to an entity that is "Accredited-Under Review." If by September 1 of the third year after being designated "Accredited-Under Review" the entity has not achieved the acceptable performance standards, SBEC's executive director may "request that the Board limit the entity to only preparing candidates for certification in specified fields and collaborate with another entity to fully manage the program" (SBEC, 1999b).

The cumulative pass rate was defined as "The number of examinations passed (by the previous year's first-time takers) within the two-year academic period divided by the number of previous year's first-time tests taken. (This pass rate reflects performance on the last time a test was taken within the two academic years.)" If a candidate passed the test outside the two-year academic window mentioned above, the candidate's score did not impact the entity for accountability purposes. Entities rated "Accredited-Under Review" were allowed to request reconsideration of that rating by the SBEC if the rating had been based upon fewer than 10 students in a demographic group (SBEC, 1999b). These provisions resulted in 16 of 87 educator preparation programs being rated "Accredited-Under Review" (SBEC, 1999a).

Based upon feedback from the field, modifications to ASEP were instituted by SBEC. For example, the 1999 ratings were based on a candidate's performances during the first academic year the examination was administered rather than on the candidate's first attempt. Likewise, it was contended that small data samples should not be considered reliable indicators of an educator preparation program's effectiveness. Consequently, the number of students in a given demographic group necessary for that group's performance to affect the accountability rating was increased from 10 to 30 (San Miguel, Garza, & Gibbs, 2000).

Still another change resulting from feedback from the field was occasioned by the public relations difficulty of an entity being initially identified as "Accredited-Under Review" but then being rated "Accredited" due to reconsideration of a rating that had been based on a small number of candidates in a demographic group. In the second year of its implementation, therefore, ASEP allowed entities to review their rating and request reconsideration prior to the rating being made public (San Miguel, Garza, & Gibbs, 2000).

The release of the 1999 accountability ratings reflected the performances of 87 educator preparation programs, 10 of which were rated "Accredited-Under Review," with 9 of these 10 entities rated "Accredited-Under Review" for the second consecutive year (SBEC, 1999d). One entity did not receive a rating because no students had been enrolled in its program for the previous two years. Caution was encouraged in comparing the 1998 and 1999 ASEP ratings because, as noted above, the criteria for those ratings had changed. A list of entities rated "Accredited" and "Accredited-Under Review for 1999 is available at http://www.sbec.state. tx.us/edprep/accred.pdf and http://www.sbec.state.tx.us/edprep/ accredur.pdf.

The 1999 accountability ratings also reflected the first time the SBEC issued commendations to educator preparation programs. For example, commendations were issued to 44 programs producing a diverse population of candidates in comparison to state or regional diversity, and to programs producing teachers in high-need subjects. Commendations for diversity were awarded to 28 entities, while 20 entities received commendations for high-need areas. Four entities received commendations in both categories (SBEC, 1999c).

As the changes in ASEP from 1998 to 1999 suggest, the accountability system is a fluid mechanism. For example, assessment of classroom teachers' performance were piloted in the 1999–2000 school year, and this process became a component of the accountability system. This process will be formative for the teachers themselves but summative for their educator preparation program. Likewise, the pass rates for meeting accreditation standards will increase, effective September 2002, from 70 percent to 75 percent for the first-year pass rate and from 80 percent to 85 percent for the cumulative pass rate. This raising of standards suggests a number of implications for educator preparation entities' approaches in terms of identification of instructor/student needs and intervention strategies to address those needs (San Miguel, Garza, & Gibbs, 2000).

Under the present provisions, sanctions will continue to play a role as standards are raised. For example, effective September 1, 2002, "If the performances of all students within a certification field fail to meet requirements . . . for three consecutive academic years, the entity may no longer recommend persons for certification in that field" (SBEC, 1999b). Being unable to certify candidates in a field or fields could negatively affect enrollment and, by extension, have substantial revenue consequences.

The twin elements of continuous improvement and sanctions have engendered considerable debate between the regulatory and practitioner elements in the Lone Star State, with some people feeling they have prodded entities into undertaking improvement efforts that would otherwise not have been attempted. A conflicting viewpoint suggests that continually "raising the bar" holds educators to a standard not expected in other professions such as the legal or medical fields and that sanctions are counter-productive in a time of significant teacher shortages (San Miguel, Garza, & Gibbs, 2000).

Case Study

There are 5 opportunities for candidates to take the ExCETs: October, December, February, April, and July. The Texas Oral Proficiency Test

(TOPT) and the Texas Assessment of Sign Communication—American Sign Language exams are offered three times and twice, respectively, during the academic year. After each administration of the ExCET, each entity receives its candidates' results via the Internet and can generate different reports with the E-Z ASEP software. This can assist the entity in identifying strengths and areas of concern. These reports include the Entity Accreditation Status Report, ExCET Results by Test, ExCET Average Scores by Domain: First-Year Takers—passed Tests Only, ExCET Average Scores by Domain: First-Year Takers—failed Tests Only, Examinee Performance Summary Report, and Student Test History. The Report of Examinee Performance by Competency or Objective is sent to the entity by National Evaluation Systems, Inc. Soon, entities will be able to receive and generate these reports on-line via the SBEC web site.

Annually, entities receive an Accreditation Summary Report (ASR) from the SBEC. For discussion purposes, two tables are shown below to illustrate with data how an entity was rated "Accredited-Under Review" for the school year 1997–98 and was able to achieve a rating of "Accredited" for the school year 1998–99.

To correctly interpret the ASR, the accountability rules and the notes below each table must be taken into account. For the 1997–98 school year, the first-time test taker line reveals that "the All Students" group and African American students did not meet the 70 percent passing rate while the other student demographic groups did. The rules call for examining the cumulative line for all demographic groups to determine if they met the minimum required cumulative standard, the 80 percent passing rate. At the cumulative line, all demographic groups met the 80 percent passing rate except the Hispanic students and females. Since one or more student demographic groups did not meet the first-time minimum standard, and since one or more of the student demographic groups did not meet the cumulative minimum standard, this entity was rated "Accredited-Under Review" for the 1997–98 school year.

The table for the 1998–99 school year first-year test takers shows that all the demographic groups met the 70 percent passing rate, except the African American student group which had a 68.99 percent passing rate. Before proceeding to the cumulative data for the African American students, the first year data for 1998–99 is combined with the first-year data for 1997–98 (not shown) to determine a combined first-year passing rate for 1997–99. This entity did not meet the 70 percent passing rate on the combined first-year line, and we can proceed to the African American cumulative data.

Dot.Com University

1997–98

	All Students	Female	Male	African American	Hispanic	Other	White
First-Time	68.55%	70.88%	73.01%	69.23%	82.64%	55.55%	93.99%
1997–98	(235)	(185)	(45)	(186)	(25)	(*)	(13)
Cumulative	82.04%	85.96%	84.22%	80.22%	79.88%	55.55%	85.07%
1996–98	(241)	(188)	(47)	(180)	(22)	(*)	(16)

Note:
- The top line shows the first-time taker results. The bottom line shows the cumulative results.
- Numbers in parentheses represent the number of individual students in each group.
- Numbers less than 10 have been masked for confidentiality.
- Pass rate percentages shown as asterisks indicate zero students in that group.
- Entities rated "Accredited-Under Review" because of their performance may request reconsideration of their rating.

1998–99

	All Students	Female	Male	African American	Hispanic	Other	White
First-Year	71.74%	71.25%	77.00%	68.99%	76.33%	88.88%	90.20%
1998–99	(275)	(181)	(41)	(200)	(23)	(*)	(30)
Combined				69.45%	77.00%	88.88%	
1997–99				(240)	(32)	(*)	
Cumulative	84.44%	85.97%	84.99%	79.00%	87.00%	89.50%	85.07%
1997–99	(237)	(190)	(42)	(170)	(33)	(*)	(27)
Combined				81.25%			94.54%
1996–99				(199)			(30)

Source: State Board for Educator Certification

First-year pass rate: The line labeled "First-Year" shows entity first-year pass rates, based on tests taken from 9/98–8/99.

Cumulative pass rate: The line labeled "Cumulative" indicates cumulative (two-year) pass rates, based on tests taken from 9/97–8/98.

Combined data: If the number of first-year or cumulative test takers in an ethnic or gender group is less than 30, the performance is combined with the performance for that group on the 1997–98 year report.

If the combined pass rate represents less than 30 test takers, the pass rate is not used in determining accreditation status; a pass rate based on 30 or more test takers is used for accreditation purposes.

The number of test takers is shown in parentheses; if the number of test takers is less than 10, for confidentiality the number is not shown and an asterisk is printed. Pass rates shown as asterisks indicate there were zero test takers in the group.

Note: The data shown are fictional and any resemblance to any entity is completely coincidental.

At the cumulative line for 1997–99, the passing rate for African American students is 79 percent and therefore, does not meet the 80 percent passing rate for cumulative test takers. When the African American students' cumulative passing rate for 1997–1999 is combined with the cumulative passing rate (not shown) for 1996–98, the combined African American students' passing rate for 1996–99 is 81.25 percent, meeting the 80 percent passing rate. This entity was rated "Accredited."

The ASEP rules have changed from one year to the next. As more data are collected by the SBEC and reviewed by the SBEC board, and with the addition of a second indicator (performance of the beginning teacher in the classroom), other rule changes may occur. In addition, the state legislature, which will meet in January 2001, may also mandate some rule changes. The ASEP is evolving and is focused on providing educators that have the knowledge and skills to make every student in the Texas public schools successful.

References

Brown, D. J. (1991). *Decentralization: The administrator's guide to school district change*. Newbury Park, CA.: Corwin Press.

Bryk, A. S., & Hermanson, K. L. (1993). Educational indicator systems: Observations on their structure, interpretation, and use. *Review of Research in Education, 19*, 351–484.

Burstein, L., Oakes, J., & Guiton, G. (1992). Education indicators. In M. C. Alkin (Ed.), *Encyclopedia of Educational Research* (Vol. 2, pp. 410–418). New York: Macmillan.

Caldwell, B., & Spinks, J. (1992). *Leading the self-managing school*. Washington, DC: The Falmer Press.

Cohen, M. (1988). *Restructuring the education system: Agenda for the 1990s*. Washington, DC: National Governors Association.

Darling-Hammond, L. (1991). *Policy uses and indicators*. Paper prepared for the Organization for Economic Cooperation and Development.

Foster, Jack D. (1991). The role of accountability in Kentucky's education reform act of 1990. *Educational Leadership, 48* (5), 34–36.

Glickman, Carl D. (1990). Open accountability for the 90s: Between the pillars. *Educational Leadership, 47* (7), 38–42.

Goodlad, J. I. (1990). *Teachers for our nation's schools*. San Francisco: Jossey-Bass.

Harrington-Lueker, D. (1990). The engine of reform gathers steam: Kentucky starts from scratch. *American School Board Journal, 177* (9), 17–21.

Hill, P. T., & Bonan, J. (1991). *Decentralization and accountability in public education*. Santa Monica, CA: RAND.

Jennings, E. T., Jr. (1989). Accountability, program quality, outcome assessment, and graduate education for public affairs and administration. *Public Administration Review*, 438–446.

Kaagen, S. S., & Conley, R. J. (1989). *State education indicators: Measured strides, missing steps.* Washington, DC: Educational Testing Service.

Lewis, A. C. (1992). House bill includes school delivery standards. *Phi Delta Kappan, 74* (2), 100–101.

National Commission on Excellence in Education. *A nation at risk: The imperative for educational reform.* Washington, DC: U.S. Government Printing Office, 1983. ED 226–006.

Odden, A. (1990). Educational indicators in the united states: the need for analysis. *Educational Researcher, 19* (7), 24–29.

Odden, A. (1992). School finance in the 1990s. *Phi Delta Kappan, 73*(6), 455–461.

Porter, A. C. (1993, June-July). School delivery standards. *Educational Researcher, 22* (5), 24–30.

Richards, C. E. (1988). Indicators and three types of educational monitoring systems: Implications for design. *Phi Delta Kappan, 69* (7), 490–498.

San Miguel, T. (1996). *The influence of the state-mandated accountability system on the school improvement process in selected Texas elementary schools.* Unpublished Doctoral Dissertation, The University of Texas at Austin.

San Miguel, T., Garza, R. & Gibbs, W. (2000, April). *Pre-kindergarten-16 educational accountability system: The Lone star State's response and is anyone listening.* Paper presented at the meeting of the American Educational Research Association, New Orleans, LA.

Smith, M. S. (1988). Educational indicators. *Phi Delta Kappan. 69* (7), 487–491.

State Board for Educator Certification. (1997). State board for educator certification. Austin, TX. State Board for Educator Certification.

State Board for Educator Certification. (1999a*). ASEP-Accredited programs under review.* [On-line]. Available: .

State Board for Educator Certification. (1999b). *1999 accountability system for educator preparation.* [On-line]. Available: http://www.sbec.state.tx.us/geninfo/rules/ch229.pdf.

State Board for Educator Certification. (1999c). *1999 accountability system for educator preparation: Programs receiving commendations for preparation of candidates.* [On-line]. Available: http://www.sbec.state.tx.us/edprep/1998_review.htm.

State Board for Educator Certification. (1999d). *1999 accountability system for educator preparation: Summary of ratings for 1998 and 1999.* [On-line]. Available: http://www.sbec.state.tx.us/edprop/commend.pdf.

State Board for Educator Certification. (2000). About SBEC: The agency's work. [On-line]. Available: http://www.sbec.state.tx.us/geninfo/about_agencywork.htm.

Wise, A. E. (1979). *Legislated learning: The bureaucratization of the American classroom.* Berkeley, CA: University of California Press.

Chapter 12

The Impact of the ExCET on SFA Departments: Stories of Alignment and Curriculum

Glenda Moss

Introduction

Readers who have read the preceding chapters in this book will have no problem framing this chapter in the bigger story of mandated systemic educational change in Texas. As already described by others, Texas responded to the nation's call for educational reform by drafting a restructuring of the entire system from the top down. Furthermore, criterion-referenced tests of accountability for teachers were instituted. The TAAS test, preceded by the TEAMS and TABS, was established as a measure of teacher success based on student learning, defined as mastery of test items. At the same time, the ExCET test for teacher certification was established. It is the impact of that test that we are primarily concerned with in this book, as we use Stephen F. Austin State University (SFA) as a case study.

The Impact of ExCET

The focus of this chapter is the impact of the ExCET on the departmental level at SFA, where I now work as a doctoral research assistant in the Secondary Education and Educational Leadership Department. Ten years of experience observing the impact that state testing has had on education at the public school level helped me to quickly recognize the signs of ExCET impact on the university departmental level last summer when I worked as a doctoral intern on another Texas university campus. The main focus of my work there was to help the Curriculum Development Team complete a year-long curriculum restructuring project in the Instruction and Curriculum Department. It was not until I started the actual paperwork of the internship that I realized we were doing the mandated realignment of course content with ExCET competencies that is required to access federal educational funding.

The process of systemic change, instituted by legislation in the mid-1980s, has now affected the university level in a fashion parallel to the effects it has had on public schools. The public has been focused on public schools for the past decade because of the TAAS, but is now turning to focus on the ExCET, which shifts or expands the focus to the university level because of concern with the number of recorded failures on ExCET tests. I simply say "recorded failures" because of the big question of what the test measures and the lack of controls in the past in terms of who could take the ExCET tests or not.

The reader needs to understand that in the past, any employed, certified public school teachers were eligible to take ExCET tests outside of their field of training. For example, it was common for physical education teachers to take the Health ExCET certification test. Many would teach the course a couple of times or read the textbook and then take the exam. Failing it once or twice was seen as a strategy for learning what one needed to know. Test takers could study on their own to master the requirements for certification. Frequently, teachers are asked by principals to go and take ExCET tests in fields where the school has a problem filling a position. Retired military personnel have been heavily recruited into alternative certification programs and teach math and physical science before completing course work and taking the ExCET. Some of them pass the Math ExCET, yet fail the Professional Development ExCET, which focuses on learner-centered instructional practices that produce student learning. They may know the academics of math but not know how to teach it.

What does that have to do with university departments? To understand the departmental effect, one must understand the domino effect of standards and performance testing. In order to take the ExCET, a student must receive a bar code from a university. This code is effectively a ticket to take the ExCET. It is also a recording device, connecting the student's score with the university issuing the code. Therefore, when a math major from SFA completes student teaching, the student registers to take the Math ExCET and the Professional Development ExCET. The bar code is issued through SFA, and the student's score is recorded for SFA. At the same time, if a practicing, certified physical education teacher decided to register to take the Biology ExCET, that teacher, in the past, could receive a bar code from SFA, even if the student had not taken biology courses required of biology majors or minors. Because of the shortage of teachers in certain fields, it has become common for teachers to take ExCETs outside their field of study to help their school fill vacant teaching positions.

Likewise, others have entered teaching through a content degree, like math or engineering, and then sought to pass the professional development portion of the certification test without actually being taught how to teach according to learner-centered principles. Since many public schools are still using traditional content-centered instruction, students entering the teaching profession through emergency certification and alternative teacher preparation programs are often influenced negatively by the teaching they have received and the content-centered teaching they observe in the school setting. This learning how to teach is not aligned with sound, research-based teaching practices that are learner-centered and aligned with the Professional Development ExCET.

Both students taking content ExCETs outside their field of study and students taking the Professional Development ExCET without aligned instruction pose a problem for university departments because the State of Texas rates colleges according to their students' performance on the ExCET. Each time an ExCET test is taken, the score is recorded for, or against, the university issuing the bar code. The data is disaggregated by ethnicity and special emphasis is placed on minority scores. For example, at SFA, the state looked at the total number of White students who took the ExCET test in a one-year testing period, September 1 through August 31, and used the number of those students who failed to determine the percentage of White failures. Likewise, the state looked at the total number of African American students taking the ExCET and used the total number of those students who failed the test to determine the percentage of African American failures. The percentage of Hispanic failures each year was similarly determined. As a result, SFA's Education Department was under review because of the percentage of failures among African American students. This has put pressure on the university to take measures to correct the situation. That has resulted in each department being required to set higher standards for entrance, aligning of course content with ExCET standards, setting higher standards of course achievement, and producing a departmental qualifying exam that must be passed before an education major will have the right to take the ExCET. In essence, departments can solve the problem by simply not letting students take the test if they cannot pass it based on their existing teaching practices.

The stories of members of various departments at SFA demonstrate the systemic effect that the ExCET is having on the dynamics of educational organization when ExCET scores are viewed from an ethnicity point of view rather than an educational point of view. The failures of candidates taking the ExCET with or without formal university preparation count against the universities where the test takers received their bar codes. According to Jasper Adams, chair of the Mathematics Department at SFA, he has been aware for years of the problem of unprepared test takers taking the Math ExCET. Pulling a bulky folder of data out of his file cabinet, he said to me, "I suggest that you delve into that." He applauds the new policy, instigated at the request of the Education Department, that each department chair sign an official document before a student is issued an ExCET bar code.

The story of the departmental effect of the ExCET is a complex one. My first glimpse of the effect came when I heard that the history department had created a new course to help students pass the ExCET. It sounded like the TAAS all over again. On the middle school level, we created TAAS writing, TAAS reading, and TAAS math in summer school nearly a decade ago. Then, similar courses began to creep into the regular school year curriculum in place of traditional electives like shop, art, home economics, and choir. On the university level it is a little more sophisticated. The senior seminar course, referred to as a capstone course, is the place where several departments have implemented a systematic review for the ExCET test.

I wondered how many departments had created courses to accomplish the same senior level goal of university education, mastery of the ExCET norm. To satisfy my curiosity, I surveyed individuals in each of the departments impacted by the ExCET. My four questions to each of the 29 field advisors, representing 62 ExCET tests, included the following: Have the standards movement, the TAAS, and the ExCET raised academic standards and achievement in your department? Has your department created any new courses, specifically designed to help students pass the ExCET? Has your faculty aligned course content with the ExCET? Has your department aligned course content with the TEKS?

My hypothesis was that many departments had created courses, restructured old ones, or created special tutorials to help students pass the ExCET. Also, I suspected that alignment had been accomplished on paper, but that nothing had changed in the classroom. Furthermore, I would not have been surprised to find out that most departmental faculty do not even know what the TEKS are, much less align their course content with the standards (TEKS) and the accountability assessement (ExCET). It may be that my questions shaped the story because the responses focused on the issue of alignment. On the other hand, Goals 2000, issued by the federal government in 1994, called for national alignment of curriculum and tied federal educational funding to standards aligned with national goals.

Realizing the Goal or Alignment?

While I doubt that anyone is opposed to increasing the learning capacity of teachers and the children they teach, and building a society of lifelong learners, the standards movement begs the question: Is the process of alignment from top down accomplishing those ends? The personal stories of several professors at SFA indicate that other results that were not intended by the plan have come about as part of the design created by the implementation of systemic change by mandate from the top down.

Dale Perritt, in the Agricultural Department, doesn't think for a moment that the designers of the Agricultural ExCET intended for him and the other faculty members in his department to take time away from their solid curriculum to teach students out-of-date information that they would need to know in order to pass the ExCET for teacher certification. Perritt is glad that the Agricultural ExCET will be eliminated as of September 1, 2000, until an up-to-date test can be written. The present test was out of date by the time it hit the press. In a society that is creating improvements in industrial technology and multiplying information at a doubling rate at 18-month integrals, is it possible to keep the test aligned with progress?

Ron Anderson, chair of the Music Department, and Mel Finkenberg, chair of the Kinesiology Department, do not know what to think about the systemic effects of a test that bases teachers' ability to teach physical skills on their ability to read. Anderson regrets that some students, who "have a wonder spark within them," "can convey a lot of information," and would "be wonderful teachers" "will be washed out of the program" because of the academic side that is tested by the ExCET. Finkenberg also laments the definition of raising standards that means setting tighter controls for admission to teacher education and teacher certification. Little has been done to address the issue of building the student learning capacity, reflective and critical thinking abilities, and creativity for problem solving needed for shaping a new and more productive public school system for the future.

Finkenberg distinguished between achievement on a test and achievement in the field as a teacher. He has no doubt that the new standards will result in the appearance of raised achievement scores. If only the students who can pass the test take it, then the new test results will give the appearance of raised standards. The state will be able to boast a rise in percentage of success on the ExCET for ethnic groups. No one outside the education system needs to know that the success was not achieved through better practice but through a "better" system of deciding who gets to take the test. Thus, the ExCET, intended to insure that all students get a better quality of education, is having the unplanned effect of reducing student enrollment and preventing students from getting an education at all. Finkenberg believes that Texans can count on a continued rise in the shortage of teachers as another effect of the ExCET and still have a system with no alignment between curriculum and instruction, the alignment that educators in the field are most concerned about.

This is the same alignment that concerns public school teachers. The middle school where I taught before entering the doctoral program at SFA was operating with two emergency certified P.E. teachers for the girls' program and one ongoing substitute in the boys' program, since the school had no qualified applicants who were qualified for permanent positions. I first got to know the lead teacher for the girls when I taught her son language arts in my seventh-grade class. He was one of only two of my students who ever correctly answered all the objective questions on the state test. He was in one of my below-academic-level classes and could never seem to demonstrate more than 50 percent mastery of any skill when tested in the format of the state test until the day that I compared the test to a Nintendo game. It took only a few practice rounds and he had mastered it. I hate to admit that I had to reduce teaching right before the TAAS test to a video game in order for my students to make a successful learning connection to the test format, but we were under the gun to raise scores. Therefore, I had no trouble making connections with Finkenberg's assessment of the newly implemented "senior seminar class" in the Kinesiology Department as "a tragedy" because "the class originally was intended to be a true senior seminar" but has "digressed and degenerated into an ExCET preparation test." Furthermore, Finkenberg thinks "it's ludicrous" to have to spend time on the senior level "preparing students to take a test." He is appalled that his department is having "to spend that kind of time and resource," but they are doing it because they have "got a gun to [their] head right now, so [they] have to do it; and [he] think[s] it's tragic."

The human side of the tragic nature of the situation, as expressed by Finkenberg, is shared in my experience with a community volunteer. A local community member, where I used to teach, raised her children in the school system, volunteered any time we needed her for a school function, prepared for teaching through the university in the city, received a degree, and has been unsuccessful numerous times on the ExCET. She had to give up her teaching position three years after her emergency certification ran out because she never could master the test.

The Impact of the ExCET on Curriculum

Mastering the test is what the curriculum is often reduced to. Many language teachers in Texas have had to reduce teaching students writing skills to teaching them test-taking wisdom for the TAAS. Using the analogy of a game-like activity, especially for the objective portion that is based on proofreading texts, is common. Though the composition part of the test has been reduced to formulas for writing success, it has been instrumental in "raising" the writing performance level of every student. Seldom does a student reach high school without having memorized the formulas for writing a five-paragraph theme—Descriptive, How-to, Compare and Contrast, and Persuasive. Ten years ago, such writing appeared to require higher-level thinking skills, but now it is obvious that the writing task is rote. Students have memorized opening and closing sentences, transition words, and how to elaborate by asking questions like who, what, when, and where.

When I first listened to Cathy Quick, professor of English at SFA, relate her typical experience with freshmen students, I knew that formula writing was common. Quick reported that since students have been "drilled on" the five-paragraph theme for the TAAS, it "colors their perception of what exactly writing an essay means." It is "very hard to get them to think in any way but a thesis and three reasons." While Quick compliments students' ability to "write good five-paragraph essays," she is concerned about their inability to write any other way or to use writing to express critical thinking. I regret that I did not focus more on helping my students to make the connection between writing skills as tools to express their thoughts, values, and beliefs rather than on writing to pass the TAAS.

Russ Cluff, chair of the Language Department, also teaches language skills, French, and Spanish. His story tells how alignment entails more than just alignment of ExCET with course content. The Language Department is affected by the contradiction between the language course requirements for bilingual preparation and the ExCET exam requirements for bilingual certification. The requirements for a bachelor's degree in Spanish and those for bilingual education are much different, yet the same Spanish ExCET exam is required. Cluff questions the shallow Spanish-language requirement for bilingual education in terms of the actual job in the field, since bilingual teachers are working with Spanish-speaking children all day long. He points out that bilingual teachers need to be fluent, but less is required for preparation to teach bilingual education than to teach Spanish to English-speaking students.

Besides having to pass the Spanish ExCET, the teachers also have to pass the Texas Oral Proficiency Test (TOPT). Cluff explained that "the state administers it" in a face-to-face setting, where an expert "takes the person as far as he or she can go with an oral proficiency test." At the argumentation stage the student has "to defend some theory, take a stand on something," or "explain a system." Students with a degree in Spanish have no problem passing the TOPT; but bilingual education students, required to take only beginning language courses, have difficulty passing the oral test, a proficiency measurement standard for certification.

A final example of the impact of the ExCET on the departmental level is one shared by the Sociology, Chemistry, Physics, Economics, Psychology, and Computer Science Departments. These departments have only up to four students take the ExCET in a given year, yet they are expected to put time, energy, and resources into aligning their curriculum to the ExCET standards. This increases paperwork for the departments and raises the issue of how to meet the diverse needs of all the students. Since all these department are already aligned with professional content accrediting boards, they are faced with the dilemma of external regulations (ExCET requirements) for the few coming to bear on the whole. The impact of the ExCET at the university departmental level raises many questions about alignment and curriculum. These are questions that need to be engaged and explored by all stakeholders in education.

Conclusion

The ExCET has taken its toll on SFA departments as seen in the necessity of creating new courses, in additional paperwork, and in the external regulations that redefine course content. However, these are not the critical issues in the ExCET's effect on university departments. The real issue is the hidden impact of the ExCET curriculum on what the departments and their professional accrediting boards have deemed relevant for their students. The ExCET drives their pedagogy and learning into the background and presses accountability issues into the foreground for faculty and students alike. The professional knowledge that the state wants replaces the knowledge deemed relevant and necessary by scholars and practitioners.

Chapter 13

Raising the Bar: How Much Should Professionals Know to Become Certified by the State?

Sharon Spall

The State of Texas Testing Agency and the Test Development Service include groups of educational professionals in their discussions when identifying the standards that students must meet at the end of educational professional preparation programs. Periodically, the state testing agency determines that the score students must achieve on the exam should be higher and that the difficulty of the exam content should be increased. When such changes are made, the state testing agency and the test development service bring educational professionals together at the state capital. These professionals represent different ethnic and gender groups in Texas. There are representatives from the major stakeholder groups, such as public schools and higher education. These professionals work with the state agency and the test service to write the standards, which are then used as the basis for the development of test items. Then, after the standards have been developed and the first exams have been held, professionals meet to review data on student scores, the exam, the test items, and the current cut score (the score a student must make to pass the exam).

One such meeting to consider raising the cut score took place in 1997. The State Board for Educator Certification (SBEC), the state agency in charge of testing for educator certification, and the test development service called professionals from across the state to review standards for educational preparation programs. I, a university faculty member in teacher and administrator certification preparations programs, was the representative of our college of education in the review of the secondary teacher

Professional Development Examination for the Certification for Educators in Texas (ExCET). This must have been one of those discretionary times indicated on the inside cover of the preparation manuals: "The ExCET program is administered under the authority of the State Board for Educator Certification (SBEC); regulations and standards governing the program are subject to change at the discretion of the State Board for Educator Certification." In the preface, the SBEC authorities state that educators participate in the test development process: "The most critical element in the process is the involvement of Texas public school and university educators." When I participated in the process, the only direction I was given by my colleagues concerning my role in this review was that I would represent the secondary teacher certification program.

All of us stakeholders received nametags at the door, and we seated ourselves around the tables (just the right number of chairs) that were arranged in a U-shape with the speakers and overhead projectors at the front. The usual round-robin introductions proved attendees included experienced teachers from secondary schools, new teachers who had recently taken the ExCET, and representatives from universities including deans, heads of departments, administrative directors, and teaching faculty. All of us seemed to be in agreement that we wanted programs that developed well-prepared professionals and that were good for our students and our schools. There was little variation in our definitions of what constitutes good preparation.

Shortly after introductions, the presenters, the SBEC and the test service, announced that we were going to take the secondary Professional Development ExCET and then examine the cut scores for possible recommendations of change. The doors were closed and test booklets passed to each of us; for approximately two hours we completed and then self-graded the exam. I passed. As I worked through the exam, I tried to visualize how a person finishing college would answer questions at this reading level, and I tried to assess the overall difficulty of the content. Our experience of taking the exam was supposed to inform us about the content as well as the level of difficulty and, therefore, help us make an informed decision regarding the level of the cut score.

The exams and all paper used during the discussion of the exam were collected and shredded. Lunch arrived, and the presenters began to explain the statistical history of student achievement over the past few years. Scores were analyzed in relation to cultural groups: Caucasian, African American, Hispanic, and other. Then the presenters led group discussion to consider possible increases in the cut score, and all present were invited to voice opinions and feelings about the proposed increase.

Tension began to rise as one by one each of us commented first about increasing the score and then about the amount of the increase. The new, young, Caucasian teacher who had just taken the exam thought that the test was manageable and that any person who was prepared should be able to pass. She felt that people who were going to be teachers should know at least what was on the exam. She described her own experience taking the test and that she did well on the exam.

One experienced teacher had been teaching in Texas schools for over a decade and wanted to uphold a high standard for teachers in the state. She expressed the need for teachers entering the profession to be well-prepared for the many challenges in the classroom. Well-prepared teachers would join the ranks of the respected, well-qualified teachers. She mentioned that public respect for the educational profession depended upon the very best-prepared persons leaving the university and entering the schools.

Another experienced teacher narrowed her eyes, tilted her head back, and said, "I think the standard should be raised." Then she turned toward one of the deans of a college of education and added, "This would show that SBEC is serious about this testing business."

These comments caused me to reflect upon my experience in Texas schools in the early 1980s. As in many other states, the teaching force comprised primarily women, who provided a second source of income for the family and who valued the summer vacation months as times to spend with the family. At that time, there had been a struggle to improve the situation for educators who were heads of households by raising salaries and health benefits and also to improve the image of professional teachers and education in Texas. On recommendations from a committee appointed by the governor and headed by a prominent businessman, the price tag for the increased salaries and benefits had been standards, testing, and accountability for all levels of education. Summer months then became time a for professional development activities. Most educators in Texas view public schools and university preparation programs meeting standards as connected to views of individuals and interest groups outside of education on teachers, public schools, and teacher preparation programs. One experienced teacher expressed the need for universities to support the maintenance of a high level of respect and professionalism, which was developing from an accountability system of testing and ranking focused on the public schools. She had witnessed the increasing accountability demands that had been placed on the public schools by the state and wanted to maintain whatever gain in respect and professionalism that had been achieved.

Besides the academic testing of students, part of the early state accountability agenda was the testing of practicing teachers. By an act of the state legislature, certified teachers practicing in public schools could only remain certified upon passing a statewide exam. On the same day at the same time, all teachers in Texas lined up outside designated testing sites to be tested in order to remain in the classroom. Some teachers viewed the exam as a way to show critics of education that teachers were qualified to be in the classroom; others felt humiliated. As a public school teacher at that time, I was in one of those lines, and the experienced teachers at this meeting who were supporting higher standards for university preparation programs were also there.

The persons from higher education were quieter. One faculty member talked about maintaining and increasing the rigor in educational courses, which would be favorably recognized by the critics of education. She felt the standardized content, detailed in the proficiencies, demanded that faculty and departments examine course content, delivery, and student outcomes. She cautioned all of us, but especially her colleagues in higher education preparation programs, to remember that these were only minimum standards.

One by one we all made comments. The primary concern that emerged was the number of minority teachers in the schools. The African American, Hispanic, and other groups' scores tended to be lower than the Caucasian scores. Raising the score could impact the diversity of public school faculties across the state. I pictured my minority students who had passed the test and were successfully teaching in the classroom. Not all were top-scoring students. Would these students have achieved the proposed, higher cut score?

Others expressed concern that one type of test was used to evaluate all students. The use of a written test alone to identify even minimum capability for students about to enter the classroom as new teachers was questioned. We reflected on the context of the questions on the exam and questioned if all students would have the same opportunity to observe such ideal situations in student teaching or during internships.

I was concerned about raising the cut score because the increase could impact individual students as well as preparation programs. My recent experience preparing students for ExCET with practice tests and review sessions raised my sympathy level for the students who were trying to finish course work and perhaps trying to finish student teaching while trying to prepare for the exam. Failure on the exam could mean that after four years of teacher education an immediate teaching position would not be attainable. Faculty members in programs across the state were developing strategies to support students, and I wondered how much more pressure faculty and programs could handle.

I listened to all the comments and reviewed the test statistics that summarized student achievement on the ExCET. The reasons given by practicing educators and the test history were not enough for me to accept that now was the time to raise the cut score. Universities were developing teacher preparation programs that included more field experiences and more contact with practicing classroom educators. An increase in the cut score would come before such new programming was securely in place.

After all of us had commented on the proposal to increase the cut score, we sat in silence for a while. In general, the practicing teachers supported the increase, and the majority of the university representatives were against it. The group would not reach consensus today.

As I pushed away from the table and looked around the room, I recalled the note in the front of the preparation manual. The ExCET was developed *with* professional educators across Texas. I thought to myself: "The SBEC and the test development service brought us here to share the responsibility for raising the cut score. Consensus was the goal. However, the decision to raise the score was made before we arrived. Am I here to be used and manipulated by the testing agency and testing service? The participants in favor of an increased score do not seem to be concerned. There seems to be a preconceived notion of how high to raise the score, although the SBEC and the test development service are apparently willing to listen and negotiate. This time, however, consensus will not be achieved." A paper was passed around the room, and each of us signed and expressed our opinions on the increase. As I returned to my university, I rehearsed how I was going to explain to my concerned colleagues the increased score and my unsuccessful attempt to hold the "line."

There are still questions in my mind about the process of raising standards. What determines when it is time to raise the cut score? What determines when it is time to increase the difficulty level of the exam? How do the state testing agency and the test development service determine the method of increasing the difficulty? At this point, the final decisions appear to be made by the SBEC.

Chapter 14

Three Perspectives on the Racial Implications of the ExCET: Anglo, Hispanic, and African American

Donnya Stephens
Sharon Spall
Sandra Luna McCune

The current accountability movement in educator preparation programs in colleges and universities across the nation is having a dramatic effect on minority students with aspirations to enter the teaching profession. In particular, the State of Texas is being closely watched nationwide for its ambitious efforts to raise the standards of educator preparation programs. The Texas legislature has prescribed "(a) the criteria for entering the program, (b) the content and number of courses offered in the program, and (c) the evaluation of the product at the end of the program" (Hollis & Warner, 1995, p. 312). Since 1986, the state has required successful completion of tests that show competence in knowledge and skills for persons certified to teach in Texas. These tests are called the Examination for the Certification of Educators in Texas (ExCET). The overall goal is to improve the performance of all children in Texas schools. In order to achieve this goal, educator preparation programs must be held accountable for the quality of teachers entering classrooms.

Because the stakes are so high, Texas colleges and universities have instituted tougher standards for their educator preparation programs. These institutions have strengthened their programs by raising the requirements for admission to teacher education, implementing field-based programs, and aligning the curriculum to become more learner-centered. In theory, the tougher admission standards are viewed as a much-needed change, which will assure that we have students in our program capable of passing the ExCET. However, at our regional university, there is concern regarding the impact of the more rigorous policies and practices on the recruitment and retention of minority students in educator preparation. Also, a high level of concern continues to exist at this regional university because a higher percentage of minority students than Anglo students have had difficulty in passing the ExCET. Minority students' difficulty with the tests resulted in "Accredited-Under Review" status for the university.

In 1998, there were 19 educator preparation programs in Texas with the status of "Accredited-Under Review" (SBEC, 2000). Educator preparation programs within the State were required to secure targeted passing rates on the ExCETs. The 1998 targets were set at 70 percent for those taking the exam for the first time, or an 80 percent cumulative passing rate for each demographic group (Female, Male, White, African American, Hispanic, and Other) taking the exam, regardless of the number of times the test was taken. Beginning in 2002, the targets have been set at 75 percent and 85 percent, respectively. In the fourth year, if a program has not met the standards, the program can lose its accreditation to certify teachers. The "Accredited-Under Review" status of our university is caused by the low performance of African Americans on the ExCET. Our university was one of 10 universities who had maintained this status in Texas for two years. This meant that by August of 2000, we had to meet the standards or accept a monitor for the educator preparation programs on our campus for the coming year. This was a concern to the entire university community because the enrollment in educator preparation programs accounts for approximately 50 percent of the total student enrollment. The loss of the ability to certify teachers would have definitely affected the university adversely.

In this chapter, three professors in the College of Education at Stephen F. Austin State University (SFA) share their perspectives on the ExCET and dialogue about differences regarding the current and future impact of the examination.

Three Ethnic Perspectives

Dr. Sharon Spall Is Assistant Professor and Coordinator of the Doctoral Program in the Department of Secondary Education and Educational Leadership

I am a member of the ethnic group that is primarily responsible for the founding of the present educational program in this country, a group that can be characterized as White, Protestant, and Anglo-European. I am also a member of the ethnic group that usually performs higher, except for the Asian groups, in academic programs and on standardized exams. Presently, I teach in a preparation program for professional educators at a small Texas state university. In this position, other faculty and I prepare students to enter classrooms as teachers as well as prepare administrators for schools. Who I am and the profession I have chosen have given me cause to critically reflect upon my relationships with students in the classroom and with my colleagues. I have recently found more reasons to question the application of mandates for professional educator preparation programs from state educational agencies. My discomfort level and self-consciousness have risen as I have examined my personal and cultural contribution to the current academic and social problems.

My colleagues and I follow all the curriculum guidelines identified by the College of Education and the standards issued by the state educational agencies of Texas, which include the State Board for Educator Certification (SBEC), the state testing agency. These guidelines and standards form the basis of what must be taught in teacher and administrator preparation programs. My assignments have included teaching courses in both the secondary teaching preparation and the principal preparation curricula. Additionally, I have volunteered to conduct review sessions, written qualifying exams for the principal program, and tutored students who have failed an ExCET. When the faculty met to align the state proficiencies based on the standards to specific courses, I actively participated, and then wrote my share of syllabi for courses. The syllabi had to be written to demonstrate the integration of specific standards with content and supporting activities.

Ideally, this all seemed to make sense at first. The state proficiencies represent minimum standards that a professional educator should reach, and practicing Texas educators developed the standards as well as the proficiencies. Each course would include specific required material as indicated on the syllabus, and the total curriculum would include all the state requirements. The faculty member teaching each course would know what proficiencies to teach in any particular course, and the students in each course would be tested to determine to what degree the course content was learned. Such steps would ensure that students were prepared for the classroom. Universities could demonstrate that students were prepared, and faculty could demonstrate how and when the specific preparation occurred. At first, all this seemed logical and appropriate.

My discomfort began to grow as the effect of the standardized minimum proficiencies, standardized curriculum, standardized syllabus, and state standardized testing settled upon the College of Education, the faculty, and the students. Upon receiving the state testing rules and procedures, the College of Education began to plan meetings in order to meet the state testing requirements. The meetings began with the convocation that welcomed faculty back to campus after summer break. State testing and test results continued to dominate faculty meetings throughout the academic year. The focus always included a review of test results, a plan for review sessions for students before the state exam, and tutoring for students. As the test dates drew nearer, the conversation about state exams and student pass and fail rates became constant and seemed to overshadow all meetings as well as consume our energies. When the state exam scores were reported and our certification programs were listed as "Under Review," the stress level increased. A continued "Under Review" status could mean program monitoring by the state and then loss of certification programs. The pressure to improve state test scores passed from the state testing agency to college administrators and faculty members. Then the faculty passed the pressure on to the students.

The new syllabi, with state standards expressed in proficiencies, were part of the College of Education plan to prepare students for the state exam. When I received the syllabus prepared by a department colleague for my course, the state proficiencies were listed there, but the activities were also indicated. I felt my academic freedom slipping away. The syllabus provided consistency between faculty members, but little room for creative, teachable moments or alternative choices for appropriate activities within the tightly-structured course plan. Standardized content and delivery forces sameness on creative faculty and marginalizes pedagogy. The state can control the content and activities of each course and eventually trace low student achievement on the state exam back to individual faculty members.

The standardized, consistent application of requirements for all students assumes that all students, universities, and geographical regions are alike. This is not true. Students come from different high school backgrounds and cultural backgrounds, and if students are teachers preparing for principal certification, the experiences within the school district vary greatly in theory and practice. The standard proficiencies and the standardized syllabi do not accommodate the student who is outside the standard, such as the student from a poor inner city school and who speaks two languages. The student group is "standardized" by raising the requirements needed to enter teacher and principal preparation programs. There are remedial programs in many departments to help students meet requirements and meet program entry requirements. Consistent application of state standards in relation to curriculum, faculty, and students will certainly standardize preparation programs. Standards mean that one plan is in place for all preparation programs and all faculty, and that all students fit into one model, one state determined model.

As the state moved toward closer scrutiny of preparation programs, the state's testing service began to analyze the scores of different ethnic groups. Now preparation programs had to show minimum achievement levels among students in each ethnic group analyzed, or the program would be cited as "Under Review." In an effort to uphold a positive image for the educator preparation programs, the College of Education tried to explain the state analysis of the "Under Review" rating by ethnic group and noted to critics that "in reality" there was only one group in jeopardy. Only one group has low scores. Only one group is a problem. Again this information is passed on to all departments in the university, to the community, and to the faculty member, and then all students know.

I have listened as the exam scores are analyzed according to ethnic group, and I have wondered and still wonder: "What is the appropriate language to use when sharing testing information? How do I sensitively discuss our program issues with my colleagues who are members of other ethnic groups? What vocabulary do I use? Perhaps this analysis of scores by ethnic group should be reserved for curriculum development within the department and the faculty only." I have noticed that close examination of all the scores of all groups has revealed that no one ethnic groups, including the privileged White group, is consistently excelling with scores in the 90s on the state exam.

I have never discussed the passing rates of different ethnic groups in my classes, but some faculty members have. The students know the exams results by group. Now I wonder how my students view each other, themselves, and me. I suspect that some students who are in the lower scoring group feel double pressure and think that there is little reason to persist because the barriers between them and success are high and uncontrollable. I suspect that the groups with higher scores acquire a false sense of security and superiority.

The application of the state standards has caused me personal and professional anxiety, which I previously referred to as discomfort. This discomfort centers on two issues: increased state control of the curriculum, which eventually controls me in my classroom; and the impact of testing and reporting of the test scores on and among ethnic groups.

Dr. Sandra L. McCune Is Professor and Coordinator of Graduate Programs in the Department of Elementary Education

Viewing it from the viewpoint of a Hispanic faculty member, the ExCET experience at SFA appears to be non-menacing for Hispanics. This small subgroup of the preservice population at the university seems to be confident in its ability to perform satisfactorily on the ExCET tests. I do not get any sense of their feeling somehow less "less educated, less educable, less worthy" than their Anglo counterparts, and I have not heard any prejudice against them voiced by their Anglo peers. This may be due, in part, to there being so few Hispanics at SFA. Overall, they comprise only about 5 percent of the university student body and represent approximately 4 percent of the ExCET test takers in the College of Education. For instance, out of the 1,006 test takers in the period from September 1, 1999, to February 12, 2000, only 42 identified themselves as Hispanic. The Hispanic preservice teachers are so few in number that they seem to go unnoticed as a separate group by their Anglo and African American classmates. Furthermore, they seldom congregate together but rather form relationships, independent of culture, with Anglo and African American students.

The Hispanic students I have worked with give me the impression that they believe they will perform as well as or better than other groups taking the tests. For the most part, this has been the case at SFA. According to Randy McDonald (personal communication, January 25, 2000), whose dissertation study examined the Professional Development ExCET scores of students at SFA, the average scores of Hispanic test takers and those of Anglo test takers are not significantly different. In other words, the Hispanic students are holding their own in the Professional Development test. Only once in recent reports has there been an indication that this subgroup might not be doing as well on the ExCET as the SBEC requires, but the subsequent test results indicated otherwise. Their performance on the test demonstrates that most of the Hispanic students have acquired the knowledge and skills the tests are designed to assess.

I am reminded of the Hispanic students I worked with at the University of Texas-Pan American four years ago. I was invited to present an ExCET workshop there and found the students to be very upbeat about their potential for success. Despite the obvious language problem that the ExCETs present, my sense that was the students felt if they studied and worked hard, they would pass. Apparently, this attitude persists there because UT-Pan American has never been on the SBEC "Under Review" list.

As for myself personally, I have not experienced any ExCET-induced untoward behavior from my colleagues. I feel we are all aware that we need to work together to help all our students achieve success on the tests. Casting blame or pointing fingers will only militate against that goal.

Dr. Donnya Stephens Is Professor and Coordinator of Secondary Programs in the Department of Secondary Education and Educational Leadership

The critical lens through which I reflect on the implication of the ExCETs is that of a female African American professor with 23 years of experience in educator preparation programs at this regional university. During my years at this university, my colleagues and I have been able to applaud our efforts to design and implement a quality educator preparation program. SFA is one of only five universities nationwide to receive the Christa McAuliffe Award for education and one of the first seven universities in the state to receive a state grant to set up a professional development school, so our educator preparation program has served as a model for other programs in the State. The University has mentored for other universities in the state, and our graduates are recruited by school districts statewide. Currently, our preparation program is accredited by the National Council for the Accreditation of Teacher Education (NCATE) but has received a status of "Accredited-Under Review" from the state, a result of African American performance failing to meet SBEC-set percentage standards. The "Under-Review" designation has sent shock waves through the university.

I have seen the climate on this campus change from one that embraces its educator preparation program to one that appears to be puzzled about why we are unable to solve the problem. Although this is actually a university-wide problem in that secondary students must also pass subject-specific examinations for the ExCET, many in the academic community view the "Accredited-Under Review" status as a College of Education problem. Policies and practices that are being implemented to solve the problem have received mixed reviews from the university community and the public. At a time when the stakes are so high, some view the changes in policies which support more rigorous admission and testing criteria as an assurance that African Americans in the educator preparation program will be capable of passing the ExCET, while others view the changes in policies as barriers to increasing the diversity of the teaching force.

I am greatly concerned because I feel that somewhere in the policy and practice debate, we must consider the impact of attaining an accredited status by more rigorous screening of the diversity of the teaching forces. At this point, I feel that we must move beyond the argument of tests as culturally biased as an explanation for lower test scores and focus on what we can do to help to solve the problem, because the testing of teacher candidates is a lucrative business, and it is here to stay. However, there are others in the African American community who feel that the standards movement, particularly the ExCET, is an intentional effort to limit the number of African Americans entering the teaching profession.

African Americans in educator preparation programs are being adversely affected by the university's status as "Accredited-Under Review." Those African American students who are capable of passing the ExCET, as well as those having difficulty passing, are experiencing negative stereotyping from the university community. On this campus, African Americans are referred to, interestingly enough, as one of our "subgroups."

The stories of African Americans' experiences include both stories of those who are puzzled because they have made good grades and have passed the ExCET yet they are referred to as members of the "subgroup," and stories of those who have made good grades and yet are having difficulty passing the ExCET. Many of them share the negative experiences they have had with peers in their classes as well as with professors across campus.

In 1996, a colleague and I set out to investigate the attitudes of African American students preparing to take the ExCET. We interviewed 5 of the 10 students preparing to take the ExCET during that time. The general theme in most of their responses was that most felt that they would perform well because they had made good grades in their course work at the university, and they had not had problems with standardized tests in the past. A follow-up study of those students' performances showed that they did indeed perform well on the ExCET. However, in the next testing period in 1996, the low performance of African Americans again became an issue for the university as the overall passing rate was below 70 percent. I have found that African American students are perplexed, in large part, because they are having difficulty understanding why they are successful in their classes but are not able to pass the ExCET. Many of them continue to try to complete their educator preparation program while others choose to graduate with a non-teaching degree.

One Saturday morning this semester was particularly memorable. I administered the ExCET qualifying examination to 24 post-baccalaureate initial certification (PBIC) students. Seven of these students were African Americans with whom I have had several conversations during the year. All seven students found themselves in a situation where they had to take and pass the ExCET or not have their contracts teaching renewed for the coming year.

Repeatedly, as I sat and held conferences with students to share the results of their performance, I felt their anguish when I had to deliver the bad news that they were unsuccessful on the qualifying examination, which is required before a student can register for an official ExCET. The pain I heard in their voices and the tears in their eyes sent me into emotional overload. All I could do was to inform them of the services offered by the university and offer to tutor them myself. Personnel director after personnel director and principal after principal call me daily to see what can be done to assist these and other teachers like them, in passing the ExCET—because these individuals are good teachers, and the school districts want to keep them. However, recently approved ExCET policies at the university state that you must pass a qualifying examination with a score of 80 or above to qualify to take the corresponding ExCET. This scenario I have described is played out after each qualifying examination.

On a personal level, I participated in a staff development activity for College of Education faculty that focused on diversity. Specifically, in multidisciplinary teams, we were asked to examine our concerns regarding diversity on campus in the context of the performance of the African American students on the ExCET, brainstorm solutions, and recommend additional staff development activities. I expressed my concern regarding the increased unwillingness of some Anglo students to dialogue about issues of diversity in my professional development classes. I explained that a response that I get repeatedly is "We are all American. Why do we have to spend time talking about differences in learning styles, expectations, language, interaction patterns?" Another member of the team said she was concerned about the African American, Hispanics, and Anglo students' segregated seating patterns in her classes. From this point on, the dialogue followed a pattern of internationalizing the problem, focusing on experiences with Japanese from Japan, Italians from Italy, Mexicans from Mexico, the hearing impaired, the gifted, and so on. The longer we talked, the farther removed we became from our original task. This dialogue is all too common. When discussing the issue of African American performance, there is concern regarding political correctness. According to Wiggins and Follo (1999), "Unless members of the mainstream culture come to understand their own place in the political, economic, and sociological mix, they have little hope of understanding the worldview of anyone from another culture" (p. 103).

African American students' experiences in predominately White colleges and universities cannot be fully understood without taking into consideration the characteristics of these colleges along with the academic and social background of the students themselves. According to Heath (1998), when there is a mismatch between the cultural experiences of African Americans and the culture of the campus, this mismatch has proven to be detrimental to students because one of the outcomes is low self-concept.

Arguments regarding the reasons African Americans do not perform as well as their Anglo counterparts vary. Some educators embrace the position of Cooper (1986) on the issue, which is that we must help students perceive themselves as capable of passing the tests, while others view the problem as one of the teacher preparation programs. Yet other perspectives, like that of Holmes (1986), view the poor performance as attributable to a lack of language skills which, in turn, causes problems with the acquisition of analytical and interpretative skills.

Dialogue from Three Perspectives

Why Does the ExCET Exist?

Donnya: The ExCET is part of the overall accountability system for educator preparation programs in the State of Texas. If we are going to require public schools to be sure that their students possess the knowledge and skills to pass an examination to graduate from high school, then we must be able to provide school districts with competent teachers and school leaders.

Sharon: About the test, some want the ExCET to assure schools that we are sending people who are quality educators to teach their children and quality administrators who are capable of leading their schools. Out of all the universities, we found that teacher preparation programs are just programs; no one gets out and leads. Faculty members know that their students will be tested on the competencies, which determine their minimum skills.

Sandra: I know from my experiences working with students over the past few years, even if they are having difficulty passing the ExCET, that most of them will become very good teachers.

Donnya: There should be a correlation between a teacher education candidate's ability to pass the ExCET and his/her performance in the classroom. I have worked with many students in our initial certification program who have received rave reviews from their school leaders and mentor teachers. However, when I visit campuses across the East Texas area, the students share with me that the ExCET is about ideal classroom practices in ideal school settings that don't seem to exist.

Sharon: People who come to our program finish our program and go back to the public schools. Students say that the public schools are really not learner-centered, and that is what the competencies are based on. And when the students sit down with a paper and pencil test, they have no experiences on which to draw, except what we give them in the classroom. Their experiences in the field have been different. So, when they take the test and try to draw from their field experience, they don't have the learner-centered model because the things they are encountering in their high school, in their field school, are not what we taught them and are not what's tested.

Sandra: It's difficult for students to answer questions that assume they have unlimited money and unlimited resources when in their own personal background, when they were going through public school themselves, they never got unlimited resources or unlimited funds. Naturally, they will have difficulty with ExCET Land—the ideal classroom and ideal school of the ExCET.

Donnya: I am deeply concerned about the low performance of African Americans on the ExCET. In working with them on preparing for the ExCET, I have found that many of them who have been unsuccessful approached the ExCET based on their experiences and practices in their schools. Those who are employed in schools that are learner-centered usually performed better than those employed in schools that do not embrace a learner-centered philosophy.

Sharon: Those students have to take the ExCET after we have worked with them in our classroom. What we need to do is to find the very best classrooms for them in our public schools for their field experience. Often, this is not possible. Of even more concern is that we have no control over them once they leave. What they are encountering on the ExCET is not what they find in the classroom.

Donnya: We have absolutely no control over where they are placed during the student teaching experience. The placements are made by the school districts. Frequently, we are responsible for helping them to develop a learner-centered mind-set before we can assist them in preparing for the ExCET.

Sharon: At one time, I thought that, to be successful on that test, students needed to know more about kids, and students needed to know more about how to work with colleagues, but I was wrong. If we want students to respond well on that test according to the way we taught them in our classes, then I think students probably need to take the ExCET before going into school districts.

Donnya: I agree with you, Sharon. I find it very challenging to provide assistance for students on the ExCET after they have experienced student teaching or a year of internship.

Sandra: Another issue is that there are questions on the ExCET about students with special needs who are in the regular classroom. For instance, they have to answer questions about English as a Second Language (ESL) students in self-contained classrooms. So they have to answer questions about situations that we have not taught them about in their classes. They're not seeing in their experiences anything that can help them answer. I don't think the internship or student teaching really helps prepare them for the ExCET. Sometimes what they learn in their internship classes and student teaching is what they shouldn't do.

Donnya: Let's focus on the current impact of the ExCET.

Sandra: It creates anxiety and frustration in our students and in the parents. We get a lot of parents calling, and they're very upset because their son or daughter is unable to pass the qualifying examination and therefore is not being permitted to take an ExCET. It's just gotten so out of hand.

Sharon: Now that we have established the policies for the ExCET we're going to do our best to carry them out. However, if a policy doesn't work, then we ought to be open to altering the policy. Remember sometimes, students are caught in the middle. For the first time since I've been at the university, parents are stepping forward with our students and talking to us as professors, whereas before we just talked with the students. When you think about students attending a minimum of four years of college and then getting to the end of their program, and they can't get certified to go out and teach, you can understand why the parents get so upset.

Donnya: I cannot tell you how many parents I've talked with this academic year regarding permission to take the ExCET and/or the performance of their son or daughter on the ExCET.

Sharon: I'm concerned that too many students, African American, Caucasian, Hispanic, think that education doesn't pay enough. So they major in business or they major in other fields. We also keep losing our best students who might do well, because they haven't had a realistic view of what might happen to them at the end of the education program, and they say, "Well, what else can I do?" They sometimes go on to another field. And I think that, for our public schools, that's sad.

Donnya: The last time I gave a qualifying exam was during contract time in public schools, and it was also the final year for some PBIC and alternative certification students to become certified. Several of these beginning teachers were in danger of not having their contracts renewed because they could not pass the qualifying examination so that they could take the official ExCET.

Sharon: I also see that there's an impact on the faculty. We spend so much of our time on tutoring, not that I don't want to tutor or don't want to help students, but the time that is taken to integrate the state standards into our curriculum and into our classroom and then support students has been tremendous. We have to give a review session; we have to give a qualifying exam Form A. If they don't pass, then we tutor them and give them a qualifying exam Form B. If they pass, then they can take the state test. Those qualifying exams had to be written and each of them is 100 questions long, and I can tell you from personal experience that implementing this process has been very costly. The time we spend with each other planning, the time we spend advising the students in addition to the tutoring part, the time we spend preparing for our classes, writing the exams, writing the syllabi, and aligning the competencies is indeed time consuming. The initial implementation of all these state standards has been costly.

Sandra: The last time we gave a qualifying exam, the students were so discouraged. They talked about how they were feeling and how frustrated they were about what has happened. I don't see that we will change our policies to be less stringent. I know that new standards are being developed, but that will affect mostly the content of our qualifying examination and probably not impact our policies significantly.

Sharon: The state will increase the difficulty of the content and increase the cut score that students must make to pass; the difficulties will increase on two levels.

Donnya: I'm concerned that we have not found the answer to how we can help our students, who find the ExCET challenging, to be successful. Overall, we have a very good pass rate. If predominately African American universities can be successful in getting the necessary percentage of their students to pass the ExCET, then we should be able to do likewise. Also, here we are, an NCATE accredited university with a highly rated educator preparation program, and many of our African American students are not meeting the state standards on the ExCET. Something is wrong with this picture.

Sharon: And if we look at our largest group, the Anglos, this group is not making really high scores on the test.

Sandra: The average score is about mid-seventies for our university, which isn't a lot to brag about at all.

Sharon: All I am saying is that we need to find the answer.

Donnya: One positive result of the circumstances we find ourselves in is that because of the "Accredited-Under Review" status, there is more collaboration campus-wide. We have been able to collaborate with academic departments and other service departments in a meaningful way to work toward solving the problem. Also, the leadership team of the College of Education has a common focus with regard to implementing strategies to help all our students be successful.

Sandra: A negative aspect is that once your image has been tarnished, even after you correct the problem, it's not recognized. It's still going to have that tarnish on it. I actually had a student ask me yesterday if I thought that she would be harmed if she stayed on at SFA for student teaching? I said, first of all, the student teaching is still part of the program, and it is best that she complete the program she started here. In the past, students have been proud to have their teacher preparation at SFA because our graduates are recognized statewide as quality candidates. These types of questions will continue to come up, and we have to be prepared to respond.

Donnya: I get similar questions from students. I was asked yesterday on the phone, "Will my degree be any good if I graduate from SFA?" The student went on to say "that knowing that I have a degree and I'm certified through Stephen F. Austin won't mean anything if I lose my current job." She apparently thought that she could lose her job because she went to school here, so it *is* becoming an issue. The fact that we have so many students in teacher education at SFA makes our image very important.

Donnya: Let's move on to the future impact of the ExCET.

Sandra: I think the future will bring higher admission standards to our educator preparation programs, which I think can be detrimental in the long run. I think that's going to impact our ability to recruit teachers.

Sharon: What about those minority students who come to the university prepared to pursue teacher certification and have the ability to do so, but because there are so few minorities in the education program and because their classmates are pursuing other programs, these students drop teacher education, too. They have heard how difficult things can be for minorities, so they wonder if that is going to happen to them. These very capable students probably will end up dropping teacher certification from their program because they do not want the hassle.

Donnya: As a result of the experiences we have had for the past three years, I see our "Accredited-Under Review status" impacting our ability to recruit both quality faculty and quality students. I see the university becoming more open to putting more resources into recruiting faculty for educator preparation programs as well as recruiting the best and the brightest students into our educator preparation programs, but it may be to no avail.

Sharon: The results could possibly result in the university tracing the competencies and proficiencies on the exam back to the courses and professors who taught those courses. Some of that is happening now in some programs at the university. This could definitely have a negative impact. On top of that, I see the state expanding the current policies and regulations more extensively.

Donnya: I do not feel that the impact of the current accountability system on educator preparation programs has caught state officials by surprise. Surely, the "powers that be" could have anticipated the negative impact on minority teacher candidates that has occurred. Nevertheless, the mood of the country is embracing the accountability movement in education in the name of a better quality workforce so that the country can be more competitive globally. I am deeply troubled about the price that will be paid for pushing this highly political agenda.

Sharon: Over time, we can see more and more and more control of education at the state level, and in reality, I feel that it will continue to increase.

Donnya: We must continue our efforts to meet the challenges that state standards have imposed upon us because apparently the standards are here to stay.

Conclusion

Our perspectives on the impact of the ExCET on educator preparation programs at this regional university have focused primarily on the impact on students in programs on our campus. Although we embrace standards, our major concern is that at a time when schools are becoming more diverse, the teaching force continues to become less diverse. We feel that the collective voices of the higher and public school education communities should be more involved in the dialogue regarding standards for educator preparation programs before our legislators vote recommendations into law. Also, we are concerned that on one hand, the State Board for Educator Certification rewards universities (and other educator preparation entities) whose educator preparation programs increase in ethnic diversity, yet it penalizes institutions whose pass rate on the ExCET falls below the state standards for accreditation. In the academic year 2003–2004, new standards for the ExCET will go into effect (Porter, 2000). Where are our collective voices regarding what we have done already in educator preparation programs to improve the quality of programs? We should be ever vigilant that opportunities are provided to all students and, particularly, that minority candidates are not inappropriately screened out from teaching.

References

AACTE/TESC (1986). *Changing course: Teacher education reform at state colleges and universities.* Washington, DC: American Association of State Colleges and Universities.

Collins, R. L. (1995). Teacher testing and the African American teacher. In S.W. Soled (Ed.), *Assessment,testing and evaluation in teacher education* (pp. 221–253). Norwood, NJ: Ablex Publishing Corporation.

Cooper, C. C. (1986). Strategies to assure certification and retention of black teachers. *Journal of Negro Education, 55* (1), 46–55.

Dometrius, M. C. & Sigelman, L. (1988). The cost of quality: Teacher testing and racial-ethnic representativensss in public education. *Social Science Quarterly, 69* (1), 70–82.

Heath, T. M. (1998). African American students and self-concept development: Integrating cultural influences into research and practice. In K. Freeman (Ed.), *African American culture and heritage in higher education research and practice.* Westport, CT: Praeger.

Hollis, L. Y., & Warner, A. R. (1996). Who should control the profession: Policy implication of assessment in teacher education. . In S. W. Soled (Ed.), *Assessment, testing and evaluation in teacher education.* Norwood, NJ: Ablex Publishing Corporation.

Holmes, B. (1986). Do not buy the conventional wisdom: Minority teachers can pass the tests. *Journal of Negro Education, 55* (3), 335–346.

Porter (2000, March 30). Minutes of TACTE/TADLAS/SBEC Conference on Certification Implementation, Omni Hotel, Austin, TX.

Smith, G. A. (1984). The critical issues of excellence and equity in competency testing. *Journal of Teacher Education, 35* (2), 6–9.

State Board for Educator Certification (2000). Programs rated "Accredited Under Review" [On-line]. Obtained February 28, 2000. Available: www.sbec.state.tx.us/edprep/accredur.pdf

Soled, S. W. (Ed.) (1995). *Assessment, testing, and evaluation in teacher education.* Norwood, NJ: Ablex Publishing Corporation.

Wiggins, R. A., & Follo, E. J. (1999). Development of knowledge, attitudes, and commitment to teach diverse student population. *Journal of Teacher Education, 50* (2), 94–105.

Chapter 15

When the Threat Hits the Fan

Fay Hicks-Townes

College enrollment of African Americans in the nation has increased nearly 34 percent between 1976 and 1996 (*Chronicle of Higher Education, Almanac*, 1998). Enrollment in college is an indication that these African American students have identified with school (Steele, 1997). They have responded to the institution of schooling with acceptance. According to Bennett deMarrais and LeCompte (1999), this "[a]cceptance involves internalization of the school's promise that academic success and educational longevity will pay off. Along with acceptance, these students, African American college students in this instance, have overcome societal influences that could negatively affect their identification with schooling, such as patterns of discrimination based on economic status and ethnocentrism. A continuation of acceptance and identification for these students is not, however, guaranteed.

The national move/trend toward more accountability for academic performance in higher education (academic performance as defined by scores on standardized tests) has made standardized test scores a do or die issue for many colleges of education in this country. It has also placed in jeopardy Black college students' acceptance of and identification with schooling. Emphasizing standardized test scores has placed a particular burden on minority students who have historically scored lower on standardized tests than their White counterparts. An additional burden for minority students is, as reported by the *Daily Sentinel* (Solis), the publication of ". . . passing rates by students in specific categories—male, female, black, Hispanic, white and other."

Stereotype Threat

"A stereotype is a one-sided, exaggerated and normally prejudicial view of a group, tribe or class of people, and is usually associated with racism and sexism" (Abercrombie, Hill, & Turner, 1988). Stereotype threat ". . . is the social-psychological threat that arises when one is in a situation or doing something for which a negative stereotype about one's group applies" (Steele, 1997). Rather than focusing on why group members may be affected by societal stereotypes, stereotype threat applies to persons who have already overcome societal limitations. These persons have overcome "inadequate resources, few role models, preparational disadvantages," low expectations, and other barriers to achievement (Steele, 1997). They have identified with the domain of school. They are college students, in this instance, Black college students who have a relational involvement with schooling. Having come face to face with a negative stereotype of their group, they risk "confirming that stereotype" for themselves and their group (Steele & Aronson, 1998). Publication of group test scores, therefore, can set the stage for stereotype threat.

Setting the Stage

In 1998, the State of Texas published the results of its Accountability System for Educator Preparation. In this first ranking, 35 out of 85 programs did not meet standards. Stephen F. Austin State University (SFA) was one of the 35 which did not meet standards based on scores from the Examination for the Certification of Educators in Texas (ExCET). As a result, the Texas State Board for Educator Certification placed SFA on Accredited-Under Review status. The local newspaper quoted university officials who stated "If only four more students in the sub-group had passed the test they too would have met the qualifications," and concerning Black students, "We found that those students weren't considering the test seriously enough" (Solis, 1998, p. 1A). The university paper reported that SFA "fell below the 70 percent standard in two demographic categories: African American and Hispanic. It fell below the 80 percent standard in only the African American category" (Burke, 1998, p. 1A).

Carolyn and Jessica (pseudonyms) were two Black female students at SFA. When the news of the university's Accredited-Under Review status hit the news, they were in their senior year completing their requirements for the teacher education program.

According to Steele (1997), stereotype threat occurs when a negative stereotype about a group you belong to becomes self-relevant. In this instance, the participants, Carolyn and Jessica, encountered a negative stereotype that affected them. The university they attended and the program they were students in had been rated as "Accredited-Under Review" by the State Board for Educator Certification. To further complicate matters, African Americans' scores were the reason. Additionally, SFA has a majority White student body and faculty. According to Steele (1997) "settings that integrate Blacks and Whites are particularly anxiety arousing." A situational contingency exists where Jessica and Carolyn face, according to Steele (1997), "the possibility of conforming to the stereotype or of being treated and judged in terms of it." The following chronicles their negotiation process through this experience of stereotype threat.

Initial Reactions

It's Our Fault!

Carolyn and Jessica expressed feelings of blame after hearing about and reading news reports of the university's status. According to Carolyn:

> Yes. I heard one report about the university losing its accreditation for teachers exclusively because of African American scores on the ExCET exam. I didn't try to read much about it or listen to it because I was tired of hearing it all around campus and then when they interviewed students on campus, they were just like, well, I did well on my ExCET and I don't know why they're doing so poorly on theirs. And, uh, it's just like, you know, we wouldn't be in trouble if the African American, you know, scores were higher. And we just kept hearing that over and over again.

Jessica echoed those sentiments:

> But . . . in the paper and everything it seemed like they were trying to throw the blame. And I heard Dr. Beaker and someone else say two, if two more would have passed. You know if two or three more would have passed. More, more what? More what? Wouldn't ever say more what. But if they would have passed, then we wouldn't have, we wouldn't have this. But, we, they just didn't. And I didn't say anything.

Burdens

Feelings of increased responsibility plagued both young women. This responsibility went beyond their individual selves. They felt responsibility for SFA and for their group. According to Carolyn:

> When I heard the news report, I felt like it was my, you know, obligation to pull us through. Us is African Americans. I felt like it was my duty that they say okay, she made it . . . . And I felt like, so much pressure and it's just like, you know if, if you fail, then it's just like, hey, your school just loses their accreditation because you

failed. You were in a position to bail us out and be a hero or heroine and, you
know, you failed us. And all this is being placed on minority students.

Jessica also talked about the additional responsibility she felt:

I felt like I took the weight on my shoulders when it was time for me to take the
ExCET test because I had double pressure. I had the pressure of the actual test
and I had the pressure of also being Black. And we, or my little part in it, I felt
then, we could lose, you know, it was so much that the Blacks, you know, if the
minority fails we're going to lose our accreditation, is basically what it's saying. So
we need you minorities to pass the test. So we won't lose it. So it's like you had
that on your shoulders. And that's about how I felt about it even when I went to
take the test. It wasn't just that, you know, you take the test. It was you have to
take it and pass it because you're a minority. You have to pass because you're a
minority.

Is It True? Self-Doubt

Soon after SFA's ratings were made public, Jessica and Carolyn took a
practice test for the ExCET in one of their education classes. After receiving scores below passing, their academic/school identification was further threatened. Carolyn related her feelings:

When I got that first practice test I was really, really discouraged. And I was, like,
what am I gonna do? Now I'm in here. They told me I was gonna fail and I failed
it. . . . But I know that when I finally . . . got the scores back from the practice test,
you know, I was really discouraged because I felt like, you know, they're right. I
can't pass it. You know I can't do this.

Carolyn had been concerned about internalizing the negative stereotypes
she was hearing. She explained:

I didn't feel like, you know, cause I, I didn't wanna keep hearing it and have it
embedded in my mind that going in there, that it didn't matter just because I was
a minority student, that you know I was gonna fail. Cause I kept hearing this. And
even though you may try not to believe it, and you try to be stronger than that, if
you keep hearing that you're no good or that you're always gonna fail, eventually
some of that starts to soak in.

Jessica had a similar reaction:

Definitely. I thought it was going to indicate what I would do on the test. I was
very discouraged. I began praying.

Singled Out

After the practice tests, Carolyn and Jessica were involved in university-
sponsored ExCET test preparation. During this time they experienced
feelings of being singled out.

According to Carolyn:

> It's like I said, it's singling out, you know, groups. We are all part of the university. We all have to take the same test. We all have to pay the same money and go through the same courses. You know we're in this together.

Jessica also felt as if she were in the spotlight:

> Because they had to have so many meetings trying to get us all prepared. Seem like they were inviting us all, but I sometimes felt like, you know, picking out the minority faces in the audience, like, okay, we need you to pass because our scores are low and if you don't pass we'll lose our accreditation.

Jessica and Carolyn felt set apart, separated from the general population of students. Steele (1997) contends that

> Negative-ability stereotypes raise the threat that one does not belong in the domain. They cast doubt on the extent of one's abilities, on how well one will be accepted, on one's social compatibility with the domain, and so on. (p. 625)

Redemption: Hope Restored

Before the semester ended, Carolyn and Jessica took another practice test for the ExCET. This time they received passing scores. The effect on both young women was positive. Carolyn recalled her feelings:

> Relieved. I felt very relieved and confident. And I was just like I can do this. I paid attention. I went back to my psych professor and I hugged him and I said I did it, I did it. You said I could do it and I did it. And I was like all that preparation, cause then it was just kind of, like, it was hey we can do this and I did prepare and I did. I felt so much better. I felt confident. I was just like, okay, it's gonna be okay. You know and the university is not gonna fall just because of my score . . . . I was just, like, I can do this. I passed the practice test. I've prepared for it. I've done what I needed to do.

Jessica also felt increased confidence. She said:

> But after I took, after I took that practice test and passed, I said I'm not going to have any problem. I'm just going to use process of elimination, use my common sense, what little I have and take this test and, you know, be done with it.

Jessica and Carolyn had reaffirmed that they belonged in the academic/ school domain.

No Time to Rest

Jessica and Carolyn continued to prepare for the ExCET exam. Although passing scores on the practice ExCET test had bolstered their confidence, they continued preparation for the "real" ExCET. Carolyn was very methodical and expansive in her approach. She stated:

> I went out and bought the 234-page manual. I completed the diagnostic as well as the practice test. I made note cards, vocabulary words. I had someone study with me. I talked to professors. I went on the Internet looking for information. Not only for my professional development but also for my subject areas. I went to the ExCET review sessions. I talked to other students who had passed it, those who had failed it.

Carolyn and Jessica also talked about thinking differently: thinking White. Carolyn said she realized that she and her White classmates "answer questions a little bit differently." Jessica felt there was a difference in the way Whites and Blacks responded to questions on the ExCET. She said:

> I've had friends that have told me that you have to think in the mind-set of a White male. You can't think like, being a Black person, well, I'm going to choose this answer because this one sounds better. But it seems like I was having to switch over to think, well, if I were White and I were taking this test, what would I choose?

Not Just for Me

Although Jessica and Carolyn were successful in passing the ExCET that spring, they weren't just happy for themselves. They believed that they had also helped their group, African American students. Jessica explains:

> And you know they really needed us to pass, you know. I kept thinking that, you know, because I didn't, it didn't feel like I was taking that test for me. I wanted to help others. Because somebody else has to come through. Somebody, you know, somebody has to start so that they will be able to. I can't, I'm not a selfish person. I always want to help everybody out. And I guess it helped me but I'm thinking it also helped someone else behind me; that has to come up.

Carolyn echoes those feelings:

> When I heard the news report I felt like it was my, you know, obligation to pull us through. Us is African Americans. I felt like it was my duty that they say, okay, she made it. And that's the way, you know, I looked at it when I talked to mostly African American students who have already taken the ExCET. I was just like, you pass it? It was like yea. Well she passed; I know I can pass. You know, or he passed; I know I can pass.

Feeling this group responsibility/obligation is characteristic of African American culture. According to Collins (1991),

Educated Black women traditionally were brought up to see their education as something gained not just for their own development but for the purpose of race uplift. . . . More recently that belief has come through the struggle to secure our own education . . . in what was formerly called race uplift but what is now called Black community development. (pp. 149–150)

Commentary

Initial reactions and responses by SFA officials to minority ExCET scores that led to an Accredited-Under Review status for the university were viewed as placing blame, increasing burdens, and singling out by Carolyn and Jessica. Unwittingly, perhaps, SFA pushed these students from a position of domain belongingness to a position of questioning their fit in education. As postsecondary education moves toward a more multicultural student population, different perspectives must be considered in policy design, instructional strategies, and policy implementation if all of the student body is to be served. To do less keeps many students, particularly students of color, in the margins of educational institutions. "To be in the margin is to be part of the whole but outside the main body" (hooks, 1984, p. ix). Using this definition to describe her life as a Black American living in a segregated town, hooks (1984) explains:

> We could enter that world but we could not live there. We always had to return to the margin, to cross the tracks, to shacks and abandoned houses on the edge of town. . . . Living as we did—on the edge—we developed a particular way of seeing reality. We looked from both the inside and the out. We focused our attention on the center as well as the margin. We understood both. (p. ix)

In a school setting, this marginality takes on a slightly different tone. Sinclair and Ghory (1987) define being marginal as "to experience a strained, difficult relationship with educational conditions that have been organized to promote learning" (p. 13). Jessica and Carolyn's relationship with SFA was strained as a result of stereotype threat relating to group ExCET scores and the accompanying responses of university officials.

SFA would do well to learn from the experience of hooks (1984) and look from "both the inside and the out" and focus attention "on the center as well as the margin" before a crisis occurs. Guinier, Fine, and Balin (1997) offer the following from their study of women in law school:

> The most important lesson we learned . . . is that we must listen to the voices of those whose experience is both marginal and central to our understanding. . . . If

we are committed to becoming a society that values inclusive decision making and genuine opportunity, the kind of we-all-can-win-something-together society to which President Clinton referred, we must learn that bringing new perspectives, especially from those who have been underrepresented, is not only fair, it is functional. (p. 4)

I suggest that even when stereotype threat hits the fan, a thoughtful and informed university response can help reduce rather than compound the potentially harmful effects.

References

Abercrombie, N., Hill, S. & Turner, B. S. (Eds.) (1988). *Dictionary of sociology* (2nd ed.). London: Penguin Books.

Burke, T. (1998, September 10). Rating of educational program 'no cause for alarm' says dean. *The Pine Log,* 1A.

The Chronicle of Higher Education. (1998). *The 1998–99 Almanac.*

Collins, P. H. (1991). *Black feminist thought: Knowledge, consciousness, and the politics of empowerment.* New York: Routledge.

deMarrais, K. B. , & LeCompte, M. D. (1999). *The way schools work: A sociological analysis of education.* New York: Longman.

Guinier, L., Fine, M., & Balin, J. (1997). *Becoming gentlemen: Women, law school and institutional change.* Boston: Beacon Press.

hooks, bell. (1984). *Feminist theory: From margin to center.* Boston: South End Press.

Sinclair, R. L. & Ghory, W. J. (1987). *Reaching marginal students: a primary concern for school renewal.* Berkley, CA: McCutchan Publishing Corporation.

Solis, T. (1998, September 2). Teacher preparation program at SFA not up to state standards. *The Daily Sentinel,* pp. 1A, 5A.

Steele, C. M. (1997). A threat in the air: How stereotypes shape intellectual identity and performance. *American Psychologist, 52,* 613–628.

Steele, C. M., & Aronson, J. (1998). Stereotype threat and test performance of academically successful African Americans. In C. Jencks & M. Phillips (Eds.), *The black-white test score gap* (pp. 401–427). Washington, DC: Brookings Institution Press.

PART FOUR

STANDARDS AND THE STATE OF TEXAS—VOICES AND CONCERNS

Chapter 16

Three Decades of Educational Reform in Texas: Putting the Pieces Together

Sandra Lowery
Janiece Buck

Since the late 1970s, Texas has evolved increasingly complex educational reforms that now impact all aspects of education. The demand for accountability and improved student performance can been seen in reform measures implemented in public schools, institutions of higher learning, educator certification, and board member standards and training, and in the transformation of the state-funded system of financing public education. The purpose of this chapter is to examine the various standards and accountability issues and put the different pieces together, describing how they all fit together for one common purpose, increasing student performance.

Texas educational systems, including public schools and higher education, are defined by their diversity. The geography of the state, from the high plains of the Texas Panhandle to the coastal cities to the semi-tropical Lower Valley, is extremely diverse.

One noteworthy aspect of diversity is the magnitude of the state; 254 counties with a total of 1,042 school districts, ranging in size from Houston Independent School District with over 200,000 students to Divide Independent School District with fewer than 20 students. Texas public schools serve almost 4,000,000 students (*Snapshot, 1998–1999 Pocket Edition*, 1999).

Texas students are a diverse population who bring to their schools a wide variety of abilities, interests, ethnic backgrounds, and economic situations. Currently, Texas public school students are 14 percent African American, 39 percent Hispanic, 44 percent White, and 3 percent Other.

Forty-eight percent of the student body is reported as Economically Dis-advantaged (*Snapshot*, 1999).

Each school district is governed by an elected board of trustees with statutory authority and limitations in governing the schools of the district. Although school districts have retained the word "Independent" in their names, more than 20 years of statewide reform, including student perfor-mance accountability measures, accreditation standards, and financial revisions have brought significant changes in every school district and eroded local control. Even with recent attention to site-based manage-ment and increased emphasis on local decision making, Texas school districts are not as independent as they once were.

The Way It Used To Be

A study of Texas reform measures can begin with the Gilmer-Aiken Bill of 1949. After World War II, the demand for quality schools increased across the state. In 1947 the Gilmer-Aiken Committee was formed and charged with the responsibility of designing a new system of financing public schools in the state (Funkhouser, 1996). The recommendations of that commit-tee included a minimum foundation program for funding public schools that was mandated by the Gilmer-Aiken Bill. A shared arrangement be-tween the state and local school districts was instituted, with the state adding to local tax revenue to fund a minimum educational program. One element of the minimum foundation plan was that school districts were responsible for meeting minimal standards for instructional programs, libraries, certification of teachers and administrators, and facilities. Local school districts were free to enrich their programs with local tax revenues and although significant local control existed, infusions of state money brought increased involvement from the state level. An old Texas saying, "the one that has the pay has the say," is another way of expressing what has happened in many Texas reform measures. Increased funding from the state level has been accompanied by increased standards and expectations.

Through the 1950s, 1960s, and 1970s, accreditation focused upon processes and procedures. The Texas Education Agency (TEA) checked school districts, monitoring rules, regulations, and educational practices. Accountability for student performance was a local issue and each school district was mostly accountable to local patrons. While the Texas Educa-tion Agency did on-site monitoring, the visits were usually focused on governance, facilities, and safety. If school districts were going through the correct processes, they were usually found to be in compliance with state accountability standards. The monitoring visits were brief and very general in content. Members of the monitoring teams often visited classrooms where the subject or grade being taught was similar to what they had taught. One of the authors was responsible for monitoring visits during this era. She recalls one team member who was more concerned about how the flags were being displayed than anything else. Product evaluation did not occur until the late 1970s with the advent of statewide testing of students.

Beginnings of Reform

The question "are schools going through the right processes?" changed to a question on expected student results: "What should students know, be able to do, and be like when they graduate from the public school system?" This new direction for Texas education actually began in the late 1970s, characterized by a change in workforce needs. The traditional Texas economy of farming, ranching, and oil and gas production changed, leading to expectations of increased knowledge, skills, and technological training.

During the 1970s, most Texas school districts were using locally developed curriculum documents with reliance on textbooks as the main resource. Although the state textbook adoption program provided each school district with textbooks for all students in all subject areas, the textbooks alone did not provide an adequate curriculum. Hass (1978) noted that schools commonly lacked a comprehensive and reasonably consistent set of objectives on which to base curriculum decisions. He also identified the importance of making curriculum decisions based on objectives that were used in teaching plans.

Significant interest in change and reform in public schools culminated with the passage of House Bill 246 in 1984. This bill established a systematic structure for the development and implementation of a curriculum that included Essential Elements of instruction for the subjects and courses that school districts were required to offer to maintain a well-balanced curriculum (Funkhouser, 1996). Prior to this law, state curriculum guides had been recommendations without the force of legislation.

Beginning with the 1979–80 school year, Texas school districts began to administer the Texas Assessment of Basic Skills (TABS). This criterion-referenced test was composed of test items directly related to the Essential Elements of the statewide curriculum that was mandated in House Bill 246 (Funkhouser, 1996). TABS results were used in both district planning and assessing individual student achievement. This clear link between testing and specific curriculum content has served as a foundation for the current Texas student assessment program.

During the 1980s, the State Accountability Standards were implemented, and school districts were monitored by the Texas Education Agency on a rotating schedule. School districts were judged by the degree to which locally developed curriculum guides, built upon the Essential Elements, or state-mandated curriculum framework, were developed and implemented. Other criteria for judging school effectiveness included class schedules and lesson plans.

Curriculum guides were developed locally, obtained from outside sources, and swapped and traded among many school districts. Dr. Janiece Buck was a consultant in the Division of Accreditation for the Texas Education Agency at that time. She noted that some districts were clamoring to obtain curriculum guides so that they would be in compliance with state standards. So great was the rush to get curriculum documents in place that this consultant observed an incident in which a school purchased a set of curriculum guides from a neighboring school district and failed to get its own name on the guides before the accreditation team arrived.

Dr. Buck visited one small school district in West Texas in the mid-1980s. As she discussed implementation of the Essential Elements with one of the teachers, he voiced his opinion that he saw no need for a curriculum guide since he had successfully used the textbook for many years. This teacher had transformed the state-issued textbook into a serviceable curriculum guide. He had noted in the table of contents the order in which he would teach the chapters, made notes on instructional strategies, and written the Essential Elements and objectives into the margins. He was commended for his work by the TEA consultant, who suggested that similar work be included in the district's curriculum planning and implementation.

There was significant resistance to change, and many educators thought the demand for reforms would eventually fade away. This school of thought was sometimes called "hunkering down"—If we just hunker down, this will blow over. Others realized early that accountability was necessary and many changes and reforms would be needed to meet accountability standards.

House Bill 72

In 1983 a committee chaired by H. Ross Perot of Dallas made recommendations for improving public education and emphasizing student academic performance that resulted in a special session of the Texas Legislature during the summer of 1984. By the end of that special session, the legislature had passed House Bill 72, the most comprehensive set of changes since the Gilmer-Aiken Bill of 1949 (Funkhouser, 1996).

Although some parts of House Bill 72 have been changed by subsequent legislation, its reform measures still in place include teacher appraisals, tutorial services, student-teacher ratio of 22:1 for kindergarten through fourth grade, limits on extracurricular activities, and the "no-pass/no-play" provision that permits only students who are passing all subjects to participate in extracurricular activities. Specifications on teacher planning time, duty-free lunch periods, notices of student academic performance, dropout reduction programs, student mastery of the Essential Elements, and the discipline management programs are other elements of House Bill 72 that have been retained (Funkhouser, 1996).

Accreditation monitoring conducted by the TEA was focused on the new legislative requirements, curriculum, and instruction. The Effective Schools Research model was recommended for implementation during this time period, especially for low-performing campuses. Tremendous pressure to teach the state curriculum was felt across the state.

Texas educators themselves were directly affected by House Bill 72. The Texas Teacher Appraisal System (TTAS) was developed for the purpose of measuring teacher performance. Every teacher was appraised using the state-mandated system. Although the Career Ladder, a merit pay system that accompanied the TTAS, was phased out in 1993, teacher salary differentials and teacher appraisals are still in place. The system has evolved into the Professional Development and Appraisal System (PDAS), which is currently used for teacher appraisals.

Every educator took the Texas Examination of Current Administrators and Teachers (TECAT) in 1985. This basic skills test examined reading and writing. Although many educators protested that their certification should not depend upon the TECAT, all Texas educators were required to take and pass the TECAT in order to retain their certification.

Another test, the Examination for the Certification of Educators in Texas (ExCET), was developed and implemented to test knowledge of specific disciplines. A passing score on the ExCET is still required for anyone wishing to obtain any certification.

The State Board of Education (SBOE) approved recommendations of the Commission on Standards for the Teaching Profession that included proficiencies describing what teachers and administrators must know and be able to demonstrate so that all children can have equal access to educational opportunities, thereby increasing student achievement. Adoption of *Learner-Centered Schools for Texas: A Vision of Texas Educators* (1996) was the first step in establishing a policy referred to as the Accountability System for Educator Preparation (Funkhouser, 1996).

Many of the House Bill 72 reforms were viewed by many Texas educators as excessively rigid, with too much emphasis on top-down control and too little input from educators, parents, and community members at the local level. Although massive amounts of data are submitted to the TEA through the Public Education Information Management System (PEIMS) and state-mandated accreditation standards are required for every Texas school district, a significant degree of decision making regarding the "how" of education has been gradually returned to local school districts.

PEIMS is a statewide data management system for public education information in the state of Texas (Texas Education Code [TEC] §42.006). School districts submit organizational, budget, financial, and staff data to the TEA through standardized computer files. Other required data includes student demographic and program participation records, and information on student attendance, dropouts, retentions, and graduation. This data is compiled and put into the Academic Excellence Indicator System Report (AEIS) (*Expanding the Scope of the Texas Public School Accountability System*, 1997).

The AEIS Report pulls together a wide range of information on the performance of students at campus and district levels every year. The origins of the AEIS Report go back to 1984 and the emphasis on student academic performance. Performance indicators such as student passing rates on the statewide academic tests, end-of-course examination scores, attendance data, dropout data, SAT and ACT participation and results, and percentage of students completing the Recommended High School Diploma are currently included on the AEIS Report for every school district.

The system of funding Texas public schools has also been characterized by change due to litigation over inequities in public school finance (*A Guide to Texas School Finance*, 1999). The Texas system of financing public schools had not undergone significant change since the Gilmer-Aiken Bill of 1949 (Walker & Casey, 1992). There were wide disparities in taxable wealth and expenditure levels among school districts due to the degree of reliance on local property taxes for funding public schools. In 1973, The U.S. Supreme Court heard *Rodriguez v. San Antonio ISD* and ruled that the issue of funding public schools was not a federal matter. This ruling brought the issue of equitable funding back to the state level (Clarke & England, 1996).

In 1987, in *Edgewood v. Kirby,* the state funding system was found to unconstitutional because it discriminated against students living in property-poor school districts (Walker & Casey, 1992). High-wealth school districts were directed to share their revenue with low-wealth districts. Commonly called the Robin Hood Plan, this system has been upheld by the Texas Supreme Court. The standard used by the Texas Supreme Court is a taxpayer equity standard, which means similar revenue for similar tax effort, regardless of the property wealth of a school district. In other words, the school finance system is to be property-wealth neutral; a district's property tax base should have little or no impact on its ability to finance the local share of the Foundation School Program (Clarke & England, 1996).

The 1990s
Senate Bill 1, approved by the Texas Legislature in 1995, began the move toward site-based management (Boyter, 1995). Advocates of site-based management contended that authority at the site level would lead to greater accountability, since improvement plans were developed locally with specific lines of responsibility established by the educators involved in implementation (Reese, 1995). Site-based decision making is a collaborative effort by which staff, parents, and community representatives assess the educational outcomes of all students, determine goals and strategies, and ensure that strategies are implemented and adjusted to improve student achievement (*Nacogdoches ISD School-Based Decision Making Plan*, 1992).

Strategic planning models were used in many school districts, using representative groups, including educators, parents, and community members in decision making. One former superintendent described this planning component of site-based decision making as "the greatest tool I have ever used for uniting people to support goals and establish strategies for improvement" (J. Buck, personal communication, April 4, 2000). Professional development changed from the inservice provision of the 1970s and 1980s in which districts had provided training on issues or trends with little regard to individual campus needs (Danielson, 1996). Administrators made many decisions about inservice without substantial input from teachers (Bergin, 1991). Texas was not unlike the rest of the nation in that practice. Goodlad (1984) found that teachers rarely had opportunities to meet with their peers to work together on problems of individual schools.

These scenarios changed in Texas public schools as site-based management was implemented and the emphasis on student achievement was moved to campus level (Downey, 1995). Campus-level teams were charged with responsibilities for improving instruction and identifying the professional development necessary for teachers to provide the necessary improved levels of instruction. In 1995, the passage of Senate Bill I mandated that professional development plans be developed by campus level teams and be directly related to campus performance objectives. The law emphasized that professional development activities must include planning together to enhance existing teaching skills, sharing effective strategies, studying curricular and instructional needs, studying research, and developing programs based on student needs.

During the early 1990s, the statewide student assessment changed to a new criterion-referenced program, the Texas Assessment of Academic Skills (TAAS), plus end-of-course examinations (TEC §39.023). The implementation of TAAS shifted the focus of assessment from minimum, or basic, skills to academic skills. TAAS is similar to TABS and TEAMS assessments that preceded it, because it is based on the state-mandated curriculum. TABS and TEAMS evolved into TAAS, a more challenging assessment involving higher-order thinking skills and problem solving.

Senate Bill I, passed by the Texas Legislature in 1995, was a sweeping recodification of the entire Texas Education Code. With its emphasis on site-based decision making and accreditation based on student academic performance measures, Senate Bill I included the return of control over many educational decisions to the local level. Senate Bill I accelerated the movement to flatten the decision-making pyramid, shifting authority and responsibility back to school districts and local educators (Kemerer, 1995). Commissioner of Education Dr. Mike Moses referred to Senate Bill I as "a contract with the people of Texas" (Moses, 1995).

Three types of charter schools, home-ruled school district charters, campus charters, and open-enrollment charters, were accepted as part of Senate Bill I. This move to give parents more options regarding the education of their children followed national trends (TEC §12.012).

Senate Bill I also provided for facilities funding assistance for property-poor school districts. This was a direct response to earlier court decisions that found the Texas system of financing constitutional only if funding for facilities was included. Eligibility for these funds was determined by a formula involving the district's wealth per student, the guaranteed wealth level, and the cost of the project (TEC §42.001).

School board members in each of the 1,042 Texas school districts have also been included in the reforms that have touched every area of education. The State Board of Education (SBOE) has been charged with the responsibility of developing a framework for governance leadership to be used in continuing education for board members. A structured system of board member training, including team building, governance issues, roles and responsibilities of board members and administrators, and other topics based on needs identified by the board members themselves, is currently in place (TEC §11.052).

Senate Bill I created a new entity to govern educator certification, removing that responsibility from the TEA to the State Board for Educator Certification (SBEC). The legislature directed the SBEC to "regulate and oversee all aspects of the certification, continuing education, and standards of conduct of public school educators" (TEC §081).

The SBEC has also had an impact on teacher and administrator preparation programs in colleges and universities, since the students trained in every institution must pass the ExCET for certification. Many Texas universities have implemented curriculum revisions, and modifications of program standards have been enacted in response to the higher accountability standards faced by all educator preparation programs. Colleges of education are now rated on student mastery of the learner-centered proficiencies required for Texas educators. This aspect of accountability and the increasing demand for well-trained, capable educators are important pieces of the big picture of reform in Texas public schools.

Where We Are Now

In keeping with the overall goal of improving academic performance for all Texas students, major changes in curriculum have taken place in both public schools and institutions of higher learning. Focus on real-world application, integrated curriculum, alignment of curriculum both vertically and horizontally, support for professional development, use of technology, and parental and community involvement are critical issues in curriculum development and implementation.

The Texas Teacher Appraisal System (TTAS), part of the House Bill 72 reforms in 1984, has been changed to the Professional Development and Appraisal System (PDAS). The PDAS was developed with notable input from educators themselves, and teacher appraisal is linked to student performance. Implementation of the PDAS and the TTAS is similar because classroom observations, written observation summaries, and summative annual appraisal reports are required in both systems. The PDAS is characterized by a higher degree of standard expectations, with all teachers expected to be proficient according to all criteria.

Well-qualified, capable teachers are cornerstones in the work to improve student academic achievement. Retention of beginning teachers and teacher shortages are concerns that have been identified statewide. A support system for beginning teachers, the Texas Beginning Educator Support System (TxBESS), has been developed to assist beginning teachers and address these concerns. A strong component of self-assessment and mentoring is reflected in the Beginning Teacher Activity Profile in Texas (BTAPT). The BTAPT provides formative information for beginning teachers for professional growth and summative information for educator preparation programs. The success of beginning teachers will be linked to the educator preparation programs where they were trained (TEC §21.045).

On-site monitoring of campuses and districts by the TEA currently includes accreditation reviews of low-performing campuses and District Effectiveness and Compliance (DEC) visits. On-site accreditation evaluations are based upon program evaluations, including establishment of criteria, gathering of data, data analysis, on-site visitation, and a written report of findings.

The DEC process is used to assess special program implementation, including special education, accelerated programs such as Title I and Migrant, Career and Technology, and Bilingual/English as a Second Language programs. The process focuses on the effectiveness of the districts efforts to improve the performance of students served in these state and federally funded programs and to ensure the district's compliance status. The report is organized into five basic areas: District Self-Evaluation, Site-Based Decision Making, District Improvement Planning, District Initiatives, and the Significant District Factors (*Accountability Procedures Manual*, 1999). This emphasis on planning and implementation of instructional programs, based on identified instructional goals for each campus, is indicative of the overall philosophy of site-based management. Although standards for student academic achievement are set at the state level by the Texas Legislature, the State Board of Education, and the Texas Education Agency, many decisions about how to achieve these goals are made at the local level. Campus planning and campus level decision making have empowered educators, parents, and community members, thereby assuring "buy-in" from these essential players in the educational improvement process.

Every aspect of education in Texas has been changed during three decades of reform. These years of change in Texas education were first characterized by rigid top-down control with multiple rules and regulations made by the legislature and state agencies. This approach was defined by increased funding, written standards, and intense pressure to change schools so that students would achieve at higher levels.

During the mid-1990s, with the passage of Senate Bill I in 1995, the Texas Legislature took another step on the path of school reform (Kemerer, 1995). The return of authority to local educational units, campuses, and districts and emphasis on innovation, including charter schools, have empowered educational improvements from the local level upward. Increased emphasis on parental involvement is a strong indicator of the swing to local decision making on how things are accomplished.

Every agency involved in education, including public and private schools, institutions of higher education, and state level entities, has been touched during three decades of change. The one non-negotiable requirement, improvement of student academic performance, remains an absolute necessity as Texas prepares students to live and work in a new century.

References

Accountability, a shared responsibility (1999). Texas Association of School Boards [On-line]. Available: http://www.tasb.org/Education/speech1.html

Accountability procedures manual for on-site evaluations 1999–2000 (1999). Austin, TX: Texas Education Agency.

Bergin, V. (October 22, 1991). *Letter to administrators in Texas.* Austin, TX: Texas Education Agency.

Boyter, G. (Winter 1995). Site based decision making: A team building process. *Insight.*

Clarke, C., & England, C. (1996). *Educational finance briefing paper: Texas public school finance and related issues.* Austin, TX: Texas Center for Educational Research.

Danielson, C. (1996). *Enhancing professional practice: a framework for teaching.* Arlington, VA: Association of Supervision and Curriculum Development.

Downey, C. (Winter 1995). Getting it off the ground. *Insight.*

Expanding the scope of the Texas public school accountability system. (1997). Austin, TX: Texas Education Agency.

Funkhouser, C. (1996). Education in Texas: Policies, practices, and perspectives. (8th ed.) Scottsdale, AZ: Gorsuch Scarisbruck.

Goodlad, J. (1984). *A place called school: Prospects for the future.* New York: McGraw-Hill.

A guide to Texas school finance. (1999). Austin, TX: Texas Center for Educational Research and Texas Association of School Boards.

Hass, G. (1978). *A new approach to curriculum.* (3rd ed.). Boston: Allyn and Bacon.

Kemerer, F. (October 1995). Senate bill I governance changes: Flattening the pyramid, chartering schools, and empowering parents. *Texas School Administrators' Legal Digest 11* (9).

Learner-centered schools for Texas: A vision of Texas educators. (1996). Austin, TX: State Board for Educator Certification.

Long range plan for public education, 1986–1990. (1985). Austin, TX: Texas Education Agency.

Moses, M. (1995). Senate bill one: A contract with the people of Texas. *Insight.*

Nacogdoches Independent School District school-based decision making plan. (1992). Nacogdoches, TX: NISD Publication.

Quality, equity, accountability: long range plan for public education, 1991–1995. (1990). Austin, TX: Texas Education Agency.

Reese, M. (Winter 1995). SBDM: Process of power or motivation? *Insight.*

Snapshot, 1998–1999 Pocket Edition. (1999). Texas Education Agency [On-line]. Available: http://www.tea.state.tx.us/perfreport/poked/99/panel2.html
Texas Education Agency §11.052.
Texas Education Agency §12.012.
Texas Education Agency §21.045.
Texas Education Agency §21.081.
Texas Education Agency §39.023.
Texas Education Agency §42.001.
Texas Education Agency §42.006.

Walker, B. (1989). *Shaping school finance policy in post-Edgewood Texas: An analytical model.* Austin, TX: Texas Center for Educational Research.

Walker, B., & Casey, D. (1992). *The basics of Texas public school finance.* (5th ed.). Austin, TX: Texas Association of School Boards.

Chapter 17

Kids, the Court, and the State of Texas: The Legal Challenge to the TAAS

Raymond A. Horn, Jr.

There are those in Texas who are very proud of the strides that the state has made in improving the quality of education. Recent editorial commentary in the *Houston Chronicle* ("Legislature," 2000, p. 20A) summarizes this pride:

> Texas public schools have come a long way in recent years in the education of children. Many had been coasting along, apparently unmindful of the terrible job they were doing. But then parents, teachers and taxpayers finally got fed up with what was going on. They began demanding that schools start teaching kids again. People were sick of students being promoted from grade to grade without having learned anything. They were sick of high school graduates who couldn't read or write. Today, Texas is moving toward making high school diplomas bona fide certificates of the fact that their recipients know a thing or two.

The central component of the Texas drive for educational quality is accountability. School boards, administrators, teachers, and parents are forced to be accountable because of a high-stakes exit-level test that focuses directly on the students. The students are the overt targets of the State of Texas. By forcing the students to pass the Texas Assessment of Academic Skills (TAAS) in order to graduate, the State of Texas is indirectly pressuring the other groups. Undeniably, by using the children in this manner, the state has motivated the other groups to take action and make educational changes. In addition, the state has provided additional support for educational change through an increase in state funding, a more equitable distribution of funds, the development of uniform state curriculum standards, stronger credentialing of school personnel, a reduction in class size, and an extension of preschool opportunities to students most in need (Cortez, 2000, pp. 1–2).

Using the children of Texas as the means to the state's ends has implications beyond what individual children score on a standardized test. The
recent court case that is the focus of this chapter, has broad implications
for not only large segments of the population of Texas, such as African
Americans and Hispanics, but for everyone in Texas. Literally everyone is
affected by the TAAS. For instance, the March 12, 2000, edition of the
Houston Chronicle included a 27-page supplement entitled, "Report Card:
Houston Area Schools." The *Chronicle* gathered test score information
and other data on all of the public schools in the eight counties that
comprise the Houston metropolitan area. School profiles were given for
each of the hundreds of schools in the Houston area. They provided the
following information: the school address; the percentage of students
passing the writing, reading, and math sections of the TAAS in 1998 and
1999; the school's accountability rating; Limited English Proficiency exemptions; special education exemptions; SAT score average; enrollment;
dropout rate; the percentage of low income students; and demographic
percentages of African Americans, Whites, Asians, Hispanics, and Native Americans.

Assuredly, information of this sort can affect people's settlement patterns. Some would argue that information of this sort, based on the results from one standardized test, could facilitate a resegregation of racial
groups. Undeniably, real estate companies include this information in
their profiles of neighborhoods given to their clients. The powerful combination of the inordinate emphasis on the TAAS and parents' concern
for the welfare of their children creates a parental necessity to focus on
the data as reported by the *Chronicle*. In the introduction to its supplement, the *Chronicle* provided a brief disclaimer about the data. "The
system, though, is not particularly simple. The information provided in
the Chronicle's report card on schools, which is based on 1999 test scores,
should be used only as a starting point in assessing performance. Schools
do get ratings—exemplary, recognized, acceptable and low-performing—
but experts say you can't rely entirely on a rating to assess the quality of
a school. In other words, a low-performing school isn't always a lousy
school. And an exemplary rating is no guarantee of excellence" (Markley,
2000, p. 2J).

Undoubtedly, this disclaimer has no chance against the powerful emo-
tions created by parents' concern about the effects of educational environment on their children. In addition, information like this acts as a
catalyst for any racist attitudes held consciously or unconsciously by parents or other members of the community.

The suit considered in this chapter, brought by seven students, who did not receive a high school diploma because they did not pass the TAAS, and the Mexican American Legal and Educational Fund (MALDEF) against the Texas Education Agency (TEA) and the Texas School Board of Education, was, on one hand, about the effects of the TAAS on certain types of students, but on the other hand it was about the effects of the TAAS on all of Texas. The plaintiffs were asking the "court to issue an injunction preventing the TEA from using failure of the exit-level TAAS test as a basis for denying high school diplomas" (*GI Forum v. TEA*, 2000, p. 2).

On January 7, 2000, United States District Judge Edward C. Prado[1] dismissed the case against the TEA and the State Board of Education. This decision greatly impacts not only Texas public school education but also all other states engaging in high-stakes testing.[2] For all concerned, the first impact is that a legal precedent has now been set that specifically supports the adverse effects of a standardized exit-level test on minority students. Secondly, despite a decision that was against the interests of minority students, the evidence provides compelling documentation supporting the deleterious effects of high-stakes testing on minority students.

My presentation of this case is centered on two documents: Edward C. Prado's opinion (*GI Forum v. TEA*, 2000) and the plaintiffs' Post Trial Brief (*GI Forum v. TEA*, 1999) submitted to the assistant attorney general of Texas. These two documents are instructive for two reasons. First, the United States District Court's decision is binding for Texas students at this point in time[3] until further legal challenges to high stakes testing are made. Second, these documents show the significant difference in political philosophy between the court and the plaintiffs. This difference is significant in understanding the current reality of our political system and the impact of this reality on disadvantaged minorities.

Supporting States' Rights

The court "determined that the use of the TAAS examination does not have an impermissible adverse impact on Texas's minority students and does not violate their right to the due process of law" (*GI Forum v. TEA*, 2000, p. 2). The court's decision was primarily based on the fact that "it is clear that the law requires courts to give deference to state legislative policy, in the educational context, such deference is even warranted. Education is the particular responsibility of state governments" (*GI Forum v. TEA*, 2000, p. 3). The court's insistence on the right of the state to set educational policy and the inappropriateness of judicial intervention unless "a state uses its considerable power impermissibly to disadvantage minority students" (*GI Forum v. TEA*, 2000, p. 3), were reiterated throughout the court's opinion as evidenced by these statements:

- This Court has no authority to tell the State of Texas what a well-educated high school graduate should demonstrably know at the end of twelve years of education. Nor may this Court determine the relative merits of teacher evaluation and 'objective' testing. (*GI Forum v. TEA*, 2000, p. 8)
- The articulated goals of the implementation of the TAAS requirements are to hold schools, students, and teachers accountable for education and to ensure that all Texas students receive the same, adequate learning opportunities. These goals are certainly within the legitimate exercise of the State's power over public education. (*GI Forum v. TEA*, 2000, p. 41)
- In addition, the Court finds that it [high-stakes testing] is an exercise well within the State's power and authority. The State of Texas has determined that, to graduate, a senior must have mastered 70 percent of the tested minimal essentials. (*GI Forum v. TEA*, 2000, p. 44)
- The Court finds that the question of whether the education of minority students is being limited by TAAS-directed instruction is not a proper subject for its review. The State of Texas has determined that a set of knowledge and skills must be taught and learned in State schools. The State mandates no more than these "essential" items. Test-driven instruction undeniably helps to accomplish this goal. It is not within the Court's power to alter or broaden the curricular decisions made by the State. (*GI Forum v. TEA*, 2000, pp. 46–47)
- In short, the Court finds, on the basis of the evidence presented at trial, that the disparities in test scores do not result from flaws in the test or in the way it is administered. Instead, as the Plaintiffs themselves have argued, some minority students have, for a myriad of reasons, failed to keep up (or catch up) with their majority counterparts. It may be, as the TEA argues, that the TAAS test is one weapon in the fight to remedy this problem. At any rate, the State is within its power to choose this remedy. (*GI Forum v. TEA*, 2000, pp. 53–54)
- It is not for this Court to determine whether Texas has chosen the best of all possible means for achieving these goals. The system is

not perfect, but the Court cannot say that it is unconstitutional. Judgment is GRANTED in favor of the Defendants, and this case is DISMISSED. (*GI Forum v. TEA*, 2000, pp. 56–57)

To minorities the implications of the court's states' rights position are clear. If minorities contest the actions of the state, they will find no relief from the court unless it can be proven that the state has used its power to disadvantage the minorities; and, of course, the burden of proof is on them, the plaintiffs.

The Case and the Court's Opinion

In this case, the court determined that " a state could overstep its bounds in implementing standardized tests as graduation requirements. Specifically, the court found that a test that did not measure what students were actually learning could be fundamentally unfair. The court also found that a test that perpetuated the effects of prior discrimination was unconstitutional" (*GI Forum v. TEA*, 2000, p. 4). In fact, the court held "that a state could violate the constitution if it implemented polices that violated accepted educational norms" (*GI Forum v. TEA*, 2000, p. 4). The court also held "that regulation, in clear, unmistakable terms, prohibits a federally funded program from implementing policies that have a disparate impact on minorities" (*GI Forum v. TEA*, 2000, p. 4).

In deciding the issue of discrimination, the court defined its task in four ways. First, the court had to consider a standardized test that measured knowledge rather than one that predicted performance. Second, the court had to decide the amount of "deference to be given to a State in deciding how much a student should be required to learn—the cut-score issue" (*GI Forum v. TEA*, 2000, p. 6). Third, the court had "to weigh what appears to be a significant discrepancy in pass scores on the TAAS test with the overwhelming evidence that the discrepancy is rapidly improving and that the lot of Texas minority students, at least as demonstrated by academic achievement, while far from perfect, is better than that of minority students in other parts of the country and appears to be getting better" (*GI Forum v. TEA*, 2000, p. 7). And, finally, the court had to determine whether the TAAS Exit Test is fair:

In relation to this issue of discrimination, the Court determined the following:

> Thus, the Court has carefully considered the claims that Texas schools still offer widely diverse educational opportunities and that, too often, those opportunities

depend on the color of a student's skin or the financial resources of the student's school district. To some degree, as discussed below, the Court must accept these claims. But that finding, alone, is an insufficient basis for invalidating this examination. There must be some link between the TAAS test and these disparities. In other words, the Plaintiffs were required to prove, by a preponderance of the evidence, that the TAAS test was implemented in spite of the disparities, and that requiring passage of the test for graduation is therefore fundamentally unfair. The Court believes that this has not been proven. (*GI Forum v. TEA*, 2000, pp. 8–9)

The court viewed this case as one that "presented widely differing views of how an educational system should work. One set of witnesses believed that the integrity of objective measurement was paramount; the other believed that this consideration should be tempered with more flexible notions of fairness and justice" (*GI Forum v. TEA*, 2000, p. 10). The judge continued:

After a review of the expert testimony the Court determined that, ultimately, resolution of this case turns not on the relative validity of the parties' views on education but on the State's right to pursue educational policies that it legitimately believes are in the best interests of Texas students. The Plaintiffs were able to show that the policies are debated and debatable among learned people. The Plaintiffs demonstrated that the policies have had an initial and substantial adverse impact on minority students. The Plaintiffs demonstrated that the policies are not perfect. However, the Plaintiffs failed to prove that the policies are unconstitutional, that the adverse impact is avoidable or more significant than the concomitant positive impact, or that other approaches would meet the State's articulated legitimate goals. In the absence of such proof, the State must be allowed to design an educational system that it believes best meets the need of its citizens. (*GI Forum v. TEA*, 2000, pp. 12–13)

It is once again interesting to note that, even though the court found "an initial and substantial adverse impact on minority students," the state's right to design and pursue its goal supersedes the impact on the minority students.

At this time, a review of the facts and conclusions of law will be conducted in relation to the court's findings and the plaintiffs' position. As determined by the court, the issues are: the test, the passing standard, objective measurement, remediation, accountability, history of testing/discrimination in Texas, educational standards, disparate impact, and dropout/retention rates.

The Test

After reviewing the construction of the test, the test's validity, and the administration of the test, the court determined that "the TAAS test effectively measures students' mastery of the skills and knowledge the State of Texas has deemed graduating high school seniors must possess" (*GI Forum v. TEA*, 2000, p. 43).

The court further determined "that the TEA has shown that the high-stakes use of the TAAS test as a graduation requirement guarantees that students will be motivated to learn the curriculum tested. (*GI Forum v. TEA*, 2000, pp. 45–46)

The court also determined that the "Plaintiffs have not demonstrated that the TAAS test is a substantial departure from accepted academic norms or is based on a failure to exercise professional judgment" (*GI Forum v. TEA*, 2000, p. 52). In arriving at this decision the court accepted the testimony of a Plaintiff-witness, that

> The item-selection system chosen by TEA often results in the favoring of items on which minorities will perform poorly, while disfavoring items where discrepancies are less wide. The Court cannot quarrel with this evidence. However, the Court finds that the Plaintiffs have not been able to demonstrate that the test, as validated and equated, does not best serve the State's goals of identifying and remediating educational problems. Because one of the goals of the TAAS test is to identify and remedy problems in the State's educational system, no matter their source, then it would be reasonable for the State to validate and equate test items on some basis other than their disparate impact on certain groups. In addition, the State need not equate its test on the basis of standards it rejects, such as subjective teacher evaluations. (*GI Forum v. TEA*, 2000, pp. 52–53)

The Passing Standard

The initial passing standard for the TAAS test was 60 percent; a year later it was raised to 70 percent. The court determined that "the TEA understood the consequences of setting the cut score at 70 percent. When it implemented the TAAS test, the TEA projected that, with a 70 percent cut score, at least 73 percent of African Americans and 67 percent of Hispanics would fail the math portion of the test; at least 55 percent of African Americans and 54 percent of Hispanics would fail the reading section; and at least 62 percent of African Americans and 45 percent of Hispanics would fail the writing section" (*GI Forum v. TEA*, 2000, p. 19). On the October 1991 exam given to 10th graders, 67 percent of African Americans, 59 percent of Hispanics, and 31 percent of Whites failed to meet the cut score (*GI Forum v. TEA*, 2000, p. 20).

The court concluded "that the passing standard does bear a manifest relation to a legitimate goal" (*GI Forum v. TEA*, 2000, p. 43), and that it is well within the State of Texas's power and authority to require seniors to attain a mastery level of 70 percent of the tested minimal Essential

Elements (*GI Forum v. TEA*, 2000, p. 44). The court's opinion was further supported by its determination that "Texas relied on field test data and input from educators to determine where to set its cut score" (*GI Forum v. TEA*, 2000, p. 45). In addition, "while field test results suggested that a large number of students would not pass at the 70-percent cut score, officials had reason to believe that those numbers were inflated. Officials contemplated the possible consequences and determined that the risk should be taken" (*GI Forum v. TEA*, 2000, p. 45).

Objective Measurement

The court recognized that "the TEA determined that objective measures of mastery should be imposed in order to eliminate what it perceived to be inconsistent and possibly subjective teacher evaluations of students" (*GI Forum v. TEA*, 2000, p. 20). Also, the TEA "presented testimony that subjectivity can work to disadvantage minority students by allowing inflated grades to mask gaps in learning" (*GI Forum v. TEA*, 2000, p. 20). They further argued that "a student's classroom grade cannot be equated to TAAS performance, as grades can measure a variety of factors, ranging from effort and improvement to objective mastery. The TAAS test is a solely objective measurement of mastery" (*GI Forum v. TEA*, 2000, pp. 42–43). Based on this evidence, the court found that "the test accomplishes what it sets out to accomplish, which is to provide an objective assessment of whether students have mastered a discrete set of skills and knowledge" (*GI Forum v. TEA*, 2000, p. 43).

In addition, the court found that the TAAS exit-level test met currently accepted standards for curricular validity, and did so with a sufficient degree of reliability (*GI Forum v. TEA*, 2000, pp. 51–52).

Remediation

The court found the evidence concerning remediation presented by the defendants' experts to be credible. Consequently, the court found that, on balance, remedial efforts were largely successful (*GI Forum v. TEA*, 2000, p. 22). The TEA's expert estimated that 44,515 minority students in 1997 were successfully remediated after having failed their first attempt at the TAAS test while in the eighth grade in 1995.

The issue of remediation was very important in the court's considerations. The court determined that "all students in Texas have had a reasonable opportunity to learn the subject matters covered by the exam" (*GI Forum v. TEA*, 2000, p. 52). The court determined that its conclusions in this case were supported by the State's efforts at remediation, especially the fact that students are given eight opportunities to pass the examination from the time of their first testing in their sophomore year to the end of their 12th year.

Accountability

The court recognized that "administrators, schools, and teachers are held accountable, in varying degrees, for TAAS performance" (*GI Forum v. TEA*, 2000, p. 21). The court also recognized that the scores are disaggregated into subgroups, "so that schools and districts are aware of the degree of success or failure of African American, Hispanic and White students.[4] If one subgroup fails to meet minimum performance standards, a school or district will receive a low accountability rating" (*GI Forum v. TEA*, 2000, p. 21).

In relation to accountability, the plaintiffs argued that the determination of the state's accountability of administrators, schools, and teachers is based on the first administration of the exit test, and that the state does not consider cumulative pass rates or final pass rates on the test when they determine whether a school district is to be rated Exemplary, Recognized, Acceptable, or Low-Performing.

History of Testing/Discrimination

The court recognized that standardized tests have been used in educational contexts to disadvantage minorities; however, the court determined that the plaintiffs presented insufficient evidence that the TAAS test is designed to or does impermissibly disadvantage minorities (*GI Forum v. TEA*, 2000, p. 22). The court agreed with the plaintiffs "that Texas minority students have been, and to some extent continue to be, the victims of educational inequality" (*GI Forum v. TEA*, 2000, p. 23). The court found the reasons for this inequity disturbing but inconclusive, and concluded "that socioeconomics, family support, unequal funding, quality of teaching and educational materials, individual effort, and the residual effects of prior discriminatory practices were all implicated" (*GI Forum v. TEA*, 2000, p. 23). In addition, the court did not comment on the argument that standards-based assessment tends to privilege particular populations, who then have access to a new form of cultural capital that is not available to excluded students, in this case, those who do not pass the TAAS.

In addition, the court found that the plaintiffs presented insufficient evidence to support a finding that minority students do not have a reasonable opportunity to learn the material covered by the TAAS because of unequal education in the past or present (*GI Forum v. TEA*, 2000, p. 23). However, the court did find that the plaintiffs presented evidence to show that, in a more general sense, minorities are not given equal educational opportunities, and that minorities are underrepresented in advanced placement courses and in gifted-and-talented programs (*GI Forum v. TEA*, 2000, p. 23). "However, because of the rigid, state-mandated correlation between the Texas Essentials of Knowledge and Skills and the TAAS test, the Court finds that all Texas students have an equal opportunity to learn the items presented on the TAAS" (*GI Forum v. TEA*, 2000, pp. 23–24). In fact, the court's opinion is "that the implementation of the TAAS test, together with school accountability and mandated remedial follow-up, helps address the effects of any prior discrimination and remaining inequities in the system" (*GI Forum v. TEA*, 2000, p. 24).

The court considered that "Texas's difficulties in providing an equal education to all its students are well-documented. It is only in the recent past that efforts have been made to provide equal funding to Texas public schools. Several schools in the state remain under desegregation orders" (*GI Forum v. TEA*, 2000, p. 55). In relation to this past history, the court "determined that the use and implementation of the TAAS test does identify educational inequalities and attempts to address them (remedial efforts help dispel the link between past discrimination and poor performance on standardized test). While lack of effort and creativity at the local level sometimes frustrate those attempts, local policy is not an issue before the Court. The results of the TAAS test are used, in many cases quite effectively, to motivate not only students but schools and teachers to raise and meet educational standards" (*GI Forum v. TEA*, 2000, p. 55).

Educational Standards

The court determined that the "current prevailing standards for the proper use of educational testing recommend that high-stakes decisions, such as whether or not to promote or graduate a student, should not be made on the basis of a single test score" (*GI Forum v. TEA*, 2000, p. 24). What was disputed at the trial was whether the TAAS test is actually the *sole criterion* for graduation. The court found that "graduation in Texas, in fact, hinges on three separate and independent criteria: the two objective criteria of attendance and success on the TAAS examination, and the arguably objective/subjective criterion of course success. However, as the Plaintiffs note, these factors are not weighted with and against each other; rather, failure to meet any single criterion results in failure to graduate. Thus, the failure to pass the exit-level exam does serve as a bar to graduation, and the exam is properly called a 'high-stakes' test" (*GI Forum v. TEA*, 2000, p. 25). However, the court determined that since students are given at least eight opportunities to pass the examination prior to their graduation date, a single TAAS score does not serve as the sole criterion for graduation (*GI Forum v. TEA*, 2000, p. 25).

Disparate Impact

Concerning the impact of the TAAS on minority students, the court came to "an inescapable conclusion that in every administration of the TAAS test since October 1990, Hispanic and African American students have performed significantly worse on all three sections of the exit exam than majority students. However, the Court also finds that it is highly significant that minority students have continued to narrow the passing rate gap at a rapid rate" (*GI Forum v. TEA*, 2000, p. 26).

In determining whether a legally significant statistical disparity did exist, the court considered the Four-Fifths Rule[5] and whether a cumulative pass rate or the pass rates on a single administration of the TAAS at the 10th-grade level should be considered. In this context, the court agreed with the plaintiffs that "on first-time administration of the exit-level test, a legally significant adverse impact exists," and that, "while an examination of cumulative pass scores in more recent years does not evince adverse impact under the Four-Fifths Rule, the disparity there, too, is sufficient to give rise to legitimate concern" (*GI Forum v. TEA*, 2000, p. 28).

The court further distinguished between the statistical impact and the practical impact. In relation to the statistically disparate failure rates, the TEA argued "that, because of the presence of largely successful remediation, the practical significance benefits minorities." (*GI Forum v. TEA*, 2000, p. 29). The court found "that the effect of remediation, which is usually eventual success in passing the examination and thus receipt of a high school diploma, is more profound than the steadily decreasing minority failure rate" (*GI Forum v. TEA*, 2000, p. 29). The court accepted the TEA argument that each individual student is given at least eight tries to pass the exam and that even though many students fail on the first attempt, many eventually succeed (*GI Forum v. TEA*, 2000, p. 39).

However, the court found "that, whether one looks at cumulative or single-administration results, the disparity between minority and majority pass rates on the TAAS test must give pause to anyone looking at the numbers. The variances are not only large and disconcerting, they also apparently cut across such factors as socioeconomics. Further, the data presented by the Plaintiffs regarding the statistical significance of the disparities buttress the view that legally meaningful differences do exist between the pass rates of minority and majority students" (*GI Forum v. TEA*, 2000, pp. 39–40). "Given the sobering differences in pass rates and their demonstrated statistical significance, the Court finds that the Plaintiffs have made a prima facie showing of significant adverse impact" (*GI Forum v. TEA*, 2000, p. 40).

Because of the prima facie showing of significant adverse impact, the court had to determine "whether the TEA has met its burden of production on the question of whether the TAAS test is an educational 'necessity'" (*GI Forum v. TEA*, 2000, p. 41). The court determined that "an educational necessity exists where the challenged practice serves the legitimate educational goals of the institution" (*GI Forum v. TEA*, 2000, p. 41), and that the TAAS test indeed serves the accountability goals of the TEA.

Drop-out/Retention Rates

The court agreed with the plaintiffs' position that "Texas students, particularly minority students, drop out of school in significant numbers and are retained at their current grade level in numbers that give cause for concern. Moreover, the Plaintiffs presented evidence supporting their contention that drop-out and retention rates for minorities are peculiarly high at the ninth grade, just before the first administration of the exit-level TAAS" (*GI Forum v. TEA*, 2000, p. 30). However, the court determined that the "Plaintiffs have failed to make a causal connection between the implementation of the TAAS test and these phenomena, beyond mere conjecture. In other words, Plaintiffs were only able to point to the problem and ask the Court to draw an inference that the problem exists because of the implementation of the TAAS test" (*GI Forum v. TEA*, 2000, p. 30).

In focusing on the state's goal of motivating students, the court determined that, even though the plaintiffs offered evidence of other approaches (such as a sliding-scale system), they could not offer evidence that these alternatives could sufficiently motivate students to perform to their highest ability (*GI Forum v. TEA*, 2000, p. 48). The court determined that "in addition, and perhaps more importantly, the present use of the TAAS test motivates schools and teachers to provide an adequate and fair education, at least of the minimum skills required by the State, to all students" (*GI Forum v. TEA*, 2000, pp. 48–49).

The Case and the Plaintiffs' Argument

The plaintiffs' position was summarized in the introduction to the Post Trial Brief:

The TAAS Exit Test wreaks havoc with the educational opportunities of the State's African American and Hispanic students. The results of the TAAS Exit Test since its implementation in the State demonstrate that African American and Hispanic students consistently do worse than whites, whether the results are viewed on a single administration or cumulative basis.

The TAAS Test has even more insidious effects on students who may not even have taken the test. Because the test is touted as a part of the State's accountability system, school districts, schools and teachers have an incentive to encourage student retention or to exempt students in order to "improve" TAAS Exit Test performance. High retention rates, in turn, have led to over-aged students in high school, which is a major reason for increased drop out rates. In addition, schools have tended to focus on the "bubble kids" on the cusp of passing the TAAS Exit Test rather than students who need much more help reaching the passing score of 70. These students—the retained, the tracked, the limited English proficient, the dropouts—all tend to fall through the cracks of the State's accountability and educational system. It is no wonder that they cannot pass the TAAS Exit Test. It is on behalf of these "olvidados" and "desaparecidos"—victims of an educational system harmful and arbitrary in its effect on minority students— that Plaintiffs seek relief from the TAAS Exit Test requirements.

The State has failed to show how the TAAS Exit Test meets the standard of educational necessity. Because the TAAS Exit Test is an invalid test, it cannot serve in a significant way the State's goals of determining whether students have mastered higher order thinking skills. The State has the duty to show that the material covered on the test is covered in the State's classrooms—including its lower educational tracks and its ESL [English as a Second Language] tracks. The Court must scrutinize the State's duty more carefully when the State has a history of past discrimination, as does the State of Texas. As described below, Plaintiffs have demonstrated that the State did not ensure that the material covered by this test was actually taught in the classrooms across the State. Plaintiffs, in turn, have met their burden of showing that there are equally effective and less discriminatory alternatives to the TAAS Exit Test.

It is important to note that the Plaintiffs are not asking the Court to diminish educational standards or to make decisions about educational policy. Contrary to Defendants' arguments during the trial, Plaintiffs are not against high standards. Fifth Circuit law governing the use of standardized tests in this context requires that Plaintiffs show that the test has an adverse impact, that there are less discriminatory alternatives, and that the test is invalid. The Plaintiffs have met their burden. On the other hand, the State has failed to show that its test is educationally necessary and that it did what was necessary to ensure that the test fairly covers what the State's children are taught. The Court has the power and the duty to strike down educational policies such as the use of the TAAS Exit Test as

a graduation requirement when those policies unnecessarily infringe on students'
constitutional and statutory rights. Plaintiffs ask this Court to take that step here.
(*GI Forum v. TEA*, 1999, pp. 2–3)

The argument of the plaintiffs, as marshalled in their Post Trial Brief, contains three parts. First, the plaintiffs argue that the TAAS Exit test has had a continuous adverse impact on Hispanics and African Americans. Second, the plaintiffs maintain that the state has failed to show educational necessity for its use of the TAAS Exit Test, in relation to the argument that there is no manifest relationship between Texas's use of the test and the State's legitimate interest. Finally, the plaintiffs assert that there are equally effective and less discriminatory alternatives to the TAAS Exit Test.

A Continuous Adverse Impact on Hispanics and African Americans

The plaintiffs argued that adverse impact can be determined by the Equal Educational Opportunity Commission's (EEOC) Four-Fifths or 80 percent rule, by statistical significance, or by practical significance.[6] The plaintiffs further argued that even under the EEOC guidelines, even ratios greater than 80 percent may constitute an adverse impact in circumstances where the differences are significant in both practical and statistical terms (*GI Forum v. TEA*, 1999, p. 6), and that, indeed, adverse impact can be proven for all three measures. The defendants' witnesses not only conceded that there is an adverse impact in the first administration of the test but also that there has been a continuous pattern of adverse impact on minorities from 1990 through 1999 in the first administration of the test.[7]

The plaintiffs noted that a defendants' witness presented evidence that there was, in fact, adverse impact on minorities at the last administration of the test. In fact, they further noted that "his materials failed to include the numbers of students who dropped out of school before the end of their senior years or students who have given up and stopped taking the TAAS Exit Test after their junior year even though they have continued to remain in school and pass their courses" (*GI Forum v. TEA*, 1999, p. 10). The record shows that the state's calculations did not include sophomore students who were supposed to take the test but didn't, sophomore students who repeated their sophomore year and again failed the test, and sophomore students who took the test but were later determined by their special education committees to be exempt from the test.[8] The former commissioner of education in Texas testified that since 1994 there have been at least 45,000 students who would have received their high school diplomas but for the TAAS Exit Test.

Concerning the adverse impact of the TAAS on minorities after socio-economic factors were removed, the plaintiffs presented evidence that after removing students who fitted the socioeconomic categories,[9] there were still violations of the 80 percent rule, the statistical significance rule, and the practical significance rule. The defendants did not criticize or rebutt either this assertion or the fact that of the remaining "cream of the crop,"—92 percent of Whites, 76 percent of Hispanics, and 64 percent of African Americans passed the TAAS Exit Test. The same pattern of achieve-ment was seen from 1993 to 1996 (*GI Forum v. TEA*, 1999, p. 13).

Evidence was presented that showed "the TAAS Exit Test has an es-pecially negative effect upon students of limited English proficiency (LEP)" (*GI Forum v. TEA*, 1999, p. 14). "Between 1994 and 1998 on all tests taken, LEP students 'improved' from 14 percent *passing* to 26 percent *passing*. During the same time, white students went from 67 percent passing to 85 percent passing" (*GI Forum v. TEA*, 1999, p. 14). In fact, one of the defendants' witness "agreed that students of limited English proficiency had problems with the TAAS Exit Test math problems even though they knew the mechanics of mathematics" (*GI Forum v. TEA*, 1999, p. 14).

Concerning the adverse effect of the TAAS on minorities, the plaintiffs argued that the TAAS Exit Test has led to increased attrition rates among Hispanic and African American students. This topic has been explored in detail in a previous chapter; however, there are additional salient points that inform our understanding of this case. The plaintiffs argued that "the increased attrition rates of African Americans and Hispanics are relevant to this case in at least 3 ways: (1) they are direct evidence of adverse impact of the TAAS Exit Test; (2) they significantly weaken the Defen-dants' claims that there has been a significant improvement in minority test scores on the TAAS Exit Test which reflects real improvement in education; and (3) they weaken the State's argument that the TAAS Exit Test is manifestly related to legitimate state goals" (*GI Forum v. TEA*, 1999, p. 15).

Both the plaintiffs' and defendants' witnesses testified that only 52 percent of the African Americans graduated in 1998 who entered high school in the ninth grade in 1995 graduated. Even the former commis-sioner of education in Texas agreed that TAAS failure can add to a student's decision to dropout. In fact, the TEA's witness "testified that TEA's dropout statistics are not valid numbers. He admitted that the TEA's dropout numbers are the biggest weakness in their accountability system" (*GI Forum v. TEA*, 1999, p. 17). The plaintiffs continued by reporting that "for example, TEA does not count a student as a dropout if the student has left school because he has not passed the TAAS Exit Test. Nor does TEA include a student as a dropout if the student left school and later passed the GED test. Defendants also admit that their dropout statistics are very weak because they are based on numbers that are self reported by school districts to TEA" (*GI Forum v. TEA*, 1999, p. 17).

Related to the dropout problem is the problem of ninth-grade student retention rates. Information presented by both the plaintiffs and the TEA showed retention rates of 25 percent of minority students in the ninth grade in Texas public schools—higher than in any other grade in the Texas public school system (*GI Forum v. TEA*, 1999, p. 17). The plaintiffs indicated that "TEA's data shows that there is a very high correlation between the students' scores on the eighth grade TAAS test and their scores on the tenth grade TAAS Exit Test. Districts have an incentive to retain students in the ninth grade who are likely not to pass the TAAS Exit Test in the tenth grade in order to improve their tenth grade exit test scores" (*GI Forum v. TEA*, 1999, p. 18). Evidence shows that overaged students are most likely to drop out of high school.

The Educational Necessity for the Use of the TAAS Exit Test

In relation to the issue of educational necessity, the plaintiffs, main points are as follows:

> The state has not come anywhere near meeting its burden to show a manifest relationship between its use of the TAAS Exit Test and its legitimate interest in high standards and accountability in education in the State. Defendants' educational necessity arguments fail for several reasons: (a) the State does not need to use the TAAS Exit Test as a diploma requirement in order to meet objectives of accountability and the legitimacy of a high school diploma; (b) the TAAS system, especially the TAAS Exit Test has many very strong negative effects on educational progress in the State; (c) the State failed to show that the TAAS Exit Test is the reason for any alleged improvements in minority achievement; and (d) the TAAS Exit Test and its use are invalid. (*GI Forum v. TEA*, 1999, pp. 23–24)

One aspect of the educational necessity issue is that of grade inflation. In other words, the grades students achieve in their courses do not reflect their real level of achievement; the grade is higher than is warranted by actual performance, and, therefore, not a valid indicator of achievement. The plaintiffs rebutted this assertion by pointing out that Texas law requires the admittance of all students who are in the top 10 percent of their high school class into any Texas university, regardless of the students' test scores, personal evaluations, or courses taken in high school (*GI Forum v. TEA*, 1999, p. 26). In addition, TEA officials admitted that they were not aware of any empirical studies indicating grade inflation in schools. In fact, nine witnesses for the defense were cited as stating that there is not a grade inflation problem in their respective school districts. The plaintiffs pointed out that "all of the Defendants' witnesses agreed with Plaintiffs' witnesses that a student's high school grades give good and reliable information [on] whether the student has mastered the state curriculum" (*GI Forum v. TEA*, 1999, p. 26).

The plaintiffs argued that the TAAS has strong negative effects on Texas schools. They reported a substantial narrowing of the curriculum in Texas, especially in minority schools. This reflects a deemphasizing of the parts of the Texas curriculum not covered on the TAAS test, and enrichment activities. The plaintiffs supported this assertion with a policy statement by the Texas Counseling Association criticizing the TAAS because of its negative effects on curriculum, and a Houston survey of 10,000 teachers that showed 68 percent of the teachers viewed the TAAS "as an obstacle to instruction and thought that the test drives the curriculum, rather than the curriculum driving the test" (*GI Forum v. TEA*, 1999, p. 28).

The argument that the TAAS is not related to real improvements in achievement is supported, first by the assertion that "much of the improvement in the scores can be attributed to the increased dropout rates and increased retention rates in the ninth grade. Indeed, a minority student has only a 45 percent chance of getting through high school without being retained one year, while Anglo students have a 72 percent chance of getting through high school without being retained one year" (*GI Forum v. TEA*, 1999, p. 29). The former commissioner of education noted "that he was very concerned about the increase in exemptions for special education in Texas schools from approximately 100,000 to approximately 150,000 in one year" (*GI Forum v. TEA*, 1999, p. 29). A second supporting point is that schools have been instructed by the TEA on how to quickly raise their TAAS scores by concentrating on the "bubble kids" (those students who are most likely to pass the next TAAS test). In addition, part of the improvement in achievement has to be attributed to the significant improvements in the equalization and level of funding in Texas's public schools between 1987 and 1995, according to the Texas Supreme Court (*GI Forum v. TEA*, 1999, p. 30).

The plaintiffs also challenged the educational necessity of the TAAS in terms of the validity of the test. Plaintiffs reported that the worse minorities do on a TAAS Exit Test question, the more likely the question is to be placed on the test (*GI Forum v. TEA*, 1999, p. 32). The defendants' psychometrician testified that she found the same correlation. In an analysis of the test questions, on one question 71 percent of whites, 44 percent of Hispanics and 32 percent of African Americans answered the question correctly. On the same test, the same objective, and the same instructional target, the passing rates of another question were 90 percent for Whites, 86 percent for Hispanics, and 84 percent for African Americans. One witness reported that "the test construction methods employed by Defendants not only fail to detect and reduce potential item bias, but actually incorporate, generate, perpetuate and enhance any existing or potential item bias and overall test bias for both African American and Hispanic test takers" (*GI Forum v. TEA*, 1999, p. 35).

The plaintiffs challenged the test construction process. The director of the organization that develops questions for the test testified that not only did she not know the qualifications of the actual question writers, but the writers did not have to come from Texas nor did they have to have any particular knowledge of the curriculum (*GI Forum v. TEA*, 1999, p. 35). In addition, none of the writers were Hispanic or African American.

The plaintiffs pointed out that the state relies heavily on revolving committees composed of about 20 teachers to review TAAS test questions for potential bias and for adequacy of preparation (*GI Forum v. TEA*, 1999, p. 36). The committee members are not experienced in statistics, question development, or test construction. The plaintiffs questioned how 20 teachers can adequately represent the 6,000 campuses and approximately 200,000 classrooms in Texas schools (*GI Forum v. TEA*, 1999, p. 36). In fact, "the committees meet for approximately two days, and on average have about three minutes to review the language and the statistics for each of the questions that they . . . review" (*GI Forum v. TEA*, 1999, p. 36).

One witness used factor analysis to "show the difference between creating items that are theoretically related to certain objectives of the State curriculum and how students actually perceive the items" (*GI Forum v. TEA*, 1999, p. 37). He found that the racial groups perceive test items differently. He summarized his findings as follows: "The Exit level TAAS administered in the spring of 1997 has such a divergent factorial structure by ethnic group, especially in the Reading and objective Writing sections, that one can only conclude that the test generally measures different factors for the different ethnic groups. Some of the problems involve both item design and selection" (*GI Forum v. TEA*, 1999, p. 37).

The content validity of the test was challenged by the admission of the Texas commissioner of education that when the test was implemented in 1990 it covered matters that were not taught in the curriculum (*GI Forum v. TEA*, 1999, p. 40). "Thus, the State validated the test and set the cut score based on a set of items which may not have been part of the classroom content at the time the TAAS Exit Test was first implemented. This fact is important. Later versions of the test are based on the subpopulation statistics developed from the field test items, so each version of the TAAS Exit Test locks in the inequities created by the first test that had improper content" (*GI Forum v. TEA*, 1999, p. 40). In addition, the curricular validity of the test was challenged by the fact that when the test was being developed during 1989–90, "Texas did not undertake any sort of comprehensive survey of school districts, teachers, students or the actual textbooks that it used in its classes in order to determine whether the TAAS Exit Test was in line with the curriculum being offered in Texas public schools" (*GI Forum v. TEA*, 1999, p. 40). The Texas commissioner of education and the head of assessment for the TEA agreed that in 1990 the TAAS Exit Test covered material that was not being taught in the public schools (*GI Forum v. TEA*, 1999, p. 41).

The instructional validity of the test was also challenged for a number of reasons. The plaintiffs asserted that "there is very significant evidence in the record that there was not an opportunity to learn what was on the TAAS Exit Test" (*GI Forum v. TEA*, 1999, p. 41). Another reason for the challenge is the significant difference between the availability of certified teachers in high-proportion minority schools versus high-proportion White schools (*GI Forum v. TEA*, 1999, p. 42). This is related to the fact that "Anglos are much more heavily concentrated than minorities in districts labeled exemplary and recognized" (*GI Forum v. TEA*, 1999, p. 42).

Finally, the issue of educational necessity was challenged when the "defense witnesses agreed that there is no information showing a relationship of TAAS test scores to performance in later life either in the work world or the college world" (*GI Forum v. TEA*, 1999, p. 46). This is discrepant with the mission of the state, which is "to create a curriculum that {will} prepare students for success after high school, and to use the TAAS Exit Test to measure that competence" (*GI Forum v. TEA*, 1999, p. 46).

Alternatives to the TAAS Exit Test
The plaintiffs presented alternatives that are less discriminatory and equally effective alternatives to the state's use of the TAAS alternatives , which also meet the state's objectives:

These alternatives fit into five categories: (1) Returning to the system used in Texas before 1987 and used in thirty of the fifty states of granting a high school diploma based upon students' successful completion of their high school course and other state requirements; (2) Using a sliding scale combining the various TAAS Exit Test scores and a student's GPA into a system which would allow a higher grade point average to offset TAAS scores below the 70 cutoff; (3) The alternatives outlined and described in detail in a 1996 TEA study of alternatives to the State's use of the TAAS Exit Test; (4) The alternatives to the State's exit test that were recommended by TEA to the State Board of Education, 1992–93; (5) Individual witness recommendations on less discriminatory alternatives to the TAAS Exit Test; and (6) Establishing parent-teacher review committees to determine whether students have mastered the curriculum despite failing the TAAS Exit Test. (*GI Forum v. TEA*, 1999, p. 48).

Plaintiffs reported that "in 1996, TEA hired a private consulting firm to present a series of alternatives to the State legislature to the TAAS Exit Test. The Texas Legislature has not adopted any of these alternatives" (*GI Forum v. TEA*, 1999, p. 50). These included the following:

- Allowing students who receive an Associate's degree to receive a high school diploma;
- Allowing students who pass the Texas Academic Skills Program (TASP) and who have met all other requirements to receive a high school diploma;
- Requiring that remediation plans be filed for students scoring below a certain level on the TAAS;
- Contracting for a professional development system to assist school districts with the development of remediation programs;
- Allowing workplace certifications;
- Judging students' performance based on portfolios of their work; and
- Basing a passing score on the TAAS on a cumulative score from the three parts of the test. (*GI Forum v. TEA*, 1999, p. 51)

Also, the plaintiffs reported that in 1992–93, TEA staff recommended to the State Board of Education a redesign that would be based on performance tasks, projects, portfolios, criterion-referenced tests, and a norm-referenced program. These were not adopted.

Questions and Commentary

After reviewing all of the legal arguments and opinions, I think that it is important to recognize that this isn't just a clinical exercise in intellectual argumentation but a situation that has adversely affected tens of thousands of people over a period of ten years. Unfortunately, most of those tens of thousands have been and will be African Americans and Hispanics. The human cost of this standards initiative is amazing; especially in light of the fact that the deleterious effects continue throughout the individual's life.

What is also disconcerting is that everyone is aware of this cost. Regardless of the court's decision, the plaintiffs raised concerns substantiated by evidence that were also recognized to be problematic by both the court and the Defendant. If the state maintains its course and does not respond to the minority concerns, will this be due to the classic bureaucratic intransigence to change, to a stubborn arrogance among the controlling majority, or to a racially motivated agenda?

This debate over standards is about more than student achievement. It is also about defining the role of minorities in Texas and in the nation. It is also about providing access to societal roles that lead to money and power. I wonder if this battle in Texas over TAAS is nothing more than an extension of the culture wars between the Right and the Left. Is this battle merely a skirmish in the greater conflict centered on cultural pluralism or the assimilation of minorities into White majority culture? It is not only unfortunate but also tragic that children are used instrumentally in this manner. Essentially, in this political context, children are objectified as commodities that can be used to promote a political agenda. Unfortunately, since these children never gain the cultural capital that is acquired by those who pass the test, in most cases, the deleterious effects will be lifelong.

From a psychological viewpoint, the standards initiative in Texas is almost entirely motivated by negative reinforcement. In classic negative reinforcement, the subject responds in the correct way (correct as determined by the experimenter) only to avoid a negative or adverse outcome. However, an argument could be made that the TAAS situation is not an example of negative reinforcement but actually of punishment. Punishment occurs when the subject cannot do anything to avoid the adverse outcome. Undoubtedly, the evidence presented by the plaintiffs clearly indicates that some children are being punished. If some children haven't been taught the test content in school, some questions are constructed in a way that means some children can't possibly answer them, and some children are not allowed to compete because they are tracked or labeled, then there is nothing that these children can do to avoid the punishment that will stay with them their whole lives. Psychologically, negative reinforcement is considered an effective behavior modification tool but less desirable than positive reinforcement, but punishment, in this case, is unconscionable. It appears that the TAAS can not only be challenged as it has been by the plaintiffs but also challenged for its poor use of psychology.

The people of Texas should be concerned about another aspect of the TAAS. As we enter the new millennium it has been made clear by pundits of all stripes that we need to move beyond the old factory system of education toward a more relevant model—one that produces autonomous, creative, and critically skilled individuals. The evidence provided by both sides indicates that the TAAS is deeply entrenched in the factory system paradigm of education. It is important for us to remember that the factory system of the past century had a strong racially biased component that was not challenged until the 1960s. Is this the direction that the people of Texas are comfortable with—the direction in which they want to go?

Finally, as I reviewed this case, I was struck how this situation represents a classic problem of our political system—right out of an old "Problems of Democracy" course. Essentially, a group of United States citizens feel oppressed by the actions of their legislative branch and unsuccessfully seek relief from their judicial branch. What is the political lesson to be learned? First, the legislature must be targeted through lobbying, campaign contributions, and voter registration drives. Second, presidential elections need to be taken seriously, due to the ability of the president to appoint federal judges. If a conservative president has the opportunity to appoint an inordinate number of young and conservative judges, the effect of his or her action will last a long time. In fact, because of the judges' ability to develop an imposing set of legal precedents supporting conservative interpretations of legislative action, the effect will indeed last long. In fact, the adverse impact will affect generations of children within and beyond the tenure of a judge.

In light of the conservative judicial position, it must be noted that on April 4, 2000, Senator Paul D. Wellstone of Minnesota and Representative Robert C. Scott of Virginia sponsored legislation that would effectively prohibit states from using high-school graduation tests. Their legislation would bar states and school districts that receive federal funds under the Elementary and Secondary Education Act from relying on any one standardized test in making decisions related to graduation, promotion, tracking, or grouping by ability of students. The National Education Association, the National PTA, the National Women's Law Center, and the Leadership Conference on Civil Rights are supporting this legislation (Schmidt, 2000).

The legal action by the plaintiffs was especially significant due to the fact that the legislature in Texas only meets every two years. Also, the position of governor in Texas is constitutionally weak. Therefore, the regulatory agencies established by the legislature have great power. Without the support of the court and with the political structure of Texas, things do look bleak for those represented by the plaintiffs.

Notes

1   The *Houston Chronicle*, on January 9, 2000, reported that "Prado, 52, a graduate of the University of Texas School of Law, was appointed to the federal bench in 1984 by President Reagan. He was one of the first Hispanics in San Antonio to ally himself with the Republican Party." The *Chronicle* also reported that "he refused to slice the Alamo Heights school district into single-member voting districts last year, which would have concentrated minority voting strength. But he also declined to free Midland public schools from federal oversight of their school desegregation efforts."

2   High-stakes testing exists when failure to pass an exit-level exam bars a student from graduation. In the case of Texas, if students successfully complete all course work and meet all other school requirements, they still cannot graduate if they fail the TAAS test. One witness testified that the TAAS is the single highest-stakes test because it not only determines who gets a diploma but because it is also used to rate schools and evaluate teachers.

3   MALDEF has decided not to appeal this decision. In an interview quoted in an article in the *Houston Chronicle* on February 8, 2000, MALDEF lead attorney Albert Kauffman stated that "this has been an extremely difficult decision for us. We feel there are serious errors in the facts and law of the decision, but we have to weigh the chances of success against the chances of creating a bad [precedent] in this area of the law." In the same article, Jim Nelson, Education Commissioner of Texas, said that "it means that the litigation surrounding the test is now over and those of us at the Texas Education Agency can concentrate on continuing to prepare our schools for the changes and challenges that lie ahead." The article included a comment on the current project of the TEA. "TEA is in the process of developing a new and more difficult exit-level test that will be administered beginning in the year 2004. At that point, a new test will be added at the ninth grade and the exit exam will be moved to students' junior year and will become more rigorous with the addition of tests in algebra, geometry, social studies and third-year English. The changes in the test were mandated by the legislature. Once they are enacted, it will mean that students face high-stakes testing from the third grade through the 11th grade."

4   In most Texas schools and communities, the problem of student achievement, which in many cases dominates the local educational system, is centered on the African American and Hispanic students. The rating of the school, which is a reflection on the community, is directly associated with those students who do not pass the TAAS test. This unequivocal focus on minority achievement is due to the disaggregation of the test results into racial categories. One outcome of this focus is to perpetuate the invisibility of Whiteness. African American and Hispanic children are perceived to be the problem due to the perception that they are *personally* unable to do what is necessary to achieve a passing grade. Rendered

invisible by this focus is the fact that the policy makers and primary decision makers of this standards system, who are predominantly White, are complicit in the problem. Because of the rules of the game, established by the White majority, minority children and poor White children are held accountable for the educational woes of Texas. The burden and pain of accountability falls squarely on the shoulders of the minorities, once again hiding the participation of the majority.

5   In 1984 the Texas Legislature passed the Equal Educational Opportunity Act (EEOA), which was designed to impose an accountability system on Texas public school administrators, teachers, and students (*GI Forum v. TEA*, 2000, p. 13). "The Four-Fifths Rule finds an adverse impact where the passing rate for the minority group is less than 80 percent of the passing rate for the majority group" (*GI Forum v. TEA,* 2000; C.F.R. § 1607).

6   The plaintiffs "defined practical significance both in terms of the number of minorities who would have passed had their passing rates been the same as whites and by the importance of the interest implicated by the test, i.e., receiving a high school diploma or being discouraged from continuing high school education" (*GI Forum v. TEA*, 2000, p. 9).

7   In Texas, a second way of satisfying the testing part of the graduation requirements is to pass end-of-course tests in designated courses such as Algebra I, English II, and Biology or U.S. History. These tests are given at the end of the courses and can be retaken if a failing score was made. The plaintiffs argued that "in addition, the results of the alternative tests, i.e., the set of end-of-course tests that a student may pass to avoid the TAAS Exit Test requirement, show significant adverse impact against Hispanic and African American students. Specifically, on the first 'live test' of the Algebra exam 40% of whites, 14% of Hispanics and 11% of African Americans passed the test. On the latest administration of the Algebra I test, 52% of whites, 26% of Hispanics, and 20% of African Americans passed the test. There was also significant adverse impact in the results of the Biology alternative tests" (p. 9).

8   The plaintiffs noted that "students who have not been identified as eligible for special education and are later determined special education exempt after failing the test raise the concern of arbitrary 'reconsiderations.' These students are also predominantly minority students" (*GI Forum v. TEA*, 2000, p. 11).

9   "These categories, often referred to as the real causes of test performance differences, include: (1) economically disadvantaged; (2) eligible for Chapter I/Title I financial support; (3) participating in special education programs; (4) identified as At-Risk; (5) participating in vocational education programs; (6) foreign exchange students; (7) participating in bilingual education programs; (8) participating in ESL programs; (9) designated as limited English proficient; and (10) designated as migrant students" (*GI Forum v. TEA*, 2000, p. 12).

References

Cortez, A. (2000). Why better isn't enough: A closer look at TAAS gains, *IDRS Newsletter*, 28 (3), 1–2, 6–9, 12.

GI Forum, et al. v. Texas Education Agency et al. (1999). No. SA 97 CA 1278EP (W.D.Tex., November 8, 1999, Plaintiffs' Post Trial Brief).

GI Forum, et al. v. Texas Education Agency et al. (2000). No. SA 97 CA 1278EP (W.D.Tex., January 6, 2000, Memorandum Opinion).

Legislature asking, "Where do we go from here?" (2000, April). *Houston Chronicle, 99* (173), p. 20A.

Markley, M. (2000, March 12). A wealth of information. . . a place to start. *Houston Chronicle*, p. 2J.

Report Card. (2000, March 12). *Houston Chronicle*, pp. 1J–27J.

Schmidt, P. (2000). Measure would end use of standardized tests as a condition for high-school graduation. *Chronicle of Higher Education.* [On-line]. Available: http://chaonicle.com/daily/2000/04/2000040502n.htm.

Chapter 18

Why Better Isn't Enough: A Closer Look at TAAS Gains

Albert Cortez

Education advocates around the United States have been told to look to Texas for evidence that education reform can indeed lead to improved student achievement. People are taking note of improved Texas academic achievement test scores, particularly gains reflected in the state's student assessment system. National studies have noted that Texas students, both majority and minority, have performed at levels above those of similar students from comparable states.

The Intercultural Development Research Association (IDRA) has examined much of the data on which those claims are based and can concur that, indeed the Texas Assessment of Academic Skills (TAAS)—the state testing measure—seems to reflect an overall improvement in student achievement. This upward trend has included all students and all grade levels.

Decades of Reforms Begin To Pay Off

Before proceeding to a detailed discussion of the improved test scores however, it is important to remember the major educational reforms (see Table 1) in Texas over recent decades that have caused much of this improvement. It is also important to note that no single reform can account for the improvements noted in Texas public schools. Rather, the progress came about as a result of the combined effects of a number of distinct education reforms.

Much of the broad improvement in Texas student performance is the result of improvements made possible by increases in state funding for elementary and secondary public education. Since the adoption of House

Table 1 Educational Reforms in Texas

1975
- Texas requires bilingual education for English language learners in kindergarten through third grade.
- Texas creates equalization aid program for low-wealth schools and creates compensatory education program.

1977
- Texas increases equalization aid funding and increases teacher salaries.

1979
- Texas creates Texas Assessment of Basic Skills—a basic competencies testing program for grades 3, 5, and 9.

1981
- Court ruling requires Texas to implement bilingual education and English as a Second Language programs for all Limited-English-Proficient (LEP) students.
- Texas revises school finance provisions.

1983
- Texas develops the Essential Elements—state curriculum standards.

1984
- Texas enacts major education reforms, including:
  - increased equalization funding
  - increased teacher salaries
  - district performance reports
  - "Career Ladder" for teachers
  - planning period for teachers
  - no pass—no play
  - exit testing for diploma
  - four-year preschool program
  - dropout reduction programs
  - teacher testing (TECAT).
- Texas increases state funding of education by more than $900 million.
- This results in upgrades in the state's basic educational program and enables local schools to improve their staff, materials, and other areas that impact the quality of instruction.
- Texas provides supplemental funding (weights) to schools based on the number and types of pupils they serve, these including students who are gifted and talented, those served in special education classes, low-income students, and LEP students.
- Texas limits class size in kindergarten through fourth grade and provides funds to schools to meet limits.

1988
- District courts mandate the state legislature to equalize funding (Edgewood I).

Table 1 Continued

1993
• Texas revises its school funding system.
• Texas's state school performance standards are used as the basis of the state's accountability system. Districts must report performance on the Texas Assessment of Academic Skills (TAAS), attendance, dropouts, and other data.

1995
• Texas moves closer to equalized school funding to better ensure that school funds are equitably distributed (SB 4).

1996
• Some funding for facilities is provided to school districts on a competitive basis.
• Texas creates State Board for Educator Certification to strengthen credentialing of school personnel.

1997
• Texas develops the Texas Essential Knowledge and Skills (TEKS)—uniform state curriculum standards that reflect high expectations for all students.
• Texas emphasizes pre-kindergarten reading.
• Texas requires students who do not pass the TAAS to be automatically retained in grade.

Bill 72 in 1984, Texas has increased state funding by over $7.5 billion. This additional money has resulted in upgrades in the state's basic educational program, providing additional opportunities for all school systems to improve their staff, materials, and other areas that impact the quality of instruction being provided to Texas students.

In a second reform area worth noting, Texas provided supplemental funding that was based on the numbers and types of "special needs" pupils being served in districts. In House Bill 72, the state created a system of funding "weights" that were calculated as an add-on based on funding provided to the regular foundation program. The actual amounts that were received by schools were based on the number of special needs pupils being served by special programs. Special needs students are those who are gifted and talented, are served in special education classes, are in low-income families, or are Limited English Proficient. These supplemental special student population funds in turn enabled school systems to provide additional resources to better serve these pupils.

While additional funding was one factor contributing to improved school performance, organizations such as IDRA, the Mexican American Legal

Defense and Educational Fund (MALDEF), the South Central Collaborative for Equity (the equity assistance center at IDRA that serves Texas and surrounding states) and others that have supported equalization of public school funding, point to the act of ensuring that the monies provided were equitably distributed as another cornerstone of key Texas educational reforms. It took a series of state court rulings to move the state legislature to revise its public school funding schemes to enable all schools to have more comparable educational resources. The fact that lower-wealth schools were finally able to offer better-quality educational programs— long taken for granted in the state's more affluent suburbs—has contributed significantly to the overall improvement of student achievement in most of the state.

Credit for improved student performance can also be assigned to the development of uniform state curriculum standards that reflected high expectations for all students. The creation of these state standards clarified what was expected from schools and students and served to create a uniform curriculum that facilitated cross-school and cross-district comparisons. The establishment of a uniform curriculum led to the creation of a new state accountability system that enabled policy makers and the public to measure individual district and state-level progress toward meeting those standards.

These curriculum standards also facilitated the development of state school performance standards that were integrated into the state's school accountability system. Incorporating comprehensive reporting and accountability requirements that not only aggregate the numbers of all pupils but also include and give equal weight to the performance of subgroups of students (for example, low-income students, ethnic minorities) have contributed greatly to raising the levels of student performance across the state.

Ongoing state attention to stronger credentialing of school personnel (reflected in the creation of the new Educator Certification Board) ongoing updating of professional skills are also factors that may be contributing to improved student performance. Additionally, the state's decision to limit class size and provide funding for reducing class sizes, particularly at the lower elementary school levels, and its commitment to providing preschool opportunities to students most in need are also seen as crucial education reform initiatives, begun over a decade ago, that are now paying dividends.

Though the state now prides itself on the national perception that it is a leader in education reform that produces impressive student outcomes, those close to the Texas education scene will attest to the fact that many of the reforms discussed above were forced on state leaders, some by court mandates (like funding equalization) and some through the intense efforts of advocates who strongly believed in the efficacy of their reforms (class size reduction and early childhood programs). Whatever the motivation or origin for the changes, many of the tumultuous reforms that occurred in Texas seem to be producing results—at least in some areas.

Overall TAAS Passing Rates

The data presented in Table 2 summarize statewide student performance on the TAAS in grades 3–8 and grade 10 for the 1994 to 1999 school years. These data reflect the within-grade-level group gains achieved by Texas students in each of the grades tested. They allow for a comparison of improvement among the major subgroups of Texas pupils for whom data are gathered and reported.

The table summarizes TAAS performance for Texas pupils over a five-year period. The data reflect the percentage of pupils passing the TAAS within each grade in which the TAAS was administered. For example, in 1994, 56 percent of third-grade students taking the TAAS achieved a passing score on the exam. In 1996, 67 percent of those tested in third grade passed, and in 1999, 78 percent of third graders achieved passing scores. The bottom row of the table reflects the net gain or increase in the percentage of pupils passing the TAAS at each grade level. Thus for third graders, the number of pupils achieving a passing score increased from a low of 56 percent in 1994 to a high of 78 percent in 1999, or a 22-point gain for that grade level over the five-year period summarized on the table.

Table 2 Percentage of All Texas Students Passing All Sections of the TAAS, 1994 to 1999

Grade	Three	Four	Five	Six	Seven	Eight	Ten
1994	56	52	56	53	53	47	50
1995	65	61	63	58	56	48	52
1996	67	63	69	65	63	55	57
1997	70	67	74	72	70	62	64
1998	73	74	79	75	74	68	69
1999	78	78	82	79	77	76	75
Gain	22	26	26	26	24	29	25

Source: Texas Education Agency

In examining the passing rates across the grade levels over the time span, we note that all grade levels reflect higher percentages of pupils passing the TAAS. Almost all grades started with passing percentages that were in the high 40s and mid-50s in 1994, and most achieved passing rates in the mid- to high-70s by 1999, an average gain of 25 points across all grades. This notable increase in the percentage of pupils passing within a grade level over time has been noted by national researchers.

The data reflect the fact that all groups, across all grade levels, have shown an increasing percentage of pupils passing all sections of the test. Changes in the percentages of students passing all segments has increased most at the eighth-grade level, followed by similar increases at the sixth-, fifth-, and fourth-grade levels. The average improvements (labeled as "gain" on the table) for all students have ranged from a 22-point increase at grade 3 to a gain of 29 points at grade 8. These improvements are part of what is drawing so much attention to the Texas education scene.

While things have gotten better in the last few years, the same data document the fact that far too many of our pupils are not performing at grade level on these measures. For example, the 3rd grade data for 1999 indicate that although 78 percent passed, 22 percent did not. In a similar vein, though 79 percent of 6th graders passed the TAAS in 1999, 21 percent failed, and though 75 percent of 10th graders passed, 25 percent failed the 10th grade exam. We can celebrate a 75 percent passing rate but should remain very concerned that one in four students fails the exit-level test. Particular concern should be focused on the exit-level test since, at this grade level, failure on the test results in the denial of a high school diploma.

While the progress reflected in the increasing passing rates across all grade levels between 1994 and 1999 should be applauded, it is important to continue our efforts to ensure that all pupils have educational opportunities that enable all of them to pass the state's criterion-referenced test. Neither Texas educators nor the public should be satisfied until all pupils tested pass the state's mandated exam for their grade level. Concern with the numbers of pupils failing to achieve passing scores on the TAAS is heightened when we examine the disparate TAAS passing rates reflected among the state's largest ethnic groups.

Ethnic Groups TAAS Passing Rates

Table 3 summarizes the TAAS passing rates for major subgroups of Texas pupils including White, African American, Hispanic, and Economically Disadvantaged students. The data here show the percentage of pupils

Table 3 Percentage of Texas Students Passing All Sections of the TAAS, 1995 to 1999

Grade	Three	Four	Five	Six	Seven	Eight	Ten
White Students:							
1994	68	63	68	67	67	61	64
1995	75	72	75	72	72	63	67
1996	77	73	79	78	77	70	71
1997	80	77	84	83	82	75	78
1998	82	81	86	86	85	79	81
1999	87	85	90	89	87	85	86
Gain	19	22	22	22	20	24	22
Hispanic Students:							
1994	44	42	44	40	38	32	34
1995	54	51	53	43	40	31	36
1996	57	54	60	51	50	40	43
1997	61	59	66	61	59	49	49
1998	65	67	72	64	63	56	57
1999	73	73	75	71	67	67	64
Gain	29	31	31	31	29	35	30
African American Students:							
1994	36	32	35	32	31	25	28
1995	46	40	42	36	33	26	31
1996	49	46	49	47	43	35	37
1997	55	50	58	56	54	45	46
1998	57	59	66	62	57	53	52
1999	59	62	68	67	63	63	60
Gain	23	30	33	35	32	38	32
Economically Disadvantaged Students:							
1994	42	39	41	37	35	29	32
1995	52	47	50	41	38	29	34
1996	54	50	56	50	47	38	40
1997	59	55	63	59	57	47	47
1998	62	63	70	63	60	54	54
1999	69	69	73	69	65	65	62
Gain	27	30	32	32	30	36	30

Source: Texas Education Agency

from within each subgroup who passed the TAAS in grades 3–8 and grade 10. As was the case with the aggregated data discussed in the previous section, all subgroups across all grade levels tested reflect improved performance on the TAAS.

The data also show that minority pupils—both Hispanic and African American—how a greater gain in the percentages of pupils passing the TAAS in each of the grades tested than do their White pupil counterparts at each grade level. While White pupils in third grade reflect a TAAS passing rate that has risen from 68 percent to 87 percent—a net gain of 19 points—the Hispanic pupil passing rate for the third-grade level increased from 44 percent passing to 73 percent passing—a 29-point gain. Similarly, while only 36 percent of African American third graders passed the TAAS in 1994, the passing rate had increased to 59 percent by 1999—a 23-point gain.

The data show that while White student gains were in the range of 19 to 24 percentage points, African American student gains ranged from 38 points at grade 8 to 23 points at grade 3, while Hispanic student gains ranged from 31 points in grade 6 to 29 points in grade 3. It is this more rapid increase in minority passing rates that has led to the statements that Texas appears to be "closing the achievement gap" between White and minority pupils attending Texas schools.

A closer look at the data shows that while there has been evident improvement and a degree of closing the performance gap between White, middle-class pupils and low-income minority pupils, we are not at a stage where the relative performances for all the state subgroups are anywhere close to being equal. While there is reason to be hopeful, the ultimate goal of having all students achieve at high levels—regardless of race, income, or ethnic background—is far from a reality in Texas. A close examination of the TAAS statewide summary data supports this conclusion.

The recently released 1999 TAAS summary data reflecting the latest round of state assessments show that, in 1999, while 87 percent of White pupils are passing the third-grade TAAS, only 59 percent of African American pupils and 73 percent of Hispanic pupils are performing as well. The differential at the fourth-grade level is similar: 85 percent of White pupils achieved passing scores, but only 62 percent of African American pupils and 73 percent of Hispanic pupils passed all sections. The same 20-point gap can be seen between White students and African American pupils throughout the grade levels tested in 1999. While the gap is somewhat smaller for Hispanic students, the differentials hover between the 12- and 22-point level at the various grades tested. The gap is smaller than it was in 1994, but very significant differences between the groups remain. No educator should be comfortable until the differences between the state's major student subgroups are eliminated.

Tracking TAAS Performance of Groups
of Pupils Over Time

Another reason for reservation is IDRA's analysis of data on specific groups (or grade cohorts) as they progressed through the Texas school system from 1994 to 1999. Table 4 tracks the percentages of pupils passing the TAAS for groups of students that were in third grade in 1994 and calculates the gains in the percentages of those pupils passing all TAAS subtests in subsequent school years. Acknowledging that the actual composition of the individual students who make up this cohort may change slightly over time, it is safe to assume that the overall group scores (given the sample size) probably reflect the overall progress of the original population. With this assumption stated, we can proceed to consider the relative changes for the state's major subgroups over time.

For minority and low-income student advocates, these analyses over a five-year span give even less cause to celebrate. According to a trend data, the percentage of White pupils passing all segments of the test increased from 68 percent in 1994 to 85 percent in 1999, a net increase of 17 percentage points. For the Hispanic pupils who were third graders in 1994, the percentage passing increased from 44 percent to 67 percent— a net gain of 23 percentage points. For this group of Hispanic pupils, there was only a 6-point reduction in the performance gap between White and Hispanic pupils over the five-year span summarized—a net gain of only 1.4 percentage points per year.

A similar analysis for students who were third graders in 1994 indicates that 68 percent of White pupils passed the TAAS in 1994 while 85 percent passed the TAAS when this group was in the eighth grade four

Table 4 TAAS Performance of Groups of Students over Time, 1994 to 1999

Grade Year	Three 1994	Four 1995	Five 1996	Six 1997	Seven 1998	Eight 1999
White Students	68	72	79	83	85	85
Hispanic Students	44	51	60	61	63	67
African American Students	36	40	49	56	57	63
Economically Disadvantaged Students	42	47	56	59	60	65

Source: Texas Education Agency

years later—resulting in a 10-point net gain. Hispanic pupils who were third graders in 1996 had passing rates of 54 percent and increased their passing rates to 67 percent when they reached the eighth grade—a net gain of 13 points.

Comparing the White net gain of 10 points to the Hispanic students' net gain of 13 points for these groups, it is evident that the gap reduction over time is also very small—a total of three points or an average of approximately one half point per year. A similar pattern emerges for the African American cohort. While the percentage of third-grade African American pupils passing all segments of the TAAS stood at 36 percent in 1994, the percentage of these students passing all TAAS sub-tests increased to 63 percent by 1999—a net increase of 27 percentage points over five years. This increase can be compared to the 17-point increase for White students over the same period. This greater proportional increase of passing students means that the gap in TAAS performance between African American and White TAAS test takers did decrease for this group over time. What should be sobering for those committed to a complete closing of the performance gap, however, is the fact that the gap was only decreased by a total of 10 points over a five-year period (percentages of the cohort passing went from 68 percent to 85 percent for White pupils—a 17-point difference as compared to a 36 to 63 percent passing rate for African American pupils—a 27-point difference), an average "gap reduction" rate of only two points per year.

Assuming that all subgroups continue to improve at rates similar to those experienced to date, with White pupils gaining an average of 3.4 points per year, Hispanic pupils gaining an average of 4.6 points per year, and African American pupils gaining an average of 5.4 points per year, it will take many years before all groups achieve parity. In fact, if White pupils continued to improve their passing percentages at similar rates, 100 percent of those pupils would pass all segments of TAAS within five years (85 percent passing rates in 1999, plus a 3.4 point gain times five years = 102). Assuming a similar annual level of improvement for Hispanic students, it would take seven years (67 + 4.6 point gain times 7 years = 99.2) for 100 percent of that same Hispanic cohort to pass all sections of the TAAS.

The problem is that this Hispanic cohort does not have eight years left in the Texas school system. If they are now eighth graders, they have only four more years to achieve parity. The percentages passing must be accelerated by three times the current rates to produce results comparable to those of their White student counterparts by graduation time, a scenario considered highly unlikely.

For African American pupils a similar pattern is noted. It would take the group of African American pupils seven more years to achieve a 100 percent passing rate. As is the case with Hispanic students, these African American pupils do not have that much time left before graduation. Their improvement rate would have to double within the four years left for them to pass at rates comparable to their White classmates. A similar pattern can be noted for economically disadvantaged pupils.

These observations, along with our familiarity with the state's tendency to try to redefine away, rather than resolve, achievement gap disparities (as is the case with dropout calculating and reporting), are the basis for IDRA's reserved response to the so-called "Texas miracle." IDRA has concluded that there is far to go and much more to do to achieve true parity in achievement for all pupils. Looking at TAAS scores within single years is one good way of assessing whether we are making progress within grade levels, and it informs us about the extent to which we are narrowing achievement differentials within specific grades in Texas. We at IDRA, like others, celebrate the progress that has been made toward educational reform. Unfortunately, as is too often the case, IDRA is one of the few to point out that while things have improved, we still have far, far to go.

This reserve is further reinforced when we analyze within-grade historical-data for grade 10—the grade level where failure to pass the TAAS results in students being denied a Texas high school diploma. According to state summary reports, the percentage of White 10th graders passing all segments of the TAAS increased from 64 percent in 1994 to 86 percent in 1999—a net increase of 22 points. Hispanic pupils went from 34 percent passing all segments in 1994 to 64 percent passing all segments in 1999—a net gain of 30 points within the 10th grade. Similarly for African American pupils, the percentage passing increased from 28 to 60 percent—a net improvement of 32 points.

Despite the notable improvement observed, the gap among the percentages of 10th-grade pupils passing all sections of the TAAS remained huge in 1999. White students passed at a rate of 86 percent, while Hispanic students passed at a 64 percent rate, and African American pupils passed at a rate of only 60 percent. The inter-ethnic group passing rate disparity in the 10th grade in 1994 was 30 points between White and Hispanic students and 36 points between White and African American students. By 1999, the 10th-grade inter-group gap was reduced to 22 points between White and Hispanic pupils and 26 points between White and African American pupils. Given that passing all sections of the TAAS is a prerequisite for receiving a diploma in Texas, this difference easily converts to an estimate of the significant difference in the graduation rates observed for Texas's major ethnic groups, a disparity long noted by IDRA.

One area of additional concern is the fact that the passing rate disparities, which are narrowing at the elementary grades, do not show the same rate of reduction at the high school level. This is despite the fact that many low-performing pupils from all three groups (but particularly from the state's Hispanic population) have already dropped out by the 10th grade, leaving the group of "survivors" to take the 10th-grade exit TAAS.

The fact that the performance gap has remained relatively constant at the high school level suggests that secondary schools have much more to do before we can assume that the differential in TAAS passing rates for the state's major ethnic groups is being effectively addressed. Since there is no inherent inequality in academic potential among different subgroups of Texas school children, we must continue to seek opportunities and programs that lead to high achievement for all pupils. There is no reason minority and low-income students should have lower levels of academic achievement.

Clearly, some Texas pupils at each of the grade levels tested are passing. This is reason for applause. But passing the TAAS reflects merely a minimum level of achievement. It is not the same as mastering school subjects. We at IDRA look forward to the days when all children regardless of race, language background, or economic circumstance are achieving at high levels. Until we get there, it is too early to host victory parades and relax.

This essay is reprinted from IDRA Newsletter, *March 2000, with permission from the Intercultural Development Research Association.*

Chapter 19

One Private School's Response to Educational Standards

Sandra Harris

In the late 1970s and early 1980s, school reform efforts in the United States primarily focused on increasing the course requirements that led to high school graduation. By the middle to late 1980s a standards-based reform began that shifted these reform efforts to the specifics of the K-12 curriculum itself. Here, the primary purpose focused on identifying what students would be expected to learn, which, of course, defined for teachers what should be taught. It was at this point that President Bush and the nation's governors established national goals for education. In 1994, President Clinton signed into law the *Goals 2000: Educate America Act* (P.L. 103–227), which encouraged states to develop their own standards for education (Jennings, 1995).

As a result, there is no doubt that education has become the number-one priority for every governor in each of our 50 states ("Honoring the Past by Preparing for the Future," 2000). Every state is involved in a rigorous examination of data and monitoring of student performance to respond to the challenge of meeting high expectations for all students (Lammel, 1999). In an effort to determine if public schools are meeting these new standards, more and more states are participating in mandatory skills testing at various levels to assure accountability. In fact, 36 states produce school-level report cards which report test scores, dropout rates, graduation rates, and other course-taking information, while the other 14 states have created other types of accountability reports (Brown, 1999). This information is reported in the newspapers, on television, and frequently on the Internet. As in the State of Texas, public schools are openly identified as "Low-Performing" to "Exemplary"; all of this is a response to the call for increased accountability in meeting educational standards.

Yet, one in four of the nation's schools is a private school, and nearly 6 million of the nation's 53 million students in grades K-12 are taught in one of the 27,000 private schools that exist in America ("Survey Profiles Private Schools," 1994). According to the National Center for Education Statistics, this number represents a 30-year high for private school enrollment, and this growth is expected to continue through the year 2007 when enrollment for public and private students is expected to peak ("Projections of Education Statistics to 2009," 1999). The State of Texas educates nearly 4 million public school students, and an additional 201,000 are enrolled in accredited private schools (Texas Education Agency, 1999). What role does the state play to ensure that private schools in America respond to the call for higher educational standards?

While states have the power to regulate private schools, this power is not without limitations. Over 80 percent of America's private schools are religious institutions; therefore, regulations must consider the First Amendment's guarantee of the free exercise of religion. Five general areas of regulation are considered by state legislatures: recordkeeping and reports, licensing/registration/accreditation, health and safety, curriculum, and public funding. Although all states appear to have limited regulations, not one of the states regulates private schools in the same way as any other (Williams, 1995). For example, Texas mandates that only one curriculum requirement is placed on private schools: they must provide instruction in good citizenship (1995). However, even though states are only minimally mandating curricular standards for private schools, because of the strong influence of the media in reporting the educational standards issue, private schools are increasingly called upon to respond to many of the accountability measures, just like their public school counterparts. Certainly, the method for reporting and the means of demonstrating accountability may be different, but no private school in America today is free from the call for accountability. (For an in-depth state-by-state analysis see Williams, 1995.) This call for accountability in the private sector is illustrated in the following case study.

The Beginning

Castle Hills First Baptist School (CHFBS) was begun in 1981 by a group of interested members of Castle Hills First Baptist Church. This was a time when there was tremendous local dissatisfaction with the public schools and, also, a time when the number of private schools was increasing by nearly 30 percent throughout the United States ("The Exodus,"1991). Castle Hills First Baptist Church, with a membership of over 8,000, is located in a growing suburban area of San Antonio, Texas. The church had sponsored a popular preschool and kindergarten for over 30 years. With the size of the church and the successful early childhood program as the base, Castle Hills First Baptist School began with grades l–6 and an enrollment of nearly l00 students. The school grew rapidly, added a grade each year, and in 1987 graduated its first class of high school seniors.

Accreditation

At the time that CHFBS began, the Texas Education Agency (TEA) accredited both public and private schools. A private school could seek accreditation from the TEA or any accreditation agency of their choice, such as the National Association of Private Schools or Southern Association of Colleges and Schools, or they could choose not to be accredited at all. At that time, CHFBS was not interested in being accredited by any outside agency because the school's leadership was very concerned with maintaining control over its own curriculum, policies, and procedures. This desire to maintain independence began to be questioned, when, in the 1980s, the strong push for educational standards—local, state, and national—began to grow (see *America 2000: An Education Strategy, 1991,* and *National Commission on Excellence in Education, 1983*). Parents, especially, brought this issue to the forefront. For example, one evening after a Parent Teacher Fellowship meeting, in the school's second year, a discussion was held on why the school had chosen not to be accredited. At least one parent withdrew his children the very next day. The more this parent thought about the school not being held accountable by any outside agency, the more uncomfortable he felt. Accreditation was seen by him, as it was by others, as a necessary protection to assure that his children would be well-educated.

While many parents at that time did express concern, the issue of accreditation continued to be debated by the school leadership. In September l987, CHFBS had its first graduating class of high school seniors. Because the school was not accredited, the students had to take the GED test and needed to meet other requirements, such as a higher SAT score than public school students, to be accepted into certain colleges in the State of Texas. Parents and students alike expressed displeasure and concern and continued to lobby for the school to seek accreditation. Due to this lobbying, the school applied to the Association of Christian Schools International (ACSI) for accreditation and, after completing an extensive self-study, was granted accreditation in 1987.

While this debate on whether "to accredit or not" was going on, the Texas State Board of Education ruled that the Texas Education Agency (TEA) would no longer accredit any private educational institution in Texas. Instead, in 1987 it created the Texas Private School Accreditation Commission (TEPSAC) which would serve as a bridge between approved accrediting groups, such as the Association of Christian Schools International (ACSI), the Independent School Association of the Southwest (ISAS), and the Southern Association of Colleges and Schools (SACS) and the TEA (Texas Education Code, TEC §53.02.12, 1987). This act gave private schools that were accredited by approved accrediting organizations recognition by the TEA and the state of Texas. This also enabled graduates of CHFBS, as well as those of other private schools, to be treated like any Texas public school student for entry into college.

Teacher Certification

The challenge of filling classrooms with properly certified teachers has resonated throughout America as a result of increased educational standards. This has led universities that prepare teachers to strengthen their programs ("To Touch the Future," 1999). Texas universities have responded to this challenge by restructuring teacher education programs in many ways, such as adding more course work. Additionally, the state now requires that teacher education graduates pass a state-mandated test called the Examination for the Certification of Educators in Texas (ExCET) in order to be state certified (TEC §21.048, 1995).

Public schools throughout the nation are having great difficulty recruiting and retaining qualified, state certified teachers. Texas, in an effort to attract and keep its teachers, has implemented mentoring programs, increased salaries, and improved staff development—as called for in the new state standards. Still, there is a shortage of qualified teachers in many subject areas, especially in math, Spanish, the sciences, and special education ("To Touch the Future," 1999).

One of the questions most frequently asked by prospective CHFBS parents continues to be regarding the school's certification requirements for its teachers. Parents want good teachers with degrees and teaching certificates. From the first year of the school's existence, the CHFBS leadership required that all full-time teachers must hold degrees from an accredited college. However, recruiting and retaining teachers who hold degrees and recruiting and retaining those who hold teacher certificates are two different issues. The school has maintained its standard in hiring only teachers with degrees. However, it is faced with an even greater challenge than the state in hiring teachers who hold state certificates, because it has an even smaller pool of teacher applicants from which to draw, with its requirement that teachers must be born-again, evangelical, conservative Christians. This factor, in conjunction with the fact that when the school opened, teachers were only paid half of the local public school salaries, has made it especially difficult for the school to recruit and retain qualified, certified teachers.

Even though, as a private school, CHFBS has no state mandate for teachers to be certified, the influence of public policy statements and parental demands that teachers be certified clearly impacted the school. In an effort to proactively meet this standard, CHFBS implemented a teacher mentoring program which had an immediate positive effect on retention of new faculty (Harris, 1995). At the same time, the school began an aggressive fund-raising campaign and raised tuition, in order to increase teachers' salaries to, at least, 75 percent of local public school salaries.

Additionally, school policy was rewritten to require that all teachers obtain ACSI teacher certification within three years of initial employment (*CHFBS Board Policy and Procedures Manual,* 1999). Typically, ACSI certification requires that teachers earn a certain number of Bible college hours, but, additionally, it requires that teachers holding degrees in subject areas but not holding state teaching credentials are required to enroll in local university programs to take specifically assigned education hours. CHFBS also added a bonus incentive of several hundred dollars to be paid to each teacher when ACSI certification is earned and upon renewal of the ACSI teaching certificate. At this time, although CHFBS does not have a written policy requirement for all teachers to seek Texas teacher certification, teachers are encouraged to seek this additional qualification. To support this endeavor, in 1999, the school also began designating gift funds to earmark for faculty to use when enrolling in certification programs and in graduate programs to seek advanced degrees. All of this reveals, once again, that the climate for national and state standards has a strong influence on Castle Hills First Baptist School.

Curriculum

Especially with the addition of the high school, CHFBS became aware of the importance of having a curriculum that allowed students to integrate with ease into the school when coming from other schools—public or private. An independent curriculum that failed to correspond in scope and sequence with those of area public and private schools or failed to address course requirements for graduation allowing its students to be accepted to their colleges of choice was not appropriate.

Therefore, the school quickly realized the necessity of aligning its curriculum with state standards.

Until it was replaced in 1998 by the Texas Essential Knowledge and Skills (TEKS), the Texas Education Code mandated a specific curriculum for the public schools called the Essential Elements (TEC §28.001, 1995). The Essential Elements covered all areas of curriculum from preschool through graduation. Through 1994–97, CHFBS chose to undertake a massive curriculum alignment with the Texas Essential Elements. Essentially, the faculty was divided into areas of interest, across grade levels. This allowed the school's curriculum to be aligned vertically, which means that teachers looked at each skill and how that skill was taught in the grades below and above their own grade. Each Essential Element that was outlined in the Texas curriculum standards was reviewed by a committee. During this comparison of the CHFBS curriculum with the Texas mandated curriculum, these questions were considered: (l) What should CHFBS be teaching? (2) What is not being taught that needs to be added? (3) What should CHFBS not be teaching? and (4) What should be taught in a different way? For example, in considering the subject of evolution, there was agreement among the faculty that students needed to have access to the same knowledge base as their public school counterparts, and therefore, evolution should definitely be taught. But, since CHFBS was a Christian school, the decision was to teach it as an important scientific theory only, not the final word in understanding the creation of the world and man.

This curriculum project led to a major change in the CHFBS graduation requirements. It was decided to adopt the Texas Recommended and Distinguished Graduation Plans (Texas Administrative Code §74.11–13, 1998). The State of Texas has three graduation plans: a minimum plan of 22 credits, the Recommended Graduation plan of 24 credits, and the Distinguished Plan also of 24 credits. The Recommended plan requires two years of the same foreign language, and the Distinguished Plan requires three years of the same foreign language. Both of these plans require advanced math and sciences. CHFBS offers only the two advanced plans, which it calls Recommended and Advanced, for graduation. This change also led the school into a partnership with one of the local community colleges to offer dual-credit courses. CHFBS was one of the first private schools in San Antonio, Texas, to consider this partnership. The dual-credit program allows qualified CHFBS juniors and seniors to participate in college courses taught on the CHFBS campus and receive both high school and college credit.

Additionally, the language of increased academic rigor has been added to curriculum areas at every level of the school. For example, in order to better meet the needs of the variety of abilities and interests of CHFBS students, enrichment activities are offered in all classes in all grades. An Alternate Instructional Method laboratory has been added to give academic support to students who have been identified as having various learning differences. Along with the changes in curriculum that resulted from the alignment with the Texas Essential Elements, the school has openly committed itself to providing increased staff development opportunities for faculty. As a result, teachers are participating at a greater rate than ever in staff development workshops so that they can be better prepared to meet student needs. Obviously, many of these academic changes are related directly to the public advocacy of higher standards.

Testing

Texas has mandated a state-wide student performance-based assessment program at several grade levels called the Texas Assessment of Academic Skills (TAAS) (TEC §39.022, 1995). This is a minimal skills competency examination and students as well as schools are rated on the results. Private schools may participate in this testing, but they are not mandated to do so (TEC §39.033, 1995). CHFBS, like most private schools in Texas, chose not to participate in the TAAS testing. However, once again, the national and state attention to assessment and the publicizing of test results continue to have an effect on CHFBS.

Giving a norm-referenced test allows schools to gauge how each student is performing in relationship to other students throughout the nation who are the same age and in the same grade. Beginning in the first year of CHFBS, and for several years thereafter, the Iowa Test of Basic Skills, a standardized, norm-referenced test, was administered. Eventually, the school began using the Stanford Achievement Test. Each year, the results of this test are closely examined by faculty not only for information about each student but for information about the school. Many curricular issues are explored, such as the importance of the curriculum allowing student exposure to a knowledge-base that is secular, even though this may offer viewpoints that are in opposition to certain Christian ideas, as with the issue of evolution. The school examines the test results and makes adjustments in curriculum and teaching needs as indicated by the test results. This testing information is also published and made available to all parents.

CHFBS also examines its students' performances on other national tests, such as the Scholastic Aptitude Test (SAT) and the American College Testing Assessment (ACT). Entry into any Texas state college requires all public and private high school seniors to take a test called the Texas Academic Skills Program (TASP). CHFBS is one of many test sites for the SAT, and the ACT and TASP are offered to CHFBS students at other locations in the city. These additional tests allow the school to examine itself closely, independently, and in comparison with the city, state, and nation. While CHFBS has always given a standardized, nationally normed test, in recent years, parents appear to be much more interested in the results of the testing of the whole school than in just their own child's results. In fact, today, even parents placing their children in the kindergarten are expressing interest in the school's overall test scores all the way through high school. Once again, this illustrates and emphasizes the far-reaching effects of the educational standards movement.

Conclusion

Castle Hills First Baptist School is just one private school. Yet, it is illustrative of many of the private schools within the United States. It reaches out to the San Antonio community, not to offer an education of exclusivity but to offer a choice to parents who are seeking a good, decidedly Christian education for their children. When the school started, it naively did not think it would be necessary to concern itself heavily with issues such as accreditation, certification, curriculum, and testing from the state or national perspective. However, CHFBS quickly learned that standards accountability has reached into every segment of our population. Even if a legislative authority is not mandating standards, the public forum in which much of this expectation is being expressed has a strong impact on the entire population, including parents who seek out private schools for their children. Castle Hills First Baptist School is just one private school. It has responded to the call for accountability, certainly because it wanted to be the best school it could be but also because the state-wide and nationwide attention to raising the academic standards of all of our schools transcends any governmental mandate. The movement to raise educational standards has opened the eyes of every parent and educator in America to the need to implement these standards in a way that leads to better schools, both public and private.

References

America 2000: An education strategy. (1991). Washington, DC: U.S. Department of Education.

Brown, R. (1999). Creating school accountability reports. *The School Administrator, 10* (56), 12–17.)

Castle Hills First Baptist school board & policy and procedures manual. (1999). San Antonio, TX: Castle Hills First Baptist School.

The Exodus. (1991, December 9). *U.S. News & World Report,* pp. 66–68.

Goals 2000: Educate America Act. Public Law 103–227, 1994.

Harris, S. (1995). A mentoring program for new teachers. *NASSP BULLETIN, 79* (572), 98–103. .

Honoring the past by preparing for the future. (2000). *Phi Delta Kappan, 81* (5), 338.

Jennings, J. (1995). School reform based on what is taught and learned. *Phi Delta Kappan, 76* (10), 765–769.

Lammel, J. (1994). Castle Hills First Baptist School Curriculum. *NASSP Newsleader, 42* (1), 11.

Texas Education Agency. (1999). *Pocket Edition: Texas Public School Statistics:1998–1999.* Austin, TX: TEA—Division of Performance Reporting.

Texas Administrative Code §74.11–13 (1998).

Texas Education Code §21.048 (1995).

Texas Education Code §28.001 (1995).

Texas Education Code §39.022 (1995).

Texas Education Code §39.033 (1995).

Texas Education Code §53.02.12 (1987).

To touch the future: Transforming the way teachers are taught. (1999). Washington, DC: American Council on Education.

Williams, P. (1995). *The regulation of private schools in America.* [Online]. Available: http://www.ed.gov/pubs/regprivschl/title.html.

Chapter 20

Examining Professional Development Standards Critically Through an Ethic of Caring

Patrick M. Jenlink
Kathryn Kinnucan-Welsch

The quest for standards in American education has prompted a cascade of activity from the public schools to colleges of education. In retrospect, the decade of the 1990s could appropriately be termed the "Decade of Educational Standards"; a decade that has poised the American public for perhaps one of its most important tasks, that of scrutinizing the impact of standards on community participation in decisions concerning education, participation that is a basic democratic principle. As McNeil (1999) cautions, "*Standardization shifts both the control of schools and the official language of educational policy into a technical mode intended to divorce the public from the governance of public schools*" (p. 230) (italics in original).

Relatedly, from the courtroom to the classroom, the assessment of student performance at the local, state, national, and international levels is being challenged. Many educators believe that increasing pressure and attention with regard to standards for improving student performance has resulted in increasing pressure and attention with regard to standards for improving preservice and inservice professional development (Edefelt & Raths, 1999). Some would argue that developing these standards is at the very heart of educational reform, extending the argument for professionalization of teachers and teaching (National Commission on Teaching and America's Future, 1996; Yinger & Hendricks-Lee, 2000). Policy makers at the state level have also participated in the standards movement through issuing initial and continuing licensure regulations based on published professional development standards.

These standards for teacher education and professional development include standards for entry into the profession, such as INTASC (Interstate New Teacher Assessment and Support Consortium, 1992). The standards also address what accomplished veteran teachers should know and be able to do (National Board for Professional Teaching Standards [NBPTS], 1994). The accrediting process for units/programs of teacher education in institutions of higher education incorporates standards developed by NCATE (National Council for Accreditation of Teacher Education, 1997). Many states have published standards affecting licensure, but in this article we use the INTASC, NBPTS, and NCATE standards as exemplars.

Many would argue that one of the routes to better teachers and better schools is to ensure adherence to the standards for teacher education and professional development for entry year and practicing teachers. Lost in the technical language and political posturing that standards levy on American educational systems, however, is a critical focus on the escalating problems faced by teachers in public schools, problems symptomatic of a society whose technological sophistication has overshadowed its focus on humanity. It has become increasingly apparent that we live in a time when democracy is tested more than ever, and our schools come more and more under scrutiny. We live in a "world fraught with violence, anguish, hatred, and disregard for life, where learning how to care for one another is critical to our survival" (Sernak, 1998, p. 146). The need for teachers grounded in not only a technical language and formal knowledge base but also in an ethic of caring challenges popular discourses on standards and redirects the questions to focus on the political purposes served by advocates of adhering to standards at the expense of preparing teachers who are caring educators.

This chapter will focus on the need for a reconsideration of the standards in American education, particularly in teacher education, seeking to illuminate the problematic nature of a standards movement that is ostensibly focused on an ideological and technical approach to professionalization. In the sections that follow, an overview of the standards related to teacher education and professional development will set the context for examining the underlying premises of the standards. Using an ethic of care as a critical lens, the underlying premises of standards will be critically examined in an attempt to problematize professional development standards. The chapter will conclude with reflections on the need for an ethic of caring as a critical consideration in the preparation and professional development of educators for America's schools.

An Overview of the Standards

In this section, we provide for the reader an overview of the three sets of standards examined in the chapter. Included in this overview are historical, organizational, and political perspectives. An extensive, although somewhat dated, review of standards for certification, licensure, and accreditation may be found the *Handbook of Research on Teacher Education* (Sikula, Buttery, & Guyton, 1996).

National Board of Professional Teaching Standards

Formed in 1987, the National Board of Professional Teaching Standards was a response to the call for reform in teacher preparation (Carnegie Forum on Education and the Economy, 1986). In the introductory paragraphs of the document introducing the NBPTS, *What Teachers Should Know and Be Able To Do*, the authors state: "If America is to have world-class schools, it must have a world-class teaching force." (1994, p. 1) The authors of this document also offer a portrait of what it is teachers should know and be able to do:

> The fundamental requirements for proficient teaching are relatively clear: a broad grounding in the liberal arts and sciences; knowledge of the subjects to be taught, of the skills to be developed, and of the curricular arrangements and materials that organize and embody that content; knowledge of general and subject-specific methods for teaching and evaluating student learning; knowledge of students and human development; skills in effectively teaching students from racially, ethnically, and socioeconomically diverse backgrounds; and the skills, capacities, and dispositions to employ such knowledge wisely in the interest of students. (NBPTS, 1994, p. 2)

It is clear from this description that the standards are designed to promote a world-class teaching force, grounded in the existing knowledge base of the profession.

The primary purpose of the NBPTS is to design standards and related assessments for accomplished teachers in 30 fields of certification. It is important to note here that these standards are voluntary and are not intended to replace the licensing function of entry-year teachers that has been the traditional and historical purview of the states. The standards are seen, however, by those involved in the development and support of, as one element of a continuous professional development system "that ensures teachers have the knowledge and skills needed to teach diverse learners so they meet high academic standards" (NBPTS, 1994, p. 28).

Interstate New Teacher Assessment and Support Consortium

In recent history, teachers have been deemed to be professionally competent to begin their careers as educators when they have completed a state-approved program of study, typically through an institution of higher education. At that point, a state body awards the recent graduate a teaching certificate. Each state has had unique requirements for certification, and transportability of the certificate from state to state has depended upon the existing reciprocity agreements. In 1987, INTASC was created to support state agencies in collaborating to formulate model policies to reform teacher education, licensing, and induction into the profession (INTASC, 1992, p. 5).

In the original document describing the role and function of INTASC, the members of the consortium made it clear that the processes in which they were engaged were in alignment with the purposes, design, and goals of the NBPTS. In fact, the INTASC entry-year standards would be "Board-compatible" and would prepare teachers for eventual acceptance as Board-certified teachers later in their careers.

Like the NBPTS, the INTASC members used as their foundation a common core of teaching knowledge and skills that should be demonstrated by all entry-year teachers. What is interesting to note about the standards as developed is that they include not only knowledge and skills, but also dispositions. The INTASC standards also suggest that although states will maintain entry licensing functions, all states should adopt the same criteria: that is, "that the entrant is prepared to practice responsibly as the primary teacher of record for students" (p. 10).

National Council for Accreditation of Teacher Education

The responsibility for licensing and certifying individuals in the profession has been articulated by individual states. Recently, NBPTS and INTASC have joined some states in the dialogue concerning the role of standards in the licensure process. Accreditation at the institutional level, however, has been the function of NCATE.

According to the NCATE primary document, "The essential function of accreditation is to provide professional judgment of the quality of the education unit and to encourage continuous improvement of the unit. Thus, *accountability* and *improvement* in teacher preparation are central to the mission of NCATE" (1997, p. 1). Roth (1996) summarized the purposes and benefits of NCATE accreditation, including creating public confidence in the program, enforcing quality control, and providing opportunity for institutional self-renewal.

In 1991, the Council of Chief State School Officers, the primary group directing the INTASC efforts, resolved to collaborate with NCATE in the development of performance-based standards with a national focus. In 1995, NCATE revised program standards to incorporate a performance-based model. They have also entered into several collaborative initiatives and partnerships with state departments of education. These joint efforts suggest that a national focus in the development of both program and licensing standards is emerging.

The Underlying Premises of Professional Development Standards

The origin of the standards examined in this chapter offers insight into the underlying premises upon which they are based.

What prompted this articulation of what teachers should know and be able to do? Retrospectively, one premise of the standards is related to professionalization of teachers through a codified knowledge base. The efforts to codify a knowledge base for teachers is not new. Going on now for several decades, these efforts are part of an evolving pattern to professionalize teachers by formalizing the learning to teach process. These efforts, however, have often privileged one source of knowledge, that of formal or technical knowledge created by university researchers, over others, more clearly aligned with the practical knowledge of teachers and the relational ways of knowing that come from experience (Cochran-Smith & Lytle, 1999). Teachers learning to teach through a formal *knowledge-for-practice* program are disadvantaged when knowledge created in other venues, such as the practical setting of the classroom, is absent from their learning.

Clearly, some educators note that the move to setting standards is a correlate of redefining what it means to be a professional in teaching (Goodson & Hargreaves, 1996). For example, the NBPTS argues that bringing standards to the forefront of our profession should be couched in the motivation to bring to teaching the respect and recognition this important work deserves (NBPTS, 1994). Zeichner (1991) argued that teaching historically has been viewed as gendered work, dominated by women, and therefore more susceptible to rationalization and external mandate. The supporters of the professional development standards maintain that the development of these standards by and for the profession is an attempt to internalize the control of the profession itself.

From another perspective, the standards developed by INTASC and NBPTS were performance-based, and as such observable and documentable through actual teaching performance. The developing notion in the profession that teaching is a set of complex behaviors left many dissatisfied with prevailing paper and pencil exams, such as the National Teacher Exams (now Praxis II), which are not capable of testing complex behavior.

Many states have a requirement that students pass a paper and pencil basic skills test, either as a condition for exit from a teacher preparation program (for example, ExCET in Texas), or as a condition for employment (CBEST in California). These requirements have more often than not originated from outside of the profession, mainly through state legislative action. The development of the performance standards can be seen as a response by the profession. As Odell, Huling, and Sweeny (2000) note, the standards were "characterized as motivated by dissatisfaction with standardized assessments, which essentially measure low-level knowledge and comprehension, and interest in developing assessments capable of measuring higher-level thinking and student use of their knowledge in authentic applications" (p. 8).

In response to these developments on the educational scene, the NBPTS has begun to develop a complex performance-based system of evaluation of teaching performance based on video, written response, and portfolio review. Many of the licensure and content areas have been fully developed and are available for teacher review; others are still in preparation. INTASC is following the same guidelines for performance assessment as NBPTS; and indeed, the request for proposals issued by INTASC for the development of its performance system banned the use of multiple-choice items entirely (Klein, 1998). The movement toward a performance-based system of assessment has not been without controversy, and recent research has focused on the issues related to performance-based standards versus paper and pencil tests and on examining the portfolio review process (Klein, 1998; Moss, Schutz, & Collins, 1998).

It seems clear, however, that many educators and policy makers have accepted the underlying premises of professional development standards. Yinger and Hendricks-Lee (2000, p. 97) suggest that standards play a dual role in the development of professions. The first role is to demonstrate to the public, including policy makers, that the profession has sufficient internal quality control mechanisms. The second role is to define effective practice in terms of desired outcomes and performance. Standards become a framework of inquiry internal to the profession. From this line of reasoning, standards define and articulate the profession, both internally and externally, and embrace the essence of what constitutes a profession. The prevailing literature has, for the most part, left these assumptions unexamined.

Furthermore, the questions that are fueling the debate about standards focus on implementation issues such as cut-off scores, dilemmas related to supply and demand, and problems related to performance assessment. We are suggesting that the move to debate the issues of implementation has left unexamined, from a critical perspective, the underlying premises of the standards. That is our purpose in this chapter.

Critically Questioning the Underlying Premises

A critical examination of professional development standards has been suggested by many educators and argued strongly by others, some of whom have spoken in this volume (see the chapters by Kincheloe and Horn). In this section, we critically question the underlying premises of the professional standards movement. We will frame this critical examination most broadly through the lens of the ethic of caring. This section is organized by three critical questions: (1) what does it mean for schools and schooling to be guided by an ethic of caring? (2) how do the professional development standards support and/or inhibit the development of an ethic of caring in schools? and (3) how does an ethic of caring contribute to questioning the established conceptualization of what it means to be professional and the correlate of that, the notion of professionalization.

The Ethic of Caring
Nearly one hundred years ago, John Dewey (1902) wrote: "What the best and wisest parent wants for his own child, that must a community want for all its children. Any other idea for our schools is narrow and unlovely; acted upon, it destroys our democracy" (Dewey, 1902, p. 3). Dewey's reference is to an ethic of caring that must pervade the public school and the practice of those who are responsible for learning. Not only is this ethic a foundation of the kind of learning that we want for all children, it is equally a foundation of our democracy. A school whose teachers are technically equipped but lack an ethic of caring presents a threat to community and democracy.

Many educators have suggested that we are facing moral, spiritual, and ethical crises in our culture and in education as a cultural institution.

Noddings (1992) admonishes us that "the need for care in our present culture is acute" (p. xi). In our examination of the ethic of caring, we draw heavily from the work of Noddings (1984, 1986, 1988, 1992, 1993, 1999). Noddings explains that "caring, in both its natural and ethical sense, describes a certain kind of relation" (1992, p. 91). Going further, Noddings (1993) states that "An ethic of care starts with a study of relation. It is fundamentally concerned with how human beings meet and treat one another. It is not unconcerned with individual rights, the common good, or community traditions, but it de-emphasizes these concepts and recasts them in terms of relation" (p. 45). How then can an ethic of caring guide teaching?

There are three broad ways of answering this question. First, an ethic of care can be used as a critical theory (Noddings, 1993); that is, it can be used to illuminate and interrogate the cultural and social contexts of teaching and to problematize teaching based on ideological and political agendas. Second, and somewhat supportive of the first, a critique by Sernak (1998) suggests that caring may be viewed as a politics of caring rather than as an ethic, thus calling into question "accepted tenets of, as well as assumptions associated with, caring" (p. 5). In this view of a politics of caring, caring as cultural understanding is rarely considered by standards or acknowledged in the organizational structures of schools. Third, teachers as carers can be guided in their individual attempts to care as educators in classrooms interacting with children from diverse backgrounds, providing a strong foundation for both community and democracy as students interact in a caring environment where the ethic of care becomes self-inscripted in each student, and, in turn in, society.

Each of the ways of describing how an ethic of care can guide teaching could provide far more extensive material than can be treated in this chapter. The importance of an ethic of caring in the larger discourse of professional development standards is offered by returning to Noddings, whose thoughts help to form the three perspectives when she notes that teachers as carers,

> want to produce acceptable persons—persons who will support worthy institutions, live compassionately, work productively but not obsessively, care for older and younger generations, be admired, trusted, and respected. To shape such persons, teachers need not only intellectual capabilities but also a fund of knowledge about the particular persons with whom they are working. (Noddings, 1988, p. 221)

The notable absence of this basic philosophy from the larger texts of professional development standards calls into question the implications of any standards wherein teachers are viewed as grounded in a technical knowledge that is decontextualized from the realities of schools. More pragmatically, caring is obviously missing from a philosophy wherein teachers are viewed as responsible only for getting students to learn particular subjects. From the perspective of caring as political, it is incumbent on teacher educators and teacher practitioners to ask whether standards privilege the political agendas of accrediting agencies while they move the politics of race, diversity, social justice and caring to the background of activity. From an institutional perspective, caring involves teacher educators as well as preservice and inservice teachers' "responding to the particular concrete, physical, spiritual, intellectual, psychic, and emotional needs" (Tronto, 1993, p. 174) of the individual within the school and of the entire school community as well. From the perspective of caring as a critical theory, "it is activated when we are challenged to justify our recommendations in light of practicalities of contemporary schooling. . . .we must transform the conditions of schooling so that teachers and students can adequately care for one another" (Noddings, 1993, p. 51).

When we adopt an ethic of caring, whether from a perspective of critical theory, politics of caring, or relationship and relational way of knowing, we are led as teacher educators to critically examine our own practice, focusing most importantly on the foundations of how we prepare preservice and inservice educators.

Professional Development Standards:
Inhibitors or Enablers of an Ethic of Caring

From the perspective of professional standards, the role of teachers in public schools is that of transmitters of objectified knowledge, and education is seen as preparation for the workforce and citizenship. Conversely, from a caring perspective, as Dewey (1902) insisted, education is life itself. But even as preparation, it encompasses far more than getting a well-paid job. "Ideally, it is preparation for caring—for family life, child-raising, neighborliness, aesthetic appreciation, moral sensitivity, environmental wisdom, religious or spiritual intelligence, and a host of other aspects of a full life" (Noddings, 1999, p. 14).

When teaching is viewed as merely a technical activity, and teachers are de-skilled by a focus on technical knowledge as most often exemplified in professional standards, the technical view of teaching deflects attention from the political nature of teaching. The political nature of curriculum and pedagogy is often silenced and hidden by the focus on teaching as a technical activity. The outcome of such silencing is that a "focus on technical competence diverts attention from an examination of, for example, the curriculum that favors the knowledge, history, and ideology of some groups over others" (King, 1994, p. 99). The privileging of one ideology (of a dominant culture) at the expense of others (of minority cultures) leads to th.e reproduction of social structures and value and belief systems that are the foundation of many of the problems in American society and in particular in education and schools.

A close examination of the professional development standards suggests a prevailing vision of teaching as a problem of technical competence, efficiency, and scientifically proven methods, masking the fact that teaching is context specific, highly unpredictable, and largely based on relationships with students. Emphasizing a technical language—language of accountability—while deemphasizing a language of responsiveness and caring suggests a lack of understanding of the sociocultural nature of schooling while highlighting a need for technical professionalization from the outside in, leaving teachers ill equipped to address the problematic nature of schools. Perhaps the most pervasive, and therein problematic, characteristic of professional development standards concerned with teacher education and professional development is that of decontextualizing knowledge from the social context in which teacher practice is carried out and in which student learning occurs—the classroom.

The question of whether professional development standards inhibit or enable an ethic of caring, when addressed from the three perspectives presented earlier, that of a critical theory, a politics of caring, and a relationship, provides a fundamental view of the standards as inhibiting an ethic of caring. The focus on technical knowledge obscures the importance of caring in teacher preparation while moving to the foreground the larger political agenda of accountability. In this view, that inhibits an ethic of caring, the standards movement is suggestive of an ideological belief focused on a technical professionalization of teaching.

Upon acknowledging "universal" standards of knowledge and technical expertise for teaching, teacher educators and preservice and inservice teachers are pressed into the cultural reproduction of a political ideology that distances teachers from relationships and relational ways of knowing their students. This cultural reproduction—where teachers are deskilled and re-skilled according to universal standards of knowledge and practice—codifies teacher preparation and commodifies teacher certification; thus difference and diversity are subverted into "universal" standards, and issues of race, equity, justice, and caring are obscured by demands for the technical professionalization of teachers.

Questioning the Conceptualization of Professionalism

The advancement of standards in America today has a long history and within this history, teacher professionalism has a presence. As such, teacher professionalism, in recent years, has increasingly become an ideology, a belief system that contains some insight but also serves to politically obscure important questions. Professionalism for teachers is an ideology that encompasses the conflicting expectations that our society has of teachers and that have become in part a form of political pressure to fix teaching and teacher preparation. The aspects of the ideal that motivate a critical assessment of teacher preparation and professional development are interwoven into the critical assessment of schools and work conditions for teachers and are linked with other values and assumptions that, in practice, impede action to improve teacher preparation and ultimately limit change in schools. "Like other ideologies, teacher professionalization reveals some issues but conceals others; it is contradictory and ambivalent in its appeal" (Burbules & Densmore, 1991, p. 47).

As an example, Hargreaves and Goodson (1996) suggest that the multiple discourses of professionalism and professionalization may, in fact, serve to both empower and exploit teachers in the prevailing struggles that characterize postmodern society. They comment as follows:

> It is our belief that such struggles should primarily be guided *not* by interests of self-serving status enhancement (as is common within classical professionalism), nor should they be confined to matters of technical competence and personal, practical reflection (as in many versions of practical professionalism).The struggle we have in mind, rather, is one which is guided by moral and socio-political visions of purposes which teacher professionalism should serve within actively caring communities and vigorous social democracies. (p. 20)

Although some proponents of professional standards have argued that standards and assessments are linked to competent, caring teachers (National Commission on Teaching and America's Future [NCATF], 1996), Andrew (1997) suggests that "although the authors [NCTAF, 1996] often call for caring teachers, their *know and can do* lingo that has emerged as the mantra of the standards movement loses the personal, ethical, and value-centered components of good teaching" (p. 167). What is the essence of the caring ethic of teaching? We have turned to Noddings (1984, 1986, 1988, 1992, 1993, 1999) work to shape our lens on the ethic of caring in education.

Indeed, as we have suggested in this chapter, Noddings (1992) fore-shadowed the emphasis on standards that was to mature in the latter part of the 1990s. She commented in 1992, "At the present time, it is obvious that our main purpose is not the moral one of producing caring people, but instead, a relentless—and as it turns out, hapless—drive for academic adequacy" (p. xii). Noddings contends that we have offered only shallow educational responses instead of necessarily deep social change. Concentrating on building an ethic of caring in schools may, in fact, support the deep social change that is called for in today's world of violence, social injustice, and enduring poverty despite visible wealth. We need to acknowledge a public responsibility for raising healthy, competent, and caring children (p. 14). Nowhere do the professional development standards explicitly address this need. Perhaps turning to a deepened and enlightened understanding of the ethic of care may do more to advance our profession than the seductive allure of uncritical compliance with professional standards.

Critical Reflections

In the ongoing debate about standards for teacher education and professional development, there are two primary considerations that must be examined in the social, political, and cultural context of schools. The first is that standards are ideologically grounded in the dominant voice of the political scene and largely contribute to cultural reproduction—the transmission to successive generations of teachers of the currently valued knowledge and resources of the culture so that these teachers can contribute productively to professionalism, in their turn, as members of the teaching profession. This view decontextualizes teaching from schools and embraces an ideological stance of professionalization of teachers that moves the political agendas of state and national agencies ahead of the local politics of difference, justice, race, and caring that are part of school cultures and communities.

The second consideration is that an ethic of caring must balance any professional development standards, leading to cultural transformation as teachers embrace caring as critical theory that enables the illumination and interrogation of political and cultural issues while problematizing schools and teaching. Embedded in this consideration is an understanding of caring as politics and an understanding that teachers must examine the social structures and political ideologies through a political lens, particularly as they continue to work through the type of professionalism they seek to embrace in a changing and challenging educational system. The place of caring as a relationship between the teacher and student—a relationship that weaves together the school community and the larger society—is at the heart of teacher education and professional development. Teacher preparation must enable the teacher to achieve her or his potential as an educator and to make original, and possibly divergent, contributions to the school community and the larger community of practice to which all teachers belong.

It is hoped that future discourses on standards and teacher education and practice will be more concerned with the question of which educational, moral, and political commitments ought to guide our work in the field, rather than merely dwelling on which procedures and organizational arrangements will most effectively help us realize tacit and often unexamined ends.

References

Andrew, M. D. (1997). What matters most for teacher educators. *Journal of Teacher Education, 48*, 167–176.

Burbules, N. C., & Densmore, K. (1991). The limits of making teaching a profession. *Educational Policy, 5* (1), 44–63.

Carnegie Task Force on Teaching as a Profession. (1986). *A nation prepared: Teachers for the 21st century.* Washington, DC: Carnegie Forum on Education and the Economy, Task Force on Teaching as a Profession.

Carnegie Forum on Education and the Economy (1986). A nation prepared: Teachers for the 21st century. Washington, DC: Carnegie Forum on Education and the Economy, Task Force on Teaching as a Profession.

Cochran-Smith, M., & Lytle, S. L. (1999). Relationships of knowledge and practice: Teacher learning in communities. In A. Iran-Nejad and P. D. Pearson (Eds.), *Review of research in education, Vol. 24* (pp. 249–305). Washington, DC: American Educational Research Association.

Dewey, J. (1902). *The school and society.* Chicago: University of Chicago Press.

Edefelt, R. A., & Raths, J. D. (1999). *A brief history of standards in teacher education.* Reston, VA: Association of Teacher Educators.

Goodson, I. F., & Hargreaves, A. (Eds.). (1996). *Teachers' professional lives.* London: The Falmer Press.

Hargreaves, A., & Goodson, I. (1996). Teachers' professional lives: Aspirations and actualities. In I. F. Goodson & A. Hargreaves (Eds.), *Teachers' professional lives* (pp. 1–27). London: The Falmer Press.

Interstate New Teacher Assessment and Support Consortium. (1992). *Model standards for beginning licensing and development: A resource for state dialogue.* Washington, DC: Council of Chief State School Officers.

King, M.B. (1994). Locking ourselves in: National standards for the teaching profession. *Teaching and Teacher Education, 10* (1), 95–108.

Klein, S. P. (1998). Standards for teacher tests. *Journal of Personnel Evaluation in Education, 12* (2), 123–138.

McNeil, L. M. (1999). *Contradictions of school reform: Educational costs of standardized testing.* New York: Routledge.

Moss, P. A., Schutz, A. M., & Collins, K. M. (1998). An integrative approach to portfolio evaluation for teacher licensure. *Journal of Personnel Evaluation in Education, 12* (2), 139–161.

National Board for Professional Teaching Standards. (1994). *What teachers should know and be able to do* [On-line]. Available: http:www.nbpts.org/nbpts/standards/intro.html

National Commission on Teaching and America's Future. (1996). *What matters most: Teaching for America's future.* New York: Author.

National Council for Accreditation of Teacher Education. (1997). *Standards, procedures, and policies for the accreditation of professional educational units (Rev. ed.).* Washington, DC: Author.

Noddings, N. (1984). *Caring: A feminine approach to ethics and moral education.* Berkeley, CA: University of California Press.

Noddings, N. (1986). Fidelity in teaching, teacher education, and research for teaching. *Harvard Education Review, 56* (4), 496–510.

Noddings, N. (1988). An ethic of caring and its implications for instructional arrangements. *American Journal of Education, 96* (2), 215–230.

Noddings, N. (1992). *The challenge to care in schools: An alternative approach to education.* New York: Teachers College Press.

Noddings, N. (1993). Caring: A feminist perspective. In K. A. Strike & P. L. Ternasky (Eds.), *Ethics for professionals in education: Perspectives for preparation and practice* (pp. 43–53). New York: Teachers College Press.

Noddings, N. (1999). Care, justice, and equity. In M. S. Katz, N. Noddings, & K. A. Strike (Eds.), *Justice and caring: The search for common ground in education* (pp. 7–20). New York: Teachers College Press.

Odell, S. J., Huling, L., & Sweeny, B.W. (2000). Conceptualizing quality mentoring. In S. J. Odell and L. Huling (Eds.), *Quality mentoring for novice teachers* (pp. 3–14). Indianapolis, IN: Kappa Delta Pi, International Honor Society in Education.

Roth, R. A. (1996). Standards for certification, licensure, and accreditation. In J. P. Sikula, T. J. Buttery, & E. Guyton (Eds.), *Handbook of research on teacher education: A project of the Association of Teacher Educators* (pp. 242–278). New York: Macmillan.

Sernak, K. (1998). *School leadership—Balancing power with caring.* New York: Teachers College Press.

Sikula, J., Buttery, T., & Guyton, E. (Eds.). (1996). *The handbook of research on teacher education.* New York: Macmillan.

Tronto, J. (1993). *Moral boundaries: A political argument for an ethic of care.* New York: Routledge.

Yinger, R. J., & Hendricks-Lee, M. S. (2000). The language of standards and teacher education reform. *Educational Policy, 14*(1), 94–106.

Zeichner, K.M. (1991). Contradictions and tensions in the professionalization of teaching and the democratization of schools. *Teachers College Record, 92* (3), 363–379.

PART FIVE

CONCLUSIONS AND QUESTIONS

Chapter 21

See Your Standards and Raise You: Standards of Complexity and the New Rigor in Education

Joe L. Kincheloe

What might a high-quality, practical, challenging, and engaging pedagogy for the needs of the twenty-first century look like? It would not look like what's presently occurring in Texas, I assert. With this in mind, chapter 21 presents a few ideas about the nature of a rigorous and equitable education. While I do not provide a blueprint—they are often absolutist and arrogant, and always reductionistic—I do offer for analysis a few suggestions for a new definition of quality education. Over the past twenty-five years, right-wing educational reformers have been able to claim the words quality and rigor, claiming ownership of an educational excellence grounded on the reductionistic features of a test-driven curriculum such as the one in Texas, teacher accountability based on a rationalistic standardization and decontextualization of practice, and an equation of issues of equity and justice with the subversion of standards.

In the name of standards of complexity, I challenge this viewpoint. In poker lingo, I "see" the assertion of high standards put forward by right-wing analysts and the Texas political and educational leadership and "raise" their ante to a much higher-level standard of educational practice. To develop a rigorous system of education, much more needs to be done; far more difficult objectives need to be delineated than most that have been implemented and proposed in the Texas case. As asserted in chapter one, any successful educational reform must be grounded on a sophisticated understanding of the relationship between rigorous scholarship, emerging social conditions, and democratic issues concerning inclusivity and quality education for all regardless of race, class, or gender. The changes in the culture of information and knowledge production are profound and must be addressed by educational reformers.

Well-educated individuals in the future must understand these complexities. Not only do teachers and students need to know how to use a variety of the emerging high-tech information technologies but they must also develop the ability to ask penetrating questions of the knowledge accessed, the dynamics involved with the interpretive process, the relation between power and information, and their own level of expertise in knowledge producing. Our concern is that such abilities be developed in the most sophisticated manner and be possessed by the largest possible percentage of the population.

The ability to ask such questions and provide sophisticated answers to them is central to the academic/practical/cognitive skills of a rigorously educated person in the twenty-first century. Such an individual understands that these academic abilities not only involve the ability to locate information but the ability to detect previously unidentified problems. At this point, rigorous scholars can both access data and deploy forms of analysis that lead to original answers.

What we are referencing here is the ability for large numbers of people to do what too few people presently can: to move beyond the information given. This aspect of rigorous scholarship in the new information society involves the development of interpretive skills that open new worlds to the analyst. Here texts begin to reveal far more than initial readings might suggest. Reading transcends the process of "information retrieval"—so typical of the Texas curriculum and many other standards-based reforms—and morphs into an awareness of the ways different interpretive schemas shape diverse understandings of particular information. In this situation the highly skilled scholars explore the process of making inference, establishing validity, evaluating significance, and discerning implications. The potential of human beings to reach higher orders of cognition is profoundly enhanced when legions of people can uncover the forces that shape what is considered knowledge. It is time for a public dialogue on this issue. This is what we are attempting to generate in standards of complexity; it is missing from the Texas definition of high-standards education.

The mismatch between contemporary society's intellectual needs and the cognitive abilities cultivated by many standards-driven systems cannot continue. The standards movement's conception of higher-order cognition simply fails to deal with the needed intellectual abilities—especially their widespread dispersion throughout the U.S. population. The editors and authors of *American Standards: Quality Education in a Complex World—The Texas Case* insist that the intellectual skills needed to cope with the emerging global informational order extend far beyond present educational reformers' call for the acquisition and reproduction of factual data on standardized tests. Such skills in standards of complexity include the acquisition and reproduction of information in a variety of contexts but also move to new levels of understanding of the production of knowledge and the assumptions that shape the form knowledge takes. The unstated assumptions behind reductionistic, technical visions of the characteristics of educated people involve a computer-like conception of the human mind where storage and retrieval of data are its central features. In this outdated mode of conceptualizing education and the information age, vision is limited to calls for all students to have computers at their desks to help them commit certain information to their memory. We conceptually move far beyond such a viewpoint.

Standards of complexity insist that education must be more rigorous than previously imagined. With this notion in mind it assembles a corps of scholars and master teachers to specify what is needed in the effort to develop and implement the vision. Educational professionals will have to be immersed in historical, social, cultural, political, administrative, psychological, philosophical, and curricular and pedagogical analyses that are integrated in a manner that provides unprecedented aid to those interested in the quest for truly rigorous educational standards for more than a privileged minority of students. I hope that the following will engage you in the excitement of such an educational quest just as others have devoted their passions to the exploration of space or the analysis of the sub-atomic quantum domain. The possibilities for human development embedded in these pedagogical explorations are infinite.

What Do We Mean by Complexity?

Teachers working toward standards of complexity rebel against the view of practitioners as information deliverers, as deskilled messengers who uncritically pass along a canned curriculum. Highly skilled, scholarly teachers research their students and their communities and analyze the curricular topics they are expected to cover. In light of such inquiry, these teachers develop a course of study that understands subject matter and academic skills in relation to where their students come from and the needs they bring to school. Such an act is highly difficult, requiring a wide range of knowledge and abilities as well as subtle pedagogical skills. If nothing else, it is complex. When this complexity is added to the complications of a deep understanding of knowledge and its production, the job of teaching to rigorous standards becomes a profoundly sophisticated task (Novich, 1996).

Educators and policy makers who appreciate complexity in the way it is employed here know that the physical world and social reality answer analysts' questions much like the oracle at Delphi—enigmatically. Rarely do top-down, technical standards take into account issues of complexity such as the following:

1. The ambiguity of language makes meaning less than transparent.
2. Individual minds rarely perceive phenomena and their meanings in the same way.
3. Meaning making is not simply a rational process.
4. The boundary between rationality and irrationality is blurred.
5. The construction of a neutral curriculum is an impossibility.
6. Researchers coming from different value positions will often produce contradictory information about a particular artifact.
7. There are disagreements about the benefits of reason. (Madison, 1988; Thomas, 1998)

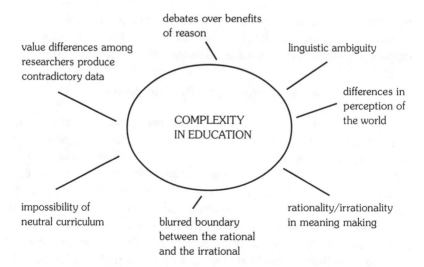

Issues Contributing to Educational Complexity

The importance of understanding these issues contributing to educational complexity revolves around the conceptual and cognitive limitations of that which comprises schoolwork. In such a context the analytical abilities of, say, an Albert Einstein would not be recognized as legitimate or relevant. Einstein would not have been a good student in schools shaped by top-down technical standards, because he was not proficient at memorizing data. When it came to viewing the world from unprecedented angles, viewing contradictions within accepted bodies of knowledge, developing thought experiments where "what would happen if . . . ?" questions were raised, transferring learning from one domain to another, or applying particular forms of knowledge to problems in the lived world, however, Einstein was undoubtedly a genius. These complex abilities were not simply not taught in Einstein's schools; they were not viewed as worthy of knowing. Unfortunately, in Texas and other technical-standards-driven schools of the early twenty-first century, they are still unrecognized (Kincheloe, Steinberg, & Tippins, 1999). Such recognitions are salient to our view of standards, as they reflect the complexity we seek.

If schools are ever to be worthy of the patronage of young Einsteins—and there are millions of students capable of Einsteinian achievements in a variety of fields—they must begin to identify the nature of the new knowledges and scholarly abilities teachers need to teach to standards of complexity. Colleges of education must play a central role in this identification and preparatory process; school districts and state departments of education must develop incentives for educators to immerse themselves in the complex task of acquiring, practicing, and teaching these high-level abilities (Elmore, 1997). Laying the conceptual foundations for these two tasks is a basic goal of this articulation of standards of complexity. One of the central understandings of these conceptual foundations involves exposing the logic behind the organization of the test-driven Texas and other school systems around the U.S. and the technical standards that guide them.

Understanding Complexity:
The Naïve Realism That Dilutes Rigor

One of the most basic assumptions embedded in technical standards is a naive realism that assumes the world is a simple system made up of entities capable of precise empirical descriptions. Such a reductionistic way of viewing knowledge (an epistemology) allows teachers, educational leaders, curriculum developers, and students to run away from complexity and hide in a shelter of mediocrity. Such low-level thinking undermines the social order on a multitude of levels and weakens the civic and democratic order. Such naive realism promotes a view of knowledge production where ancient Greek notions of "gaining insight" are replaced by an obsession with following the "correct" method. Here, knowledge production is *reduced* to a notion of rigor that relies exclusively on fidelity to a technical method. Thus, knowledge production is no longer an act of insight, contextual analysis, intuition, and creative brilliance, but a *procedure*.

Viewed as a procedure, knowledge production turns away from concern with the multiple relationships between entities, the larger processes of which they are a part, the new understandings to be gleaned from examining the same thing within different contexts. Instead, naive realist or reductionistic knowledge producers focus on understanding the objective world and its contents as isolated entities, things-in-themselves. In this epistemological framework, these things-in-themselves wait around for a knower to arrive and "discover" them by using the right procedure. Such a way of perceiving shapes not only knowledge production but knowledge reception as well. Assumed in the realist scheme is the belief that knowledge discovery is the end of the process—after we "know" one of these things-in-themselves, there is nothing more to learn. Thus, the purpose of a school or of educational standards grounded in this construct is simply to obtain the knowledge already produced—a.k.a., the truth.

All this talk about analysis, complexity, relationship, insight, creativity, and higher-order thinking is a waste of time in the context of naive realism. The work has already been done and the knowledge has been produced by the experts. Schools need only some dedicated teachers to simply induce students to commit the truth to their memory banks. This is one aspect of the logic that serves to dumb down technical teacher education and public education at the beginning of the twenty-first century. In philosophical language this influential concept of thing-in-itself has been referred to by its detractors in the Western tradition as the category of substance. In this disciplinary lexicon, substance implies that what we know has a material quality, it is *something*. The traditional dissenting viewpoint asserts that what is ultimately important in worldly affairs is immaterial, is the *no-thingness* of relationships and connections between things. A relationship or a conceptual connection can many times not be expressed in an empirical manner. From the naive realist perspective, this renders it irrelevant.

Realist truth claims are riddled with problems as the aforementioned issues contributing to educational complexity are ignored. The content that realist methods produce is not the neutral result of objective procedures. A plethora of value choices and subjective judgments have gone into the production of the final product of inquiry (Madison, 1988; Thomas, 1998; Ward, 1995). This final product (data) is the result of a procedure-driven chronicling of the decontextualized thing-in-itself. Removal from the various contexts that shape its meaning renders such "validated knowledge" less trustworthy than scholars and teachers have traditionally assumed. Andrew Murphie (1998) labels knowledge produced by more contextualized and complex methods as "objectiles." An objectile escapes the realist thing-in-itself reductionism and simplification and comes to be defined by its movement and change and its connections with other objectiles. The researcher, knowledge analyst, teacher, and learner can use the insights gained from the notion of the objectile to become far more sophisticated knowledge workers and thinkers. They understand that objects in both the physical and social worlds are not merely solid and independent entities. Learning that recognizes complexity is more concerned with an object's connections to other objects than with its substance.

There are numerous examples of the importance of connection in the world around us. Art has always had objectile properties, as the positioning of images in relation to one another is seen as more important than the isolated image. In contemporary electronic reality, hypertext, with its series of links from one site to another, well illustrates connectivity. In hypertextuality the site possesses no presence that transcends its reference to somewhere else (Murphie, 1998). In this cyber-context, connection and relationship take on a new importance as we construct various web sites and seek knowledge on those already created. Maybe the best way to illustrate the importance of connection vis-à-vis a realist conception of the thing-in-itself is to follow the way it helped shape Albert Einstein's development of the General Theory of Relativity. In this example one can see the way this epistemological dynamic separated Einsteinian from Newtonian physics and opened not only a window to a new and more complex view of the universe but a window to higher orders of cognition.

Einstein, Connection, and Complexity:
Moving to a New Cognitive Domain

Working in an Austrian patent office in 1905, Einstein sought to understand the Newtonian force of gravity and the limitations of Newton's theory.

Something about the theory didn't make sense to Einstein and he wanted to know what it was. When Newton developed his Universal Theory of Gravitation in the 1600s, he focused on gravity as a thing-in-itself. If gravity, as he believed, was simply a force, why would one look at it in any other way? Thus, he and especially those who followed him employed the emerging scientific method and removed gravity from its context so it could be efficiently analyzed. And this was exactly their mistake.

Instead of searching for gravity as a *thing*, Einstein saw it as a *relationship*. He saw gravity *in relation* to other aspects of the universe. Indeed, he understood that the relationship between matter and space is exactly what makes the world what it is. What we experience as gravity is not a force made up of tiny gravitons but a reflection of the structure of the universe moving us along a path existing in curved, multidimensional space. Space, he figured, is not the package in which the universe is stored—it is a central part of creation. For those who understood the basic idea of Einstein's theory, the world could never be viewed the same way again (Woods and Grant, 1998). A new, more complex view of the physical world was emerging. The way Einstein uncovered this complexity provides insight into cognition, education, and the quest for high standards in the twenty-first century.

An analysis of the genesis of the General Theory of Relativity helps us make sense of the need for standards of complexity. Einstein used the notion of a rubber sheet stretched over a baking dish to explain the complex notion of space. When a bowling ball or a BB is placed on it, the sheet is bent or warped around the object. This distortion exemplifies what massive objects such as the sun or the moon do to the fabric of space. This is one of the basic concepts of Einstein's General Theory of Relativity. The rubber sheet is flat when no objects are placed upon it; Einstein referred to this as the absence of gravity. When the bowling ball depresses the sheet, the curvature around the depression represents a gravitational field. A BB rolled along the sheet will fall into the trough just as an asteroid will fall to Earth if it gets too close to its gravitational field. The more massive the object the greater the bending of space. The bowling ball will distort the rubber sheet more than the BB.

So, according to Einstein, mass causes a depression in space. If a comet, for example, moves too close to a star it is drawn into its gravitational well and seized. Thus, entities in space follow the shape of the universe when they fall to Earth. They are not pulled by some gravitational force! While the rubber sheet is merely a metaphor and reduces the complexity of Einstein's relativity, it does help us appreciate the structural unity of space, matter, and motion. Gravity, therefore, is simply a part of the structure of the universe—and, amazingly, Einstein figured that out. Objects fall into the valley in space-time produced by the bowling ball/ sun. In this context the orbits of the sun's planets can be better conceptualized: Mercury and Venus as well as Neptune and Pluto "roll" around the indentation in space caused by the sun's gravity trough.

As Einstein sought to understand the force of gravity, he discovered that there is no such thing as "nothingness" in the structure of the universe. Space like everything else *is something*—it is an integral part of the fabric of the cosmos. Space is neither empty or separable from matter. The *relationship* between space and matter is central to making the universe what it is. Despite sci-fi's fascination with anti-gravity machines, Einstein's General Theory of Relativity contends that gravity can't simply be turned on and off. To do so one would have to change the nature of the universe. Gravitational change, Einstein asserted, would involve a geometrical change. Thus, the General Theory of Relativity with its insightful notion of space as a rubber sheet forces us to change not only our view of the universe but also, I argue, our conception of the microcosms of the social, the psychological, and the educational—to name only a few. Drawing on Einstein's emphasis on relationship in the physical universe and moving it to an appreciation of interconnectedness in infinite domains helps us reconsider the notion of complexity, higher-order cognition, and rigorous standards.

Einstein's connectedness in the physical universe revived numerous concerns with the limitations of Western logic and its tendency for thing-in-itself reductionism. Ignoring the importance of relationship, many Western scholars disregarded the wisdom produced in numerous ancient traditions regarding the interaction between entities as a "living process." In such a process, all things in the world were affected and shaped by all other things—just as in Einstein's theory, mass worked on space and space worked on mass. Thus, all things of the world are "in process," parts of larger activities. The role of scholars changes with this idea in mind from one of discovering things (the force of gravity) to one of gaining insight into the way things fit into larger processes, relationships, and structures.

Obviously, this notion is extremely important in teaching and learning. When the world is viewed in this manner, Western commonsense linearity, notions of cause and effect, begin to break down. For example, does gravity cause the apple to fall and hit the observer on the head? Not exactly, if the question is answered with the General Theory of Relativity in mind. Such a recognition of complex new ways of seeing not only the physical but the social and psychological worlds as well is central to our standards of complexity. Viewing Newtonian realism—gravity as a thing-in-itself—through Einsteinian eyes we come to appreciate the forms of knowing that can change the world. Such a knowing does not involve merely accumulating so-called facts and data that make us "educated"; it involves creating conditions where everyone can participate in the analysis of relationships and the subsequent creation of meanings that connect us to the complexity of the world (Apple, 1993).

Implementing Standards of Complexity in Complex and Diverse Classrooms

When the standards advocated here reference complexity, they are not only hailing complexity within an Einsteinian world of content but also in the complicated world of teaching with its diverse cultural settings and wide range of student backgrounds that face Texas and all educational domains. Advocates of technical standards assume that if we lay out the minimum content requirements that all students must meet and then teach everyone in the same way, schools will be improved. They don't seem to recognize the diverse needs and dispositions toward the schooling process that different students bring to the classroom. Would we teach the same skills and content in the same way to a group of students in a classroom where most students read below grade level as in a classroom where all students read above grade level? How do we develop and teach standards that take into account this and 1,000 other levels of diversity? Standards that don't address such issues are mere window dressing, public relations campaigns for particular political operatives.

Such questions and concerns, ironically, take us right back to Einstein. The great physicist's relation to complexity doesn't end with his revelations of a universe far more perplexing than previously imagined. Einstein the young student also provides lessons concerning the complexity of the teaching act. The strict, authoritarian German schools of Einstein's youth provided him with carefully delineated content goals—specific subject matter standards—that his teachers insisted he commit to memory. Reflecting on his primary, secondary, college, and graduate schooling in his later life, Einstein saw years of wasted time in which he was forced to memorize large quantities of data that were fragmented to the point of meaninglessness. None of the abilities that he used to develop his insights into the universe were cultivated in school. Instead, his efforts to employ such budding capacities were squashed by a system that saw them as irrelevant and even at times disrespectful.

Einstein represents only the tip of the diversity iceberg. His difference was *psychological* in that he learned in quite unique ways. His verbal ability was slow in developing and because of this he told interviewers that he thought in pictures and "thought experiments." The rubber sheet and the bowling ball constituted a thought experiment that led to the General Theory of Relativity. Obviously, there are thousands of different ways to learn, and teachers must gain an awareness of such cognitive differences in their efforts to teach in more sophisticated ways. Often these cognitive differences are connected to cultural issues such as race, ethnicity, socioeconomic class, gender, religious beliefs, and other factors. Any articulation of rigorous standards must understand the effects of these contextual factors, in particular their effects on school performance. Without such an understanding, cultural and cognitive *difference*, as in Einstein's case, is confused with academic *deficiency*. Learning to make this distinction and then developing a pedagogy to address the difficulties students experience is a necessary teaching ability in standards of complexity.

At the beginning of the twenty-first century, classrooms are structured by multiple layers of complexity. Typically ignoring this reality, reductionistic technical standards often view the educational world as one homogenous group. Even relatively simple distinctions such as the difference between the goals of elementary and secondary education are often overlooked by the present standards conversation. Elementary educators teach all subjects and are expected to be content generalists. Of course, secondary teachers teach particular subjects in the present school configuration and are expected to be content specialists. Elementary teachers are now being presented with stacks of content standards in a variety of fields with little, if any, help in integrating them or making sense of how these bodies of content might fit into an elementary education.

Secondary teachers are now being provided with large collections of technical content standards in their disciplines. If such teachers possess the skills such standards dictate, then advocates of technical standards are demanding that these teachers discard their disciplinary knowledge and experience and embrace without question a body of externally imposed data. In Texas's TAAS prep courses there is a need for dumbed-down teachers who never think of the issues delineated here. All teachers deserve to be a part of the conversation about standards, not deskilled functionaries who mechanistically do what they are told by external inquisitors. In standards of complexity, teachers must not only engage in a dialogue with standards devisors but buy into the logic of such rigor if improvements are to be made. Advocates of standards of complexity must be prepared to convince teachers that such goals are worthy. Such advocates must be prepared to help teachers move from their present understandings to a more complex view of the teaching act. Standards of any type cannot work if teachers are excluded from the negotiations about their development and implementation.

Many advocates of reductionistic technical standards hold a romanticized vision of a common American culture that fails to understand cultural diversity and the educational complexity it establishes. If we don't address linguistic diversity, students whose first language is not English will be left behind—as, of course, many Mexican American students in Texas have been. If we don't address economic diversity, students from poor and unschooled families will rarely perform as well as students from more privileged backgrounds. Such equity concerns have infrequently bothered advocates of technical standards. Faced with such questions, many proponents of technical standards have argued that we should simply raise the requirements and everyone will fall in line. Such a position again ignores complexity—in this case the multitude of socio-educational forces that operate to undermine the performance of students who fall outside the mainstream in some way or another (Elmore, 1997; Apple, 1993).

Thus, if we expect standards to work and improvements in education to be made, we must give teachers much assistance. Advocates of standards of complexity must make sure that all teachers gain the academic skills necessary to understand and teach standards of complexity. Just as importantly, teachers need help in the perplexing task of taking such knowledge and abilities and connecting them to the particular circumstances of their diverse classrooms. Anyone who fails to recognize the complexity of this task has not sufficiently analyzed the teaching process at the beginning of the new century. Educational and political leaders who view standards-based reform as a narrow process of specifying a specific body of content to be covered will find teachers rebelling as they attempt to implement such dictates amidst the chaos of contemporary schooling. Such narrow standards *are not designed to help teachers accomplish their difficult tasks.* Too often, as the Texas case illustrates, they are designed amidst calls for accountability, to simplify the complex task of reporting school performance. In this way public uncertainty is reduced and the *illusion* of accountability is created.

Judging by the experiences of professional groups, especially in history and English, in their attempts to insert the complexities of professional knowledge into the standards debate, the struggle to move beyond narrow technical standards mandating subject matter reflecting one group's view of truth will be difficult. The history standards debate turned into a simple ideological fight over whose history would be taught. Questions concerning reflection on the debate itself, issues of historical knowledge production, the purposes of teaching history in the first place, the ways schools might deal with ideological diversity, the role of teachers in shaping content, and ways to help educators connect standards to classroom practice were ignored (Elmore, 1997; Zabierek, 1998).

Contextualizing Standards

In order to make sense of the current standards debate and to rethink educational standards in rigorous ways that take into account issues of complexity, analysts must understand the multiple contexts in which standards operate. Since most standards being pushed on schools are of the specific content variety that mandate the teaching and learning of unexamined subject matter, it is important for political and educational leaders to appreciate the context in which such official data are generated. The way such information originates and is canonized is not a simple, linear, or innocent process. Instead, that information which becomes the content standard is produced in a complex interplay of researcher perspective, experiential background, observation, and values vis-à-vis the ideological interests and educational goals of standards makers (Bridges, 1997).

Teachers and students in standards of complexity—not to mention educational and political leaders and standards devisors—need to understand this complex process. A manifestation of their grasp of complexity involves the ability to uncover the ways particular epistemological and cultural assumptions have always shaped the information societies value. Tracing this process and understanding the context in which it takes place prepare students to make huge conceptual leaps, to push the cognitive envelope. In this process of analyzing the context of knowledge production and the construction of standards, students learn the invaluable lesson that multiple logics of inquiry coexist in any scholarly domain. Such contextual study helps students identify the implicit logics within that which is presented as neutral, transcultural, and even timeless. Technical standards are often offered in this naive and neutral manner, erasing in the process the complex social, political, and epistemological dynamics surrounding them. Most of those who are forced to teach and learn them are "protected" from the forbidden knowledge of such rationalities and logics.

Such erasures constitute a dumbing-down process in American schooling. Those who are concerned with truly challenging our students run with these contextual understandings of knowledge production, taking them into unprecedented levels of thinking, teaching, and learning—they deploy them as part of the process of breaking the presently perceived limits of human possibility, human achievement. Armed with such contextual knowledge, teachers and learners can begin to expand what it means to learn. In simple terms they not only possess knowledge but they know where it came from, the conditions of its production, the ways it can be used to bring desired states into being, the problems its unexamined use may create, and alternative information that may exist about similar topics produced by differing logics of inquiry.

Concurrently, the context of interpretation of data is studied in light of the questions raised by standards. Too often the centrality of the interpretive act in knowledge production is lost in traditional schooling and technical-standards-driven lessons. Again, we observe the process of simplification at work, as education that disregards the interpretive context confuses the event/act/text with the interpretation. The meaning of the object of study rests not on the object itself but in the less-than-innocent act of its interpretation—and if nothing else, interpretations are always open to challenge. If students view any interpretation as an act of myth making, they may be better equipped to demystify the authority and expose the invisibility of the interpretive aspect of knowledge production. Moving to this deeper context of information analysis, the process of interpretation is opened to the light of day. Advocates of standards of complexity consider this exposure of the subjective nature of interpretation as an indispensable feature both in understanding the construction of standards and in the education of top-quality teachers and wise students (Degenaar, 1995; Lester, 1997; Madison, 1988).

Contextualizing/Diversity

Advocates of standards of complexity understand these dynamics; they understand that knowledge producers, standards writers, teachers, and students perceive the world from a center located within themselves, shaped by the social and cultural context in which they operate, and framed by languages that contain within them tacit views of the world. As they dig deeper into the contexts surrounding standards, analysts sensitive to complexity find that students from different racial, ethnic, and class locations will relate to standards in different ways. If students who fall far from the middle-class, White, English-speaking mainstream are not provided with assistance by insightful teachers, they will be the victims of decontextualized content standards. These students will not fail to meet the standards because of some inability or lack of intelligence but because of a set of forces unleashed by their relation to what is often labeled the "common culture." The more standards advocates use the term "common culture" in an unexamined way, the more those students who fall outside of its boundaries will fail.

Educators who understand contextual complexity appreciate the notion that American culture is not a homogeneous way of life but a domain of difference shaped by unequal power relations. They understand that social and educational analysts and professional practitioners must act on an appreciation of the way these differences shape people's relationships to various institutions. If everyone is seen as a part of some narrow articulation of a common culture, then those who don't fit the mainstream criteria will find themselves looking into the society's institution as unworthy outsiders. Rigorous standards understand these important social tendencies and make sure that steps are taken to include everyone in a high-quality education (Kincheloe & Steinberg, 1997; Apple, 1993).

The way these factors play out in the everyday life of school is multidimensional, complex, and always significant. When classroom instruction is driven by technical standards with their fragmented factoids, the same pedagogical actions take place repeatedly without regard for who succeeds and who fails—in particular, what social groups succeed or fail over time. A creative way of merely *delivering* content, no matter how ingenious it may be, still works to produce much the same results as long as the epistemological assumptions are the same. Thus, to avoid falling into these age-old traps, teachers must understand both the social context that shapes learners and the epistemological context that molds the way knowledge is viewed and thus educational goals are forged in the classroom. Such contextual awarenesses provide teachers with a monitoring system that allows them a cognizance of the multidimensional effects of their pedagogy. Of course, Texas and U.S. education in general didn't need top-down, content-based standards to fall into the trap of delivering a decontextualized, standardized body of unproblematized data to diverse students with long-term predictable patterns of success and failure.

Indeed, teachers taught *de facto* content standards by teaching the subject matter of market-driven textbooks. Questions concerning the writing and production of the textbooks were generally not asked. Thus, teachers teaching a rigorous curriculum are reflective professionals who bring an awareness of the multiple contexts of the teaching act. Insights derived in this contextualizing activity allow teachers to engage in and share with students the higher-order cognitive activity of reframing knowledge and skills. This reframing process moves them to ask questions of belief and value: Do we believe what this author is telling us about the meaning of the short story? Do we see this description of Western expansion in the nineteenth century as a balanced account of the process? Is this a comprehensive depiction of Darwin's theory of evolution? Is the data presented in the chapter on quadratic equations worth knowing at this point in our study of math? Why is quantum mechanics not included in our physics textbook? (Elmore, 1997; McLaren, 2000)

The ability to employ contextualization in the pursuit of multiple perspectives is an important skill of teachers who embrace standards of complexity. As students begin to see the multiple perspectives that always surround any topic, they examine such viewpoints in relation to one another. The insights derived from such an activity lead directly to cognitive growth and an appreciation of the complexity of the cosmos. When specific content standards are implemented on the national or the state level, the ability of teachers to take the multiple contexts of schooling and its students into account is undermined. Their capacity to study the context in which knowledge is produced and validated is subverted. In such a simplified, standards-based classroom it doesn't matter who students are or what their specific needs may be—the curriculum has already been mandated. It doesn't matter who produced the information covered or the contextual conditions of its construction—the point is to commit it to memory.

Contextualizing the Contemporary

In this decontextualized format teaching and learning are less immediate, less connected with the conditions of the community, less involved with what motivates students, less concerned with moral and ethical issues in the life of the school, less connected with other bodies of knowledge produced in different situations. Moreover, technical standards that decontextualize remove schooling even further from the socio-economic and cultural changes surrounding it. As the information society changes the nature of jobs and the tools required for them, not to mention producing the need for new citizenship skills in a new globalized knowledge order, teachers and students drift along in low-level memory work far removed from the commerce of everyday life. Standards of complexity understand the context of socioeconomic and cultural change, so that teachers and students can keep ahead of it and help direct it in positive, democratic, and just ways (Norris, 1998).

Educational reforms based on technical content standards remove teachers and students from a knowledge of and input into the compelling problems of the day. This is a fatal pedagogical mistake as it sets up a dichotomy between school and the "real world." Such a division will always undermine motivation, as teachers and students come to see the mandated activities of school as trivial and irrelevant. Such an observation should not be taken as an argument for a non-historical, presentist education. The point is not that we should ignore the past and the various traditions of knowledge produced by human beings in a variety of cultures around the world. The concern is that standards of complexity operate to help teachers and students integrate this knowledge and the skills obtained in their study with an understanding of current affairs and the "changing nature of change" in the electronic context of the new century. The subtle ability to make this connection is one of the most important and complicated aspects of standards of complexity.

To integrate these understandings, educators must appreciate the way the world has changed in the last few decades. The rate of socio-economic and cultural change has accelerated, and in this process identities are no longer as stable, as individuals are bombarded with information to the point of incomprehensibility. Traditional forms of problem solving where variables are limited and are assumed to act in predictable ways are less useful in an era marked by the complexity of multiple causality and as many have termed it, chaos. With globalization and new forms of information production and communication, individuals in various fields have been confronted with more ill-structured and divergent problems, cultural misunderstandings and value conflicts, and problems of power inequities. It is apparent that a rigorous education would include an understanding of this new context and the forms of knowledge, skills, and cognitive abilities needed to deal with it successfully (Kincheloe, Steinberg, & Hinchey, 1999; Lester, 1997).

The era of images and pictorial representations ushered in by television has never been adequately addressed—if it has been addressed at all—by schools. Media literacy, a set of skills so central to citizenship and an understanding of the contemporary world, is rarely observed in schools. When such imagery is not integrated with hypertext and cyber-virtuality, schools fall even further behind cultural and informational change. Those students who are conversant with such dynamics learn about them on their non-school time. While their insights and abilities often border on genius, there are still many aspects of the contemporary techno-electronic landscape that are missed by such students. Nevertheless, the technological abilities obtained by such students—typically, economically privileged ones with access to computer equipment at home—exacerbate the gulf between the haves and have nots in alarming ways. Technical standards that emphasize memorization of data are devised as if we are still living in an oral culture. The cognitive and pedagogical processes required by such decontextualized standards hark back to medieval schooling where students memorized texts because there was so little literature in print.

The printing press made texts far more available and changed our relationship with information. The information revolution, made possible by personal computers and hypertext, modifies our interaction with knowledge even further. Albert Einstein understood this informational dynamic in the second decade of the twentieth century. When he stepped off his ship on his first trip to the United States, he was bombarded with questions by reporters anxious to engage the genius who had just won the Nobel Prize in physics. One blurted out the question: "Dr. Einstein, what is the speed of sound?" Einstein humbly admitted that he didn't know. Perplexed, the reporter followed up: "You're the smartest man in the world, how could you not know the speed of sound?" Einstein replied, "If I ever need to know it, I'll look it up." The great physicist understood his relation with information in an era with an abundance of printed literature. In electronic reality, schools must rethink and continue to analyze the nature of our relations with data and their implications for pedagogy and cognition.

In the context of cyberspace we possess less and less knowledge of the cultural location, the human contributions, the sociopolitical and economic interests that shape information. In those few classrooms where students are asked who produced the data they downloaded off the Internet the night before, they are often at a loss to answer such a query. They have never considered such a question or its multidimensional implications. Information in such situations has lost its borders; it moves and flows in the non-linear and instantaneous ways that human thought operates. Traditional forms of knowledge as it is organized in books and official interpretations are undermined in this new context. A subversive element implicitly operates that challenges the informational status quo but at the same time allows power wielders who control informational pipelines to covertly promote data that serves their economic, social, and political interests (Murphie, 1998). Obviously, such a dangerous reality demands new forms of knowledge work, education, and cognition. In an era where the power of economic institutions—especially in relation to control of information—has risen to unprecedented heights, the development of our ability to delineate the hidden interests of the knowledge that cyber-technology provides us so abundantly is crucial to the future of democracy. Standards of complexity understand these threats and strive to overcome the technical rationality and reductionism that blinds educational leaders to them.

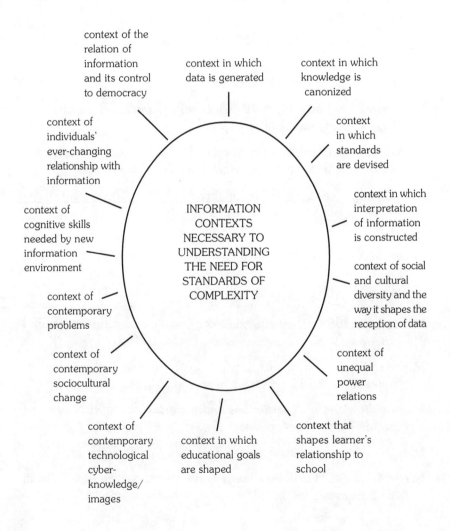

context of the relation of information and its control to democracy

context in which data is generated

context in which knowledge is canonized

context of individuals' ever-changing relationship with information

context in which standards are devised

context of cognitive skills needed by new information environment

context in which interpretation of information is constructed

context of social and cultural diversity and the way it shapes the reception of data

context of contemporary problems

context of contemporary sociocultural change

context of unequal power relations

INFORMATION CONTEXTS NECESSARY TO UNDERSTANDING THE NEED FOR STANDARDS OF COMPLEXITY

context of contemporary technological cyber-knowledge/images

context in which educational goals are shaped

context that shapes learner's relationship to school

References

Apple, M. (1993). The politics of official knowledge: Does a national curriculum make sense? *Teachers College Press, 95* (2), 222–241.

Bridges, D. (1997). Philosophy and educational research: A reconsideration of epistemological boundaries. *Cambridge Journal of Education, 27,* 2.

Degenaar, J. (1995). Myth and the collision of cultures. *Myth and Symbol, 2.*

Elmore, R. (1997). *Education policy and practice in the aftermath of TIMSS* [On-line]. Available:

http://www.enc.org/TIMSS/addtools/pubs/symp/cd163/cd163.htm.

Kincheloe, J., & Steinberg, S. (1997). *Changing multiculturalism.* London: Open University Press.

Kincheloe, J., Steinberg, S., & Hinchey, P. (1999). *The post-formal reader: Cognition and education.* New York: The Falmer Press.

Kincheloe, J., Steinberg, S., & Tippins, D. (1999). *The stigma of genius: Einstein, consciousness, and education.* New York: Peter Lang.

Lester, S. (1997). *Learning for the twenty-first century* [On-line]. Available:

http://www.devmts.demon.co.uk/lrg21st.htm.

Madison, G. (1988). *The hermeneutics of post-modernity: Figures and themes.* Bloomington, IN: Indiana University Press.

McLaren, P. (2000). *Che Guevara, Paulo Freire, and the pedagogy of revolution.* Boulder, CO: Rowman and Littlefield.

Murphie, A. (1998). *Cyberfictions and hypertext: What is happening to text?* [On-line]. Available:

http://wwwmcs.elm.mq.edu.an/staff/Andrew/307/hypeprt.html.

Norris, N. (1998). Curriculum evaluation revisited. *Cambridge Journal of Education, 28,* 2.

Novich, R. (1996). Actual schools, possible practices: New directions in professional development. *Education Policy Analysis Archives, 4,* 14.

Thomas, G. (1998). The myth of rational research. *British Educational Research Journal, 24,* 2.

Ward, S. (1995). The revenge of the humanities: Reality, rhetoric, and the politics of postmodernism. *Sociological Perspectives, 38* (2), 109–128.

Woods, A., & Grant, T. (1998). *Reason in revolt: Marxism and modern science.* [On-line]. Available: http://www.easyweb.easynet.co.uk˜zac/chapter7.htm.

Zabierek, H. (1998, November 25). Whose history is it? *Education Week* [On-line]. Available: http://www.edweek.com/ew/vol-18/13zabier.h18.

Chapter 22

The Moral and Ethical Implications of Educational Standards: Commentary and Questions

Raymond A. Horn, Jr.

American Standards is a brief look at a highly complex phenomenon in American education, one that is currently dominating education in Texas. We have discovered that there are different types of standards, each representing a different way to view the world and each demanding different things from our children. We have discovered that standards are inextricably linked to political interests whose agendas strive to construct a society in their image. Finally, we have discovered that minority segments of our student population are the targets of these political agendas.

The reader is now aware that the standards movement in Texas is more than "content to be learned" and a "test to measure the learning." Through the analytical lenses provided in chapter 3 and through the broad contextualization provided by the other chapters, American standards, as exemplified by the Texas case, have deep systemic, political, social, and personal implications for the whole school system; and, for the other social and community systems that are part of our societal environment.

Cleo Cherryholmes points out that "educational practices result from choices. Choices cannot be made without reference to a value, set of values, criteria, or interests" (1988, p. 4). The choices represented by current Texas standards are sedimented values from an earlier time that now need to be transcended. Current Texas standards and the values that they represent are affected by the discursive practice of the past. Past educational discourse and practice in Texas was inherently racist in its segregation of minorities and in its emphasis on vocational training for minorities that resulted in a social class system with the minorities on the bottom. Times are different, and the past discursive practice of Texas education has been modified by the contemporary context provided by the larger systemic environment and by the desire of Texans to transcend this aspect of their history. However, history weighs heavily on all change initiatives.

By history, I am referring to Cherryholmes' (1988) idea that power arrangements inherent in our systemic structures affect what we think and how we act. Cherryholmes argues that "ideology intertwines with power as individuals accept, believe, and internalize explanations and justifications for the asymmetries of their social world" (1988, p. 5). Power is manifested as rewards and punishments that can be externally imposed on individuals by others acting as agents of the bureaucratic and systemically entrenched ideology or world view. The ideological history of ideas and attitudes about different types of people and the capability of people as individuals to rise above any adversity, merely through their personal strength of will, are remnants of the past discursive practice that still haunts the present. It is this thinking that needs to be post-formally exorcised. Cherryholmes points out that the structures of a system are perpetuated by the system's ability to regenerate and reproduce its structures. If Texas is to qualitatively evolve its educational system, then the process of reproduction needs to be scrutinized as closely as the more visible manifestations of the process. This reproduction of systemic structure can be most effectively scrutinized by looking at the choices that we make: choices based on what we value, and how we determine what is true.

An Analysis of Truth

One last lens needs to be added to our post-formal analysis, for a consideration of the morality and ethics of the standards movement. The specific lens that I will use to explore the morals and ethics of standards in Texas will be Parker Palmer's (1993) idea that education is a spiritual journey. Many have written about the moral implications of educational leadership (Sergiovanni, 1992), and the need to focus on the development of egalitarian community in schools. Peter Senge's (1990; Senge et al., 1999) work concerning schools as learning organizations, or Nel Noddings (1992; 1995) idea of schools as caring places would also have been appropriate because in the literature of this type the essential element is about the relationships—the equitable and caring relationships between all members of the community.

However, I have selected Palmer because of his avowed Christian context. Those familiar with Texas understand the Texans' ardent pursuit of their faith. With respect, in this moral context, I find it ironic that the inequities revealed in *American Standards* are occurring. To further broaden our understanding of this phenomenon, one last look at Texas standards, through the lens of ethics and morality, is necessary.

Initially, we must all agree that students are instrumentally used as objects or means to secure other people's ends. Instead of focusing on resources or instruction, the burden falls on the students. Often in the newspapers we see the editorial cry for more experienced and better-educated workers. The litany invariably includes commentary that either overtly states or alludes to the opinion that our ability to compete in the global market place is at risk because of the poor job that schools are doing in producing skilled workers. Seldom, if ever, does the litany include a call for governmental and community accountability in the form of equitable funding. In this case, once again the schools and students are objectified or commodified as instruments whose primary value is economic.

Martin Buber (1988) characterizes this instrumentality as an "I-It" relationship between people, in which a person or a group of people is isolated and objectified in the relationship. Buber's concern was the domination of society by the state, or in this example, by economic and political interests. The problem that ensues is the "weakening of the spontaneous basis of social relationships and cultural creativity. In its more severe forms, the domination of state over society can lead, as we have witnessed in the current century, to the disintegration of social life and culture" (Eisenstadt, 1992, p. 13). I am not suggesting that the instrumentality observed in the Texas situation will have such drastic effects. However, with significant numbers of minority and disadvantaged students being forced out of the educational system, this instrumentality certainly and significantly perpetuates the culture of poverty and isolation of these people.

Buber's concern about the loss of cultural creativity is ironic, in relation to the need for highly skilled creative workers, in that technical standards taught in a regressive system are not the answer. Only standards of complexity, propagated in a positive and nurturing environment, can achieve this kind of work force.

Returning to the lens of morality and ethics, Buber sees a dynamic social relationship between people, in which we move back and forth between an "I-It" and an "I-Thou" relationship. In the "`I-Thou,' the I risks his or her security by listening as well as speaking, ready to receive something new and to respond in a new manner" (Buber, 1988, p. xii).

Buber sees the "I-Thou" relationship as the essential characteristic of situations conducive to creativity. In this relationship, there is dialogue and communicative openness, which allows people to transcend the institutional and formalized frameworks that isolate them (Eisenstadt, 1992, p. 11). Being a religious philosopher, Buber proposes this kind of transcendent relationship as in the realm of the sacred that leads to the development of a common discourse with a search for ultimate values between a person and God, but he also regards this relationship as the essential element "for holding society together, for meeting conditions conducive to cultural creativity and for counteracting the possible stagnative or destructive forces that are endemic in any society" (Eisenstadt, 1992, p. 11).

Using Buber's work as a moral lens focused on the standards issue raises significant questions about who we are and the relationships that we foster. What kinds of relationships exist and are fostered by a technical-standards-driven educational system? What values are promoted in our children by these kinds of relationships? Are these the values that will best serve our children and us?

Palmer also stresses the importance of transcendent relationships. Palmer writes of education that is characterized by "knowing" and "truthful" relationships. "Education of this sort means more than teaching the facts and learning the reasons so we can manipulate life toward our ends. It means being drawn into personal responsiveness and accountability to each other and the world of which we are a part" (Palmer, 1993, pp. 14–15). Accountability is not primarily directed toward economic or political interests but toward truthful relationships with others with whom we are intimately bound (Palmer, 1993). This kind of accountability leads to communities of faithful relationships where the primary bond is not of logic but of love (Palmer, 1993, p. 32).

The antithesis of this kind of community is the modernistic community that still embraces the Cartesian separation of emotion and reason, the kind of community that is steadfast in its commitment to this seemingly objective path, further strengthening its refusal to be "drawn into personal responsiveness and accountability to each other and the world of which we are a part" (Palmer, 1993, p. 15). A community of this type refuses to allow a moral lens to mediate its view of a situation. Regarding the case of the Texas standards, the state's response to the problems of the *Others* is a lack of compassion, involvement, and accountability. The state's involvement is one of clinical detachment, which allows the state to fail to recognize its own complicity in the problem. Parker refers to this condition as the ethic of detachment and manipulation. Is this the kind of ethic that we want to instill in our children?

In a discussion of the mutuality of truth, Palmer asks the question, "What does this encounter reveal about me?" (1993, p. 60) By this he means that, as we seek truth, there is the potential of ourselves also becoming known. He likens this to "an 'inter-view,' a way of looking into other people's behaviors and attitudes that opens our own lives to view" (1993, p. 62). As you engaged the stories, court case, factual explanations, and interpretations of the Texas case, what did you learn from this pursuit of truth about the storytellers and information givers and, most of all, about yourself? As our children interact with our standards-driven educational system, what truths are they learning about others and about themselves?

In dealing with obedience to truth, Palmer writes that "suspicion of obedience is especially pronounced among the cultural minorities of our day, among groups such as blacks and women and Jews who will rightly ask, 'Whose truth are we being told to obey?' These groups know what it means to live under other people's 'truth' in an obedience not freely chosen but coerced" (1993, pp. 65–66). In an analysis of the root of the word "obedience," Palmer found that it means, "to listen." If those who fail in our standards-driven system only learn to be obedient when coerced, will they ever really "listen" in later life?

In the Texas standards system, everyone is held accountable for student achievement as measured by the standardized tests. Through the lens of Palmer's definition of accountability, how truthful are the relationships in Texas between those in control and those who must be obedient? If the situation were different and the accountability demanded by the State of Texas required obedience to truthful, faithful, and loving relationships, how different would the outcome be in terms of the types of standards, the assessment tools, the failure rates, and the dropout rates? If the Texas standards initiative was centered in a "mutuality of truth," how would the standards and their assessment be different? Once again, how would this difference be reflected in failure and dropout rates?

Since the focus of much of this book has been on the minorities and disadvantaged, Palmer's comments concerning a pluralistic society are instructive. "In a pluralistic society, the way to truth is to listen attentively to diverse voices and views for the claims they make on us" (1993, p. 67). He continues by suggesting that "paradoxically, as we listen obediently to the voice of the other, our own speech becomes clearer and more honest; through the other we learn much about ourselves" (1993, p. 101).

Unfortunately, there are no spaces where the educational policy makers and the minorities can dialogue about the former's need for standards and the latter's need for equity. The courtroom provides such a space; however, the conversation that occurs in that venue is inherently dialectical, not dialogical; and once one side wins, the other no longer has the option to engage in even that kind of conversation.

The problem is that in most cases only those who have the power can open up the conversational spaces. In the case of Texas, the members of the dominant culture not only control the access to these spaces but also control the agenda for how these spaces are used. In these tightly structured spaces, conservative political pressure dynamically molds the space in such a way as to dictate the conversational flow, topic, and outcomes (P. Jenlink, personal communication, March 30, 2000). However, this presents a moral dilemma for those in power—protect their own interests by refusing to dialogue with the others, or embrace the egalitarian principles of our democracy and include everyone in the conversation? It also presents a moral dilemma for the disenfranchised—enable the perpetuation of the conversational inequity, or create their own space for conversation, as did Civil Rights leaders like Martin Luther King, Jr.?

Once spaces conducive to dialogical conversation are created, Palmer proposes a "consensual inquiry" where people "learn by listening and responding faithfully to each other and to the subject at hand" (1993, p. 94). This "consensual process of truth seeking is based on the simple assumption that all of us thinking together are smarter than any one of us thinking alone—as scores often demonstrate" (Palmer, 1993, p. 94).

Finally, Palmer suggests that in education there are really three parties to any conversation: the teacher, the students, and the subject itself (1993, p. 98). *American Standards* has provided space for the three parties related to this issue to be heard—the State, the minority view, and student achievement. The readers' task is to assess what each party is saying; especially what is said by the subject—student achievement. What is the significance of what each party says in relation to its own position, separate from the others, and then in relation to the systemic knowledge that they are all interrelated? How do these conversational parties play out against the perspectives and lenses provided by *American Standards*? What questions are raised about community, the kind of educational system that we want, inequity, the role of minorities in our society, and our own personal role in this controversial issue? Finally, readers need to examine their own voices and then to add their voices to the conversation. When you next talk with others about this issue, what will you say?

An Analysis of the 1968 Goals for Public Education in Texas

To conclude this examination of American standards, especially in the case of Texas, I want to briefly return to the 1968 goals (Operation PEP, 1968) that provided the foundation for today's standards. Politically, this is important because as the Reagan Revolution swept across America, conservative educational reform was carried in that wave. Assuredly, what was occurring in Texas influenced, in many ways, this phenomenon. Embedded in this conservative wave are certain values that have great moral and ethical implications for everyone who is a part of, or affected by, the educational system.

Nested in the intellectual discipline goal is the phrase—"help each child to accept responsibility for self-evaluation and continuing self-instruction." One interpretation of this phrase is that people are directly and personally responsible for themselves. Therefore, regardless of race, gender, ethnicity, or social class, if you fail the TAAS or ExCET, it is because you haven't done what you need to do to pass. The responsibility is yours, and only yours. If you have chosen to not be accountable for this responsibility, then you have ethically, morally, and academically abdicated your responsibility. It is obvious that this is the state's position, and that the state is comfortable with it due to the intense emphasis on remediation. However, in terms of good and bad or right and wrong, this is an inordinately more complex situation than such a simple phrase indicates. Moving away from right/wrong and good/bad considerations of standardized testing itself, more important considerations are about right/wrong and good/bad in relation to concerns about bias and equity as they relate to the type of standards, the type of assessment, and the procedures of the assessment. Here is where the lens of morals and ethics needs to be applied.

Dealing with the moral questions raised about these considerations of standards is the essence of the debate surrounding American standards. In the case of Texas, because of the current structure of the standards, the assessment, the assessment procedures, and the accountability procedures, some of the original goals are not being met. Within the economic and vocational competence goal, the state declared that it wanted to provide all students with usable vocational skills to equip them to find employment. Obviously, that is not occurring with large numbers of minority students. Within the citizenship and civic responsibility goal, the state wanted to equip each child for intelligent participation in the democratic process. Obviously, not only is this not occurring with all students, but also what message is sent to these people about the relationship between them and their government? Within the competence in human and social relations goal, the state wanted to assist the children in making a place for themselves in the community. Isn't the place in the community for many of these children being predetermined by the nature of the standards and their assessment? Within the same goal, the state wanted to help develop in all children a respect for the rights of others as individuals and as groups. If the state continually refuses to critically and morally examine the effects of its program on minorities, what is the message that is sent to all the people in Texas about respect for others?

The last two goals deal with instilling moral and ethical values and promoting the mental and physical health of the children. As more and more children fall by the wayside, how can we expect them to view life through the moral and ethical lenses that are appropriate for their own welfare and that of society? The lessons that many learn are not those conducive to the development of the kind of community that we want to foster. Can we say that the mental anguish that the children must suffer as they struggle with each testing situation, through no fault of their own, promotes this goal of mental and physical health? As children fall by the wayside and end up in low-end jobs with few or no medical benefits, can we say that we have met our goal of promoting their physical health?

In order to understand teachers' professional knowledge, Jean Clandinin and Michael Connelly (1995) utilize the idea of a landscape as a metaphor, which allows them to conceptualize this knowledge in terms of space, place, and time. To borrow their metaphor allows us to view Texas education as a landscape and to see how the standards initiative has postformally affected place (Texas and specific schools), space (areas contested by various interest groups defined in terms of race, gender, age, and social class), and time (the past, present, and future). In relation to the nature of theory and practice in this landscape, Clandinin and Connelly (1995) use the metaphor of a funnel, in which theory is poured into the landscape from an agency such as the state or a school board. The theory that is funneled into an educational system or community becomes the sacred story that is deeply engrained in the consciousness of the people to the point that it is taken for granted to the degree that it becomes invisible (Clandinin and Connelly, 1995). Sacred stories also include related cultural, political, and economic beliefs that support the professional theory. The idea of sacred stories is akin to what critical theorists call grand narratives, or the great stories/myths that provide a center for people to use in making moral decisions. The moral orientation and sense of certainty of people "are due to the sacred story, which requires that the descriptive 'is' of theoretical knowledge be transformed into a prescriptive 'ought' in practice" (Clandinin and Connelly, 1995, p. 11).

A second story is the secret story. Clandinin and Connelly (1995) propose that the classroom within the professional landscape is a safe place, a "private place in the sense that teachers and students work behind a closed door" (p. 12), "a safe place, generally free from scrutiny, where teachers are free to live stories of practice that are essentially secret ones" (p. 13). Secret stories differ from sacred stories in that they more closely approximate what actually is occurring.

The need for cover stories arises when the teacher is confronted with the "out-of-classroom" part of the landscape: situations in which the teacher must deal with parents, administrators, state officials, the public, and other teachers. To reconcile the difference between the sacred story (the official version of what goes on) and the secret story (what is really happening), the teacher needs a cover story. "This is not a language of story, it is a language of abstraction. The language of abstraction, a rhetoric of conclusions, is propositional, relational among concepts, impersonal, situation-dependent, objective, nontemporal, ahistorical, and generic" (Clandinin and Connelly, 1995, p. 14). In other words it is decontextualized (shorn of the rich details that make it true in the eyes of the teacher) and the origin of the knowledge supplied by the cover story is not disclosed or is not linked to the real events of the classroom. On the other hand, language of the secret story is "prototypical, relational among people, personal, contextual, subjective, temporal, historical, and specific" (Clandinin and Connelly, 1995, p. 14). This is the rich story that can provide a thick description of reality as critically constructed by the teacher. The difference between the sacred story and the secret story is illustrated by Clandinin and Connelly thus: "returning to the classroom from a staff meeting on a new board of education curriculum plan, . . . is a move from a place of abstractions and propositional reasoning to a place where the prototypical life unfolds" (1995, p. 14). To extend their example, when the teacher must represent how she reconciles the abstract theory of the sacred story with her secret story of what really happens, she creates a cover story that accommodates the creators of the sacred story and the people of the out-of-classroom part of the landscape. In reporting on what teachers have told them, Clandinin and Connelly (1995, p. 15) write:

How do teachers manage this dilemma? Increasingly, teachers tell us they live and tell cover stories in the out-of-classroom professional knowledge landscape, stories in which they portray themselves as characters who are certain, expert people. These cover stories are a way of managing their dilemma. The tension in managing their dilemma in this way is what we first noticed in teachers' feelings of being disturbed on the landscape.

Now that we have post-formally worked through the context, origin, and interpretations of standards in Texas, we can make one more sweep through this book and attempt to see it differently through the stories that emerge from this landscape. However, each story is essentially a morality tale, in which we can discern how right and wrong and good and bad are construed. Using social justice and caring as a central point, upon which to compare each story, how are social justice and caring portrayed in each story? How does each story reconcile the moral and ethical propositions of the other stories? In looking at the three types of stories in this light, how are our own moral positions that we have constructed on the Texas standards issue affected?

We hope this is another useful lens that can be added to the others provided by *American Standards* for you to post-formally employ in understanding educational standards within Texas and within your context. As you read the final chapter, see how these three stories play out against the commentary provided in that chapter. In addition, we hope that we have problematized your prior understanding of the standards movement in America and Texas. Whether your decision making is guided by considerations of self-interest, the common good, or idealistic principles, our hope is that your new understanding of standards in America is complex and compassionate.

References

Buber, M. (1988). *Eclipse of God*. Atlantic Highlands, NJ: Humanities Press International.

Cherryholmes, C. (1988). *Power and criticism*. New York: Teachers College Press.

Clandinin, D. J., & Connelly, F. M. (1995). *Teachers' professional knowledge landscapes*. New York: Teachers College Press.

Eisenstadt, S. N. (Ed.). (1992). *Martin Buber: On intersubjectivity and cultural creativity*. Chicago: Chicago University Press.

Noddings, N. (1992). *The challenge to care in schools*. New York: Teachers College Press.

Noddings, N. (1995). A morally defensible mission for schools in the 21st century. *Phi Delta Kappan, 76* (5), 365–368.

Operation PEP: A State-wide Project to Prepare Educational Planners for California. (1968, December). *Goals for public education in Texas: A report by the subcommittee on goals to the governor's committee on public school education*. Redwood City, CA: County Office of Education.

Palmer, P. J. (1993). *To know as we are known: Education as a spiritual journey*. San Francisco: HarperSanFrancisco.

Senge, P. M. (1990). *The fifth discipline: The art and practice of the learning organization*. New York: Doubleday/Currency.

Senge, P., Kleiner, A., Roberts, C., Ross, R., Roth, G., & Smith, B. (1999). *The dance of change: The challenges to sustaining momentum in learning organizations*. New York: Currency Doubleday.

Sergiovanni, T. J. (1992). *Moral leadership: Getting to the heart of school reform*. San Francisco: Jossey-Bass.

Chapter 23

Coda: Personal Opinions in a Public Forum

Raymond A. Horn, Jr.

The following commentaries appeared in Texas newspapers as editorials, letters to the editor, or articles. Obviously, these are not intended to be a comprehensive sampling of the issue in the press; however, perhaps it is best to let these writers have the last word.

I don't understand. They had the same classes. They take the same preparation and the practice test. Why are the black kids not doing as well on the TAAS? It is a simple test. Why are we not passing it? Where is the school failing us? March 1, 2000, *The Daily Sentinel*, Nacogdoches, Texas

I just read the article in Thursday's paper about Central Heights School system doing so well. I have children there. They should really do well academically. They study about half the year for one simple TAAS test, and usually they review last year's test, the old TAAS test, to study for the new test for this year. I think they should do well. If I studied half the year for one test, I would do well. February 7, 2000, *The Daily Sentinel*, Nacogdoches, Texas

"NHS is 'Exemplary Bound': TAAS training preparing students for February testing." Students at Nacogdoches High School are "Exemplary Bound," and teachers and administrators are doing everything they can to help them reach their destination. "We're going on a TAAS hunt! Exemplary Bound" is the theme of an intensive TAAS training and incentive program under way at NHS to help students be successful during February TAAS testing. The theme and incentives were developed by a committee of students, teachers, and parents. "We're in our third week of intensive training for ninth- and tenth-grade students utilizing TAAS materials," TAAS specialist Dianne Baker said. "Intensive training" means that a portion of each class period is devoted to discussing certain objectives Monday through Thursday of a six-week period leading up to the February test days. Each Friday, students are given a test on the TAAS materials covered. "Sophomore students who are not successful on the Friday test will have individual or small group assistance to let them know what they didn't do correctly," Ms. Baker said. While the TAAS training is taking place, eleventh- and twelfth-graders who have already passed the test will receive ACT/SAT preparation training for college testing. Feb. 22, 23, and 24 are important dates for NHS sophomores, and NHS is providing a few incentives to encourage students to take the TAAS seriously and pass all three parts of the exit test the first time. Homework passes, tardy passes and added points on a daily grade are among the incentives. "It's been successful in the past, and we were so close to being a recognized campus last year," she said. A TAAS coaching team has been established to oversee teacher efforts to provide personal added incentives for students. Each teacher has been assigned three-to-four students to encourage one-on-one to do well on the TAAS. January 30, 2000, Robbie Goodrich, Sentinel Staff, *The Daily Sentinel*, Nacogdoches, Texas

The majority of schools are administering the TAAS test April 11 through 14. With all the past concerns with who is to blame for poor test results, maybe the baseball and softball associations along with parents should consider this when scheduling games on the nights before the tests. As a classroom teacher I have four students that have games scheduled on Monday and Tuesday nights. Maybe it is time we decide where our priorities really lie. April 8, 2000, *The Daily Sentinel*, Nacogdoches, Texas

"TAAS testing begins at NHS." TAAS testing for students at Nacogdoches High School will be administered today through Thursday with the following schedule:

TAAS testing—7:45 to 11:05 a.m.
Third block—11:10 a.m. to 1:10 p.m.

This schedule will affect early release, late arrival concurrent and co-op students. Working students will need to notify employers about the change of the school day as soon as possible. Co-op students and teachers will need to make arrangements with employers for these days. Students enrolled in college courses will need to notify your professors and make arrangements with your teachers at NHS and your professors. Students may not automatically leave for early release at the regular time on the TAAS testing days since the times for classes are different on these days. The student is responsible for making arrangements with teachers and employers for the special schedule on TAAS testing days. All teachers need to make every effort to help these students with arrangements. April 11, 2000, *The Daily Sentinel*, Nacogdoches, Texas

Sheriff's deputies are investigating a reported assault that occurred Thursday at a local residence. According to the report, a man became angry when he went to his residence to pick up his son and was told by his ex-wife the boy had to complete TAAS tests that day. The report said the man became more angry after learning that a television had been broken. The report said the arguing continued, and the man allegedly threatened to. . . . February 26, 2000, *The Daily Sentinel*, Nacogdoches, Texas

"Spring hopes to get a jump on TAAS." The Spring school district is looking to get a head start on a new state law that requires students to pass the TAAS before they are promoted. Spring's proposed policy, which goes before the board for a final vote March 7, starts phasing in the new promotion standards in 2000–2001, two years before the state standards take effect. Under the state policy, all Texas children starting kindergarten this year will have to pass the reading section of the TAAS at the end of the third grade and the reading and math sections at the end of the fifth and eighth grades. Spring Superintendent John Folks said the district's proposal, drafted by a committee of principals, affects more grades than the state's plan and offers summer school to students who need extra help meeting the promotion standards. "We are doing it to help the kids, to identify them and help them get into a program where they can receive the instruction they need to be successful," Folks said. Under the proposal, third-graders at the end of the 2000–2001 school year would have to pass the reading portion of the TAAS before being promoted. The testing requirement would be expanded to the fourth grade in 2001–2001 and the fifth grade in 2002–2003. Beginning in 2003–2004, fourth- and fifth-graders also would have to pass the math portion of the TAAS. A diagnostic test developed by the district would be used to determine if first- and second-graders are ready for promotion, beginning in 2000–

2001. The Houston Independent School District last year required students in the first through third grades to pass a test before they could be promoted, and this year the policy will affect all schoolchildren through the eighth grade. February 11, 2000, Melanie Markley, *Houston Chronicle*, Houston, Texas

Kindergarten used to be a time when small children learned a little about reading and math, but mostly they played, took naps and learned to get along in a classroom setting before their success was measured by grades and test scores. Now it's become a time for 5-year-olds to prepare for the state's barometer for student success—the TAAS. Instead of taking a pencil to paper on the TAAS, kindergarten students now undergo a variety of assessment tools, including a test known as the Texas Primary Reading Inventory (TPRI). It measures their ability to recognize letters, detect sounds, understand rhyming words and comprehend the spoken word. Performance on the TPRI and other forms of testing is used to determine where the students need additional work. It's intended to help prepare this year's kindergarten students for the 2002–2003 school year, when they will be in the third grade and their score on the TAAS will decide whether they go on to the fourth grade. At Olmos Elementary School in the North East School District, Elsa Gutierrez is in charge of the reading program and spends much of her time giving tests to the 700 students in kindergarten through fifth grade. With the 5- and 6-year-olds, she makes an extra effort to avoid test anxiety. Students are not told they are taking a test, but are encouraged to show off their knowledge as she sits down with them one by one to go through an assessment tool given every eight weeks in addition to the TPRI. "Give me five," she said Thursday as she raised her hand to congratulate 6-year-old Armando Roman after he successfully struggled through the word "must." The heightened emphasis on testing at the kindergarten level is the result of a law passed by the Legislature last year to stem social promotion, the practice of passing students who are not academically prepared for the next grade level. The law calls for students to be held back if they do not pass the TAAS, starting with third-graders in the 2002–2003 school year and continuing with fifth- and eighth-graders in subsequent years. Opponents argue that holding students back discourages them from finishing school and would contribute to an already high dropout rate, but proponents said enough measures were put in place to make sure most students would pass. The result is a succession of tests, assessments, and remediation beginning with kindergarten students this year and extending to the first, second, and third grades in the next three years. The effort to end social promotion now makes all students, no matter how young, an integral part of the state's accountability system, said Bertha Perez, a reading specialist and an associate dean at the Downtown Campus of the University of Texas at San Antonio. She praised the state for placing a priority on reading, but she said the TPRI and a tendency to teach to the test are at odds with good reading instruction. "It goes counter to all the research we have learned from the past 20 to 25 years on how children develop language and literacy," she said. Schools are not required to give the TPRI, but it's increasingly becoming a common practice and a driving force in kindergarten classrooms. Schools give the test midway though the year and again at the end of the year. February 25, 2000, Lucy Hood, *San Antonio Express-News*, San Antonio, Texas

"Mixed grades for TAAS Test scores up, but critics fear students are shortchanged." Beverly Nabors' third-graders don't do as many science experiments as her students did a decade ago. Instead, they're busy learning to pick out "code" words they'll see on the TAAS test. Nabors flashes math worksheets on an overhead projector for the first 15 minutes of class each day. On one morning, the test-taking drill explains that the phrase "how many altogether" means that students should add up the numbers in a problem. The goal is to raise low math scores at Oakhurst Elementary in Fort Worth. But because of the TAAS drills, students spend less time studying the solar system and get a shorter lesson on Greek mythology, which used to mesmerize her classes, Nabors said. "My fear is that these kids are going to grow up and realize they didn't learn about some interesting things," said Nabors, who has been teaching in elementary schools for 33 years. "There is a lot to get into one day, and TAAS is the priority." Many teachers, parents and students complain that the TAAS is taking freedom and fun out of teaching and learning. They say it narrows instruction, puts too much emphasis on one test and doesn't necessarily produce a better education. Indeed, some college officials and business leaders say that steadily rising TAAS scores have not guaranteed better students and workers. . . . Retired Fort Worth teacher Sherry Ware said: "It has not done anything to improve the overall performance of students. It was meant as a guideline, and now it has become the Ten Commandments."

Hot tubs and test scores. On a rainy day last fall, Lori Golden was repeating herself for the tenth time as her eighth-graders at Riverside Middle School in Fort Worth fiddled with pencils and leafed through folders.

They didn't know it, but Golden is responsible for improving the school's passing rate on the math section of the TAAS. Low scores caused the school to lose its acceptable rating and drop to the low-performing category on the state's performance scale last year. Ever since Riverside got the test results last spring, Golden and other faculty members have been analyzing what went wrong. Besides math, Golden is focusing on vocabulary. The school's analysis of test results suggests that some students, even native English speakers, are stumbling and getting stuck on unfamiliar words. For example, last year a question about circumference began with an example of a tarp covering a circular swimming pool. "They have a formula chart. I couldn't figure out why they couldn't find the formula for circumference," Golden said. "Then one of my kids asked, 'What's a tarp?'" Golden wasn't allowed to answer that question during the test. Afterward, she told the class that a tarp is used to cover pools, or hot tubs, or cars. "But how many of my kids have seen a hot tub?" she asked. "That has nothing to do with a child's intelligence. It has to do with their experiences." Golden believes that this difference is what handicaps her students and poor kids in general compared with their wealthier peers. Golden said she believes that schools should test students on what they should know. But the way people make judgments about schools based on the TAAS results is unfair, she said. "Does it totally judge what my kids know? No," she said. "Does it tell us who are good test-takers? Probably. Does it say that Grapevine-Colleyville is a better district or that their kids are smarter or their teachers better? Or does it tell you their parents have more power and better transportation to get their kids to tutoring when some of my kids ride the city bus and can't stay after dark?" "These kids in Grapevine-Colleyville know what a tarp is because they have pools and hot tubs," she said. "It's just a fact that you're going to have children in the suburbs who have more advantages than inner-city kids." The consequences of failure—there is hell to pay if students don't pass the TAAS. Students who complete high school can't graduate unless they pass the exit test. Teacher evaluations are linked in part to their school's overall performance. Superintendents re largely judged by their districts' scores. February, 22, 1998, Michelle Melendez, *Fort Worth Star-Telegram*, Fort Worth, Texas

I rarely agree with the editor of this newspaper, but on Tuesday, April 11, your opinion on TAAS testing is the same as mine. The TAAS test tells us only one thing about a student, how well he takes tests. If your child thrives on competition, chances are he will do well. If your child isn't a great student, has been teased about his grades and enters each test with fear of failure, that result will show. The enormous amount of time spent preparing for TAAS and the pressure put on both students and teachers is a terrible waste of resources. April, 14, 2000, *The Daily Sentinel*, Nacogdoches, Texas

Out of curiosity I looked up the data from our superintendent's former school on the TEA web site. I was rather surprised at what I found. According to the data on that Web site, 38.9 percent of African Americans were ARD-exempt; that means they did not have to take TAAS. In fact, 44.4 percent of African American children did not take TAAS at all. In our town, the ARD-exempt students are quite a bit lower than that. I don't know the percentage offhand, but it is quite a bit lower. I am just wondering whether he is planning on lifting us up or pulling us down to the level he came from. April 15, 2000, *The Daily Sentinel*, Nacogdoches, Texas

As a retired school teacher I must apologize for the statement made by one of my own in the Wednesday, March 15, paper stating that the blame for the low TAAS scores belongs with the parents and the children, not on the teachers. I'm afraid that the direct responsibility does lie with the teachers. I must commend Dr. Riehl and the school board for taking strong action that needed to be taken and is long overdue. Thank you. March 18, 2000, *The Daily Sentinel*, Nacogdoches, Texas

I'm responding to the retired teacher who blames the parents and students for poor TAAS scores. You want to play the blame game, look in the mirror. You are the reason I am homeschooling my child today. March 18, 2000, *The Daily Sentinel*, Nacogdoches, Texas

Getting rid of the principals is not going to solve the problem of the TAAS test. It is a tradition of low expectations that some of the teachers have for black success. It also stems from the fact that at home the parents are not able to help their children beyond a certain point with their homework. Smart students reflect smart parents. Let's face it, we are all born equal, but we don't remain that way after we are born. Until we can get homework assistance centers set up within each community to assist with homework and until we can have high expectations for all children and until we can believe that all children can learn and eliminate social promotions and watered-down courses to get minority students through school and out of a discipline problem we will never solve the problem. March 17, 2000, *The Daily Sentinel*, Nacogdoches, Texas

"Basic Skills: Notion minority students cannot pass TAAS is insulting." Trial got under way this past week in San Antonio on a lawsuit filed by a prominent civil rights organization that wants the state to stop with-holding diplomas from students who cannot pass the TAAS. The MALDEF based the suit on the contention that the test is discriminatory because minority students have trouble passing, a notion that is insulting to black and Hispanic students. MALDEF contends minority students consistently perform "significantly worse" than white students on all sections of the TAAS. But surely members of this organization neither believe nor mean to promote the belief that there is a genetic basis for minority students' lower TAAS passage rate. Furthermore, active encouragement of the idea that the intellectual capacity of young people is determined by skin color is offensive. On the first day of trial, a Boston education expert testified on MALDEF's behalf that requiring the TAAS for graduation has a "per-vasive" impact, labels minority students failures and drives them to drop out of school. The TAAS did that? Of course that is absurd. Barring disability any student who possesses the basic academic skills that give a high school diploma value ought to be able to pass the TAAS. Those students who do not possess those skills—even if they took all the re-quired classes and completed all their coursework—will not be able to pass the exit exam and should not be granted a diploma. Texans should wonder how thousands of students can satisfactorily meet all other re-quirements for graduation and still not be able to score at least 70 percent on a test of rudimentary math, reading and writing skills. In fact, one of the most valuable uses of the TAAS is as a check on the effectiveness of Texas schools, curriculum and teachers, as well as of the students' own diligence. MALDEF forgets the students of all ethnicities who take school more seriously because they know a final test stands between them and a diploma. The organization also ignores all the students who are prompted by a failed TAAS to take remedial courses to learn what they missed the first time. Most of those students on whose behalf MALDEF is fighting probably realize that if they cannot pass the TAAS, they do not possess the skills a high school graduate is expected to have. There are no doubt many reasons that some minority children do not perform well on the TAAS, including, perhaps, inferior schools, lower expectations from adults and poverty that precludes their participation in enrichment activities. And, like white students, black and Hispanic students who do not apply themselves to their studies will tend to fail. What surely is not a factor in minority student failure on the exit exam is inherent intellectual limitation. Texas ought not give up on a worthwhile test on this faulty and objection-able premise. September 27, 1999, Editorial, *Houston Chronicle*, Houston, Texas

The court battle over the TAAS test is really sad. I took the TAAS in 1992, and it was a complete joke. I was shocked at the absurdly low academic expectations for Texas students. If they can't pass the TAAS, they should not receive a diploma, because they obviously are undereducated. Let's not devalue the worth of a high school diploma by eliminating a test that is already way too easy. October 3, 1999, *Houston Chronicle*, Houston, Texas

"TAAS language-dependent." In the September 27 editorial, "Basic skills: Notion minority students cannot pass TAAS is insulting," the *Chronicle* Editorial Board grossly misrepresented the case by the MALDEF against the TEA and the State Board of Education. First of all, MALDEF has contributed significantly to a long tradition of fighting in the courts for the civil rights of Mexican-American children in Texas. It is inconceivable that it would file a frivolous lawsuit, as you suggest. Also, it is condescending to characterize MALDEF's explanation of the problem as a matter of genetics or skin color. Finally, the editorial is preposterous when it turns everything upside down and tries to make MALDEF the source of the problem by calling its suit an insulting and offensive affront to minority youth. "Inherent intellectual limitation," as the editorial writers framed it, is hardly MALDEF's premise in the case. MALDEF has brought the lawsuit on behalf of minority students and their families because the 10th grade-exit test is having a discriminatory effect on their future educational and employment opportunities. Specifically, tying scores to the receipt of a high school diploma has far-reaching implications for the current generation of Texas youth. According to the 1995 TEA interim Report on Texas public schools, failing the TAAS was listed as the second-highest reason students drop out of school. The editorial writers presume that since they have ruled out both genetics and race (understood narrowly in terms of skin color), then other grounds for discrimination do not exist. According to their logic, TAAS performance is therefore reducible to individual motivation. However, this explanation is found wanting when a full 85 percent of those who fail the 10th grade exit TAAS are either African-American or Hispanic. The MALDEF case looks closely at the impact of linguistic, cultural, and economic discrimination. They provide credible arguments for the high failure rate on the TAAS exam by limited English proficient students. Of all special subpopulations on which the TEA collects data, theirs are consistently the lowest scored—ranked next to special education students. Despite numerous opportunities to pass the test, they fail at excessively high rates, in great part because of their lack of fluency in English and not because of a lack of motivation. Many of these students, who so often possess such incredible potential as segments of Mexico's and Latin America's "brain drain," cannot possibly carry the entire burden of responsibility for their low scores when performance on the TAAS test is so language-dependent. Exams which serve as benchmarks for student performance may be helpful, but when these exams work to determine the destinies of children and not of schools, we are condoning irrecoverable harm to both our children and to society. October 10, 1999, Angela Valenzuela, Editorial, *Houston Chronicle*, Houston, Texas

"Good Judgment: Ruling affirms that test standard for all not discriminatory." Judges are supposed to interpret the law fairly, intelligently and without regard to an ideology or agenda. But plaintiffs who sought a federal judge's ruling that Texas' high school graduation test discriminates against black and Hispanic students seemed to be asking the judge to forgo those standards, as well as the use of sound judgment, also a key element of a jurist's duty. U. S. District Judge Ed Prado rejected the claim by lawyers for the Mexican American Legal Defense and Education Fund that the TAAS should be banned as a requirement for graduation because black and Hispanic students disproportionately fail the test. Prado did agree that a substantial number of minority students are not granted diplomas because of the TAAS. But he did not agree that that undesirable outcome outweighed the positive effect of the test as an objective standard for graduation. MALDEF attorneys alleged the TAAS is discriminatory in its construction. Surely these lawyers do not mean to assert that a flaw in the brains of black and Hispanic students hinders their ability to satisfactorily complete a test that many white students pass. The fact that plenty of minority students do pass the test points out the defect in that argument. The plaintiffs' own numbers point out that 80 percent of black and Hispanic students ultimately pass the exit test. The lawyers' second argument, that schools attended mostly by minorities tend to be low performing and do not offer an equal opportunity to learn, is stronger. But here, too, the TAAS, which is administered as a graduation requirement and at various points in a student's academic career, provides more help than hurt to black and Hispanic students. The TAAS is the cornerstone of Texas' education accountability system. Without it, it would be harder for teachers, parents and the public to know how well schools are passing on basic skills and knowledge to students. The fact that the gap in TAAS achievement between minority and white students steadily is narrowing indicates that the test is prompting districts to devote more attention to under-performing schools and is requiring teachers to expect more from minority students. Two Harvard University studies of Texas education raise some troubling warnings, however. That research showed that teachers are spending an inordinate amount of classroom time drilling students on test-taking skills instead of teaching academic subject matter. Also, schools are encouraging teachers to eliminate lessons that teach skills not specifically tested by TAAS. Another just-released study, by the Thomas B. Fordham Foundation, shows Texas is one of only five states that combine high standards with robust accountability. Texas would be moving in reverse, and doing a disservice to its minority students, if it backed away from that potent combination on the false presumption that minority students cannot meet high measures for success. And it is clear that much more emphasis needs to be placed on helping minority students from the outset so that when the testing and accountability systems do begin to measure their progress, they are better equipped to measure up. It is not the standards that should be lowered, but the effort to better educate all students in Texas that should be stepped up. January 9, 2000, Editorial, *Houston Chronicle*, Houston, Texas

I agree with the court ruling, the decision on the TAAS case. The fact that a person is Hispanic doesn't change history. George Washington is still the first president of the United States. The fact that a person is black has nothing to do with English. A participle is still a participle, a noun is still a noun, a verb is still a verb. January 18, 2000, *The Daily Sentinel*, Nacogdoches, Texas

An article in the *Chronicle* September 21 told how TAAS testing failures lead to dropping out, but I wonder if the TAAS is as hard as people are led to believe. If a minority failed the TAAS would it cause him to drop out? I don't think so. The TAAS holds the fate for each student's graduation. Of all the students who take the test in schools, only about 20 percent of students do not pass all of the objectives. Those who have to retake the test in the summer or the following year have to pass the objectives they failed. The public is led to believe that minorities have a problem passing the test because the test is too difficult for them to comprehend. If Hispanic students who don't speak English very well were given the test in Spanish, they would perform better than they do, and this would not hold the Hispanic students back from graduation. As a recent high school graduate and a minority, I did not find the test to be that hard. Other minorities who took the test with me did not fail any objectives and also received national recognition in more than one objective. The TAAS is only as difficult as the student makes it to be. October 3, 1999, *Houston Chronicle*, Houston, Texas

To say that the TAAS test discriminates against minorities is simply ludicrous. If someone takes the test 12 times and does not pass, how can that possibly be because of race? Not passing after 12 attempts is a lack of preparation—a lack of studying. The TAAS is "a basic skills exam." To remove it as a requirement for a high school diploma trivializes the entire educational process. Do we really want students to have a Texas diploma if they can't pass a test of basic skills? We must also ask how someone can complete the course work for a high school diploma and still not pass the test. A great majority of Texas students are able to pass the test. Why, then, would someone who has completed the same course work fail? I think the answer is study habits. Many students simply "cram" the night before an exam, are able to pass it and then immediately forget the information. Still others choose to cheat. The TAAS requires students to actually remember the information they learned. All students able to complete the required course work in high school have gained enough information to be able to pass the TAAS. If they can't remember the information, the only one they can blame is themselves. October 3, 1999, *Houston Chronicle*, Houston, Texas

"TAAS not accurate gauge of a child's knowledge." With all the emphasis placed on the TAAS, what type of an education are children receiving in other areas? So much rides on the outcome of a single test that teachers spend hours doing nothing more than teaching the TAAS test itself. And—why not?—teacher pay, bonuses and other incentives often are based on this test. For years the TAAS test has been under fire for having too much emphasis placed on it. Why should one test get all of the credit for what a student learns throughout his or her educational career? Just because a student performs poorly on the TAAS test, does that mean they should not be allowed to graduate? And why should a teacher's salary or a district's funding be linked to something that really has no bearing on whether a student received a quality education? Straight-A students have been known to fail the TAAS. Sure, there is an argument that if a child can pass the TAAS test, then he can be adequately scaled as to where he is in the educational process. But think about this: If you were taught the same thing over and over, every day for six months, wouldn't you perform well? Aside from the topics you covered in that six-month period of time, what else did you learn? While everyone is happy that test scores are going up, the students are losing out because they are not receiving a truly rounded education. Instead, teachers receive copies of previous tests or sample tests in some cases and repeatedly pour this information into a child's brain. But the fault does not lie with the teachers. They are just doing what comes naturally. It is human to ensure self-preservation, and these teachers need a job. In many cases, if a teacher's class performs poorly on the TAAS, his or her career could be in jeopardy. School administrators may deny that, but it can happen. Even the administrators, who come down hard on teachers and principals when a school performs poorly, are not solely to blame. They are in the public eye and they know that if the district is going to appear successful, then it must have high scores on the TAAS. No, the blame lies with the legislators who sit in Austin and think they can come up with a single idea that hasn't been thought of before. The legislators want the schools in Texas to score well against other states. They want to be able to puff their chests out and say "Hey, our standardized test scores are better than yours." So, what do they do? To ensure that districts focus on the test, legislators go out and pass laws tying half of all money allocated to a school district to a single test. It is time that everyone should realize that the final effect of a complete education cannot and should not be placed solely on the outcome of one test. April 11, 2000, *The Daily Sentinel*, Nacogdoches, Texas

Index

Raymond A. Horn, Jr. is Assistant Professor of Secondary Education and Education Leadership at Stephen F. Austin State University in Texas. He teaches critical theory and research methods to graduate students, and is the author of *Teacher Talk: A Post-Formal Inquiry into Educational Change* (Peter Lang, 2000).

Joe L. Kincheloe is Professor of Education at the Graduate Center at the City University of New York and Professor of Education at Brooklyn College, where he has served as The Belle Zeller Chair of Public Policy and Administration. He often works with his partner, Shirley Steinberg, editing series such as *Counterpoints: Series in the Postmodern Context of Education* for Peter Lang Publishing. Dr. Kincheloe's books include: *How Do We Tell the Workers?; Critical Politics of Teacher Thinking; Toil and Trouble* (Peter Lang); *Contextualizing Teaching;* (with Shirley Steinberg and Patrick Slattery); *Changing Multiculturalism* (with Shirley Steinberg); *Thirteen Questions: Reframing Education's Conversation* (with Shirley Steinberg; Peter Lang); *Getting Beyond the Facts* (Peter Lang, forthcoming); and *Teaching Social Studies in the Twenty-First Century*.

Studies in the Postmodern Theory of Education

General Editors
Joe L. Kincheloe & Shirley R. Steinberg

Counterpoints publishes the most compelling and imaginative books being written in education today. Grounded on the theoretical advances in criticalism, feminism, and postmodernism in the last two decades of the twentieth century, Counterpoints engages the meaning of these innovations in various forms of educational expression. Committed to the proposition that theoretical literature should be accessible to a variety of audiences, the series insists that its authors avoid esoteric and jargonistic languages that transform educational scholarship into an elite discourse for the initiated. Scholarly work matters only to the degree it affects consciousness and practice at multiple sites. Counterpoints' editorial policy is based on these principles and the ability of scholars to break new ground, to open new conversations, to go where educators have never gone before.

For additional information about this series or for the submission of manuscripts, please contact:

Joe L. Kincheloe & Shirley R. Steinberg
c/o Peter Lang Publishing, Inc.
275 Seventh Avenue, 28th floor
New York, New York 10001

To order other books in this series, please contact our Customer Service Department:

(800) 770-LANG (within the U.S.)
(212) 647-7706 (outside the U.S.)
(212) 647-7707 FAX

Or browse online by series:
www.peterlang.com